MW00851285

ABRAHAM
KUYPER

Collected Works in Public Theology

GENERAL EDITORS

JORDAN J. BALLOR

MELVIN FLIKKEMA

ABRAHAMKUYPER.COM

OUR PROGRAM

A CHRISTIAN POLITICAL MANIFESTO

ABRAHAM KUYPER

Translated and edited by Harry Van Dyke

LEXHAM PRESS

ACTONINSTITUTE
FOR THE STUDY OF RELIGION AND LIBERTY

Our Program: A Christian Political Manifesto

Abraham Kuyper Collected Works in Public Theology

Copyright 2015 Acton Institute for the Study of Religion & Liberty

Lexham Press, 1313 Commercial St., Bellingham, WA 98225
LexhamPress.com

All rights reserved. You may use brief quotations from this resource in presentations, articles, and books. For all other uses, please write Lexham Press for permission. Email us at permissions@lexhampress.com.

Originally published as *Ons Program*. Tweede druk (2nd ed.) © Amsterdam: J. H. Kruyt, 1880. First published unabridged in 1879.

This translation previously published in 2013 as *Guidance for Christian Engagement in Government* by Christian's Library Press, an imprint of the Acton Institute for the Study of Religion & Liberty, 98 E. Fulton Street Grand Rapids, MI, 49503.

Unless otherwise noted, Scripture quotations are from The Holy Bible, English Standard Version® (ESV®), copyright © 2001 by Crossway Bibles, a publishing ministry of Good News Publishers. Used by permission. All rights reserved.

ISBN 978-1-57-799655-2

Translator and Editor: Harry Van Dyke
Acton Editorial: Nienke Wolters, Paul J. Brinkerhoff, Timothy J. Beals, and
    Stephen J. Grabill
Lexham Editorial: Brannon Ellis, Lynnea Fraser, Scott Hausman, Justin Marr,
    Jesse Meyers, Abigail Stocker, Joel Wilcox
Cover Design: Christine Gerhart
Typesetting: ProjectLuz.com

CONTENTS

GENERAL EDITORS' INTRODUCTION

In times of great upheaval and uncertainty, it is necessary to look to the past for resources to help us recognize and address our own contemporary challenges. While Scripture is foremost among these foundations, the thoughts and reflections of Christians throughout history also provide us with important guidance. Because of his unique gifts, experiences, and writings, Abraham Kuyper is an exemplary guide in these endeavors.

Kuyper (1837–1920) is a significant figure both in the history of the Netherlands and modern Protestant theology. A prolific intellectual, Kuyper founded a political party and a university, led the formation of a Reformed denomination and the movement to create Reformed elementary schools, and served as the prime minister of the Netherlands from 1901 to 1905. In connection with his work as a builder of institutions, Kuyper was also a prolific author. He wrote theological treatises, biblical and confessional studies, historical works, social and political commentary, and devotional materials.

Believing that Kuyper's work is a significant and underappreciated resource for Christian public witness, in 2011 a group of scholars interested in Kuyper's life and work formed the Abraham Kuyper Translation Society. The shared conviction of the society, along with the Acton Institute, Kuyper College, and other Abraham Kuyper scholars, is that Kuyper's works hold great potential to build intellectual capacity within the church in North America, Europe, and around the world. It is our hope that translation of his works into English will make his insights accessible to those seeking to grow and revitalize communities in the developed world as well as to those in the global south and east who are facing unique challenges and opportunities.

The church today—both locally and globally—needs the tools to construct a compelling and responsible public theology. The aim of this translation project is to provide those tools—we believe that Kuyper's unique insights can catalyze the development of a winsome and constructive Christian social witness and cultural engagement the world over.

In consultation and collaboration with these institutions and individual scholars, the Abraham Kuyper Translation Society developed this 12-volume translation project, the Abraham Kuyper Collected Works in Public Theology. This multivolume series collects in English translation Kuyper's writings and speeches from a variety of genres and contexts in his work as a theologian and statesman. In almost all cases, this set contains original works that have never before been translated into English. The series contains multivolume works as well as other volumes, including thematic anthologies.

The series includes a translation of Kuyper's *Our Program* (*Ons Program*), which sets forth Kuyper's attempt to frame a Christian political vision distinguished from the programs of the nineteenth-century Modernists who took their cues from the French Revolution. It was this document that launched Kuyper's career as a pastor, theologian, and educator. As James Bratt writes, "This comprehensive Program, which Kuyper crafted in the process of forming the Netherlands' first mass political party, brought the theology, the political theory, and the organization vision together brilliantly in a coherent set of policies that spoke directly to the needs of his day. For us it sets out the challenge of envisioning what might be an equivalent witness in our own day."

Also included is Kuyper's seminal three-volume work *De gemeene gratie*, or *Common Grace*, which presents a constructive public theology of cultural engagement rooted in the humanity Christians share with the rest of the world. Kuyper's presentation of common grace addresses a gap he recognized in the development of Reformed teaching on divine grace. After addressing particular grace and covenant grace in other writings, Kuyper here develops his articulation of a Reformed understanding of God's gifts that are common to all people after the fall into sin.

The series also contains Kuyper's three-volume work on the lordship of Christ, *Pro Rege*. These three volumes apply Kuyper's principles in *Common Grace*, providing guidance for how to live in a fallen world under Christ the King. Here the focus is on developing cultural institutions in way that is consistent with the ordinances of creation that have been maintained and preserved, even if imperfectly so, through common grace.

The remaining volumes are thematic anthologies of Kuyper's writings and speeches gathered from the course of his long career.

The anthology *On Charity and Justice* includes a fresh and complete translation of Kuyper's "The Problem of Poverty," the landmark speech Kuyper gave at the opening of the First Christian Social Congress in Amsterdam in 1891. This important work was first translated into English in 1950 by Dirk Jellema; in 1991, a new edition by James Skillen was issued. This volume also contains other writings and speeches on subjects including charity, justice, wealth, and poverty.

The anthology *On Islam* contains English translations of significant pieces that Abraham Kuyper wrote about Islam, gathered from his reflections on a lengthy tour of the Mediterranean world. Kuyper's insights illustrate an instructive model for observing another faith and its cultural ramifications from an informed Christian perspective.

The anthology *On the Church* includes selections from Kuyper's doctrinal dissertation on the theologies of Reformation theologians John Calvin and John a Lasco. It also includes various treatises and sermons, such as "Rooted and Grounded," "Twofold Fatherland," and "Address on Missions."

The anthology *On Business and Economics* contains various meditations Kuyper wrote about the evils of the love of money as well as pieces that provide Kuyper's thoughts on stewardship, human trafficking, free trade, tariffs, child labor, work on the Sabbath, and business.

Finally, the anthology *On Education* includes Kuyper's important essay "Bound to the Word," which discusses what it means to be ruled by the Word of God in the entire world of human thought. Numerous other pieces are also included, resulting in a substantial English volume of Kuyper's thoughts on Christian education.

Collectively, this 12-volume series will, as Richard Mouw puts it, "give us a much-needed opportunity to absorb the insights of Abraham Kuyper about God's marvelous designs for human cultural life."

The Abraham Kuyper Translation Society along with the Acton Institute and Kuyper College gratefully acknowledge the Andreas Center for Reformed Scholarship and Service at Dordt College; Calvin College; Calvin Theological Seminary; Fuller Theological Seminary; Mid-America Reformed Seminary; Redeemer University College; Princeton Theological Seminary; and Southeastern Baptist Theological Seminary. Their financial support and partnership made these translations possible. The society is also grateful for the generous financial support of Dr. Rimmer and Ruth DeVries and the J. C. Huizenga family, which has enabled the translation and publication of these volumes.

This series is dedicated to Dr. Rimmer DeVries in recognition of his life's pursuits and enduring legacy as a cultural leader, economist, visionary, and faithful follower of Christ who reflects well the Kuyperian vision of Christ's lordship over all spheres of society.

Jordan J. Ballor
Melvin Flikkema

Grand Rapids, MI
August 2015

TRANSLATOR AND EDITOR'S INTRODUCTION

The text that follows is a translation of the book *"Ons Program"*, written by Abraham Kuyper (1837–1920) and first published in 1879. In it Kuyper offered a running commentary on the draft program adopted and published on January 1, 1878, by a provisional central committee located in Amsterdam. This committee offered advice during election time and served as a national clearinghouse both for locals of the Anti-School Law League and for antirevolutionary voters' clubs active in their respective electoral districts throughout the Netherlands. The draft program was originally prepared by Kuyper himself and only slightly amended after consulting law professors De Geer van Jutphaas of Utrecht and Gratema of Groningen as well as Alexander de Savornin Lohman, a prominent attorney in 's-Hertogenbosch.[1]

Kuyper's draft also gained the public endorsement of prominent pastors of the Secession Church and was praised in the weekly *De Bazuin* of that denomination's Theological School in Kampen.

---

1. To the original eighteen articles Kuyper added articles on justice, public decency, and public hygiene (chaps. 14–16) before embarking on his commentary. These articles are placed in square brackets at the beginning of their respective chapters.

PURPOSE

The Program was intended to serve as a common basis for participating in general elections. In April 1878 Dr. Kuyper began to publish a commentary in installments in his daily *De Standaard*, the newspaper he founded in 1872. In March of the following year it appeared in book form under the title *"Ons Program"* ("Our Program"), now divided over twenty-two chapters in 328 numbered sections.[2]

Its author stated in the preface that the commentary had a twofold purpose: to serve antirevolutionaries as a guide for promotional activities and to prepare them for the formal establishment of an Anti-Revolutionary Party.

Kuyper's wider aim with the publication was "to show likeminded citizens that our political creed is sound, consistent, and wholesome," and in addition, "to make it easier for those of other minds to understand our aspirations and intentions."

THAT CURIOUS NAME

One of the principal ideas to be developed in the commentary immediately explains the curious name of this political movement: to be *antirevolutionary* was to be uncompromisingly opposed to "modernity"—that is, to the ideology embodied in the French Revolution and the public philosophy we have since come to know as secular humanism. Kuyper reminded his readers that on almost every important question in society and politics the antirevolutionary movement stood opposed to both liberals and conservatives. Both camps, he explained, based themselves—consciously or unconsciously, enthusiastically or half-heartedly—on the fundamental worldview that was spawned by "the Revolution." Thus, in this commentary the term "the Revolution" stands for the enduring values and assumptions that had inspired the French Revolution, to be sharply distinguished from the passing upheavals in France of 1789, 1830, and 1848.

No further identification of "the Revolution" was needed. Readers knew that Kuyper was referring to the Revolution of the previous century, that is, to the intellectual and spiritual transformation which during the Age of Reason had ushered in a whole new way of seeing the world and shaping life and society throughout Western Europe.

---

2. In actuality, there are 326 sections since section numbers 15 and 16 were inadvertently skipped. See chap. 2n1.

Antirevolutionaries stood for a broad alternative to the secular, rationalist worldview, the set of beliefs that had issued in humanity's proud declaration of independence during the Enlightenment. This secular worldview, with all its political and moral implications, had been put into practice in the great Revolution of 1789, and a century later seemed to be a permanent feature of public life, adapted to the times but basically unchallenged. To those beliefs, to that worldview and that practice, the journalists and the readers of *De Standaard* could only be opposed root and branch.

THE PREFACE

Kuyper's five-page preface that appeared in the published book is mainly of interest today because of the disclaimers it contains. First, the author wrote (and I paraphrase in the first person): My commentary is scarcely exhaustive. At this point in time, no one should expect an erudite and scholarly treatise on the political philosophy underlying the antirevolutionary movement. Even if that were available, the nature of the present work is intended first of all to be popular and practical, and thus it avoids concepts and definitions from political and legal philosophy.

Furthermore, (Kuyper explained), I could not hope to strive after completeness: too many details lack consensus among us and beg for more study in the future. Like every political movement, the antirevolutionary "party" has always had its right and left wing: one tendency sides more with a strong state, and the other relies more on a free society.

The right wing at this time on the Continent was conservative and favored a more interventionist state, whereas the left wing was more progressive and championed individual freedom and private initiative. Kuyper wanted to be reckoned among the left, but he assured readers that he welcomed principled and constructive criticism from the right.

Finally, the preface cautioned that this work ought not to be regarded as a definitive statement, as though it were the "only orthodox" interpretation of the Program. The author would not want to be accused of such foolish and laughable arrogance. Take this commentary, he wrote, as my own personal contribution to staking out our place in politics. I alone am responsible for it, so feel free to agree or disagree with it.

That said, Kuyper was careful to mention that the late Groen van Prinsterer (d. 1876) expressed his overall agreement "in outline and substance" with a sketch of the same ideas that are here given much more extensive treatment. Kuyper did not identify the "sketch" further, but one can be quite certain that he was referring to a rather lengthy memorandum, dated February 4, 1874, which he submitted to Groen for approval and which summarized his intended line of conduct and legislative goals should he be elected to the lower house (a distinct possibility at the time). For Kuyper to be able to boast of having the stamp of approval imprinted on his ideas by the revered pioneer of the antirevolutionary movement would certainly help him recruit endorsers and fend off detractors.

THE INTRODUCTION

Following the preface and before offering his commentary on each of the twenty-one articles in the Program (originally listed first altogether and then piecemeal as chapter epigraphs), Kuyper wrote a helpful six-page introduction, covering §§ 1–4. Here he explained the difference between various forms of what might pass for *programs* of a political party.

There are first of all "campaign manifestos," which are retired once the elections have been held. Then there are more formal "government platforms," which the party, if it wins the elections, will incorporate in the Speech from the Throne. An intermediate form is a "program of action." A fourth form is the kind of program that the present work is a commentary on, a "program of principles," one that aims to nurture and develop political awareness and involvement on the basis of deeply held beliefs about the nature of the world, the character of human society, and the task of government. Articulating such foundational principles as the basis for organizing a political party made it necessary to identify the root cause of one's discontent and to offer an honest appraisal of the historical past from which one now had to move forward. In addition, Kuyper explained, such a program should begin to develop "secondary" principles that logically derive from the foundational ones.

LAYING THE GROUNDWORK

Beginning then with § 5 and continuing through to § 84, Kuyper's commentary on the opening seven articles of the Program laid the groundwork for the thoroughgoing alternative that state and society clearly needed. As he set out to explain what an antirevolutionary party should affirm as its political philosophy, Kuyper began by assuming that his country was a Christian nation. At the same time he was careful to put "Christian" in quotation marks. The modifier "Christian," besides denoting people's subjective faith and membership in a church, can also be used as a political concept, meaning that Christian traditions and Christian values can be ingrained in the life of a nation apart from any church connection. He made a clear separation between church and state, in effect endorsing the slogan gaining ground in Europe at the time: "a free church in a free state," with the proviso that the two should engage in correspondence with one another on a regular basis. Thus he rejected both the secular state and the theocratic state.

While he managed to include many of the usual issues when Christians engage in politics and aspire to the seats of power, he did so on the grounds of *natural theology*, referring to the Epistle to the Romans about the works of the law that are engraved in the hearts even of the Gentiles. (Over time, Kuyperians would begin to speak of *general revelation* that impinges on all mankind and is heeded in greater or lesser degrees thanks to *common grace*.) Every government, asserted Kuyper, of whatever kind or conviction, will heed the truths manifest in reality itself if it knows what is good for it and good for its subjects. Thus he argued, for example, that Sunday observance is not just beneficial for Christians but for the whole nation. Similarly, maintaining law and order, upholding capital punishment, administering the oath, curtailing prostitution, and the like, are all policies that recommend themselves to the state and its citizens upon thoughtful reflection and commonsense realism.

After elucidating the first seven articles in eight chapters (article 4 received two chapters), the rest of the commentary discussed the remaining fourteen articles of the Program.[3] In bold strokes, alternated by detailed proposals based on precise calculations, Kuyper sketched the implications of the fundamental starting points. With patience and deliberation, in piecemeal steps, he developed, each time from first principles, what the "antirevolutionary principle" demanded for the country's constitutional arrangement and the various government departments.

The work *"Our Program"* illustrates how Kuyper became the emancipator of the then still disenfranchised middle and lower classes in his country by first of all becoming their teacher and educator. He set forth what his people ought to believe and understand on the basis of Scripture,

---

3. Between § 324 and the final four sections (§§ 325–28), the publisher inserted a related series of sixteen articles written a year later in 1880 and entitled "*Antirevolutionair óók in uw huisgezin*" [Antirevolutionary also in your household].

sound reason, and common sense. He reminded them that they are Dutch Calvinists, offspring and heirs of the freedom fighters against Spanish tyranny in the sixteenth century. But he concluded, wisely and perhaps not redundantly, that in their day and age they should not strive for a "Calvinist utopia" but rather for a pluralist state, one in which all groups enjoy a level playing field as they try to enlist support for their vision of a just society.

THE DUTCH PARLIAMENT

For a better understanding of some of the sections, notably §§ 93–109 and 319–324, the reader may welcome a brief note about the main features of the parliamentary system in which the Anti-Revolutionary Party hoped to be involved.

Only partly modeled on the Westminster system of the United Kingdom, the Dutch system had a distinctly *dualistic* character. The parliament of the Netherlands, composed of a legislature of an upper and a lower house of elected representative and called the "States General," was and still is strictly separated from the government, which consists of the Council of Ministers or cabinet.

Cabinet ministers may be chosen from among the elected members of parliament or from nonmembers (extra-parliamentarians) considered especially suited for certain government departments or ministries. If a party (or an informal group of like-minded parliamentarians, as in the days when Kuyper's Program was published) wins a majority or plurality of seats and forms the government, it contributes members to the cabinet who then give up their seats to sit behind the government table. The number of seats thus vacated is replenished through by-elections, or, since 1920, by other members on a party's national slate of candidates. The government does not vote on the bills and budgets that it tables in parliament. If the lower house votes down a bill, the act may signal a growing lack of confidence in the sitting government. If the lower house votes down the annual budget, the government has lost the confidence of the house and "falls," whereupon the Crown issues a writ for new elections to be held.

In theory, the government rules for the benefit of the whole nation, not in the interest of a party. Should a party ride roughshod over the rights and religious beliefs of the minority—as antirevolutionaries claimed the liberals were time and again guilty of, notably with regard to the question of primary education—then spokesmen like Kuyper did not hesitate to speak of "partisan government" and "party tyranny." The hopeful ray in this somber scene during the last quarter of the nineteenth century was that the silenced majority in the country, including the antirevolutionaries, belonged to the lower middle class and the working class. They by and large still attended church, Reformed or Roman Catholic, and were shut out from the political process due to the limited franchise based on the *census,* or amount of taxes paid annually. Thus, any enlargement of the voter base by expanding the franchise would only work in favor of these classes and strengthen informed participation by Christians in the political process.

As is to be expected after a century and a half, quite a few, if not many, of Kuyper's notions, suggestions, and concrete proposals would be unworkable today. The value of his musings, dreams, and reasoned alternatives lies in the backdrop against which he approached the whole area of practical politics—his biblical common sense, fair-mindedness, indignation at patent injustices, zeal for genuine liberty, and freshness of ideas.

EDITING METHOD

My translation follows the second edition of 1880. The first edition of 1879 was almost three times as large because each chapter was followed by an extensive appendix containing articles from various sources in which the author had earlier enlarged further on the topic at hand. These were removed in the following year from what the publisher styled a "second printing" that was intended to put a cheaper "popular edition" on the market. It is this work that is here presented in translation. The items deleted from the first edition were of local, contemporary interest, but are now dated and too detailed to be of much use today. Other printings of *"Ons Program"* followed in 1892, 1898, and 1907, bringing the total number of copies printed at 5,350. All printings are virtually identical; I have noted the few variants in the footnotes. Brief editorial notes have been added throughout in order to identify persons, schools of thought, or events mentioned in the original that might be unfamiliar to contemporary readers. Although few in number, Kuyper's original footnotes have been retained, brought up to contemporary bibliographic standards, and clearly marked as *Note by the author*.

Other stylistic alterations have been made for ease of reading and for the sake of appearance. Italics are used less frequently in the translation than appear in the original. The original text, being newspaper articles, is replete with separate paragraphs; without eliminating all of them, I have sometimes fused shorter or even one-sentence paragraphs to keep related thoughts together, but I have retained most paragraph divisions to reflect their original provenance.

Now and then I have omitted an adverbial or adjectival phrase in order to keep a sentence from being overloaded; in all cases, however, the context ensures that nothing is lost of Kuyper's argument and very little of his colorful prose. Use of square brackets to enclose material added to clarify the translation of the original has been kept to a minimum.

As for word choice, I have tried to reflect the semipopular journalism that Kuyper practices here. One of his key terms, *"levens en wereldbeschouwing,"* I have rendered by the single word *worldview.*

Dutch currency references are prefixed with a florin (*f*) to indicate the basic monetary unit of the Netherlands (replaced by the euro in 2002) or include the word "guilder(s)," which is the English translation of the Dutch *gulden*, from Old Dutch for "golden." British currency in pound sterling (£) also appears in a few places. Distance, area, and weight are usually given in U.S. customary units and metric equivalents.

References to titles, offices, and names of organizations such as governmental bodies or political organizations and movements were sometimes capitalized and other times lowercased in the original, though not consistently. Thus for consistency a principled "down" style was applied so that many of these terms are now lowercased in keeping with standard editorial conventions. All references to "liberals" and a "liberal party," and similarly to "antirevolutionaries" and an "antirevolutionary party," are spelled lowercase to indicate that they were not organized groups but *schools of political thought* and *currents of opinion* in the country, the antirevolutionary current being the one that Kuyper wanted to gather into a well-constructed organization. When he succeeded in establishing the Anti-Revolutionary Party shortly after publishing *"Ons Program,"* he had in effect become the founder of the very first modern political party in his country.

A special word of thanks is due to George, Hans, and Rimmer as well as to my patient editors Nienke Wolters, Paul Brinkerhoff, Tim Beals, and Stephen Grabill. My gratitude also goes to the Stichting Doctor Abraham Kuyperfonds for their generous financial support of this volume.

Harry Van Dyke
Spring 2013

CHAPTER ONE

OUR MOVEMENT[1]

The antirevolutionary or Christian-historical movement represents, insofar as it pertains to our country, the keynote of our national character as this received its stamp around 1572 under the leadership of Orange and the influence of the Reformation, and wishes to develop this in accordance with the altered circumstances of our nation in a form that satisfies the needs of our time.[2]

ARTICLE 1

I. OUR NAME

ANTIREVOLUTIONARY[3]

§ 5

Our movement has two names: either antirevolutionary or Christian-historical, depending on whether you focus on what we oppose or on what we wish to promote.

---

1. "Our Movement" here translates the original *Onze richting*, that is, our school or persuasion (in this case, regarding political thought).
2. William I, Prince of Orange, also known as William the Silent (1533–84), was the leader of the Dutch Revolt against the Spanish Habsburgs. See also below, § 10.
3. The first four sections (§§ 1–4) were the author's introduction. As summarized in the editor's introduction above, they spelled out at some length the difference between four possible types of political "programs," the fourth being a "program of principles" on which this book is a commentary.

Our movement's *first* name, given its origin, is "antirevolutionary." It took its rise from opposing something offensive, something that clashed with what is just and sacred.

We are therefore at heart a *militant* party, unhappy with the status quo and ready to critique it, fight it, and change it.

What we oppose is "the Revolution," by which we mean the political and social system embodied in the French Revolution. Contrary to what is imputed to us, we do not oppose each and every popular uprising. We recognize that national leaders are sometimes called upon to put an end to destructive tyrannies, and so we honor, for example, the Dutch Revolt against Spain, the Glorious Revolution under William III, the American war of independence from Britain, and our overthrow of the Napoleonic regime in 1813.

Those events, after all, do not represent destruction but restoration, not the overthrow of a nation's laws but their reaffirmation, and thus not a forsaking of God but a return to him.

What we combat, on principle and without compromise, is the attempt to totally change how a person thinks and how he lives, to change his head and his heart, his home and his country—to create a state of affairs the very opposite of what has always been believed, cherished, and confessed, and so to lead us to a complete emancipation from the sovereign claims of Almighty God.

The French Revolution was the first and most brazen attempt of this kind. Thus, like Edmund Burke, we do not hesitate to focus our attack on this monstrous Revolution. To forestall any misunderstanding, I ask only of my readers, be they adherents or opponents, to bear in mind that the enduring power of an *idea* is different from its fleeting *expression* in that one event.

As an idea, the Revolution turns everything topsy-turvy, such that what was at the bottom rises to the top and what was at the very top now moves to the bottom. In this way it severs the ties that bind us to God and his Word, in order to subject both to human criticism. Once you undermine the family by replacing it with self-chosen (often sinful) relationships, once you embrace a whole new set of ideas, rearrange your notions of morality, allow your heart to follow a new direction—once you do this the Encyclopedists will be followed by the Jacobins, the theory by the practice, because "the new humanity" requires a new world. What the philosophers, whose guilt is greater, did to your minds and hearts with pen and compass and scalpel (and would like even more boldly to do to your children) will be carried out by the heroes of the barricades with dagger, torch, and crowbar.

CHRISTIAN-HISTORICAL §6

But it is not enough to know what you are against. To wage war with prospects of victory, our people needed to become aware of the sacred stronghold for the sake of which we entered the fray. To indicate that, we called ourselves *Christian-historical*. The ideology of the Revolution, after all, is anti-Christian in its starting point and therefore much worse than the worldview of paganism.

That is why the *Christian* banner had to be lifted high again. Not only did it announce an Evangelical program, but it also affirmed specifically that the battered condition in which the eighteenth century had handed Europe over to the age that followed, was not the fault of Christian principles having failed us but of our failure to live up to those principles.

We condemn outright the abuses that were customary in 1789, though there was exaggeration in the way revolutionaries depicted them. We fully agree that things could not go on that way. And even in the unholy and shameful upheaval that brought all the dregs of human passions to the surface, we revere God's guiding hand in delivering Europe from those abuses.

But when revolutionaries now tell us: "Everything used to be Christian, so your religion was responsible for those abuses, and abandoning the Christian religion and switching to our humanist beliefs is the only permanent remedy"—then everything in us protests against such calumny. On the contrary, after comparing the historical record with the demands of the gospel, we contend that this godless tyranny, this level of infamy to which men had sunk, this whole situation so unworthy of humanity, would never have come about if the nations of Europe had not time and again put the candle of the gospel under a bushel.

We contend that to stray onto the slippery paths of the philosophy of humanity will not stop the flood of iniquity. Instead, that would make it wash over us even more frightfully and before long confront us with such calamities that the blood-red luster of 1789 and 1793 will pale by comparison.

We contend, after consulting our beliefs, examining our personal lives, and listening to the past, that there is no other cure to be found for Europe's malady than under the auspices of the Man of Sorrows.

If "Christian" therefore stands opposite "humanity," the addition "historical" indicates that our situation *cannot be created by us* at will. It is the product of a past that, independent of our will and apart from our input, is fashioned by him in whom we live and move and have our being.

Whoever respects the rights of history places himself under a law and acknowledges that his will is bound by the will of former generations and is tied to the interests of the generations to come. In short, with the hallmark of history on our labors, the crown that we took for ourselves is laid down again and, alongside our forefathers and surrounded by our present adherents, we go on our knees in order to give glory, not to the creature, who is nothing, but to him whose holy footsteps you hear rustling through the pages of history.

§ 7   THE DIFFERENCE BETWEEN THE TWO

From this short exposition it is clear that "antirevolutionary" and "Christian-historical" are words of almost identical meaning. It betrays a lack of familiarity with the meaning of these terms when people give out that they are willing to be called "Christian-historical" but not "antirevolutionary."

Granted, there is more durable content in a label that states positively what you are for, than in a term that merely indicates what you are against. Also, the terms *Christian*[4] and *historical* sound more familiar and positive and speak more to your inner life than the cold foreign term *antirevolutionary*. In addition, the label "Christian-historical" would remain relevant even if the Revolution were vanquished and the term "antirevolutionary" had outlived itself.

The reason why we often prefer the name "antirevolutionary," as one can readily see, is that it is more energetic and more compelling. When someone tells you, "I am an antirevolutionary" you know at once where you are at with him, whereas "Christian-historical" still leaves you wondering.

Let's make no secret of it: it takes more courage to be an antirevolutionary.

---

4. *Note by the author:* Historically, in the Netherlands, the adjective *christelijk* [Christian] denotes whatever is based on the Reformed religion.

Oh yes, our day and age will let you have your label "Christian-historical," provided nothing further is specified about it. You can be Christian-historical without any consequences to speak of. With nothing but that title you will even be admitted to the circle of full-blooded radicals as a person open to change.

But when you declare yourself an antirevolutionary—that is, when you consciously and stoutly oppose the prevailing ideas and trends in legal thought; when you carry forward your Christian and historical convictions onto the political and social domains and consider it an honor to belong to that group in society that is targeted for oppression if not destruction—then your opposition provokes resistance and you are in for a political fight to the death.

II. THE KEYNOTE OF OUR NATIONAL CHARACTER

THREE BASIC TYPES OF NATIONALITY   § 8

Three national types vie for dominance in the bosom of our nation: the Roman Catholic type, whose image and ideal lie in the Middle Ages; the Revolutionary type, whose ideal and type are found in the model states of the French or German doctrinaires;[5] and in between these two the Puritan type, which is represented by our movement and whose flowering coincides with the glory days of the Dutch Republic.

Each of these three types have always displayed the same national character, but each time with a different keynote, depending on the principle animating it and the aims pursued by it.

The old Netherlandic people stayed the same; the nation was never uprooted. Yet in the sixteenth century and again toward the end of the eighteenth century, this people underwent a remarkable transformation and renewal in its character and qualities, a change that, depending on your sympathies, you will either praise as having rejuvenated and ennobled the nation or else denounce as having perverted and degenerated it.

The weakest type to develop was the Catholic one. During the years that Rome flourished, any political and cultural unity in the Low Countries

---

5. Doctrinaires were those who wished to reconcile monarchical institutions and old-regime values with the new political realities brought on by the French Revolution.

burgeoned only briefly and proved incapable of inspiring a comprehensive national sense through a single national will.[6]

Of greater influence was the liberal keynote that was imposed upon our national character after the revolution of 1795, when national unity was consolidated as never before and the systematic breakup of our liberties and privileges began in earnest, following foreign examples. It had greater influence in part because already during the Dutch Republic a powerful group had wanted to enter upon a course that could now be taken unhindered under French auspices. The influence was greater above all since Roman Catholics, in a natural reaction to the anti-Catholic nature of our former republic, initially aided the revolutionaries.

But the type to develop most richly, to blossom most abundantly, to ripen to nationality most fully, was the Puritan Christian type that our people took on during the Republic. The Catholic type had been impressed only briefly on the newly formed nation. The Revolutionary type has been operative for only eighty years. The Puritan type, by contrast, has had two full centuries to unfold its splendor.

The age in which that keynote came to dominate was the heroic age of our nation, or if you will, that mysterious moment when all the hidden treasures of our nationality suddenly burst to life and everything seemed to have become great, causing the nation to outdo itself, even as mutual trust and confidence redoubled the effect of the nation's strength.

It is a matter of record that at that time the Netherlands was at its peak, was most itself in every field and every domain of human endeavor, of learning, and of life. All Europe acknowledges that we were then the most refined and the most richly organized region of the whole continent.

And the memory of that former greatness is still so overpowering that our "revolutionaries," rather embarrassed by the traditions of their own forefathers (the terrorists of the French Revolution), preferably parade in garb stolen from the wardrobe of our history and act as if a Marnix of old and a Kappeyne of today resemble each other like two drops of water.[7]

---

6. Kuyper refers here to the years ca. 1430–1530 when the Low Countries collectively were ruled by the Burgundians and the Habsburgs.

7. Philip of Marnix, lord of St. Aldegonde (1540–98), was a Calvinist theologian, scholar, Bible translator, poet, political activist during the Dutch Revolt, and diplomat in the service of William the Silent. Johannes Kappeyne van de Coppello (1822–95)

Toward the end of the eighteenth century the Puritan type was removed from our emblem. At first, admittedly, the attack on this national type seemed to have succeeded all too well, especially after the annexation of the southern provinces of North Brabant and Limburg.[8] There were those who believed that the vibrant life of earlier days was totally choked and crushed and could never again become a national movement. But events soon proved that they had cried victory too soon.

On the contrary, no sooner did the faith of our fathers surface again in the *Réveil*,[9] the *Scheiding*,[10] and the reaction to theological modernism, than it became evident that the old sympathies were back and people longed for the social and political ideas from days of yore.

Indeed, our party is not a "school party," destined to disappear again once the education question is off the table. Nor are we a group of the "orthodox" party whose political sympathies are yet to be born and who exist only as a *church party*.

On the contrary, our party's strength lies precisely in the fact that we know ourselves to be heirs of a political program that once aroused the admiration of Europe, made the Netherlands a world power, and if developed in accordance with our times still has promise for the future.

Groen[11] therefore understood very well that his strength lay as much in our national history as in our school system, and that the [Christian day] schools, which he provisionally named "Christian-national" schools,[12] could flourish only if they were grafted onto the root of this Puritan history.

---

was a talented parliamentary leader of the Dutch liberals and notorious sponsor of the Primary Education Act of 1878 against which Kuyper organized the People's Petition (*Volkspetitionnement*).

8. These provinces, whose populations were and still are predominantly Roman Catholic, were incorporated in 1815 into the United Kingdom of the Netherlands.
9. *Réveil* refers to the Reformed-evangelical revival of the early 1800s.
10. *Scheiding* refers to the Secession of 1834 from the national church.
11. Guillaume (Willem) Groen van Prinsterer (1801–76) was the leading member of the "confessional" party in the Dutch Reformed Church and founding father of the anti-revolutionary movement in Dutch politics, essentially Kuyper's political godfather.
12. In 1861 Groen van Prinsterer helped establish the Association for Christian-National Education in support of financially struggling "Christian-national" primary schools, while in 1868 a second federation, the Association for Reformed Education, was founded to support "schools with the Bible." The schools of both organizations competed with the publicly funded schools that were mandated by law to inculcate "Christian and civic virtues" yet without use of the Bible or reference

§ 10   THE CONSTITUTIONAL CHARACTER OF THE REFORMED TYPE

The Puritan type of our national character was formed during the revolt against Spain, after being prepared by the ferment of the Protestant Reformation. Thus it came into being as early as 1520, became self-conscious in 1568, and was the first in 1572 to scuttle the ships and burn the bridges behind it, marking the irrevocable changeover of the nation to a new direction in life. It traveled the moral high road by putting the entire life of the nation in the service of one sacred, lofty cause. It has rightly been said that in our country the church was not established within a state, but inversely, that the Republic of the United Netherlands was set up as a protective wall around an already existing church and therefore as part and parcel of that church.

Consequently, the mission of our republic was to use its armies and fleets and its commercial influence to protect the free course of the gospel throughout Europe and other continents and to safeguard the free course of the gospel at home in accordance with freedom of conscience for everyone.

The inspiring ideal of our nation at that time was *civil liberty*, not as a goal in itself but as the vehicle and consequence of that much higher liberty that is owed to men's conscience.

And so people knew what they lived for; they knew the purpose of their existence. They believed, they prayed, they gave thanks. And blessings were plentiful: the country enjoyed prosperity, happiness, and peace.

William of Orange was the spiritual father from whom this type grew and who preserved it from those excesses of the left and of the right that led similar efforts in Westminster and New England to such totally different outcomes.

Orange represented more than the small number of heroes who lived up to the reputation of that noble house. In the nation's eyes, a Prince of Orange represented a mystery, a star of hope that was safe to follow, a precious treasure because he was so evidently provided by the Lord.

---

to Christian doctrine. Kuyper agreed with Groen that the teaching of such values deprived children of the motive to honor them and the strength to persevere in them. See also below, § 156.

The motto *Hac nitimur, hanc tuemur*[13]—leaning on the power of God in his holy Word and deeming liberty a priceless good—was a marvelous and meaningful expression. When struck on coins it was a cautionary reminder for a trading nation that this treasure of Orange was to be deemed of greater value than all the spices from the Orient.

THE UNFOLDING OF THIS TYPE IN THE ANTIREVOLUTIONARY MOVEMENT §11

The antirevolutionary party indeed adopts an exalted standpoint when it declares that it represents "the keynote of our national character as this received its stamp around 1572 under the leadership of Orange and the influence of the Reformation." Yet this stance becomes practical only when it adds at once that it "wishes to develop this in accordance with the altered circumstances of our nation in a form that satisfies the needs of our time."

We refuse to join the revolutionaries in sliding toward their godlike *power state*. We refuse no less to join Rome in returning to the Middle Ages. And against their united or separate attempt to eradicate the Puritan type from our national character, we shall continue to defend the latter tooth and nail.

Yet not by repristination.

We wish to recover nothing from the past that has proved unusable, nothing that we have outgrown or that no longer fits our circumstances. None of us dreams of visiting the museum of antiquities to bring back the old, clumsy, rusty state machine that had begun to creak on all sides.[14]

We also accept the fact, without mental reservations, that North Brabant and Limburg are now parts of our country and will be constitutive elements of our future nationality.

And, to put to rest once for all: we ourselves react more strongly than anyone to the idea of re-establishing a Reformed state church. On the contrary, we demand the strictest application of the principle that the state shall not itself promote "the saving faith."

But the chief goal that is nonnegotiable for us is this: (1) Our country as a state shall not be placed in a hostile position over against the living God.

---

13. "On this we rest, this we defend," translates this Latin motto that appeared on early-sixteenth-century coins depicting the maid of Holland leaning on a Bible and holding a spear topped by a liberty cap.
14. Kuyper makes reference here to the highly decentralized, oligarchic government of the Dutch Republic.

(2) Our country shall not go back and exchange the Puritan political principles for the Catholic ones. (3) Our country shall not surrender its native institutions in favor of models from abroad.

That was the threefold goal for which our fathers, under the leadership of Orange, fought against Rome and Spain and equally against the Arminians and the States.[15] That same threefold goal we are committed to pursue for our time. To forestall any misunderstanding, we hasten to add that the manner in which our fathers tried to realize that goal can no longer be fully ours.

What we must pursue today is to gain acceptance for those political ideas that will enable our citizens, endowed with equal duties and equal rights, be they Catholic, Puritan, or Revolutionary, to contribute, each in their own way and for their part and in their measure, to the formation of a higher national type that will restore the unity of our national consciousness.

III. OUR MOVEMENT IN OTHER COUNTRIES

§ 12   IN CATHOLIC COUNTRIES

Our Program states correctly that the antirevolutionary party represents the Puritanism of the sixteenth and seventeenth century "insofar as it pertains to our country" and that it cannot be tied to such a narrow definition beyond our borders.

In other countries the antirevolutionary party determines its relations on the one hand according to the position taken with respect to the Revolution, and on the other according to the felicitous or less felicitous manner in which the confession of the gospel was brought into agreement with the defense of freedom of conscience.

This last point needs to be added in this last quarter of the nineteenth century, lest by steering clear of the Revolution we should fall into the hands of Rome.

As is well known, after 1815 it indeed seemed for a long time that all Christian elements in Europe, whether they still remained in the Catholic

---

15. "Against Rome and Spain" means against the Inquisition introduced by Charles V and intensified by Philip II; "against the Arminians and the States" means against the government that used its political power around 1610–18 to privilege free-will Calvinists over sovereign-grace Calvinists, a bias that was reversed by Prince Maurice, son and successor of William of Orange.

church or flourished in the churches of the Reformation, could make common cause against the godless drive of the Revolution.

The spokesmen for Rome took up a very moderate position. They mostly emphasized the Christian faith and pushed the specifically Romish element to the background. In a very engaging manner they approached you with open arms, inviting you to do battle together for Throne and Altar. Their political writers did what was necessary to achieve success in this reconciliation. Their sincere and winning ways persuaded the old Protestant leaders to see benefit in closing ranks and recommending a new approach to politics.

Dedicated to pushing back the Revolution and granting equal status to both confessions, this approach—called "antirevolutionary" in Germany and "legitimism" in France—seemed to offer a basis for a modern reconstruction of the Christian state. Stahl, and even more Gerlach, were the talented advocates of this splendid illusion.[16]

Following the reaction of 1813, a number of confessors of Christ also in our country were infected by this naïve theory, and in some backward regions of the country one can still point to traces of the political paralysis inflicted on its blind followers. Precisely for this reason it cannot be praised enough in Groen that he never just imitated Edmund Burke or Gentz, Haller or Leo,[17] or even Stahl and Von Gerlach, but increasingly pressed toward the more Puritan standpoint, the standpoint on which one extends the hand to the Catholic Christian yet opposes the ultramontane element in his politics.[18]

In other countries, however, men did not sober up until Rome dropped her mask and everyone could see how the Jesuits, even as Catholics and Protestants were beginning to form a united front, quietly and

---

16. Friedrich Julius Stahl (1798–1861), professor of jurisprudence in Berlin and member of the Prussian diet, defended "the monarchical principle against the Revolution" and famously stated that if the Revolution should ever triumph, Catholics and Protestants "would mount the scaffold together." Ernst Ludwig von Gerlach (1795–1877), another member of the Prussian diet, crossed over from the Evangelical conservative party to the Catholic center party in the 1860s in protest over Bismarck's power politics.

17. Kuyper lists off leading conservatives: Edmund Burke in Britain, Friedrich von Gentz in Austria, Karl Ludwig von Haller in Switzerland, and Heinrich Leo in Prussia.

18. Ultramontanism was Catholic political action that recognized the supreme authority of the pope in Rome.

imperceptibly, behind our backs, were aiming at our destruction and using us to have Rome brazenly triumph in the end.

§ 13   AGAINST THE MAY LAWS

Accordingly, almost nowhere do orthodox Protestants and Catholics travel together anymore. Everyone knows this about France. In Germany one leading paper has written off the Evangelical party as a "lemon sucked dry" and another paper never even considered a merger with Rome. Since the death of Von Gerlach we can safely say that as a result of Rome's untrustworthiness there are no proponents left of a political prospect that, however appealing, brought nothing but cruel disappointment for our German friends.

That said, the rise of ultramontanism may have caused us to stop believing in one big worldwide Antirevolutionary Party composed of Catholics and Protestants, yet one should not infer from this that we are indifferent to every effort undertaken by Rome. On the contrary, in her struggle against the terribly unjust May Laws, the Center Party in Germany has our fullest sympathy.[19] Rome's exertions, both in Germany and in France, against secular public education and secular socialism remind us of our own long-standing efforts. The introduction of free universities in France, though initiated by Rome, has our warm approval. And even when a somewhat rigid and too virile ultramontanism in the republics of South America tries to bring healing in a situation of chronic civil war, the endeavor probably has ulterior motives yet we applaud what is commendable in it.

But nowhere do we recognize *kindred spirits* in the ultramontane party. We were never one, we are not one, and we shall never be one. And should there be instances, such as those mentioned above, when we choose for Rome against the Revolution, there are other cases, no less important, when we would favor liberalism over Rome. In both cases, meanwhile, we would be navigating our own vessel between a rock and a hard place rather than acting from affinity and principle.

---

19. The May Laws were enactments by the Bismarck government during the 1870s by which religious orders were abolished, and Catholic clergy were excluded from the education system and trained and appointed subject to state supervision.

We recognize only two types of political parties as like-minded with ours: (1) those that flourish in countries where the French Revolution never infiltrated; (2) those that oppose this Revolution within their borders on the basis of the Word of God.

To the first category belong the political parties in Britain and the United States. In neither country was society unhinged in order to replace it with a new one after the French model. In both countries government still stands on the foundation of God's Word and the historic rights that have roots in the nation's past. The only exception is the Radical group in England, especially the Birmingham club.[20]

If asked whether our sympathies in British politics then lie with the Tories or the Whigs, one can already infer from our "leftist trend" (as it has been called) that we lean toward the Whigs. We admit that, to the degree that different countries can be compared, the domestic politics of Forster and Gladstone has virtually the same intentions as what antirevolutionaries aim at in the Netherlands. This explains why one of our conservative dailies could write recently that a liberal like Gladstone in no way resembles a Dutch liberal and that the real Puritans in Britain almost to a man support Forster.[21]

In America it stands to reason that we side with the Republicans against the Democrats. The Republicans are the spiritual offspring of the old Pilgrim Fathers, the heroes of the Anti-Slavery War, the adversaries of Catholicism, and the spokesmen of that true civic spirit that arose especially in New England.

As for the second category, with respect to Germany it should be kept in mind that not the *Kreuzzeitung* but the *Reichsbote* with its much purer tone is the paper of our sympathies. By this we do not at all deny that the *Kreuzzeitung* has stoutly revenged itself for its moral lapse brought on by Bismarck's reckless action of 1866. Still, we are sorry to say that this return to better paths was never resolute and energetic enough to enable it to compete with the *Reichsbote*. Germany's antirevolutionary party, particularly since the "Christian socialists" have taken the bull by the horns,

---

20. Kuyper refers here to a movement for "secularism" founded by George Holyoake (1817–1906), a British utopian socialist.

21. William Edward Forster (1818–86) was a member of British prime minister William Ewart Gladstone's first ministry, whose Education Act of 1870 protected denominational schools and permitted religious instruction in government schools.

has been moving on firmer ground and is gradually freeing itself from the bad repute of the Junker party.[22]

As far as Catholic countries are concerned, they leave us almost cold— especially now that in France even a Broglie[23] has been chased from the scene as a "conspirator" and a Gambetta,[24] now master of the situation, looks like the calmest man in the world. Little can again be expected from the colorless constitutionalists, and the legitimists have forfeited their honor by allying with the republicans. He who loves France and fears God turns his eyes away from this sorry spectacle of human self-abasement and dreams nostalgically of what France might have been if only she had not listened to the Sorbonne but instead to the man from Geneva.

The same is true, *mutatis mutandis*, of Austria, Italy, Spain, and Belgium. We are keenly aware that the clerical parties in these countries would like to prevent free proclamation of the gospel, while the radicals on that score are favorably disposed towards us. But in these exclusively Catholic countries this is such a minor issue that it would be very superficial to let that determine our sympathies—all the more so after it became clear how badly we would compromise ourselves in the company of atheists from Antwerp who misuse the name "Beggar" and of radicals in Brussels who misuse the name of our Marnix of St. Aldegonde.[25]

Finally, the fact that we often judge the actions of the Russian government more positively is easily explained from the circumstance that every attempt at converting Russia into a state after the revolutionary model has thus far been resolutely resisted. The conviction that "Russia must seek its own form of government along its own paths without allowing itself to be seduced by foreign utopias" is a thoroughly antirevolutionary idea (although this certainly does not stop us from severely condemning

---

22. The Junkers were the landowning aristocrats of Prussia who supported Bismarck's aggressive foreign policy, which was also endorsed by the conservative newspaper *Die Kreuzzeitung*.

23. Albert de Broglie (1821–1901), a three-time conservative prime minister of the Third French Republic, was denounced as a "traitor" by the royalist party for supporting President Mac-Mahon (1808–93) in 1877 in his controversial dismissal of the Chamber of Deputies known as the "coup d'état of May 16."

24. Leon Gambetta (1838–82), a radical leader in the Third French Republic, converted to "moderate opportunism" after 1877.

25. "Beggar" here translates the original *Geuzen* (from the French word *gueux*, "beggars"), a term of contempt, but later the honorific label for participants in the Dutch Revolt.

what happened, for example, in Poland).[26] Add to that the fact that the Russian Empire, as a patron of the Christian religion, has always opposed Islam both in Europe and in Asia. As well, the person of the czar offers a valuable counterweight to the pope of Rome. Understandably, a mighty empire with such desirable traits has always enjoyed a measure of sympathy on the part of antirevolutionaries. Thus in its present struggle Russia enjoys the moral support of Gladstone and Forster, of the Republicans in America and the antirevolutionary party in Germany. And all who were called "Christian-national" in our country have always, spontaneously and unanimously, sided with Russia.

---

26. In 1831, and again in 1863, the czarist regime squelched uprisings in Warsaw with a heavy hand.

CHAPTER TWO

AUTHORITY

The party locates the source of sovereign authority not in the will of the people, nor in the law, but solely in God, and therefore it rejects popular sovereignty on the one hand and on the other it honors the sovereignty of Orange that under God's guidance is rooted in the history of our country and was brought to development by the men of 1813 and confirmed as such in the Constitution.

ARTICLE 2

I. SOVEREIGNTY

§ 17   ABSOLUTE AUTHORITY[1]

Sovereignty in an absolute sense occurs only when there is an authority that has no other authority over it, that always commands and never obeys, that does not admit of restrictions or allow competition, and that is single and undivided for all that has breath.

I am sovereign in an absolute sense only over that with which I can do what I please. Since as a human being I never possess such unlimited power over anything, it is out of the question that I shall ever possess original sovereignty.

---

1. When the original manuscript for the book was assembled from *De Standaard* newspaper articles, section numbers 15 and 16 were inadvertently skipped; that no actual sections are missing is confirmed by original publication dates for the articles constituting the prior and subsequent sections. See introduction, note 2.

Just because I can draw or write anything at all on the piece of paper in front of me still does not mean that I am a sovereign over that piece of paper. For that paper is hard or soft, fibrous or smooth, of a certain thickness and length, and so on, and I am bound to all these properties. They restrict my power and force me to conform to them. To be sovereign in this case I would personally have to be the maker of that paper, this pen, and that ink, and I would have to make them each time again in order to have them serve my purpose and remove every impediment to my will.

But even if you think that this would be conceivable, I still would not have sovereign power over that piece of paper, since in making it I would find myself bound by the materials and the tools commonly used for the papermaking process, and I would often bump up against the limits of what is possible when I try to introduce still one more improvement or remove one last flaw. I would have to have complete control over those raw materials and those instruments. Assume for a moment that even if that were possible and that in the making of pen and ink I disposed over the same creative freedom, then just to be sovereign in the mechanics of writing I would have to be able to freely determine or alter the laws governing the adhesion of the ink to the nib and the flow of the liquid onto the paper.

Only Possible with God §18

Transferring this special case to the general situation, we can see that the following is required for wielding absolute sovereignty over any object: (1) that I have this object completely in my possession; (2) that I have made it with my own hands as I saw fit; (3) that calling the necessary raw materials into being depends on my omnipotence; and (4) that it is up to me to set the laws that will govern its action and regulate its relation to other objects.

Now then, since no man, however celebrated, talented, or powerful, will ever have such power at his disposal, it follows that no ruler can ever be truly an absolute sovereign over his people. Similarly, no father can ever really be an absolute sovereign over his family, and no farmer can ever be a truly absolute sovereign over his animals. Thus any ruler who nevertheless arrogates such a right to himself only does so against right, by abusing power and destroying the mental and spiritual development of his people. Any father who exercises such exorbitant powers over his wife and children can only do so in spite of right and fairness and at the price of the more noble aspects of family life. And the madman who lays violent hands on his animals violates a higher law-order and lowers himself to the rank of a brute.

Sovereign authority over nations presupposes sovereign power over the families, and thus over the people that make up these nations. It can therefore reside only with the one who created these people, families, individuals—created them according to his good pleasure, without being bound to anything other than the laws and ordinances that he himself had earlier decreed according to the demands of his own being and for the benefit of people's flesh and blood as well as their heads and hearts, their tastes and feelings, and their moral and religious development. The possession of their whole person would be his as well as their very existence. From him would be the substance of their material and spiritual being, and from him also the laws that govern the life and development of their entire human personhood.

Who else, pray tell, can this be but the supreme, holy, almighty God?

Furthermore, sovereign power is exercised in the home of your neighbor on the left and in the home of your neighbor on the right, and the unity of the two is found in the mayor of your village. But next to that village lies another village, and the union of their sovereignties automatically points to the regional government. Yet your region, too, is surrounded by other regions, and the union of all these regions flows down from a single central government. At this point, however, you cannot go any further on earth; you run stuck. For next to your own country are other countries where sovereign authority is exercised, just as in yours. If you then look around on earth for the unifying point of all those lines, you will be hopelessly disappointed. So you must look higher, to a power to which all these countries are equally subservient! Now then, who else has power over all the nations of the earth but the Lord our God?

Add to that the current state of the different nations: their condition has come about as a result of what was done in the past. The generation now living was not free to choose; willy-nilly it had to accept the national heritage in the form as it was enriched or impoverished by an earlier generation. And that earlier generation, too, did not do so in complete freedom, but in turn found itself restricted by what a still earlier generation had done. And so history shows continuous, ceaseless change that shapes political authority in every country and for which all generations together are responsible.

If here I look again for the origin of sovereign authority, then of course I have to find a power that could govern all these generations combined; a power that held in its hand the entire history of our nation and other nations; in short, a power not for one age but for all ages. And again we ask: who else could possess such power but God?

In sum, sovereign political authority that is exercised among the nations of the earth has to cooperate with the laws that govern the life of mankind; with the laws that regulate air and soil and the life of animals in their development; with the laws that have guided the history of our nation and other nations. And only when this entire complex of laws—including the laws for thinking (*logic*), willing (*morality*), feeling (*aesthetics*), and eternal life (*religion*)—interacts and works together in good order and harmony, does the wheel of life revolve majestically around sovereignty.

All Sovereign Authority Derives from God   § 19

On this account we wholeheartedly confess what Jesus' apostle has put on the lips of every Christian: namely, that the governing authorities "that exist have been instituted by God";[2] or, to use the words of our Program: that the source of sovereign authority does not reside in the law or the will of the people but in God.

And truly, either one has stopped thinking or one must admit that only the atheist can dispute the truth of this premise. Whoever acknowledges that God exists cannot but profess that he is the Almighty One, and that this structure we call *world*, and that other structure we call our *country* or *nation*, is dependent upon him.

A political authority decides on questions of justice and injustice. It determines what shall count as acceptable and unacceptable in civil society. It will have a say over your possessions, in some cases over your house, sometimes even over your personal freedom—in fact, over the life of your children by having them draw lots.[3] How then, we ask, would anyone ever wish to constitute such an authority and yet *not* have that authority derive from God, flowing from him and willed by him?

For if not, you would get a godlike power next to your God; or rather, your God would cease to be your God. To ask for your rights from the state on the one hand, and on the other to ask for healing from your God in

---

2. Rom 13:1.
3. "Drawing lots" refers to the method of deciding who should be conscripted for military service.

times of illness—that is not the religion of robust folk! That is to play with words in days of health and to toy with one's heart when ill. That is poetry, not a reality that will see us through. Or if you will: it is to pose as a citizen without God at one time, to be inconstant in our piety the next.

II. ITS HISTORIC DEVELOPMENT

§ 20   SOVEREIGNTY IN EVERY DISTINCT DOMAIN OF LIFE

For this reason we must look for the source of all sovereign authority in the living God alone, since he alone has at his command every creature and every order of things and every kingdom in the natural world. To use a word from Scripture: "the pillars of the earth are the Lord's, and on them he has set the world."[4]

Sovereign authority, flowing from that source, flows out over all creation, not just in the political field but in every domain. Laws of nature exercise authority over matter, and in matter the strong elements over the weak. Authority is wielded by climate and soil over the world of plants, and in that world by the laws that govern its life. Authority is also wielded by nature over the animals; in that animal world by one animal over another; in some of their packs by their leaders; and over all of them by mankind. Similarly, control, command, power, and authority are wielded among people by people, in every domain of human life.

There is an authority, a power, which our body, our blood and nerves, must obey if we are not to grow wanting and weak. In the domain of thought there is the authority of the laws for thought, the power of logic that must govern the formation of every judgment. Talent exercises authority in the area of science, genius in the area of art. Authority is indispensable and exists wherever people are active, be it in industry or agriculture, in seamanship or commerce. And all these varieties of authority are established, maintained and exercised, not by convention or legislation, but only by "God the Father, almighty, creator of heaven and earth."

One cannot do with one's body as one pleases, but must obey God in it. One cannot think arbitrarily, but must do so as God has ordained the power to form judgments. And so also in the areas of scholarship and business nothing remains but to trace the laws and relations that God has laid in them.

---

4. 1 Sam 2:8

In the same vein, authority exists also in the moral and spiritual domain. Moral life, just like physical life, is subject to laws and influences that are determined by God, not man. We are all obliged to follow those laws and obey those influences, on pain of moral death. This is a rule that holds even more strongly for our spiritual, eternal growth, which—depending of course on God's counsel and decree, his foreordinations and spiritual laws—is subject in the strictest sense of the word to his absolute sovereignty.

SOVEREIGN AUTHORITY IN THE POLITICAL DOMAIN   § 21

Political sovereignty, therefore, is not an isolated case but merely one link in the great chain that causes the whole creation to cohere and exist by the ordinances of God.

Nevertheless, there is one important difference between all these sovereignties and sovereignty in the political domain. In the political domain God delegates to humanity the power to exercise this supreme power consciously and purposefully. An artist like Raphael exercised as much sovereign authority as a statesman like Bismarck, but with this considerable difference that Raphael did so unconsciously and unintentionally whereas Bismarck does so only through deliberate acts.

In every other domain of life, authority is exercised simply by letting the ordinances of God take their course and by acting as a personal link in that. But in the political domain the sovereign himself is invested with the making of laws that determine what is just, and he is charged with the right to enforce those laws.

So we repeat what we said at the outset of this article: sovereign authority flows out from God Almighty *to all parts of his creation*—to air and soil, to plant and animal, to a person's body and a person's soul, and in that soul to one's thinking, feeling, and will; and further, to society in all its organic spheres of scholarship and business; and finally, to families, to rural and urban communities, and to the sphere that encompasses all these spheres and has to safeguard them all: to the state.

Thus political authority operates alongside many other authorities that are equally absolute and sacred in the natural and spiritual world, in society and family. Every attempt by political authority to try and rule over one of those other areas is therefore a violation of God's ordinances, and resistance to it is not a crime but a duty.

Moreover, when a country's political authority defines by law the boundaries where a different sovereign authority stops and its own begins, then this in no way restricts that sovereignty but merely indicates its natural limits.

Conversely, to surrender, be it to society or the family or nature, any portion of what belongs to political authority is not an act of liberality, but is sacrilege.

What the doctrine of sovereignty requires is simply this: (1) to recognize that sovereign authority obtains in every domain of life; (2) to fully grasp that political sovereignty has its own distinctive character; and (3) to include under it whatever belongs to it and exclude from it whatever does not belong to it.

§ 22   HISTORICAL GROWTH OF POLITICAL SOVEREIGNTY

The particular manner in which God Almighty transfers sovereign political authority may vary. Sometimes this happens as a result of the passage of time after violent conquest. Sometimes this happens through an agreed upon settlement. Sometimes it is done by orderly mandate, be it through popular acclamation of the people or in a solemn assembly of its leaders. And finally, as far as the personal bearers of the Crown are concerned, the transfer of political authority occurs chiefly through inheritance after a death.

None of these ways and means lies outside divine dispensation. Here too God's rule uses the sins of the nations and the crimes of the powerful. During such transitions, the one holding the power has to be respected as the bearer of sovereignty as soon as his sway, as a result of gaining recognition or else through intimidation, reaches far enough to cause his laws to be legally binding before the conscience of the nation.

Exactly *who* becomes bearer of the sovereignty as a result of these events is neither here nor there. Sovereign political authority can flow from God Almighty to the heart of a single man or to a dynasty of heroic men. But it can also descend upon an institution of which consuls, dictators, viceroys, or, if you will, presidents of a republic, are merely the temporary occupants. In fact, one is so little bound to a single individual that sovereign authority can reside, as it did in the former Dutch Republic, with the estates of the realm, or even, as is the case in more than one country in the Americas, with the voters themselves.

But no matter what the scenario, one must make sure that people fully acknowledge that this sovereign authority is from God and not from man. The destructive delusion of popular sovereignty must be permanently abandoned and remain banned. If a people imagines it can *grant* sovereignty it will also view itself as supreme; then it will want to dominate instead of obey, and "sit in the seat of God."[5] And if one tries to camouflage popular sovereignty with milder expressions like "the social contract shall be supreme" or "all authority resides in the law," it would not eradicate the root of godlessness. Even under a social contract the human creature continues to say: "I do these things at my own pleasure" and so he lays the foundation for a state that must end with enmity toward God and his Word.

And when "more respectable" men today go on driveling about "the law" as the source of authority, this too is nothing but a fiction in order to escape the will of the people that presumably is not aristocratic enough. As these gentlemen themselves profess, what is that law to which they will swear an oath other than the pronouncement in dignified form of what the *pays légal*[6] has willed.

In the face of these fictions and monstrous theories we resolutely maintain the following three propositions: (1) political authority, like every other form of sovereign authority in life, flows from the living God; (2) for the transfer of this authority in the course of history the Lord uses both lawful and unlawful deeds of men; and (3) the transfer takes place to single individuals, to dynasties, to institutions, or to the nation as a whole.

REVOLUTION §23

However, some people will ask, is it not the people themselves that create a new sovereign authority whenever a new state is established or a revolution is successful? We would agree *qua* form, but we deny it on principle.

If the executor of an estate liquidates a deceased's assets and distributes the proceeds, was he then the owner during those weeks or months? Or, stronger, if you find a briefcase on the sidewalk filled with banknotes and after many days return it to its rightful owner, are you then handing him a gift from your possessions?

---

5. Ezek 28:2 (KJV).
6. The term *pays légal* refers to the nineteenth-century franchise, that is, that fraction of the nation that had been given the vote based on the level of taxes one had paid.

No one would dream of asserting such an absurd idea. Why then view it as anything other than the act of an executor when a nation transfers or commissions sovereignty to a ruler? When that nation on behalf of the Almighty delivers this precious jewel to the ruler, is the messenger or the agent then the owner of the sovereignty?

And if we are then pointed to scenes such as those that existed under the Paris Commune and slyly asked whether that too was the exercise of sovereignty, then we venture a counter-question: if you are unconscious and delirious with fever, are you then still there, and will you come out of it as a human being?[7] Everyone will answer that during such a delirium not the conscious person is speaking but rather his senses that are set adrift. In the same way we judge of the Commune and similar travesties that this was not the execution of sovereign authority but the sick and deadly ravings of an alien intruder.

III. THE LEGAL BASIS OF SOVEREIGNTY IN THE NETHERLANDS

§ 24   THE SOVEREIGNTY OF ORANGE BASED IN HISTORY

As in any state, a political sovereignty is also operative in the Netherlands. This authority determines what will be just and unjust. It combats injustice and upholds justice, if need be with force. It represents the nation abroad. Domestically it seeks to confirm, improve, and enlarge the opportunities and conditions by which Dutch national life, and with that the personal lives of people, can flourish.

Now then, with whom does this political sovereignty reside, this supremacy by the grace of God?

All will agree that the answer cannot be: with the mass of the people. Nor with the voters. Certainly not with the ministry or the States General.[8] And to say that the sovereignty lies with the law is as absurd as to say that the nightingale is in its song. The sovereign, after all, is the one that must give the law.

---

7. The Paris Commune was the name of the provisional government of Paris during the working-class uprising in the spring of 1871, marked by hastily improvised measures in keeping with socialist ideals.

8. The "ministry" refers to the council or cabinet, consisting of the heads of government departments. The "States General" refers to parliament, consisting of a First (upper) and a Second (lower) Chamber.

This alone makes it apparent that in fact the sovereignty, which must reside somewhere, can have no other address than the *House of Orange*. Such is our provisional conclusion, one with which the annals of history fully agree.

In the year 1813, the son and heir of Orange was proclaimed Sovereign Prince by common consent and with a level of enthusiasm that would have smothered every protest (assuming there had been any) with the cry "God wills it!" This event was recorded in the Constitution of 1814 in the following words: "The sovereignty of the United Netherlands is and remains assigned to the Prince of Orange Nassau, to be heritable by his lawful descendants." The Constitution of 1815 expressed this almost verbatim, replacing only "sovereignty" with "Crown," to prevent any misunderstanding and rule out any sort of absolutism.[9]

This was a view that was still shared in 1848 by the then sitting cabinet when it used these words in its program of May 13: "The nation feels deeply that, just as it owes its independence to the ruling dynasty, this independence remains tied to *the preservation of sovereignty in that House*." The revised Constitution of the same year again used the selfsame formula: "The Crown is and remains assigned..." This, we believe, raises above suspicion the conclusion that the framers of our fundamental laws, both in 1815 and in 1848, as in 1814, only meant to give constitutional form to the historical fact that was accomplished in 1813. The Constitution assigns nothing; it merely notes that the Sovereignty, the Crown, before the framers of the constitution ever met, "*had been* assigned," not in order to have the Constitution take it back again, or alter it or transfer it, but to have it *remain* so assigned.

THE SOVEREIGNTY OF ORANGE IN 1813   § 25

Now for the historical event of 1813. Were the leaders of the day—Van Hogendorp, Van der Duyn, Van Stirum, along with De Kemper and Falck—were they in possession of the sovereignty and did they tour the country in search of a prince? Hardly. As the kingdom of the Netherlands was being set up, Orange was by rights not a pretender to the throne but the only rightful and eligible candidate.

---

9. This revision, so soon after the Constitution of 1814, was necessitated by the merger of the Northern Netherlands with the Southern Netherlands (now known as Belgium) to create the United Kingdom of the Netherlands.

To be convinced of this, all you need to do is draw up a list of foreign princes or local grandees who might have been named alongside Orange as serious candidates—I do not say with a chance of success, much less with a semblance of right, but at least with propriety. Doing so, you will realize at once that below the name of Orange this list would have had to remain blank. Admit, then, that the Triumvirate had no choice, given the situation, but to go by the unquestionable option that was unmistakably indicated by the sum and substance of our historic and political past.

Nonetheless, what was arranged by the men of 1813 reflected what our Program rightly calls "a development" of what was available in that situation. The situation called for three things. First, it was impossible to restore the political framework of the Union of Utrecht.[10] Second, it was essential to curb factionalism by establishing a unitary, hereditary form of government. Third, it was a duty of gratitude to assign this unitary authority to the House of Orange.

But this threefold result of history was developed by the men of 1813 in such a way that for that unitary administration they chose the form of monarchy and from the start pressed the Netherlandic stamp upon that monarchy by setting it up as a *shield for*, not a *bulwark against*, the rights and liberties of the nation.

Later we will deal with the question whether they acted beyond reproach and did not give in too much to the seductive idea of "having a king like all the other nations."[11] Just this: if a less exalted title had been chosen, the House of Orange might well have gained in splendor, and political wisdom might have found the means to introduce in the Constitution of 1814 what turned out to be unattainable even in 1848. It would probably have spared us the upheaval of 1830[12] and the desperation of 1848.[13]

---

10. The Union of Utrecht (1579) regulated the political relations among the towns and territories that were in revolt against Spain. It laid the groundwork for the later republic of the Seven United Netherlands that carried on as a highly decentralized federation that in time often frustrated united action and also facilitated the predominance of the province of Holland.

11. See 1 Sam 8:19-20.

12. In 1830 the Belgian Revolt led to the breakup of the United Kingdom of the Netherlands.

13. In 1848, the "year of revolution" that rocked Europe as crowds demonstrated and thrones toppled, panic gripped the Dutch government. The conservative Dutch

The main thing, apart from the actual sovereignty of Orange, is the *manner* in which it was politically embodied and formulated. In the words of our Program, this took place "under God's guidance." We cannot but speak here of the guidance of God, because the creation of great men, more than anything else, is an immediate act of the "Father of spirits."[14]

Add to that the fact that a single family produced a succession of men without equal, such as William the Silent, Maurice, Frederick Henry, and William III, to name just the stars of the first magnitude.[15] Admired by all Europe, they joined the glory of a princely house to the splendor of their character and personality. Each was a hero and a genius, inspired by one grand idea and devoted to one and the same noble cause. More than once they saved the sinking fatherland from ruin and raised it from those depths to unknown heights of power and glory. They set the moral tone of our national life and gave it moral leadership. As dynasty and nation grew together, they mutually sealed this intimate partnership in the struggle for a sacred ideal with the noblest of blood.[16] Very well, in the historic rise of such a dynasty we are naïve, superstitious, and old-fashioned enough to honor the slow action of God's providence for the sake of preparing for himself a bearer of his sovereign authority over these lands.

No ruling house in Europe experienced the kind of opposition that Orange endured. That opposition was locally planned, systematically fostered, and brilliantly organized.[17] Yet in spite of opposition and adversity, the moral influence and reputation of this house continued to rise, even under descendants who could not match their great forefathers. The indispensable role of the house of Orange was more and more recognized. In the natural course of events, without intent or intrigue, its members were eventually raised to the office of hereditary stadtholder. Given these

---

king surprised his ministers by declaring that he had become a liberal overnight and by appointing a committee to revise the constitution in a liberal sense. See below, § 83n11.

14. Heb 12:9.

15. These men were princes of Orange, stadtholders of the Netherlands; William III was also king of England (1689–1702).

16. This "sacred ideal" in Kuyper's reading of Dutch history was to champion freedom of conscience and offer asylum to religious refugees.

17. Kuyper makes reference to the periodic opposition to the status of the princes of Orange waged by the urban oligarchy of the upper-middle class known in history as the States party.

facts, is the phrase "rooted in our national soil" too strong an expression for the history that Orange went through in these lands?

If we are then asked whether we want to surround the Orange dynasty with a halo of mystery, then we answer without hesitation: with a mystery, yes—the mystery of a higher guidance than is customary in the affairs of men; the mystery of a hidden power that, through changing persons and events, has destined our nation for one grand purpose and never ceases to enrich us with these eminent princes for attaining that purpose. It is a mystery—if we are pressed to come out and say so—which still today contains the secret of the slogan "Up Orange!" and offers hope for the future happiness of our country.

This belief (for that is what it is) in no way diminishes our vigilance and realism in the political domain. We want to make sure that the constitutional supremacy assigned to Orange does not, according to Groen's witty saying, degenerate into a sovereignty "that is at home in China, Japan or even Russia," but remains the kind of sovereignty that alone could be assigned in our country: "a genuinely Netherlandic sovereignty over the Netherlands."

CHAPTER THREE

THE ORDINANCES OF GOD

It professes the eternal principles of God's Word also for the political domain, yet in such a way that the authority of the state is bound to the ordinances of God neither directly, nor by the pronouncement of any church, but only in the consciences of those in government.

ARTICLE 3

I. KNOWABLE ONLY FROM GOD'S WORD

THE MAKING OF LAWS IS BOUND TO GOD'S WILL   § 27

Government has the competence to determine the law of the land, and government has the duty to uphold that law, if need be by force.

This raises the question by what standard a government ought to establish the law. No one would say that this can be done in an arbitrary way. A government that creates capricious ordinances, declares its whims to be the rule, and raises ill-considered ideas into law would judge itself and could not stand.

Government is to make just laws, but it can only do so on the basis of assuming that justice already exists. It exists before government considers and passes laws. Government's contribution is confined to having its laws *reflect correctly* what objective justice is as required by the principles of justice. Knowledge of those principles is therefore the sovereign's starting point for all good legislative work. In the measure that his insight into those principles grows and improves, in that measure he secures and sanctifies his institutions.

It is our conviction that sound and comprehensive knowledge of those principles can only be attained by studying God's Word and researching God's ordinances.

The criteria that others recommend for determining what is just and unjust leave us unsatisfied: neither history nor legal science nor philosophy of law, as far we can judge, offers a reliable starting point for knowledge of the true, sound, eternal principles of justice.

Not history! For although we would agree at once that a nation's manners, customs, and usages express its sense of justice, and legislation that failed to take tradition into account would be without any basis—yet history cannot be the test of principles for the simple reason that it never *formulated* the principles of justice, even though it is a record of their constant *application*. And if that were no objection, still we could not be certain that justice applied might not have been justice perverted or justice denied.

Nor can we go by legal science. For although we would concede that a nation's sense of justice undergoes constant development, and that legal science, by tracing this development, can in part discover along what lines justice unfolds from its principles—yet any scientific conclusions could never provide us with the criterion for justice, because humanity's sense of justice is disturbed by sin, and the outcome in the non-Christian nations of our continent (ancient Rome not excluded) remains absolutely unsatisfactory, for example, with respect to the rights of the human person.

And to seek the help of philosophy is the very error of the revolutionaries. We need only point to the arbitrary systems of Rousseau and the Encyclopedists, followed by the systems of the democrats, next of the respectable constitutionalists, and today of the radical socialists and doctrinaires of every description. They remind us where humans end up if they presume to *decree* principles instead of *seeking them out* and to press God's creation into the straitjacket of a self-constructed theory.

No, as soon as it is a question of justice you have to choose for or against the living God. If he lives, and if we and our nation and all the nations of the world are subject to him, then his alone is the right to determine what is just and unjust.

You cannot be a human of one piece, a person of character and intelligence, and still allow yourself to be tempted to split your conscience in two, professing your God in one half and in the other half bowing before laws that have nothing to do with him. That does not comport with reason, nor does it square with your conscience.

If God is truly God, then all determination of law proceeds from him, and all that remains for us to do is to ask with holy reverence for the road that can lead us to the purest knowledge of what God Almighty has stamped as justice for the whole of his creation—as eternal justice for every creature.

God's Ordinances for Nature and Human Life §28

If we may refer to these as "ordinances of God" then it follows that there are ordinances for soil and climate, for the products and resources of our country, and for the animals over which we were given dominion. But there are also ordinances of God for *human life*, for body and mind, for the development of our human capacities, for blood relations and kinship, for commerce and industry, for our calling and destiny as a nation. In short, there is a will, a command, an ordinance of the Lord for everything that people can have two opinions about. According to the firm principles that flow forth from God's holy Being, one will be commendable, the other unacceptable.

Naturally it would be easiest for us if God had decided to communicate all these ordinances to us in clear statements. But that was not what he decided, and it behooves us to acquiesce in that decision.

Most ordinances, in fact, can only be made out from reality itself. In the case of the natural and material life of man and beast, empirical research is the only way to discover them—but we hasten to add: since no human willing, and therefore no sin, comes into play here, such research almost always suffices.

The real difficulty begins in that part of life which involves human will and which requires not just observing positive facts but also drawing positive conclusions. The inevitable result of our sinful condition is that time and again we draw the wrong conclusions and despite the best of intentions stray from the path of righteousness. Even so, rulers and peoples retain some natural knowledge of God, some moral law in their conscience, some sense of what is shameful. This safeguards virtue. But however much these supports of righteousness are to be valued, they do not lead to correct knowledge of God's higher ordinances. This is sufficiently plain in the history of the most outstanding nations in antiquity and still today in the wretched condition of life in, for example, China, Siam, or Baluchistan.[1]

§ 29   THERE IS A REVELATION OF GOD'S WILL

If there were no revelation, we too would have to put up with similar conditions and resign ourselves to bearing the consequences that sin brings in its train. Sin is a divisive, darkening, and disruptive force in every domain of human life, not least in the area of justice.

But no, as Christians we confess that there is such a revelation. The divided and dispersed nations of the world are not left to their own devices. To check the effects of sin, God Almighty has in a special way revealed himself "at many times and in many ways."[2] We have access to a Word of God in a narrow sense that spreads considerable light on those eternal principles and indicates to a considerable degree those divine ordinances for human life.

To be sure, we understand perfectly well that there are people who do not embrace this revelation as coming from God. But what we do not understand is that there are people who accept this Word of God with deep reverence and yet do not want to involve its directives in political administration, legislation, and the justice system.

That is worse than being inconsistent. That—we do not hesitate to say it—is tantamount to professing a truth while not really believing it, to be guilty of moral fence-sitting that is bereft of all sincerity; or if you will, it is playing with the sacred that is unworthy of a person of character.

We antirevolutionaries do not wish to become accessories to such vacillation and half-heartedness. In defiance of prevailing ideas, we pride ourselves on fine-tuning our convictions in accordance with the following propositions:

(1) All law that is to pass for just law on earth must pass the test of justice.

(2) God alone determines what is just, in accordance with his holy being.

---

1. "Siam" refers to Thailand; "Baluchistan" refers to the southwestern province of Pakistan.
2. Heb 1:1.

(3) Insofar as human life is concerned, pure knowledge and firmness of these divine ordinances were lost as a result of sin.

(4) Natural theology and natural morality, however much to be appreciated, are therefore insufficient for getting to know the eternal principles.

(5) The special, supernatural revelation of God's Word has spread important light on those principles, including principles relevant to civil life; and it is therefore our calling to confess, also in the political domain, the eternal principles revealed in that Word.

II. WORKING THROUGH THE CONSCIENCE OF THE GOVERNMENT

HOLY SCRIPTURE AS THE RECORD OF THAT REVELATION   § 30

If God invests governments with sovereign power to determine what the law shall be, and if he wills that they should not do this arbitrarily but in accordance with the eternal principles that he has set, then we must ask: By what means can governments get to know what those eternal principles are?

If this arrangement had stayed the way it was originally, if sin had not disrupted this wonderful organism, and if it still ran the way God had made it run from the beginning, then the answer to this question could have been: earthly governments know those eternal principles from what they see all around them, from the course of life itself, from the way things work!

Just as an experienced watchmaker gets to know the principles according to which a watch is made when he takes the watch apart, or just as a chemist learns the composition of a substance through analysis, so in the same way governments would get to know the proper course of life through simple observation—would learn the principles that underlie those laws which are just.

That is exactly what most people believe, now that fewer and fewer people recognize the reality of sin. An odd conclusion, since if there were no sin and everything ran well, government would not exist. If everything worked properly on its own, well then, it would work by itself and would need neither guidance nor correction by some external power.

The Reformers saw correctly that government is only there because of sin and that as a result all politics divides into two broad streams: former ages acknowledged the sins of persons and nations; our age attributes them to immaturity and judges that the time is not yet ripe for the just society.

We for our part would violate our conviction if we weakened the awesome fact of sin. Sin is a disruptive and destructive force for decay. Thus we are obliged to open another path that can guide government to knowledge of the ordinances of God. We open this path by pointing to the holy ordinances that nature still teaches us for unfree (that is, material) life and what God's Word teaches us for free (that is, moral) life.

Yet even that does not resolve the difficulty. It would, if Holy Scripture were composed like a law code, so that one could look up the various titles and articles and find there the rules that are to govern relations between government and subjects and the mutual relations among subjects.

But that is not what Scripture is. It is not a repository of legal provisions. Rather, it is the certified record of one mighty revelation about life spanning a history of centuries. Scripture contains God's ordinances— that is, his eternal and unchangeable principles—but mostly in mixed form, like nuggets in a gold mine.

§ 31   Exegeting Scripture. Theocracy

This raises another, no less weighty question. In what manner are governments to obtain knowledge of the eternal principles presented to us in God's Word?

Three answers are conceivable. First, one might say: The task of the church is to show in what manner. This is the answer given by Rome.

Rome has never denied that government has a right to independence of judgment in its own affairs. But as soon as it is a question of primary, eternal principles, Rome has always reserved the final decision to herself. Reserved to herself, not just in the acceptable sense of recommending and urging her decision, but of wielding an authority that is rightfully hers. This authority may factually be set aside, but never with impunity from a spiritual point of view. Think of Syllabus and Encyclical![3]

Now then, we are diametrically opposed to this solution. We do not wish that any Reformed church be given the right to decide what the divine ordinances for government are.

---

3. This is possibly an allusion in particular to the *Syllabus of Errors* (1864) against secular liberalism and the encyclical *Quod nunquam* (1875) against the May Laws in Prussia, both issued by Pope Pius IX. See below, § 80n7.

To have an opinion is the church's right. Her right to propagate her views within the spiritual sphere remains undisputed. And on occasion nothing prevents the church from approaching the government with a petition or a complaint regarding political issues.

But the church can never be given the authority *in her own right* to determine what should obtain for the state. That would cause a terrible confusion of the two spheres of life.

In a mixed community we do not desire a theocracy; rather, we oppose it with all our might, for two cogent reasons: (1) Wherever such church rule was established, it always ended in tyranny and the corruption of a people. (2) The church lacks the gifts required for giving laws for civil society that evince intimate knowledge and understanding of civil life.

CAESAROPAPISM   § 32

A second answer might be: Let government itself be the church! This solution is known as caesaropapism and has been adopted especially in Russia. The Russian czar is emperor and pope, that is, sovereign and high priest, or if you will, government and church, combined in one person.

This prevents clashes. The church retains its influence but cannot exercise it except through the sovereign. Its influence, therefore, is a sham.

In Russia it is indeed the czar, either in person or through his agents, that determines what shall count as divine ordinance in his realm. The Russian church serves only to accredit this for the common laity.

On a different scale this caesaropapism was also introduced by Protestant rulers, particularly in Germany, and it must be said to our shame that during the events of 1816 even our foremost pastors were far from unwilling to follow King William I on his questionable steps toward caesaropapism.[4]

This system, too, we reject most resolutely. It can only lead to the spiritual death of the church and thus to loss of spiritual knowledge of God's Word as it pertains also to government. Caesaropapism deprives the church of Christ of her freedom of movement, which is one of her vital conditions. It turns her pastors and teachers as if by magic into vapid and haughty magistrates, and turns believers and their church government

---

4. Kuyper alludes here to the reorganization in 1816 of the Dutch Reformed Church under newly issued Rules providing for a synod and church courts appointed by the state.

into each other's enemies. This weakens the church, causes her to pine away, and numbs her spirit.

Just look at what is left of vitality in the Greek Orthodox church! Consider the piteous state of the Evangelical churches in Germany. Remember how fatal the tender embrace of our national church has been as practiced by our ever so religion-minded government.

When the church languishes, we lose that fresh spiritual atmosphere in which alone the sound interpretation of the Word of God can flourish. What we end up with is the drone of Byzantine chanting or, as in our country, with Jewish teachers educating our youth in "Christian" virtues.[5]

We want to be inspired, not put to sleep. We seek God's glorious ordinances, not hollow words or empty phrases. We therefore oppose this second, even worse solution with conviction and force.

§ 33   The Conscience of the Government

The antirevolutionary party has always given the third answer: government authority is bound to the ordinances of God by way of the conscience of the government.

We are well aware that the possibility exists that a government's conscience is totally inaccessible to influences of God's Word. It is possible that the government even of a "Christian" nation falls away from the faith altogether and blatantly turns against the Christian religion, or under a Christian mask wages an even more bitter—and more dangerous, while hidden—war on whatever lives by God's Word. But this problem cannot detain us, for the obvious reason that this possibility exists just as much with the two previous solutions, only here in a more hideous, offensive, loathsome manner.

The problem is not due to the system but to the wretchedness of our conditions. Barring exceptional circumstances, it is a case of one of two things: either it is the natural chastening by which a nation that has forgotten God's Word is driven back to that Word; or else, if the confessors of God's Word form only a small minority in that nation, it is the heaven-sent spur to work hard for enlarging its influence.

How we conceive of the operation of God's ordinances on the conscience of the government will be shown in our concluding article.

---

5. By the Primary Education Act of 1857, all public school teachers without exception were obliged to educate the children in "Christian and civic virtues."

III. IN ITS OWN DISTINCTIVE WAY AND UNDER SOCIAL INFLUENCES

THE FACT OF SIN   § 34

In his fine book on education, *Nos fils*, the French author Jules Michelet makes a most valid observation. He writes, "The great divide in life occurs when you acknowledge or deny the fact of sin. You must choose, and depending on whether you proceed to the right and acknowledge it, or to the left and deny it, you will land on totally different shores."[6]

We can only affirm this truth. Also for politics.

If humans are sinners, there can be no question of deriving the eternal principles of justice from their sinful minds, and there is an imperative need for a direct Word of God to indicate the basis of law. But if people are merely undeveloped creatures, then their sense of justice, though not yet entirely clear, can still be correct and reliable, and there will be no need for a special Word of God since it would be available in the word of man.

The same contrast occurs among those who are in agreement about accepting God's Word as a rule for conduct also in politics. There too you will find those who first profess the reality of sin and then lose sight of it again, as Rome and the caesaropapists do, while the advocates of Protestant politics on the other hand continue to reckon with this fact.

If you proceed further while ignoring the profound significance of the fact of sin, as theocrats do, then you deem the sinner quite capable of acquiring firm, correct, and keen knowledge of what God's Word reveals about civil life. Then you are prepared to have a spiritual caste or a clique of court theologians establish these principles, thus crushing their tender shoots with the rigid fingers of the jurist.

But if you do not want this, if you remain mindful of the fact that you are dealing with sinners—with a sinner on the throne, with sinners in the assembly hall, with a sinner in his study, with sinners at the voting booth and in the homes—then you can only come to the frank admission, whether you like it or not, that the Word of God, however perfect in itself, yet precisely because it finds only sinners, can never be fully understood. You will recognize that it is impossible to formulate with fixed certainty, and lay down for all ages and all countries, the principles or ordinances of justice revealed in that Word.

---

6. See Jules Michelet, *Nos Fils* (Paris: Librairie Internationale, 1870), 10. Kuyper appears to be paraphrasing.

Because of this, we refuse to be blinded by an illusion of certainty that yields no security whatsoever and, content with more modest results than aimed at by czar or pope, we acquiesce in the effect which that Word exercises on the conscience of the people in government.

§ 35   DIVISION OF LABOR

By *the people in government* we mean the sovereign with all his subordinates. This includes at once a hierarchy of civil servants and bureaucrats. These may on occasion be in a position to persuade the sovereign, even one whose conscience is blunted, to make laws in conformity with God's Word, laws that he would never have discovered on his own.

It also includes all those officials whose conscience can inspire and pervade the interpretation and enforcement of the laws, even a lifeless law, with the eternal principles of justice.

It includes as well the whole body of government in all its branches, which can gradually form a tradition of nourishing a holy sense of justice. That sense can serve as a criterion when choosing new officers and can help a new generation uphold certain general concepts that are to govern the government bureaus.

We certainly do not mean by this that every civil servant is to consult the Bible when carrying out his task.

Such a superficial idea is furthest from our mind.

That every civil servant reads his Bible at home, to find therein food for his soul and dedication for his life's task—excellent! But the task of mining God's Word for the right principles and applying them to their specific portion of the public service far exceeds the power of ordinary civil servants.

That would lead to a morbid dilettantism that, as in the case of the Barebones Parliament, dissolves itself after a brief trial period.[7]

No, everyone should stay in his station.

To the legal scholars, the political philosophers, and the thinkers among our statesmen falls the weightiest task. They have to work very hard in order to be able to demonstrate with scholarly rigor that the principles

---

7. The Barebones Parliament, or the "parliament of saints," was installed in England in 1653. It was dominated by men with little or no political experience, and its incessant infighting caused it to be dissolved after less than half a year to make way for Cromwell as Lord Protector of the Commonwealth of England, Scotland, and Ireland.

they defend before a higher forum bear the hallmark of stemming from God's Word.

The practical statesmen, the popular tribunes, and the leaders of public opinion, armed with those principles, have to offer ceaseless criticism of the injustice present in the status quo and help improve the situation in keeping with the ordinances of God.

From the civil servants and bureaucrats, finally, after they have been inducted into that circle of ideas and breathed that atmosphere, no higher demand can be made than that they do their work *conscientiously*, lest the spirit of these higher principles is lost.

THE CHURCH AND THE PRESS   § 36

If, in conclusion, you ask just how the influence of God's Word operates on the consciences of those in government, then we must distinguish between a direct and an indirect influence.

The influence is direct when government officials who occupy the highest rung of the ladder personally glean from God's Word, in their private studies or in the cabinet, what they will champion in public as a responsible system of statecraft.

The indirect influence, by contrast, comes in many forms and is exerted by the church, the press, public opinion, and world opinion.

Later we shall discuss the range and limits of the church. Here we are only concerned with the calling of the church. The church is called to devote special spiritual care to those people in government who belong to her membership. The church should also nurture sound theological studies so that the political theorist, too, is able to study God's Word. And, last but not least, the church should resist the fundamental error of one-sided spiritualization, as though civil society did not concern the Christian.

After the church comes the press. The press is a kind of mediator, an unofficial interpreter if you like, between nation and government. If the press suggests day in, day out that you can engage in politics apart from Christ and that you should lean on your own understanding and rebuff God's Word, then this will dull the conscience of those in government, and they too will come to love wandering on self-chosen paths. But if daily newspapers appear that dare once more to base themselves on the Word of God, which recommend again the principles of that Word for the political domain and remind king and country of their duty toward the divine ordinances—then increasingly the conscience of the people in government will at first be shocked and provoked, and before long challenged, and the ordinances of God will gain in influence during their deliberations.

No less strongly, in the third place, does *public opinion* exert influence on the conscience of those in government.

If a people is serious, its government cannot be light-hearted. A people that seeks after God cannot be governed unless the sovereign allows himself to be governed by God's Word.

The spirit of a nation and the spirit of its government may be distinct, but they are not hermetically sealed from one another. They interpenetrate.

Thus if a government knows that enacting laws according to the demands of God's Word will meet with reluctance and resistance, it will be tempted to go astray itself and burn incense before the idols of the day. Conversely, if folk songs and folk sayings, days of prayer and national holidays, petitions and elections encourage a people to raise the level of seriousness, ennoble national life, and praise the Almighty—then it will automatically motivate government, if only to satisfy the nation, to inquire again after the ordinances of God.

§ 37   World Opinion

Finally we mentioned world opinion,[8] a factor that is overlooked much too often.

For consider: whatever people in London, Paris, or Berlin think, ponder, and believe has such a preponderant influence on the whole of Europe's press and literature, ours included, that one can literally observe a shift in public opinion and a reversal in prevailing views in all the smaller countries of our continent the moment a great metropolis takes the lead. Think of the recent May Laws and the growth of state absolutism.[9]

And this is perfectly natural. The influential people in our country read almost nothing else than books from abroad. Their study aids come from abroad. So does their recreational literature. So do the models they imitate. Even our leading papers contain little else besides echoes of what the leading dailies contain in France, Germany, or Britain. And in our clubs and ladies' salons and in our secondary schools it is always a foreign product that occupies and captivates the minds. Really, our own indigenous life of the mind is so small. It is small in size and often smaller in quality.

---

8. In the original: "…the opinion of Europe."
9. The May Laws were repressive laws in Germany aimed at Catholics and socialists. See above, § 13n19.

It cannot stand against the mighty stream from abroad. We just drift with the current.

Now that this stream runs almost entirely counter to Christ, it is only natural that the general way of thinking is increasingly deteriorating and affecting the conscience of the people in government for ill rather than for good.

But imagine instead that this mighty stream ran with pure water in the direction of God's Word, then the effect on those in government would be incalculable, and the influence that traveled furthest would nevertheless soon appear the most powerful.

What all this suggests for the duties of Christians in the area of politics, journalism, and international relations would no doubt provide material for a most important study, but that lies outside the scope of this work. It was our task to set forth in what way we antirevolutionaries would wish God's Word to have real influence on political life without infringing on freedom of conscience or independent scholarship. Our reward will be more than abundant if we have at least succeeded somewhat in that endeavor.

CHAPTER FOUR

GOVERNMENT

It teaches that in a Christian nation, that is, a nation not without God, government is a servant of God and duty-bound to glorify his name.

ARTICLE 4A

I. THE STATE IS A MORAL ORGANISM

§ 38   GOVERNMENT HAS DOMINION

The antirevolutionary party confesses the reality of an *Overheid* and values the continued presence of the term *Overheid* in our country's Constitution.[1]

This title denotes what our fathers, borrowing a term from Latin, called the *Magistrate*, that is, a power in the land that has the right to command and the right to demand obedience.

Thus at the head of the state stands not a set of bureaucrats, a hierarchy of appointees or functionaries—as in that wretched system that dared to call even the king "the first functionary of the commonwealth"[2]—but "a power placed over us," which we are to honor.

---

1. *Overheid* (German: *Obrigkeit*) is the term Kuyper uses here to emphasize that government stands over or above society. Often rendered "the civil magistrate," it is here translated as "government."
2. This was a designation of King Louis XVI by the legislative assembly during the French Revolution.

Even the president of a republic, once he has been elected, is to act with the authority that is derived from God and not from those who voted for him.

At issue is the principle of authority. If government officials are a kind of eminent domestic servants in a public household—useful men that are enlisted in the country's service as doctors and nurses in a hospital, or to use a more modern image, a kind of managers of a large hotel with its staff of chefs and waiters and maids—then of course there can be no question of authority.

Then it is a matter of employment, arrangement, agreement, contract—and not a shadow of the high status of government remains.

Living together in one state then becomes a network of interpersonal relationships, a partnership of peers, a mass of independent individuals who *formed* the state by coming together and uniting on certain conditions.

People will then obey because there has to be order, after all. They will obey with self-control as much as from self-preservation, not because it has been so ordained but because, regrettably, it just can't be helped.

In contrast, antirevolutionaries confess that the state is a moral organism, by which they mean that the various relationships that are manifest in the life of the state did not arise by agreement but were ordained as powers over us, apart from us, and for a sacred purpose.

THE STATE AS AN ORGANISM   § 39

Every living thing is an organism, and the peculiarity of an organism is that all its parts, members, joints, and ligaments are potentially present in it before they can be seen. They gradually unfold and take on the fixed forms in which the strength of the whole will be displayed. Likewise, the forces that will operate in those members and the laws that will govern those forces are firmly established, without the will or contribution of the living thing and with such spontaneity that they will always turn out to be identical, no matter how altered the circumstances.

Such an organism is a moral affair if the purpose for which it was created is not a material, earthly, perishable one, but a noble, lofty, sacred goal.

The organ of the human heart, for example, is an organism because it consists of elements that it did not choose itself but which it received. It works with forces and obeys laws in spite of itself. And if things are to be well, all its parts must be directed toward a single goal.

But in addition the human heart is a *moral* organism, because the purpose for which the heart was composed and endowed with powers is not fleeting enjoyment or momentary splendor. Its purpose is to be a process that, rooted in the holy things of God, far transcends the boundaries of this life.

In the same way, we consider the state an organism. First of all, the people and the identity of these people, their connections and the resulting relationships, and all the social forces that reside in them—including a link with the soil they live on and the whole physical environment that must be taken into account—have not come together by chance but have depended on each other from the first and belong together by virtue of their nature. Furthermore, the laws that the state obeys as it lives and develops cannot be arbitrarily determined but (barring some necessary correctives) are given with the nature of the state.

It is our conviction, therefore, that the life of the nation that comes to expression in the state is not an aggregate but a living whole. Families and kinships, towns and villages, businesses and industries, morals, manners, and legal customs are not mechanically assembled but, like groups of cells in a human body, are organically formed by a natural urge that, even when degenerate or deviant, is generally obedient to a higher impulse.

What may never be omitted, however, is that the will of a higher power, which made everything thus suited to each other, designed it for a *moral purpose*.

The state is not just there so that there can be a state.

A state is not an end in itself. On the contrary, the life of a state, too, is only a means to prepare for a communal life of a still higher order, a life that is already germinating and someday will be gloriously revealed in the kingdom of God.

In that kingdom there will be perfect harmony. Tensions between maximum freedom for the individual and optimal development of communal life will there be replaced by the worship and adoration of God.

To prepare for that, and to contribute to the coming of that kingdom, the state has the calling to provide already now that higher form of community life that can do what family life is not able to do: namely, to ensure a social life where human persons can deploy their latent strengths in the most untrammeled fashion possible.

Of course there are stages in all this.

There are states where this goal has been attained to a very limited extent only. Others have progressed further. There are constitutional states where living conditions have reached a very desirable level. But in the two continents that count here, even the best-governed countries never saw more than a feeble glimmer of what the life of the state is to become in its ideal development.

But whatever unknown paths and unforeseen and unfamiliar struggles the state will traverse as it approaches that ideal, yet it can already now serve its ultimate goal in part by its incredible influence on individual persons as well as the respect it evokes for the law.

What we mean by this last point will be explained later. For the present it is enough if we recognize that to acknowledge the state as a moral organism means to acknowledge that government has the right to wield authority over us.

Our readers will not find this difficult to accept.

The people that make up an organization recognize the difference between the power assigned to one member and that assigned to another. The twig has power over the leaf dangling from it; the branch over the twig; the trunk in turn over the branches; while inside that trunk the fibers govern the bark and the sap that flows beneath the bark governs the formation of those fibers.

In a horse, to use a more telling example, the brains and nerves control the head, and the head controls all the muscles of that magnificent body.

And—to use an even stronger example if possible—we all experience personally that one part of our body is better, stronger, and more influential than another, and that heart and head (at least under normal conditions) direct our whole person toward our will.

Transposing this to the social organs, the child, growing up within the family, meets its father as head and governor. Father was there before the child was born. Father is a power under which the child is born. The child did not place itself under him; it came to be under him.

Naturally, in a well-developed organism of national life, too, there must be some members who have almost no influence, and next to them members of some influence, and above them members of still greater influence, until finally there must be one all-controlling member who has power over all the parts and knows how to steer and guide the whole.

Without this the state could not even be an organism. Thus both our premises—that the state is a moral organism, and that at the head of the state is an authoritative government—are the two interlocking truths essential to the state.

II. GOVERNING

§ 41   THE CALL TO GOVERN

Government has the right to exercise dominion. It is a governing, not an administrative organization. Thus it lacks backbone if it effaces itself and abandons its calling—if it lacks the courage to act with commanding authority and coercive force.

Be aware that the antirevolutionary believes this not because his system happens to demand it and therefore the defenseless people will have to be sacrificed to it, but on the contrary, because it is his deepest conviction that upholding that authority makes a people happy and abandoning it causes a nation to pine away.

Any form of government, however tyrannical and despotic, is still preferable to complete anarchy. And anarchy, we all know, can be created not only by a revolution with incendiary bombs and pavement stones in the palace courtyard, but just as well by a revolution with slogans and ideas aired in cabinet or parliament!

Government is quite different from administration. The deteriorated constitutional situation into which we are gradually entering increasingly encourages putting administration in the foreground and leaving genuine governance in the background, as though it represents an abuse of power or a luxury we can do without.

This shift does not exalt society but ruins it. There is no unhappier family than one with a weakling for a father: it resembles a team of galloping horses without a bridle. Similarly, there is no more miserable people than one left to itself, without authority: it feels the nerve of its national strength flagging more and more. Letting go of the high authority of government strikes at the root of a nation's sense of duty and breaks the nation's moral energy.

Most people lack an independent moral life. One may lament this, but that does not alter the fact. The sinful inclination to follow one's lusts, to live for material things and not care one whit about the higher interests of the whole—that is the spur and motive of most inhabitants of this good land. Only a small core of the nation rises to the standpoint of doing their duty "for God's sake."

Precisely because this surrender to the *immediate* authority of God is the exception of nobler minds among people everywhere, the *mediated* form of that authority through government should not be absent, lest all sense of duty slacken.

Nor should we forget that any slackening of the sense of duty is an ill that reveals itself very quickly as the mother of all sorts of other ills in the life of a nation. If the holy spur of "thou shalt" or the still holier incentive of "thou shalt not" grows weaker, a nation loses its moral compass and forfeits strong, salutary, sterling characters. And since life must be lived and a solution must be found, a sad transition takes place to a totally different view of life, one that soon tips over the nation's moral stance: among the sensuous natures toward love of pleasure, and among the finer spirits toward an overestimation of learning and culture. Today our country is passing through this deplorable process, a process that finds its pitiful slogans in "popular amusement" and "public education"—pitiful because it bypasses the human heart.

TYRANNY   § 42

The antirevolutionary party therefore urges the restoration of authority. Government should be affirmed again as vested with authority. We ought to return to the conception of government as wielding dominion, a conception that a people cannot do without if it is to maintain its moral character.

Our party urges this, not to introduce tyranny but to check tyranny. A child who is raised well does not think it annoying or demeaning when father or mother orders him to do something. He does not call that tyranny but rightful exercise of parental authority. And it does not fill him with resentment but with a sense of duty.

But do you know when his heart fills with resentment and blood rushes to his face? That happens when father and mother are absent and a sibling, who is not his superior, tries to lord it over him, vents his lust for power on him, and treats him as an inferior and a subordinate. This the best child cannot stand. His sense of justice will protest against it with repugnance and rancor. This, he knows, is tyranny—a tyranny of the worst kind, an evil that he cannot and will not abide.

Alas, that is exactly the sad situation we have arrived at in the political domain. In the absence of a government that governs, some "siblings" in our society have conspired to lord it over other "siblings" whom they do not like. Since they are superior or stronger or cheekier, they try to keep the others down, tyrannize them, oppress them.

The power that government let slip away is picked up by the least scrupulous group of citizens, to play it off against their fellow citizens who are supposed to be in everything their equals. Thus some sort of governing is going on in any case. Only, it now operates in such a way that the holy authority of government has deteriorated into the very unholy authority of party tyranny. The rule of the powers that be, instead of fostering morality, corrupts the national character, pits citizen against citizen, and feeds the fire of rancor and resentment.

It is precisely in order to put an end to this situation and leave no future opening for such unbearable wantonness that our party calls again for *government*, for a government that bears the title of government and acts like one. It calls for a power that we acknowledge as standing over us because we know it stands over everyone and by rights makes its coercive power felt, now on the oppressing group, now on the oppressed group, in fair and equal measure.

§ 43   Government the Servant of God

We desire such a government, however, only if it rules as the servant of God.

Rules *over* us, but *under* God. Subject therefore, along with us, to God alone. Since he is God, he alone can give the right to enforce the right that is derived from him.

Thus the persons in government remain for us perfectly ordinary people who in themselves have not the least to say, not even over the least of the subjects, and who in their own littleness are on the same level as the day laborer and the beggar.

For this reason we reject and combat, with shock and indignation, every notion that a ruler—a human being, hence a sinner—is a different, better, higher sort of creature than the ordinary person. We object when princes and governors are not held to God's holy law and allowed to follow a different set of norms in their private lives. And we refuse, like our fathers, to let go of our firm conviction that as a private person even the mightiest potentate on earth is subject to the law and not a law unto himself.

Only God can command. A human being can command only insofar as God himself has invested him with authority and made him accountable before his holy judgment seat.

A husband and father, by the grace of God invested with authority as head of a family, is not just *allowed* to command; he is obligated to do so. A sea captain can say: "I, next to God, master of my ship." A king, if he wears the crown not as a result of a conspiracy or by popular acclamation but in accordance with what he and his people confess, can say: "I, king *by the grace of God.*"

III. THE RELIGION OF THE NATION

THE RELIGION OF THE NATION   § 44

Government is always the servant of God, without fail—among all nations, in the person of all rulers and men of power, throughout the ages. Government is the servant of God in the sense that, willingly or unwillingly, it is and remains dependent on God. It received its power from him and it serves his counsel.

But if we understand the intention of the Central Committee well, then the tenor of our Program, when it uses the term "servant of God," goes beyond mere dependence.[3] With this term it insists that the government must acknowledge its calling to serve God and behave as an obedient servant of God. Hence the explicit addition: "in a Christian nation, that is, a nation not without God, government is a servant of God and duty-bound to glorify his name."

The point is the insertion "in a Christian nation, that is, a nation not without God."

For in a nation whose people had remained alien to the true God there could be no question of a government that served God in the narrow sense of the word. Only the religion of the nation can enable even the best of governments to fulfill its duty with an intentionality that is rooted in personal faith. This is a link in the whole of the antirevolutionary system that cannot be emphasized enough.

It is not uncommon for us to meet up with, say, a liberal and to have thrown in our face, in all seriousness and not without some justification:

---

3. Kuyper was chairman of the central committee of the antirevolutionary party *in statu nascendi* (that is, in its formative stage) and also the author of the first as well as the final draft of the party's Program laid out in the present work.

"Why form a separate political party rather than joining us? After all, you want the same things as we do."

Mind you, he will then hasten to add: "Your dogmatic premise and your view of history is diametrically opposed to ours; but surely," he will continue, "that does not warrant fundamental opposition in practice, since you are for freedom, emancipation, and principled politics, just as we are."

To this our answer has always been twofold.

First of all, our demands no doubt agree at many points with the *theory* of the liberals, but not with their *practice*, where their application tramples their own principles underfoot, for example, in the schools question.[4]

Secondly, as the saying goes, when two people say the same thing, it does not always mean the same. What divides liberals and antirevolutionaries has always been religion.

During a naval battle, after all, two rams, built exactly the same way, can batter and pound each other in an attempt to sink each other. Yet nothing stops them from being built at the same shipyard, by the same builder, according to the same model. It is even conceivable that the engines powering the two monsters are of the same type and were built at the same factory. Indeed, their identity can extend so far that the pieces these rams carry are poured from the same mold, with metal from the same foundry. And yet those two ships are diametrically opposed to each other, simply because they display a different flag in the topmast and have a captain on the bridge who is wearing different insignia on the brim of his collar.

In the same way it would be conceivable that the vessel launched by the liberals and the ship we are busy preparing looked so perfectly identical that a person could not possibly distinguish one from the other, and that nevertheless the two were called to wage a war to the death simply on account of the flag that was raised aloft and that our side displayed the unmistakable color of religion.

§ 45   RELIGION IN A NATIONAL, NOT ECCLESIASTICAL SENSE

However—and it seems that people just refuse to understand this—when we speak of religion in the political domain it has nothing to do with our confession of the mysteries of salvation. It is meant as a purely political concept.

---

4. Liberal governments had privileged publicly funded common schools while other widely-supported educational options were left to fend for themselves.

As little as a gardener can tend a garden without taking into account the nature of the soil in which his plants are rooted; as little as a farmer can prepare healthy dairy products for us without taking into account the nature of the soil on which his cows are grazing; and as little as a builder can put up a sturdy, well-constructed house unless he adjusts to the type of soil on which his building lot is situated—so little can a government make a nation flourish, and in that nation make justice flourish, unless it takes into account the spiritual soil in which the nation is rooted and on which justice is founded. Now then, in a Christian nation that spiritual soil, the basis of its very life as well as the bedrock of its system of justice, is religion.

"The bedrock of its system of justice," indeed. For when today's politicians keep telling us that what matters is to consolidate the *just state*,[5] then honesty demands that they also tell us where the pivot of justice is found. In our chapter on the ordinances of God, it became abundantly clear that for those who still hold to the reality of sin there is no other test of what is just—according to the eternal principle of justice—than the test of religion.

But now in the second place, religion is also the soil in which a people is rooted. This does not refer, of course, to a people's outward appearance—to the body, the food, the climate, and so on. That these are certainly related to it becomes immediately apparent during an outbreak of the plague or a cholera epidemic. But all this touches too exclusively the lower, animal side of life to be decisive for a people *qua* people.

An advanced people can be rooted only in its nobler, conscious, moral life.

Now one of two things: either a people stands on the foundation of an autonomous morality, a morality that can flourish without being grounded in a religion, or it confesses the motive of morality to proceed from the living God. In the first case a people's deepest foundation is philosophy; in the second it is religion.

BELIEVING IN THE LIVING GOD § 46

No one can deny that it is impossible to profess belief in God and at the same time anchor one's life in something other than this God.

---

5. The "just state" here translates the original "*rechtsstaat*," the constitutional state, or rule of law.

Everyone realizes that *God* means "deepest Origin," "Fountain of life," "First Cause." Thus it amounts to effacing God Almighty in his divine quality if one will not, or dare not, acknowledge that the ground, the foundation, the very terrain on which our nobler, conscious, moral life flourishes is the belief that God is there and that he is active everywhere.

This is why antirevolutionaries assert that this belief, this religious faith, is the nerve center of the political organism by which a government rules a nation.

Imagine if you had to deal with a people that did not believe in the living God, hence a people that did not believe it was duty-bound, for his sake, to submit to the laws he has ordained and to obey the ordinances he has established—what might possibly motivate a people like that to obey its government?

Do not, to escape the force of the argument, point to pagan nations. Their submission to law hinged on their belief in the gods— and surely you do not want to return to those idols? In fact, this example could be turned against you by reminding you that when these nations abandoned their gods but had not yet embraced the living God, all authority, in Athens as well as Rome, collapsed and the people turned out to be ungovernable.

And you can learn a lot but take little comfort from what we have witnessed among "modern enlightened nations," that is, from governments by avowed atheists who had the opportunity to rule to their heart's content— for example, governments under the Sansculottes and the Communards.[6]

Then it was made clear that when religion is gone, nothing remains to force people's compliance but brute force—the force of the guillotine or the firing squad. And because it is force it cannot govern; at most it can struggle and fight, until a still greater force, until a Napoleon or a Thiers, acts to crush the political monster.[7]

It follows logically from all this that there is no other cement to keep the walls of the edifice standing than religion. Essential is the belief that there is a God who has ordained principles of law, right, and justice that one must honor, and a government that one must obey.

---

6. The Sansculottes and Communards were the most radical of the ideological parties in France, responsible, respectively, for the reign of terror of 1793/94 and the Paris atrocities of 1871.

7. Napoleon's rise to power after 1795 marked the end of the Reign of Terror. Adolphe Thiers led the government of Versailles that crushed the Paris Commune in 1871.

If that element is missing in a nation's consciousness, forget about governing. If that element is present but only weakly, governing becomes difficult. Only where the religious element is still the mainspring of national life can there be strong government. For then a government can expect to find in the nation: (1) persons who as civil servants will maintain the law from a sense of justice; who will insist on compliance without elevating themselves; who will respect the limits God has put on their authority; and (2) an inclination among the people to obey the law without fear, from a sense of duty; a willingness to bow to the laws for God's sake; a public spirit in which justice can begin to flourish.

These conditions are indispensable for enabling a government to govern in that higher sense as "servant of God." And so we have demonstrated as well that the banner of religion in politics contains not a single ecclesiastical thread.

IV. A CHRISTIAN NATION

CHRISTIAN, AS OPPOSED TO NON-CHRISTIAN § 47

The state is a moral organism. Hence the state, like every other organism, has a head. This head we call the government, since it wields authority and dominion. Both organism and head have been placed by God in a reciprocal relationship. Not only, therefore, must the state honor God Almighty, but the government must be viewed as none other than a servant of God.

Having come to this point, we explained in the previous article that there can be no question of this moral, noble conception of the state unless religious faith is at the heart of a nation. We showed as well that "faith" in this context does not at all refer to any ecclesiastical confession but solely to a solid sense that there are eternal, unshakable principles of justice grounded in God's will and essence, and in that connection, to a deep-rooted conviction that one must obey government, not because it would otherwise use force to coerce compliance, nor because there could be no public order otherwise, but solely and exclusively because God Almighty has laid this obedience upon human beings.

That the above is still applicable to our own state, at least for the time being, can be demonstrated by explaining in what sense we believe we are justified in claiming that we are still a "Christian nation."

That should not be difficult.

Our people as a nation either still takes religion into account, or it does not. If the Dutch nation does reckon with religion, no one in his right mind will think of the Buddhist, Muslim, or Jewish religion. The only religion that applies is Christianity.

That simplifies the issue.

For it confronts us with this pointed question: Does our national life rest on metaphysical presuppositions that deny Almighty God; or does it rest, as Christians would put it, on fundamental beliefs that honor God as "God" in his glory and majesty?

This is a question that cannot be decided by conducting a poll—by counting noses. In the case of a moral organism, the rule applies that questions of character and conviction are decided only by its nobler parts, and the less noble parts are simply ignored. When a martyr for the faith mounts the stake, his whole person and all his members, including his imagination and his intelligence, vote *No!* because they shrink from pain and shun fire and recoil from death. Only his moral will, which honors a higher principle and therefore obeys a higher law, says *Yes!* And even though all the other parts are opposed, the martyr gives himself over to death, and all who witness the scene are jubilant that this person, this "organism," has proved his Christian character in a most glorious way.

Similarly, it is irrelevant if the moral organism of the state contains, numerically speaking, a few, or many, or even a majority who have no personal relationship with Christ. To answer the question that we are here considering, one must look only to the driving force of the more noble members of the nation who impart forward movement to the whole.

§ 48   CHRISTIAN IN A NATION'S LOFTIER APPROACH TO LIFE

Where the whole person or the entire nation is involved, one cannot in the first place understand the "more noble" members to be the intellectual circles, or the self-complacent aristocracy, or, if you will, "the thinking portion of the nation."[8] The nation is not an intellectual organism but a moral one. Hence one judges its noble or less noble members by a moral standard.

Erasmus of Rotterdam was a thousand times more learned than Jan de Bakker, and yet not the "prince of the humanists" but the priest from the humble town of Woerden was the spokesman of what moved the nation at

---

8. This translates the original *het denkend deel der natie*, an expression used by Dutch liberals to denote the "enlightened" sector of the population, which included themselves.

the time.[9] A century later, Hugo Grotius was at least twice as intelligent as Johannes Bogerman, and yet the "father of international law" stood outside the current of national life.[10] Still later, Spinoza without a doubt far surpassed Witsius in flight and boldness of thought, yet he was scarcely in touch with the nation's aspirations, of which Witsius was such a splendid mouthpiece.[11] In the same way, it is undeniable that also today, and even more so, the self-satisfied thinkers among us who deny the Christ and critique revelation are superior in intelligence and erudition; yet this fact in no way proves that therefore the current of national life has already been diverted from the Christ and now flows out of philosophy.

To decide this, one needs to look at other signs. One needs to view the nation not as an aggregate, that is, by numbers, but as an integral whole, an organism. And this organism needs to be viewed, not just as it is now, but in connection with the life of centuries past that put its stamp on it and shaped its character. One needs to look at the nation, thus understood, in light of its public holidays, the anthems voicing its deeper life, the forces driving it today, and the ideas current among its population.

If one can approve of this criterion (as we think in all honesty one should), then it is permitted to ask: Did the people of the Low Countries not leave their barbarian state behind and gradually develop into national elements when at last they abandoned their heathen idols and adopted the cross as their symbol? Did these elements not give rise to an energetic national unity when the war against Spain received its consecration in the struggle for the gospel? Did every powerful commotion that rocked these lands not always have the interest of the Christian religion at its core? And as for our own time: did our people as they experienced events like 1813 and 1830, or as they were seized with fear at the approach of menacing forces or the threat of epidemics, not spontaneously cry out to God before they even realized it?[12] Are Bilderdijk, Da Costa, Beets, and Ten Kate, our best poets, not men who refused to forsake the Christ; and did the

---

9. Jan de Bakker, the Dutch name of Johannes Pistorius (1499–1525), a priest, was the first martyr in the Northern Netherlands to be burned at the stake for his Protestant beliefs.

10. Johannes Bogerman (1576–1637), a leading Calvinist pastor and Bible translator, served as president of the international Synod of Dort (1618/19).

11. Herman Witsius (1636–1708), a pastor and theologian of the Second or Puritan Reformation in Holland, was the author of a mediating "covenant theology."

12. The year 1813 marked the end of the French occupation; 1830 marked the outbreak of the Belgian Revolt.

verse of Tollens and De Genestet in a parallel stream of great poetry not always try to pluck the harp of religious sentiment? And further, do the no-popery movement of 1853 and the schools question since 1857, particularly around the great People's Petition of 1878, not offer incontrovertible proof that the struggle for the Christian religion and the Bible stirs our national life most deeply? And finally, are the common ideas, even among the unchurched, about home life and marriage and the duty to bear children and the dignity of women and other notions of that sort, not closer to the fundamental law of Christ than to the eccentric dogmas of philosophers like Van Houten?[13]

Very well, if a negative answer to the above series of questions is scarcely conceivable, does that not prove our case and vindicate the Christian character of our national life?

Even if unbelief were to penetrate still deeper than today and apostasy took on still more appalling proportions, would the Christian character not remain undiminished so long as the liberal leadership in press and parliament did not succeed in replacing the old way of life with a modern way of life and imbuing it with a new spirit?

Two more comments, to prevent misunderstanding: (1) We are looking at this question from a political point of view, so have deliberately not talked about the Christian churches and their influence, their practice of baptism, and their rootedness in the life of the nation. (2) Given our political point of view, the presence of Jewish citizens, which is often used as an argument against the Christian character of our nation, can be left out of consideration. These individuals count only if one goes by numbers, not when the nation is looked upon as a moral organism.

---

13. Samuel van Houten (1837–1930) was a progressive member of parliament and propagator, among other things, of birth control.

CHAPTER FIVE

NO SECULAR STATE

It teaches that in a Christian nation, that is, in a nation not without God, government as a servant of God is duty-bound to glorify his name and accordingly ought to (a) remove from administration and legislation anything that impedes the free influence of the gospel on the nation; (b) abstain from all direct meddling with the spiritual formation of the nation, being absolutely incompetent thereto; (c) treat all denominations or religious communities, and moreover all citizens, regardless of their views about things eternal, on a footing of equality; and (d) acknowledge in people's conscience, provided it does not lack the presumption of respectability, a limit to its power.

ARTICLE 4

I. THREE SYSTEMS

IGNORING RELIGION

§ 49

We have seen what government is: a *servant of God*. Now we come to the question: What should government do and not do to be found faithful in the service of God?

Following the tenor of our Program, we answer: Government has both direct and indirect duties toward God. The direct duties are either of a negative or a positive nature. Negatively, government is bound to allow unrestricted freedom for (1) the gospel's influence; (2) people's spiritual formation; (3) the manner in which people choose to worship; and (4) people's conscience. Positively, government is duty-bound to (1) maintain law and order; (2) honor the oath; and (3) dedicate one day a week to God.

We are well aware that these brief indications throw into sharp relief the difference between the kind of state the liberals want to establish and the kind we antirevolutionaries aspire to.

This is best seen if you take the trouble to think for a moment about what the liberals want. Their state is a state without God; it is a *secular state*.[1]

This does not mean that each and every liberal wants to be irreverent and disrespectful toward God. It only means that in their opinion religion belongs to the realm of the inner life and that the state as a political power must avoid as much as possible all contact with this inner life. They feel that the situation will not be ideal until the point is reached where in government circles no mention is ever made of God, religion, or church. Whatever traces might remain of that sort would gradually need to be eliminated. Kingship by the grace of God would have to go. So would prayer for God's guidance in the Speech from the Throne. So would a prayer for God's blessing when tabling legislative bills. Sunday observance would have to go. Every connection with the church would have to go. So would the oath. And so on.

This is true of our liberals as well as our conservatives. Not if you look at what they say, but at what their principles prescribe. Those principles leave no room for serving God. At most, as a result of inconsistency or for the sake of party interest or the theory of Hobbes, they allow for God Almighty to serve as "the invisible police that casts fear into the multitude."[2]

The basic error of this political system is the claim that one cannot really know if there is a God, hence that nothing objective can be established in regard to religion, and that this whole feature of the inner life of

---

1. The original reads: "Hún Staat is los van God, een état athée."
2. English political philosopher Thomas Hobbes (1588–1679) defined religion as "*feare of power invisible.*" Thus he contends that "before the time of Civill Society, or in the interruption thereof by Warre, there is nothing can strengthen a Covenant of Peace agreed on, against the temptations of Avarice, Ambition, Lust, or other strong desire, but the feare of that Invisible Power, which they everyone Worship as God; and Feare as a Revenger of their perfidy." See Thomas Hobbes, *Leviathan*, ed. A. R. Waller (Cambridge: Cambridge University Press, 1904), 1.14.96.

human beings belongs to the subjective, personal, at most domestic and ecclesiastical domain.

Modern subjectivism—the false theory that religious sentiment is a separate capacity which, like musical talent, is stronger in some than in others—and in connection with that theory the false notion that we are able to ascertain what the human person *thinks* of God but not whether he exists or who he is—this way of thinking could not but lead with logical necessity to this God-less political system. It is a system that no longer has any room for prayer in the council chambers nor for national days of prayer. It is a system which prescribes that everything that is state must, *qua* state, ignore the living God.

A STATE CHURCH   § 50

In opposition to such a system, the antirevolutionary party asserts that religion is not solely subjective but in fact is first of all objective. It contends that the knowledge that there is a God and that we have to do with that living God is firmly established and must be acknowledged, independently of our feelings. It holds that the state, too, as "the moral organization of the people as a whole," is obliged to reckon with this foundation and fountainhead of all moral life.

The party bases this claim not on revelation but on natural theology—on the knowledge of God that can be gathered from what is seen of God in creation, particularly in the human person, and not least in the national organism as well.

In this, it consciously follows the tradition of our Reformed theologians, who held fast to this natural theology precisely for the sake of that which falls outside the kingdom of heaven. At the same time, to add one more note, the party was completely vindicated in this view by Max Müller's recent lecture series on religion.[3]

This natural knowledge of God, not the knowledge from revelation, has compelling force for every person. Certainty about the first kind of knowledge does not require what the second requires, namely, supernatural illumination.

For this reason the non-confessional government has the absolute and direct legal competence as well as the obligation to take as its official rule

---

3. Max Müller, *Voorlezingen over de wetenschap van den godsdienst* ('s-Hertogenbosch: Van der Schuyt, 1871). ET: Max Müller, *Lectures on the Science of Religion* (New York: Charles Scribner, 1872).

of conduct the first (natural) knowledge of God, but not the second (revealed) kind.

This last would only be possible if there were an extraordinary, supernatural organ that could decide with absolute certainty what the revealed knowledge of God demanded in a given case. Such an organ, however, is lacking. And *had to be* lacking, otherwise either the state would become *spiritual* or religion would become *profane*.

Accordingly, any attempt to call such an organ into existence regardless, as was done by Rome, has foundered miserably and corrupted state and church alike. Things of a different nature just cannot be mixed.

The state is not the kingdom of God, and the kingdom of God cannot be pressed into the confines of political life. We resolutely reject every attempt at reviving a "Christian state" in this sense, just as we resolutely turn against men like Rothe whose theory lacks all boundary lines and has the church flow into the state and then the state into the kingdom of God.[4] Such unsound confusion of ideas must not be tolerated. It obscures clear thinking and causes the worn-out minds to sink back into the mysteries of the "unconscious" life and unsteady "feelings." And that must not be. We have to use our understanding, our thinking, our reason in what we do, and the laws for our thinking do not allow for such a chaotic muddle.

§ 51 STATE AND CHURCH INTERRELATE, EACH ROOTED IN ITS OWN PRINCIPLE

The state is intended for the present dispensation and has at most preparatory significance for the eternal household of humankind. The kingdom of God, on the other hand, derives its purpose and character from the coming dispensation and at most *uses* earthly things for the things eternal.

This gives rise to two different sets of ideas that increasingly follow their separate ways and therefore ought not to be confused in our minds.

Government is directly rooted in the natural life and as such has no other than a natural knowledge of God. The kingdom of God is a supernatural realm where supernatural knowledge of God shines undimmed.

Thanks to its natural knowledge of God, government knows (1) that there is a God; (2) that this living God governs the fate of everything created, hence also of the state; (3) that this all-governing providence desires

---

4. Richard Rothe (1799–1867), a German theologian, taught that history was gradually replacing piety by morality and the church by the Christian state, ending in a universal absolute theocracy.

justice and is therefore an avenger of injustice; and (4) that sin is operative among human beings, from which higher intervention alone can save.

Now it is on the basis of this purely natural knowledge of God that the state comes to honor God in its public actions; to invoke God's holy name in state documents; to respect the oath; to dedicate a day of rest to him; to proclaim national days of prayer during disasters; to practice justice even with the sword; and to allow free course to the gospel.

Three systems therefore:

(1) There is the God-less state of the liberals, who reject both the natural and the revealed knowledge of God and whose motto is "leave God out of it." (2) There is the theocratic state of Roman Catholics and inconsistent Protestants, who base the state *qua* state directly on both the natural and the revealed knowledge of God and consequently make the state function as the active promoter of the kingdom of God, as for example in the Middle Ages and still partly in Prussia.

And finally (3) there is the political and yet God-honoring state of the Reformed or Puritan nations, who base the state directly on the natural knowledge of God and accordingly have government proceed *actively* as a servant of God in the sphere of the natural knowledge of God but *passively* in the sphere of the revealed knowledge of God. An example here is the United States of America, where on the one hand government prays, proclaims days of prayer, and honors the seventh day, while on the other hand it conducts itself in a more neutral fashion *vis-à-vis* the churches than any country in Europe.[5]

II. THE DEVELOPMENT OF THE REFORMED POLITICAL PRINCIPLE

INDIFFERENTISM
§ 52

The whole difference between us and the liberals about religion in the public domain is that they regard religion in all its life-expressions with suspicion as a dangerous intruder, whereas we consider religion as a member of the family whose presence and influence we value highly.

---

5. *Note by the author:* The conception, held by some Reformed theologians, of government as a servant of God *within the church* can be left out of consideration here, since it holds only for countries of unmixed populations and for nations who really want to be simply a church, with a police force to maintain law and order.

Both of us judge that government has to abstain as much as possible from interfering in matters pertaining to "the salvation of souls." But with the liberals this judgment is based on the view that politics is superior to religion, and with us on the conviction that religion is superior to politics.

Our opponents exhort to noninterference because it would corrupt government. We recommend noninterference because meddling with this most holy domain would corrupt religion.

Liberals underestimate if not disdain the Christian faith, whereas we love and respect it. They advise abstention in order to keep religion within the narrowest confines possible. We advise abstention in order to have faith's sanctifying influence work as purely, as powerfully, as widely as possible.

The result is that liberals adjust their form of government to suit atheists. Of course, we know better than to assume that most liberals are atheists. Many appreciate forms of piety. But as much as this may be true for their private life, their ideal in politics is the atheist ideal.

Their political ideal would be met beautifully by a nation consisting exclusively of atheists. Gone would be all those thorny religious issues. Gone all those problems with conscientious objectors and all that opposition to a strictly neutral government school for all children. Gone all that trouble with religious processions and popular petitions. No more disruptions of the steady pulse of the pure magnetic-liberal current.

§ 53   THE REFORMED PRINCIPLE

We, by contrast, wish to structure our state in such a way that political life and national life match. And since we are not a nation of atheists but a Christian nation, we want to give the state a structure that matches that situation in practice—a structure in which the Christian feels at home and which continually reminds the atheist of the undeniable fact that not the Christian, but he, is the exception and that he is accommodated, to be sure, but only by way of exception.

In taking this stance we proceed from the obvious fact that the form of government is not designed for the blind, the deaf, or the cripple, but for the ordinary citizen who can see, hear, and walk. Just as government seeks to assure the best possible existence for the atheist, so it will for the blind, the deaf, and the cripple, yet an existence that will always be the exception, never the rule.

If it were the case that religion benefited from state propaganda (which we deny), we would even go so far as to spite the atheist by allowing the state to engage in religious propaganda. If history taught that state intervention to spread the faith and keep it pure is effective, then the honor of God and the salvation of sinners would so trump everything for us that we would not hesitate for a moment to call in the power of the state. So greatly do the honor of God and the glory of his name surpass constitutional form and parliamentary interest that hesitation would be a sin if one knew that state compulsion could add to that honor.

Similarly, the redemption of souls, the salvation of sinners, the introduction of sensuous humans to the higher powers of heaven is such an eminently holy cause that we would straightway surrender every political interest to it if state interference had proved effective in helping reach this goal.

No one should suspect us, therefore, of timidly hiding our agenda or half-heartedly taking up with theories that are foreign to us. No, we will never break up the wheel of life and we resolutely oppose every revolution that wants to overturn that wheel.

That which is on top should stay on top. For us, the name of God Almighty stands high above all creatures, including the creature called the state. They are all mere instruments that must together serve his honor and praise.

Compulsion Proved Unprofitable   § 54

Thus, if state compulsion were helpful, we would not shrink for one moment from state intervention (provided personal and domestic life remained untouched).

That we do recoil from it—in fact protest against it with all our might and oppose with all the influence at our disposal those who still pin their hopes on state meddling in this matter—it is solely and simply because of the overwhelming evidence that state meddling with the salvation of sinners always degrades the honor of God instead of exalting it and chokes the life of piety instead of causing it to flourish.

It was tried for centuries—among all peoples, in every region, in all sorts of ways, under all kinds of circumstances. It was tried with cunning and ulterior motives, yet mostly with sincerity and earnestness. Even the victims (among others Servetus) acknowledged the fairness of the policy, although they challenged the correctness of its application.[6]

And the unquestionable result of all these attempts was grievous. God's name was robbed of its splendor. The saving of souls was obstructed and disrupted. The religious and moral life of the nations did not advance but regressed. The gospel, instead of gaining in influence, saw its impact decrease to its lowest level.

If there is one lesson from history that we cannot question, it is this one. If there is one thing that we know for certain, it is the knowledge, bought too dearly at the price of much precious and sacred blood, *that compulsion clashes with the very nature of all higher life, and hence clashes most vehemently with the character of the Christian faith.*

§ 55   REFORMED THEORY AND PRACTICE

It is for this reason that we saw ourselves obliged by God to develop our position on this crucial point more consistently[7] and to deviate from the line of conduct followed by our political forefathers. In practice they rarely followed it otherwise than with moderation, but in theory they invariably recommended it as good and sound.

Their system, as found in Article 36 of the Belgic Confession, as soon as one wants to apply it in countries of mixed populations, degenerates again into the system that Rome conceived, introduced, and maintains to this day.[8] On the basis of this theory, Maresius, as late as the seventeenth

---

6. Michael Servetus (1509/11–1553) was famously executed as a heretic in Geneva during the time of John Calvin.

7. *Note by the author:* See my *Het Calvinisme, oorsprong en waarborg onzer constitutioneele vrijheden* (Amsterdam: B. van der Land, 1874). [ET: "Calvinism: Source and Stronghold of Our Constitutional Liberties," in *Abraham Kuyper: A Centennial Reader,* ed. James D. Bratt (Grand Rapids: Eerdmans, 1998), 279–317.]

8. The reference is to italicized words below in the description of the task of civil governments in Article 36, "The Magistracy (Civil Government)," of the Belgic Confession: "Their office is not only to have regard unto and watch for the welfare of the civil state, but also that they protect the sacred ministry, *and thus may remove and prevent all idolatry and false worship, that the kingdom of antichrist may be thus destroyed* and the kingdom of Christ promoted." In 1905, Kuyper persuaded his denomination to remove these words and amend the confession. Most sister and daughter churches have since followed suit.

century, reminded government of its duty to execute heretics, albeit with various restrictions.[9]

There is therefore no need to debate this further. The student of history is also familiar with this story—we do not say our shame, but still our short-sightedness and blindness.

In actual practice, all Reformed nations, churches, governments, and canonists, Voetius at the head, protested and agitated against this system, even though they adhered to it in theory.[10]

To act according to the demand of their system, after all, had been from the beginning a rare exception. Even the government edicts against Rome usually were nothing but paper scarecrows. And if asked what emerges from the religious history of the Reformed nations in Switzerland, Holland, Scotland, England, and America, it is that exceptions to the theory multiplied steadily, and freedom of conscience and freedom of religion were increasingly respected in all kinds of ways.

It *had to* come to this because the Reformed people had the will to push through their protest against human authority in religious matters. It cannot be emphasized enough that the English revolutions of the seventeenth century, thanks especially to the energy of the Independents, promoted freedom of conscience as the maturing fruit from the Reformed tree.

Without disguising the fact or sounding a retreat on this point, therefore, we break with the imperfect political theory of our fathers and condemn what they perpetrated in Geneva, England, and partly also in our country. They acted on the strength of a faulty theory, contrary to their own principle. As for us, we accept, in all sincerity and with utter conviction, that other principle: *the state shall allow, no less but also no more, freedom for the development of the Christian religion.*

III. FREE COURSE FOR THE WORD OF GOD

FREEDOM FOR THE GOSPEL §56

Government, as we saw, stands outside the domain of revealed religion. It possesses natural knowledge of God, not the supernatural kind, at least

---

9. Samuel Maresius (1599–1673) was a French theologian who was a pastor of Walloon churches in the Low Countries and a professor of systematic theology in the University of Groningen.
10. Gijsbert Voetius (1589–1676) was a prominent Reformed theologian who was a professor in the University of Utrecht.

not directly. This means that with respect to supernatural revelation it has only duties in a negative sense and is bound to observe positive duties only on the strength of the natural knowledge of God.

Government is aware, thanks to this natural knowledge of God, that this knowledge does not suffice but presupposes, rather, a revelation that is supernatural. It is aware that the subjects it governs are *human beings*, beings of a higher order, created for more than one life, who are in need of still another guide, another aid, another light than government can provide.

Traditionally, the government of a Christian people is aware as well that this higher light is not found with Confucius or Buddha, nor with Darwin, but only with Jesus Christ or, if you will, with the eternal gospel. But government has no decisive answer to the question in what way this gospel is to be brought to the people and what obligations the gospel imposes on them. It is powerless to find an answer because the gospel lies outside its domain and beyond its reach. Nor can it adopt the answer of others because those answers vary and government lacks the spiritual competence to choose from among them.

On this ground, therefore, we confess that government may only conduct itself negatively in regard to the gospel.

It must not favor it, but even less must it discriminate against it. Its attitude must be that of respectful treatment and benevolence, but with a benevolence that refuses, precisely out of pious respect, to do anything it cannot do.

Accordingly, the Program speaks, quite correctly in our opinion, of four different obligations.

(1) The gospel shall have free course.

Government must not obstruct the proclamation of the gospel. There are to be no restrictions or hindrances to the preaching of the Word. Every agent of the good news must be able to see in the behavior of the government and its officials that it wants to be a friend of the gospel and never an enemy—that far from obstructing God's Word, it paves the way for that Word.

Governments can transgress this rule both directly and indirectly.

Ours did so directly in 1816 by becoming the guardian of a mighty corporation in the heart of the nation, the Dutch Reformed Church, striking a once vibrant body with absolute impotence and causing it to suffocate in a bureaucratic straitjacket.

Our government has also done this in a direct and shocking way by preferably appointing assailants of the gospel in almost every department of our universities and making the founding of free evangelical universities as impossible as it could make it. This has impeded the course of the gospel among senior civil servants as well as the educated classes.

Likewise, it has done so in an indirect way through its cool and surly behavior, in fact—why not say it?—through the ungracious conduct of its civil servants, creating the impression everywhere that it had rather *not* give free course to the gospel.

This cannot be tolerated. This must change. We ask no favors, but neither obstruction. Government shall give free course to the Word of God.

No Counter-Gospel   § 57

(2) Government shall not introduce and protect a counter-gospel.

The gospel can be combated in two ways: by attacking the Christian religion openly, or by balancing it with a Religion of Humanity or some other belief system.

When the state does the latter it is no less an enemy of the gospel of Christ. It may take on the air of being neutral, but in fact it undermines the power of Jesus' gospel. It achieves the same goal as under open attack, but now in a covert, noncommittal, hypocritical manner.

That we have arrived at this situation in our country hardly needs mention. It is as clear as day to everyone that the circles of the educated and erudite in our larger cities have attempted with growing determination to supplant historic Christianity with a kind of philosophical morality that closely resembles the ideas prevalent among the cultured circles of Rome and Athens in the days when Jesus was born in Bethlehem.

In accordance with our system the government was obliged to give free rein to this conspiracy against historic Christianity, but at the same time it should have viewed it with regret and never have favored it. That would have been the only appropriate stance.

Instead, our government has from the beginning taken the side of these enemies of historic Christianity, smuggled virtually every post of any influence into their hands, incorporated more and more of their ideas in legislation, and last but not least, placed millions from municipal and national treasuries at their disposal in order to push through this systematic undermining of Christianity by means of the public school.

§ 58   Equal Rights for All

(3) There shall be equal rights for all in religious affairs.

No matter how much the government may sympathize with the gospel, it should never allow itself to be tempted to banish or bind preachers who wish to *combat* the gospel.

If a Jew wishes to take exception to the Messiah of the Christians, or a Muslim to Holy Scripture, or a Darwinist to the idea of creation—or for that matter, if a positivist wants to protest against the root which for all things holy lies in faith—all should be free to do so.

Free, because once government starts to weed, it can easily mistake wheat for tares. Free also, because once these opponents of Christianity are beaten back, they can boast that they were not beaten fairly but only yielded to force. Free above all, however, because Christianity itself needs this constant dueling with champions from the other camps and must prove its moral superiority by triumphing in a strictly *spiritual* battle.

Again, associations of like-minded people, too, should be left free. Even the question whether such an association takes the name of church, communion, or society should be immaterial to government. Even if a church of atheists should want to establish itself, it would have to be tolerated. No special protection, but neither prevention or repression. What shoots up and is able to grow should be allowed to grow. Leave it to Christian believers, if need be to Christian martyrs, to have the honor of demonstrating the intrinsic emptiness of non-Christian spiritual life.

We must not shrink from allowing freedom for believer and unbeliever alike, or else the strength on which we want to lean will appear to be another than the strength of faith.

And if all this holds for opponents of the gospel, it should hold all the more for the different, diverging, sometimes even bizarre forms under which the proclamation of the gospel appears.

A Baptist should not be favored by government over an Irvingian, and an Irvingian not over an Arminian. Government never chooses sides between church and church, no matter under what motto or creed it operates.

Roman Catholics should not be granted anything that is withheld from the Reformed. Nor should they be subjected to pressure, burdens, or curtailment of rights that we would not tolerate for ourselves. Even if Rome should provoke or taunt us ten times worse than it has thus far, it would still behoove us to stay calm and not deviate an inch from our principle that prescribes government nonintervention in the domain of revealed religion.[11]

Finally, also in regard to private life and citizenship, all citizens, regardless of their views about things eternal, ought to be treated on a footing of equality. That is to say, no one, for example, should be excluded from appointment to a certain post merely on the basis of what he believes or does not believe. And in the case of the oath, a means must be found to remove an atheist's spiritual blindness as a handicap for him in the field of politics. In the same vein, it is not right systematically to exclude people of our persuasion from the governing boards of the universities; this system, still defended recently in the liberal press, bears the shameful mark of flaming illiberality.

(4) Conscience shall never be violated.

There should be freedom of expression, freedom of belief, freedom of worship; but above all, the root of all these freedoms: freedom of conscience. This broad subject requires a separate article.

IV. FREEDOM OF CONSCIENCE

Conscience: Sovereign in Its Own Sphere   § 59

The conscience marks a boundary that the state may never cross.

The limits to state power reside in the will of God. Government has as much power as God has assigned to it. No more; no less. It sins if it leaves unused a portion of the power assigned to it, but also if it arrogates to itself any power that is not assigned to it.

---

11. Kuyper may be thinking, among other things, of the bull *Ex qua di arcano* of March 4, 1853, in which the pope announced the restoration of the episcopal hierarchy in the Netherlands and which not only referred to Jansenism as a "monstrous pest" but spoke of the "violent assault" of the "Calvinian heresy" that inflicted grievous losses on those flourishing churches once founded by Saints Willibrord and Boniface: "a hostile man did his utmost to destroy that precious vineyard of the Lord." As earlier in England, the episode led to a vehement no-popery movement lasting several months and resulting in the resignation of the government, which would not back down on respecting the constitutional right of Catholics to organize their church.

There is only one power without limits, the power of God, whence it is called almighty power. Anyone who accords the state the right to exercise power as if it had no limits is guilty of deifying the state and favoring state omnipotence. That is not indulging in oratorical phraseology but simply indicating a purely logical concept.

The moment one no longer speaks of "God" but of "an institution that he called into being," one is alluding to a distribution of power that has taken place. God called institutions of all kinds into being, and to each of them he granted a certain measure of power. In other words, he distributed the power that he had to assign. He did not give all his power to one single institution, but he endowed each of those institutions with the particular power that corresponded to its nature and calling.

It was this distribution of power that created boundaries, just as breaking up the commons gave rise to individual plots of land. Thus if the issue of power concerned things tangible and material, there would be no debate about the limits to state power. God would once for all have delineated the boundaries of each of his institutions. He could have given us a description of those boundaries, and whenever a quarrel arose we would be able to settle the issue (if we may be allowed to put it that way) by consulting this "divine registry."

But such is not the case.

The various entities—human persons first of all—which God called into being by his creative powers and to which he apportioned power, are almost all, in whole or in part, of a moral nature. There is a distinctive life of science; a distinctive life of art; a distinctive life of the church; a distinctive life of the family; a distinctive life of town or village; a distinctive life of agriculture; a distinctive life of industry; a distinctive life of commerce; a distinctive life of works of mercy; and the list goes on.

Now then, next to and alongside all these entities and ever so many other organizations stands the institution of the state.

Not above them, but alongside them. For each of these organizations possesses *sphere-sovereignty*, that is to say, derives the power at its disposal, not as a grant from the state but as a direct gift from God.

Fathers have power over their children, not as a gift from the state but by the grace of God. The only right the state has at most is to codify the right that fathers have received from God and, should a father want to injure the rights that God has also given to the child, to restore the situation as God has intended it.

The state is differentiated from all these other organizations by the fact that government alone has public power, whereas all other organizations in and of themselves are of a private nature.

Later we shall discuss the nature of this difference. For now it is enough to note that only the government has been given the power, when rights are under dispute, to impose on organizations and individuals what it deems to be just—if need be by the strong arm and, if it comes to that, by the sword. At the same time—and this especially should be noted—government has been assigned the duty, as much as is feasible, to jump in whenever these organizations and individuals neglect their natural life-task.

Conscience: the Limit to State Sovereignty§ 60

In practice, three examples of this kind of negligence can occur that involve these organizations (and individuals).

One of them may transgress its bounds and harm another. In that case government must push back the intruder.

Or one of them simply supplies what another left unused and undone, in which case government need only guard against chaos and confusion.

Or, finally, one or more organizations leave undone what another does not supply, and then government, if it is a matter of essentials, has to consider how it will jump in and in the meantime how it can stimulate the energy of its citizens so that this intervention need only be temporary.

From this it follows that a government has a twofold task, a normal and an abnormal one. Its normal task is to till its own field; its abnormal task is to look after neighboring fields to the extent that those neighbors let them lie fallow and to take care of them for as long as they neglect them.

Thus, in a nascent society, the state will have to do almost everything. In the measure that the energy of the citizenry awakens, government will more and more be relieved of abnormal action. And things will not be right until the citizen's energy breaks out in all directions and creates the opportunity for the state to do nothing extra and to focus exclusively on cultivating the field it was assigned.

Now if there were a still higher judge on earth who could pronounce a verdict in any disputes between the state and the other organizations (or individuals), and if that judge at the same time had the power to enforce compliance with his verdict, then there would never be any problem about this *negotiorum gestio*.[12]

But there is no such judge on earth. In disputes of this kind, government is judge in its own cause. This opens the source for the unfair treatment and abuse of power that governments time and again are guilty of.

Time and again governments, represented by sinful people, abuse their exclusive prerogative to compel by force.

They do so in three ways: (1) by pretending that they have the competence to grant power to the other organizations; (2) in disputes between these organizations, by favoring the party that is sympathetic to them; and (3) by gradually acting as owners of fields of which they are only the temporary caretakers. For this threefold abuse there is no other cure than absolute and full respect for freedom of conscience.

The sense of justice does help. But lately it has become more evident than ever in our country that government has makeshifts at its disposal to dull even this sacred sense.

The Constitution is also helpful. It is the charter of our civil rights. But we know how the interpretation of the Constitution has served as the magic formula for nullifying the Constitution.

Public opinion also helps. But May Laws and Socialist Laws have made it abundantly clear how one energetic government leader can reverse all of a country's public opinion in the space of three years.[13]

And therefore the only point of support that has ultimately proved invincible and indomitable over against the power of the state is the conscience.

§ 61   Conscience Cannot Be Coerced

Conscience is the most intimate expression of the life of a human being. Conscience knows that it has received its power directly from God. Conscience revolts against every unjust verdict that ends a dispute. Conscience will not cease to badger government whenever it acts as the owner of a field of which it is only the temporary caretaker.

---

12. *Negotiorum gestio* refers to an agent, recognized in Dutch law, who acts on behalf of a principal, for the benefit of that principal, but without that principal's prior consent. The reference here is to the government's temporary role in non-government areas.

13. Kuyper makes reference here to repressive laws under the Bismarck government in Germany during the 1870s. See above, § 13n22.

These excellent traits derive from the fact that conscience is the immediate contact in a person's soul of God's holy presence, from moment to moment. Withdrawn into the citadel of his conscience, a person knows that God's omnipotence stands guard for him at the gate. In his conscience he is therefore unassailable.

If government nevertheless dares to push through its abuse of force, the end will be a martyr's death. And in that death government is beaten and conscience triumphs.

Conscience is therefore the shield of the human person, the root of all civil liberties, the source of a nation's happiness.

To be sure, we are very much aware that in our sinful conditions two wrongs can occur in connection with conscience: (1) that one misuses his conscience as a hypocritical pretext; and (2) that one's conscience errs in what it wills. Thus we understand very well that the authorities would love to use this circumstance to overrun this last bulwark of resistance by telling us that it is beneath a government's dignity to yield to consciences that are so unreliable.

Nevertheless, although we admit the reality of this problem, we would rather needlessly step aside ten times to a false conscience than even once repress a good conscience.

Ten times better is a state in which a few eccentrics can make themselves a laughingstock for a time by abusing freedom of conscience, than a state in which these eccentricities are prevented by violating conscience itself.

Hence our supreme maxim, sacred and incontestable, reads as follows: as soon as a subject appeals to his conscience, government shall step back out of respect for what is holy.

Then it will *never* coerce. It will not impose the oath, nor compulsory military service, nor compulsory school attendance, nor compulsory vaccination, nor anything of the kind.

When it comes to fighting for the homeland to defend its freedom, the country's independence will be ten times safer with a robust sense of conscience in the nation than with the addition of a hundred conscientious pacifists in uniform.[14]

---

14. The original reads: " ... than with the addition of a hundred Mennonites to the ranks."

Our Program makes only one exception, and not unjustly it would seem: an appeal to conscience is to be honored provided it does not lack the presumption of respectability. A swindler, a reckless rogue, an unscrupulous wretch should not have the right to appeal to that forum. Granted, this is a limitation, but not an unfair one. If you want to preserve your right of conscience, it is not too much to ask that you be willing to renounce whatever is shameful.

CHAPTER SIX

"BY THE GRACE OF GOD"

It affirms that government rules by the grace of God and, thus authorized to rule, has the right to demand the oath and is obliged, as much as is feasible in all its branches—after amending the existing Lord's Day Act for the sake of keeping the Lord's Day free, hence also in the interest of the people—to rest on that day as well as to stipulate in its concessions to transportation companies a complete or partial cessation of activities on that day.

ARTICLE 5

I. THE STANDPOINT OF THE LAW

GOVERNMENT UPHOLDS THE LAW OF GOD

§ 62

Article 5 of the Program imposes three duties on government: to exercise authority; to maintain the oath as the cement of the state edifice; and to keep the Lord's Day free. It affirms as well that the competence to do all three derives from ruling *by the grace of God*. Let us start with the first duty: to exercise ruling authority, by virtue of the grace of God. A shorter way of saying this is: government must uphold the law of God.

A government by its very nature and calling is appointed to take the standpoint of the law, not of grace; and it inflicts incalculable harm on the nation if it abandons the sphere of law and infringes on the domain of pastoral care and sentiments.

It may not do what governments long arrogated to themselves, namely, to constitute themselves priests in Christ's church, housekeepers of the kingdom of God, and in the meantime to allow the meaning of right and law to grow dim by mixing constitutional law with concepts that derive from the covenant of grace.

But neither must it do what governments have more and more taken the liberty of doing since the spread of the Revolution's ideas, namely, to encourage the notion that all law is merely conventional, that obedience to the law can only be the result of voluntary consent, and that therefore lawbreakers do not need punishment so much as correction.

Both departures cause government to cease being sovereign in its sphere, cause the sense of justice to dull and erode through its laxness, and cause its authority to lose dignity and respect.

To be sure, there must be preaching of the kingdom of God and correctional programs for the criminal; but neither the one nor the other is the business of government.[1]

Government has its own calling and honorable task, and for this distinctive calling it has been assigned a separate domain, a separate sphere of life and a separate instrument for realizing its purpose.

Hence its standpoint can be no other than the standpoint of the law and—since it does not rule on its own authority but by the grace of God—of the *law of God*.

§ 63   MORE PARTICULARLY THE MORAL LAW

By "law of God" we do not mean the Ten Commandments but the universal moral law that was ingrained in man before his fall into sin and which nevertheless, however weakened after the fall, still speaks so sharply, so strongly, so clearly among even the most brutalized peoples and the most degenerate persons that Paul could write: "For when Gentiles, who do not have the law, by nature do what the law requires, they are a law to themselves, even though they do not have the law. They show that *the work of*

---

1. Most of Kuyper's contemporaries would have agreed with him that both correctional and rehabilitation programs for ex-convicts are the concern of philanthropic agencies.

the law is written on their hearts, while their conscience also bears witness, and their conflicting thoughts accuse or even excuse them."[2]

Even Calvin, in his naturally very theocratic essay about the Magistrate, pointed out that even in pagan lands governments uphold this universal law of God and take it as their guide. Just how unfeasible it is to place government formally on the standpoint of the revealed law of the Ten Commandments (other than through the personal influence by those in government) can be shown no more clearly than by recalling what sanctions our old theocrats proposed for government to apply in case of transgressions of the tenth commandment, "You shall not covet."[3]

Moreover, in light of what we said in connection with Article 3, it hardly makes any difference to us whether one assigns government the task of upholding the revealed or the universal moral law. After all, in a Christian nation, in the measure that the church of Christ upholds religious consciousness, the dictates of the moral law in people's hearts will be purified and sharpened by the higher standpoint occupied by the Ten Commandments.

But even if this were gradually to become less true due to decreasing church attendance, this should not tempt us, on grounds of utility, to deviate from the only sound path.

In political matters, too, you have to make up your mind and decide clearly whether or not you would have government, officially and as a body, act as the interpreter and defender of *revealed* truth.

But whatever choice you make, be consistent and act accordingly. If you think government can be mandated to uphold the revealed knowledge of God, then submit the whole of revelation to government—not just the Decalogue but also the gospel, hence also the preaching of the kingdom of God; in other words, return to strict theocracy and with that to the Roman Catholic principles of politics.

---

2. Rom 2:14–15 (author's emphasis).

3. Kuyper's point here is related to his earlier discussion of the traditional Reformed understanding of the duty of the civil magistrate to punish heretics. In another work, the *Tractaat van de Reformatie van der Kerken* (a treatise on the reformation of the churches, included in the "On the Church" volume in this series), Kuyper goes into more detail concerning the argument involved in Article 36 of the Belgic Confession, and lists a number of figures after Calvin whom he may have included here among "our old theocrats," including Theodore Beza (1519–1605), Samuel Maresius, Gijsbert Voetius, Francis Turretin (1623–1687), Johannes à Marck (1656–1731), and Bernardinus de Moor (1709–1780).

But if you do not want this, then don't do halfway what you say you reject on principle. Instead, choose consciously and resolutely for the opposite standpoint, and stick to it no matter what difficulties you may then face. Acknowledge that government is responsible for the *natural* knowledge of God but not (at least not directly and only via personal conscience) for the *revealed* knowledge of God. State plainly that government is to act as defender, not of the Sinaitic laws but of that deeper moral law which according to Romans 2 underlies the conscience of all people. The Ten Commandments merely affirm this moral law with divine guarantee, intensify it with a view to the gospel, and articulate it in accordance with Israel's needs.

Thus government must uphold the moral law, but as little in that most concrete form of the decrees of Mount Sinai as in the form, favored today, of human approval—the latter least of all.

The law has power to command and coerce only because it is the law *of God.* That is why our Program correctly reminds us that government must uphold the law but that it can do so only *by the grace of God.*

In sum, we must hold to this proposition: Government, acting as a servant of God, must place itself on the standpoint of the law and so must uphold the authority of the law on the strength of its mandate to rule by the grace of God according to the guidelines of the universal moral law and with obligations to revealed truth only insofar as the people in government affirm it in their own conscience.

§ 64   For the Glory of God and the Benefit of Church and Kingdom

We place special emphasis on government's task to uphold the standpoint of the law. That alone honors God.

That standpoint says: you are not your own lord and master. There is a power above you, a power that also concerns your moral life and prescribes the law, not according to your pleasure but according to the unchangeable standard of eternal Right. That standard demands that you give account of yourself, and it punishes you if you disobey. It is the eminently practical message that says, "You are men, and I am your God."[4]

Furthermore, this standpoint alone prepares the whole of life for the kingdom of God.

---

4. See Ezek 34:31.

The law is the "schoolmaster to bring us unto Christ"[5] and only if government vigorously sticks to the standpoint of the law are the souls of people overcome by that wholesome fear that in the end makes them bend to the fullness of the Sinaitic commandments and moves them to that awareness of sin and misery from which they will cry out for deliverance.

It follows that the church is enabled to fulfill her grand task far more through this particular government task than through any privileges that government might want to bestow on her. If government takes care that respect for the law revives in the land and that awareness of an all-controlling sacred Right can take root again in the conscience of the people—then, but then most certainly, people will be open to the fear of the Lord, and abandoning all false piety and minimal virtue, will allow those other and higher aspirations of the heart to surface, aspirations that are attuned to the gospel and cause people to thirst after reconciliation.

And finally, something one should especially not undervalue: when government itself upholds the law as the law of God and compels respect for a right that comes from God, it inscribes the standpoint of law, which a higher power commands and a lower power is to obey, so deeply into national life that, imperceptibly and automatically, discipline in the home is restored, honor for parents increases, respect for one's superiors improves, deference among the younger generation for the elderly rises—in a word, that strength and seriousness enter again into all those bonds of social life that today have lost their energy and fail to function because government stopped upholding the law as the *law of God*.

II. THE OATH

The Oath Is Out of Place in Revolutionary Constitutional Law §65

The oath is out of place in a state after the liberal model, but it does belong in antirevolutionary constitutional law.

True, most liberal constitutions maintain the oath, but that is an inconsistency—it is shrinking back from the consequences of one's system and hanging on to the old routine. As a result, liberals are always pushing for reducing the use of the oath. They first cheapened the taking of the oath by making the ceremony as thoughtless and irreverent as possible. They then prescribed it for so many occasions that it became a meaningless formula for countless government officials. And now they have advanced

---

5. Gal 3:24 KJV.

to the position that the oath is optional. If this process succeeds and the principle of "oath *or promise*," as currently on the books, is sustained, the oath will gradually fall into disuse and the day will arrive when this remnant of former narrow-mindedness will be transferred from the statute books to the museum of historical antiquities.

That it will come to this, if nothing intervenes, follows directly from the liberal principle, for the simple reason that its point of departure is "to leave God out of it." To make room for invoking God's name is then a patent absurdity, an internal contradiction, and an offense against the harmony of the whole.

But there is another reason as well.

As we have shown more than once, the basic concept of the liberal state is the *contract*. The liberal state chooses its starting point in human free will. It honors Pelagius as its spiritual forefather and therefore has the Arminian (that is, the semi-Pelagian) Hugo Grotius as its scholarly patron. The state is said to arise from a contract. As does government. The basis of marriage is a contract. A position of service rests on a contract. And so on.

Thus for this kind of state, the will and word of man is the origin of all things. Obviously, then, it will not do, on the one hand, to attach such overriding importance to a person's expression of his will—that is, his word—that it is viewed as the source of every possible legal relationship, and on the other hand, in subordinate interests, to show such distrust in a person's word that it should still need the affirmation of an oath.

To the extent, therefore, that our Constitution and our political system not only continues to have room for the oath but even has the bond between the king and his people rest on it, to that extent our constitutional law is not liberal but definitely antirevolutionary.[6]

§ 66   THE OATH IS A REQUIREMENT OF ANTIREVOLUTIONARY CONSTITUTIONAL LAW

If one affirms, as we do, that government only has power as servant of God to uphold divine justice among men within the limits determined by God and with accountability to his lofty Majesty, then it follows at once that every relationship between government and subjects is at one and the same time a relationship in which both stand before God.

---

6. This is an allusion to a monarch's oath upon his investiture to uphold the constitution.

In a court of law, the state enters not only in a relationship with the accused and with the injured party, but at one and the same time with God, whose justice the magistrate is to uphold. Similarly, the plaintiff or the witness does not merely enter into a relationship with the state but at one and the same time with the God who has given him the rights that he alleges have been abridged.

Similarly, when government administers a pledge of loyalty to a soldier or a civil servant, or when a king binds himself to his people as a constitutional monarch, it is not just a question of concluding a contract but of recognizing a relationship that was ordered by God in the course of events and of mutually binding oneself to fulfill all the obligations that God has attached to this relationship.

Both in a court of law, therefore, and in establishing a relationship between a government and a subject, there is always and invariably at the basis of the relationship between the two persons a relationship of the two parties with the living God. That is why it is good and right and just that both parties also solemnly acknowledge this relationship with the living God as the basis of their action, and that they not bind themselves to each other but to him who knows the hearts.

Accordingly, we do not just put up with the oath but demand its preservation as the cement of the State.

The Commandment Not to Swear   § 67

The commandment of Jesus not to swear does not in any way relate to the civil oath.[7] That commandment was given to the narrow circle of his disciples and therefore holds for the church, where the oath should never be admitted. But it does not hold for civil society in relation to the state. Jesus himself swore an oath before Caiaphas.[8]

This cannot be otherwise.

If the oath is a mutual reminder that what one is doing is being done while accountable to the living God, then of course there can be no question of the oath in the church, that is, in a domain where one is expected to be very much aware of standing before the face of God. But the oath cannot be done away with in civil society, where the rough and the sensuous intermingle with the spiritual and the pious. Particularly not in a law

---

7. See Matt 5:33–37.
8. See Matt 26:62–64.

court, where every lawsuit and every criminal case is a constant reminder that many do not live in communion with God.

The error of forbidding the oath was understandable among the Anabaptists, who confused state and church. But for us, who distinguish state and church as two altogether divergent life-spheres, this error would be unforgivable.

§ 68   THE OATH AND ATHEISTS

We strongly urge that the oath be maintained, though with the following provisos:

(1) The oath ought to be administered as solemnly as possible and be preceded at a minimum both by asking the person who is to take the oath whether he believes in the living God and by reading a brief formulary that clearly explains the meaning of an oath.

(2) The oath ought to be administered only on the most important occasions and not be robbed of its power and gravity through too frequent use.

(3) A member of a denomination or association that out of respect for God and his Word, even if misunderstood, considers the taking of an oath unlawful, ought to be allowed to replace the oath with a promise, provided such a person (a) produces a statute of his society that condemns the oath *out of respect for God and his Word*; (b) submits a written statement that he personally shares this objection *on the same grounds as his society*; and (c) submits a written testimony that the promise he wishes to give binds him toward God in the same way as he would be bound if he were free to take the oath.

(4) Atheists, that is, exceptional people who do not unconditionally declare that they believe in the living God, ought not to take the oath, nor give a promise as outlined under (3), but ought to be treated in the following manner: an atheist should state that he is prepared, to the satisfaction of the state in case it so requires, to be represented by a respected person—whom the state may likewise challenge and of whom it is established that he has known the party involved well enough and long enough—and to have that person declare under oath that in the case at hand he has no reason to doubt the love of truth of this atheist.

As one can see, it is our intention in every way to show up atheists to be *exceptions* and to make sure, in the interest of the state, that also in the case of nonbelievers there is always a guarantor who does believe in God.

This is only fair. There are, after all, *very few* atheists. Population statistics bear out that after subtracting Plymouth Brethren and other Christian sects there are at most two or three hundred persons in our country who do not belong to any church. Such exceptions barely count.

And if it is pointed out to us that many atheists are hiding in the church, then our answer is: "Any atheist dishonest enough to take on the appearance of worshiping God is the last person that deserves to be trusted as someone who loves the truth and keeps his word."

Thus we do not believe that the number of atheists is considerable; there are so few of them that it is scarcely worth the trouble to make an exception for their group. But rather than doing too little, we have indicated even for this exceptional group of citizens a method for reconciling as best as possible the indisputable right of the state with their private interest.

III. SABBATH REST

SOCIAL AGITATION FOR A SEVENTH DAY OF REST § 69

Quite correctly, it seems to us, our Program does not link the Sunday issue to the social question but addresses it in the present article that deals with the obligations of government toward God.

A day of rest can easily be imagined even in a nation of atheists. Labor without letup would gradually exhaust atheists too. And when you are at the end of your tether you will instinctively look to rest as the natural means to restoring your strength.

The only disagreement might arise over the question whether one ought to be "idle" every six, seven, or ten days. As is well known, the French Revolution, in order to erase from the life of society every last remnant of Scriptural marks as a toxic virus, actually created weeks of ten days, changing "six days shalt thou labor" into a nine-day workweek.

Such a day of "idleness" is coming into vogue again among the extreme left of our liberals. After indulging for half a century in poking fun at "Sabbatarianism" and taking offense at an official Sunday, the social democrats in Germany and the Aart Admiraals and many others in our own country are turning up with sentimental articles about work stoppage on

Sundays, articles that our large liberal dailies lift up to be brilliant specimens of spanking-new wisdom.[9]

We must confess that we have very little sympathy for this movement. Those who put taking care of the body higher than honoring God should not take it ill of us that we have a rather low view of their lofty ideal. And it makes little difference to us when they add some silver lining by noting that it would enable people to visit museums, enrich family life, and engage in "culture." All these modern frills have proven only to lead to more vaudeville, more trains, more concerts, and more pubs and taverns, and the higher inspiration that is sought apart from God does not issue from "the Spirit" but from "new wine."

§ 70   CELEBRATING THE SABBATH FOR GOD'S SAKE

In one respect only we do appreciate this new agitation. It reveals that we are right in deducing Sunday observance from the "natural knowledge of God" on which government too is based. It reveals that the ordinance of resting on the seventh day was "ingrained" in the very creation of man. "Ever since the creation of the world," writes Paul, "his invisible attributes, namely, his eternal power and divine nature, have been clearly perceived."[10] Once again we see that from the very constitution of the creature called man it is seen and understood that the Lord willed that this creature rest every seventh day.

In addition, thanks to a tradition dating back to paradise, the memory of this day of rest has stayed alive among virtually all peoples. The effect still shows that the peoples who strictly observe the Sabbath are the most energetic and the most stalwart. And as we know, the commandment to keep the Sabbath day holy, again according to the Sinaitic law, is not based on God's secret will but on the fact that the Lord made heaven and earth in six days and rested the seventh day—and made man after his image and likeness.

For this reason we maintain that government certainly has a duty toward God to honor the seventh day. That our "seventh" day is the Sunday is the result of history. It was in the course of history that our nation

---

9. Aart Admiraal (1833-78) was a freethinker, regular contributor to the anarchist journal *De Dageraad*, and author of booklets with titles such as *Zondagsviering* [Sunday observance] (1877) and *Dr. A. Kuijper is geen vertegenwoordiger van het Nederlandsche volk* [Dr. A. Kuijper (*sic*) does not represent the Dutch people] (1875).
10. Rom 1:20.

became a Christian nation. And given that among Christians the day of the resurrection is the symbol of the new life in Christ, whoever considered establishing a seventh day of rest but on another day than Sunday would violate history and with that our national character.

Thus the childish objection that we should really hallow the Saturday rather than the Sunday does not affect us at all.

Even if we were officially to place government on the basis of the special revelation in Scripture (which we do not), even then it ought to be known in a Reformed country that the ceremonial law has been abolished and only the moral law remains, also in the fourth commandment. But on our standpoint that remark can be omitted, given that we base official Sunday observance on these three grounds only: (1) the natural knowledge of God; (2) the history of a Christian nation; and (3) the influence of the Word of God, including the Ten Commandments, on the conscience of the people in government.

It is important to emphasize, therefore, that by hallowing Sunday the state first of all performs an act of reverence toward the living God, and only thereafter acts in the interest of the people.

Upholding the honor of God always serves the interest of the people as well. In defining the present issue, however, everything depends on not overturning the wheel of life, as the Revolution does, but leaving on top what belongs on top, namely, the honor of God.

APPLICATION OF THIS PRINCIPLE   § 71

Once government takes this stand on Sunday observance, the next question is: What can the state do to discharge this duty? We offer the following suggestions.

(1) Keep the seventh day free for the undisturbed work of the church in sanctuary, hall, or home. Government itself is powerless to administer spiritual food to the people, but that is exactly why it is part of government's duty to create opportunity for others to do so. That requires a day set apart, a day when nothing disrupts or diverts, so that people can give themselves wholeheartedly to it.

The main goal should not be physical rest or family life, but the nurture of godliness among the people; the rest will follow but should not be in the forefront.

The body will then automatically come to rest. But family life is destroyed rather than built up by an empty Sunday if the wellspring of godliness begins to dry up in the heart of the nation.

Thus, hands off the Lord's Day! This is the policy of *dies non*, as in the American system, signifying a day of which government acknowledges that the state does not own it and has no jurisdiction over it.[11]

That day is set apart for the service of God, precisely so that the other six days may be spent in service to society.

(2) Abstain from all state business, as a government rule. Government consists of people and employs people, and those people too have an account with their God. The state may not impose rest on others unless it takes the lead by abstaining from work itself.

No work ought to be done by government agencies, nor by the state-owned railways, postal services or telegraph offices, nor by the militia and armed forces, nor as little as possible by the police. These bodies of people must not be used as mere tools but must be respected as human beings with obligations to God.

We know that this is not feasible in any absolute sense. On Sundays, too, guards and police have to be on duty. We also know that a sudden cessation of telegraph and postal services on Sunday would meet with strong resistance.[12] But all that concerns the *modus quo*, the manner of application, not the end goal to be pursued: *absolute abstention*.

(3) Shut down all events that would normally be open only under government license but which run counter to the purpose of Sunday.

Theater productions, traveling shows, public casinos and concerts, and so on, do not belong on Sunday.

Similarly, permits for houses of prostitution, gambling, or alcohol consumption should never be more than a license for six weekdays, never for Sunday as well.

Closure during worship services means nothing: nowadays services are conducted at any hour of the day; and the underlying notion, "first to church, then to the pub," is unworthy of a Christian government.

---

11. Kuyper refers to the principle of *dies non (juridicum)*: a day when courts do not sit and no legal business of any kind is carried on.

12. At this time, in the larger cities, mail was delivered two or three times a day, seven days a week.

(4) Enforce even more strictly than usual the laws that regulate public decency and morality.

Creating a disturbance, breaching the peace, gathering in crowds, and brawling in the streets are not becoming on Sunday.

Loitering along the street in a state of intoxication, singing obscene songs in public, shamelessly soliciting prostitution, and the like, should never be tolerated, but especially not on Sundays.

A nation must have rules for the public domain. Not for the home, where people are personally responsible to God. But certainly in the public domain, which falls under the responsibility of the state.

(5) Prohibit Sunday labor in all workplaces of industrial or commercial establishments that operate under government license.

This has to be done, if for no other reason than to be rid of the noise and clamor caused by many factories, the offensive displays of many stores, the impudence of carts laden with freshly slaughtered meat making their way through throngs of churchgoers, and whatever other inconveniences are commonly caused by ongoing activity of workers and vendors.

But this has to be done even more so because of the obligation that rests on government to uphold, in the interest of the workingman against the possible greed of employers, the ordinances established by God for all that is human.

(6) Cut back on public transit operating under a public concession.

To foster fear of God demands serenity, and you do not establish serenity but eliminate it when you allow people to scatter in all directions on Sundays. Then on Monday morning people are not rested but more tired than ever. Then your Sunday does not sanctify the common people but makes them lose their senses and weans them from discipline and order. If the current Lord's Day Act fails on this noble standpoint, it ought surely to be annulled.[13]

Of course, only a thoughtful, deliberate, and gradual transition could hope to reform habits and customs in this area.

---

13. One of Kuyper's first acts as prime minister in 1901 would be to ask Tiemen de Vries, who had defended a doctoral dissertation in the law faculty of the Free University on the history of Sunday legislation, to compose a draft for a new Lord's Day Act.

As well, Sunday observance along these lines may require that the working man be given another half day for recreation. But we shall deal with that when discussing the social question.

Finally, for the sake of completeness, we add only that we consider keeping the *Christian holidays* advisable from a historical point of view, yet we would never dream of placing them on a par with observing the Lord's Day.

CHAPTER SEVEN

FORMS OF GOVERNMENT

While it deems no form of government the only serviceable one, it recognizes the constitutional monarchy that has gradually evolved in our country from the republic of the previous century as the most suitable form of government for the Netherlands.

ARTICLE 6

EVERY FORM OF GOVERNMENT IS SERVICEABLE   § 72

What we need to say about the form of government can be dealt with in a single article.

All we have to do is point out two things: (1) which form of government to choose is relatively immaterial; and (2) constitutional monarchy is the preferred form for our country.

In regard to the first point, antirevolutionaries have always maintained that in itself the form of government does not matter and that it is possible to have a democracy or a republic or a monarchy in which God is honored and the form of government proves conducive to the true happiness of the people. This conviction flows from our firm belief in the almighty power of God and is confirmed by the lessons of history.

God's absolute power has to be respected even in the means he chooses. Everything depends, after all, not on the means he chooses but on the purpose he intends.

God, not the government, is our real ruler and king. Just as it is immaterial in a monarchy whether the ruler exercises his dominion through officials who bear the title of grand vizier, councilor, or civil servant, so in the great divine monarchy it is a matter of indifference whether the Lord of lords wishes to exercise his rule over us through servants, authorized and installed by him, who bear the title of king or mighty lords or popular representatives.

Experience confirms this. There have been (and still are) monarchies that thrived and flourished, others where life stood at a standstill, and still others where the monarchy was a scourge and an affliction.

Equally, history can tell you of republics that shone gloriously, republics that presented a miserable spectacle, and republics that ruined land and people.

And the same goes, finally, for democracies that remind you by turns of the glory of Athens, the weakness of present-day Switzerland, and the horror of the Paris Commune.

This fact warrants the conclusion that none of these vicissitudes were due to the form of government but instead depended on the people who ruled, on the people that were to be ruled, and on the circumstances that made that rule easy or difficult.

§ 73   THE DOCTRINAIRES

For this reason we must protest against both doctrinaire royalists and the even more insufferable doctrinaire democrats.

Doctrinaire royalists consider monarchy the only sound form of government because it guarantees a single head of state and hereditary succession. They are fanatic about a version of divine right that diminishes the human worth of people in order to be able to honor a more than human worth in the royal person.

Imperceptibly they have cultivated a spirit of slavish flattery and unmanly pliancy. By honoring the people at court without daring to critique the lifestyle of the court, they foster a moral decadence that desecrates a people from the top down. They unconsciously promote a kind of militarism when it comes to authority, and a worship of opulence as compared to society's needs. This can only break manly civic spirit.

But even worse are the doctrinaire democrats. They want to impress upon you that things will never be good or will never get better, in your country or anywhere else, so long as you do not dare to embrace the one holy catholic democratic state as the cure-all for all civic ills. This system is the logical consequence of the Revolution principle of utter self-sufficiency, which teaches the people to throw off all authority and to honor no other guide or leader than the one they have created themselves and will continue to create in order to perpetuate their state.

We will have nothing to do with this doctrinaire democracy, not for anything in the world. It is the incarnation of our enemy. Its principle is absolutely incompatible with the exalted nature of the honor of God.

When Calvin writes that if he had to choose he would prefer aristocracy, because "in the light of sin, authority is safer in the hands of many than in the hands of one," then we agree, although it should be remembered that he placed his aristocracy over against the absolute monarchy of his day and at bottom simply had in mind our tempered monarchy.[1]

THE FORM OF GOVERNMENT FOR OUR COUNTRY   §74

If we now address our second point—the form of government to be preferred for our country—then we do not hesitate to state that we would just as soon have seen a continuation [in 1813] of the hereditary title of *stadtholder*, with improved constitutional guarantees, than the adoption of the title of *king*.

We are not all that much attached to titles.

Small countries like Belgium, Bavaria, Wurtemberg, Saxony, and our own may even be too small for the splendor of kingship. Moreover, all that opulence and glitter of a royal train, which a king simply must have, is seldom good for the moral standards of a people. The people of a residential capital are usually inferior in moral fiber to those of other cities. And what especially weighs heavy with us is that the magnificent name of Orange might have derived more distinctive, more historical, and hence more hallowed luster if it had continued to wear its historic garb.

But now that the men of 1813, and at their initiative the nation, and at the call of the nation the prince of Orange himself, judged otherwise, now antirevolutionaries have no difficulty whatsoever in extending their undivided sympathy to our constitutional kingship, and we are of the view

---

1. See John Calvin, *Institutes of the Christian Religion*, vol. 2, ed. John T. McNeill, trans. Ford Lewis Battles (Philadelphia: Westminster, 1960), 4.20.8.

today that every attempt at altering the status quo would be to insult the House of Orange and to tamper with the state edifice, hence to commit a crime against the nation.

Furthermore, a republic, which today, given the prevailing ideas, would automatically assert itself in a revolutionary form, could not bring us a sound government because it would immediately degenerate into a party regime. This would undermine the already weakened sense of justice among the people, which is an essential condition for establishing a viable government by the people.

And whoever would be foolish enough to dream of a democratic form of government for our country—in all seriousness, such a one would completely overlook that a democracy is impossible without a strong public spirit and that a public spirit of the political kind runs counter to the national character of the Dutch people.

With gratitude and affection, borne up by both political and historical conviction, we range ourselves with those who will support nothing but the constitutional monarchy, for as long as God allows us to have the House of Orange.

In the Germanic period of our history, our forefathers governed themselves as in a people's democracy. In the best period of our history they maintained a republic. Today we stand behind our constitutional monarchy—not by preference, but because the faults of the past and the upshot of history landed us at this crossroad.

Let there be a monarchy then, *constitutional* in its exercise of power because it is constitutional in nature and origin.

But then let it be a constitutional *monarchy*, with a king not just in name but a king who is the bearer of sovereignty, who can make laws for his people, and who therefore can also, when party tyranny violates justice, protect justice with his royal shield.

German notions of monarchy, as held in Berlin today, are foreign to us; and extravagant claims like those of the seventeenth-century Stuarts will never become indigenous here.

All false royalism, all attempts at having some kind of "throne worship" take root in our country, must be resisted tooth and nail.

Orange, once the founding father of our glorious republic and advocate of our civil liberties against the absolutistic monarchy of Philip II of Spain, will never wear any other crown in the Netherlands than the crown that has its diadem of gold wreathed with leaves of oak, symbol of patriotism in defense of civil society.

Groen van Prinsterer always insisted on this. Happily, our Program does the same. We never spoke otherwise.

And if it has recently, on the occasion of the People's Petition, been thought fit (this time by liberals as formerly by conservatives) to suspect us of being sympathetic to the use of unconstitutional means, even of speculating on a coup d'état, then he who dared suspect a serious-minded group of Netherlandic people of such treasonous intentions has tarnished his own proud name of Netherlander.[2]

2. The *Volkspetitionnement*, submitted to the king in August of 1878, asked him not to give his royal assent to the Primary Education Act passed by both houses of parliament a month earlier. The petitioners believed a king of the House of Orange had a right, if not a historic duty, to do so, for the sake of protecting freedom of conscience. The king and his advisors decided, however, that a royal veto would not be in keeping with constitutional practice.

CHAPTER EIGHT

OUR CONSTITUTION

It accepts, as a starting premise, the Constitution as revised in 1848, in order to attain through legal avenues a reformation of our political institutions in keeping with Christian-historical principles.

ARTICLE 7

I. ACCEPTING THE CONSTITUTION

§ 75   A CONSTITUTION IS NEEDED

We accept the Constitution, but do so in order to reform it.

We accept it because we consider it superior to its predecessor, and also because its stipulations as a whole do not constitute a hindrance for us to swear an oath on it.

The antirevolutionary party, too, desires a Constitution. Not a so-called Charter, but a Constitution in a real sense. Not a vague theory for all nations and peoples, but one demanded by our existence as a Netherlandic people and born of the history of our people.

We are not in favor of a Constitution in an absolute sense. A Constitution is unthinkable among people at a low level of development. Even today it would be an *hors d'oeuvre* in Russia. And Turkey, by introducing a Constitution in its dying hours, made itself the laughingstock of all Europe.

What is more, there are peoples who can bear the grant of a Charter, but not a Constitution.

The difference between the two, as everyone knows, is that a Charter is granted by an absolute monarch. He is not obligated to grant one, but from pure kindness he freely and voluntarily limits his power as far as he thinks fit and gives his subjects permission (with the right to revoke it, hence only temporarily) to enjoy a measure of freedom that suits his royal pleasure.

A Fundamental Law or Constitution, by contrast, is the recognition by two parties of each other's rights and the regulation of their relationship on the basis of these rights.

Thus there can be no question of a Constitution unless the bearer of sovereign authority and the people's representatives have developed themselves as two separate powers in the realm which in the course of history and as a result of their struggles have arrived at boundaries that limit each to its own proper sphere.

Conversely, however, you have to have a Constitution in a country like ours, where society no longer lives almost unconsciously in an embryonic state but has arrived at a self-conscious stage of development. Here all factors are present to properly delineate the boundaries that will indicate where sovereign authority ends and the sovereignty of the social spheres begins. Every attempt to go back to a granted Charter is to betray both the nation and its history.

THE 1848 CONSTITUTION BETTER THAN THOSE OF 1815 AND 1840 §76

Although it is inconceivable for us to live without a Constitution, we would not want to return to the Constitution of 1815 (or 1840).

The list of our rights and freedoms that was handed us in 1815 was far from complete and no more pure than that of 1848 in the matter of principles.

It was incomplete because, compared to our ancient privileges, it spoke more of curtailing than expanding our national rights and civil liberties. It regarded the people as very immature, and it conformed more, in tenor if not in tone, to German constitutions (*Verfassungen*) than to the political character of the Dutch nation. More than is sometimes realized, it contributed to disrupting the political fabric of our nation, leading us back to the chaotic situation in which the nation's energy, as bitter experience is teaching us these days, is being spent in a pointless endeavor to get the country moving again and to escape the evil of party tyranny.[1]

We do gratefully acknowledge that the excellent qualities of our first king initially tempered much of the attendant evil; but neither may we be silent about the fact that many things that were undeniably good about King William were in contrast with not a few questionable policies that he pursued. In any case, thirty years of lack of political progress, particularly after the political blight of French domination, was injurious to our ability to operate under constitutional government, an injury from which we have still not recovered.[2]

It would be a mistake, therefore, to think that we are unhappy with the Constitution of 1848 because we have a greater preference for the earlier, more openly absolutistic constitution.

If we had to choose I wonder if we would not, to a person, reject the one of 1815, since it proved unprofitable as well as ill-suited for the free development of the nation. At least, we must never forget that under the Constitution of 1815 the hardest blows were struck against the Christian religion in the land: the revival of the Christian element with its own organization was continually obstructed,[3] and the public school of 1806, lacking in positive objectives, is proving to be, with the clarity of hindsight, more the mother of the neutral government school than of the free school that is free to honor Christ.[4]

The source of our dissatisfaction, therefore, is not that the Constitution of 1815 was revised, but that it was not revised *in a better spirit*.

What was on the books could not be kept, but it should have been replaced by something better than we have now. For thirty years Groen devoted his best efforts at fighting the spirit that obstructed something

---

1. This article was originally written on July 9, 1878, during preparations for the People's Petition against the bill on Primary Education then being debated in parliament.
2. French domination lasted from 1795 to 1813; William I was king from 1814 to 1840.
3. For almost a decade, worship services of the *Afscheiding* (Reformed congregations that seceded from the national church in 1834) were forcibly broken up, troops were quartered in members' homes, and ministers were fined and imprisoned.
4. The Education Act of 1806 first introduced instruction in "Christian and civic virtues" as the overall aim of primary public education. The phrase was retained in the Acts of 1857 and 1878. "Christian virtues" soon proved equivalent to the values of an autonomous morality, divorced from Bible or Christian doctrine. Kuyper agreed with Groen van Prinsterer that the teaching of such values deprived children of the motive to respect them and the strength to persevere in them. See also below, § 156.

better, and faithful to his memory we shall do the same, to the best of our ability.

Antirevolutionaries May Swear an Oath on the Constitution §77

That brings us to the third point we indicated: "its stipulations as a whole do not constitute a hindrance for us to swear an oath on it."

An antirevolutionary, too, can swear an oath on the Constitution in good conscience and in good faith, without any mental reservations whatsoever.

He can do so even better than many an atheist.

After all, the confession of God Almighty as the source of all authority is so clearly and strongly interwoven with our Constitution that we can scarcely imagine an atheist who, as a minister, member of parliament, or civil servant, can swear an oath on the Constitution and yet remain an honest person in his own eyes.

But even apart from the excellent and positive antirevolutionary components still present in goodly number in our Constitution, our contention that every antirevolutionary can swear an oath on it simply rests on the threefold consideration: (1) that one's oath does not exclude but includes the article that indicates how it may once again be revised; (2) that in applying the Constitution one is bound to its text and not to a liberal interpretation of it;[5] and (3) that our political creed is anything but opposed to its basic thrust. Allow me to briefly explain each of these three considerations.

The Constitution Is Open to Revision §78

First of all, the Constitution, revised in 1848, can be revised again. Whether it will in fact be revised depends not only on you but far more on other factors. You therefore do not commit an immoral act, nor contradict yourself, if you take the oath on the Constitution and then go on to use all your influence, including the influence gained by that oath, to agitate against it.

In 1847 liberal candidates swore an oath on the Constitution of 1840 with the express purpose of setting it aside as soon as they got elected. Yet no one dreamed of condemning their action.

We find ourselves in the same situation today.

We, too, make no secret of the very grave objections that we nurse against the Constitution of 1848. We have no hidden agenda. Whoever

---

5. One decade after this was written, liberals conceded in a parliamentary session that public funding for non-government schools was "not necessarily unconstitutional."

administers the oath to us knows that we do not plan to leave it undisturbed. And so long as we comply with it while it is in force, we must be allowed the unabridged and unimpeded right to make use of the means provided by the Constitution itself to implement its closing articles when the opportunity presents itself.

§ 79   THE CONSTITUTION, NOT INTERPRETATIONS OF IT

Secondly, we swear an oath on the Constitution, not on someone's interpretation of it.

An antirevolutionary, too, can in good conscience, quite apart from his right to work for a revision, swear an oath on Article 194 because nothing binds him to the interpretation of this crucial article that liberals read into it.[6]

Our oath does not even bind us to the historical interpretation of the article in question as commonly presented.

To present a historical interpretation that relies on statements in a certain report or speech or pamphlet, without taking into account the spirit in which it was approved even by that uncertain vote without whose cooperation it would never have been enacted into law—to present such an interpretation, we say, is tantamount to presenting, if not a falsification of history, a history so full of holes that any oath could circumvent it.

As long as we enjoy the indisputable right to set *our* historical—and in fact more stringent—interpretation over against the prevailing one, so long shall we also take the liberty, in the solemn moment of taking the oath, to call to mind what we think is the true interpretation, rather than the reading that always roused our protest.

§ 80   ITS BASIC THRUST IS STILL IN PART ANTIREVOLUTIONARY

Thirdly, we are not diametrically opposed to the basic thrust of the Constitution.

Our situation is entirely different from that of Rome. No *Syllabus* exists for us, and more than one article that the *Syllabus* condemns in our

---

6. Article 194 contained the clause ("the wretched clause," as Groen and his fellow supporters of free, private schools came to call it) that "government shall everywhere provide adequate public primary education." The clause was cited to forbid government support of any kind for non-government schools, and on occasion was used by the authorities to justify establishing tuition-free, one-room schoolhouses in areas where the population used only private schools for their children. But see also the previous note.

Constitution is affirmed and defended by us as a sound political idea.[7] Like others, we fail to understand how our Roman Catholic politicians square their loyalty to the *Syllabus* with their oath on the Constitution. Not even if we give full due to the negative character of that papal document. In fact, we for our part would consider our oath less than genuine if we held to the *Syllabus* and nevertheless swore an oath on the Constitution with the intent to execute and apply it.

But that is not our situation. There is much in the Constitution, also after its revision in 1848,[8] that is sooner antirevolutionary than liberal. The liberalism still present in it virtually nowhere carries the mark of state omnipotence and occurs mostly in moderate form. And where the impure principle still crept in, it was mostly attached to policies that cannot be imposed by legislation anyway but are simply governed by practice.

II. ITS REVISION

APPROPRIATE AND ADVISABLE § 81

We desire: (1) a general revision of the Constitution; (2) achieved along legal avenues; (3) in the spirit of Christian-historical principles.

As we know, our Catholic countrymen do not share our desire for a general revision. They were the ones who in 1848, with the help of the liberals, pushed through the present Constitution, taking care that its main provisions agreed with *their* views by ensuring a legal advantage for themselves and crippling the development of the Protestant element in the nation. Naturally, our Catholic politicians cherish their own creature and want to keep their advantageous position.

Still, that advantage is not by itself enough to explain Rome's intractable antipathy to every notion of constitutional revision. In addition, no doubt, the Catholic politicians are afraid, given the unfavorable times, that recasting the Constitution in a newer mold would enable unbelievers to make its provisions still more radical and, no less, give antirevolutionaries a chance to somehow defraud Rome again of the equal rights it acquired in '48.

This fear seems to us ungrounded.

---

7. The reference is to the *Syllabus of Errors* attached to the 1864 encyclical of Pius IX, which condemned eighty propositions held by secular liberalism. See above, § 31n3.
8. *Note by the author in later editions:* And in 1887.

As far as antirevolutionaries are concerned, people can know, if only from our Program, that we wish to enhance "equal rights for all" rather than curtail them. And although we do not deny that in certain backwaters of our country voices are sometimes raised for restoring the official Reformed character of our state, as of old, and to place Roman Catholics outside the common law, nevertheless we can assure them that these stray voices of an irrevocable past are becoming weaker all the time; they are opposed on principle by our more influential members and are scarcely of any weight in discussions of a general political nature.

As for the other fear of revision in a more radical spirit, we acknowledge fully that the political climate does tend in that direction. Yet it is legitimate to ask, with a reference to '48, whether one honestly believes that this danger can best be warded off through passive resistance.

It seems to us, much rather, that this slide toward radicalism cannot be stopped anyway and that all passive resistance will have to admit defeat in the end. Conversely, by taking action and setting program against program, one gains a voice at the table at crucial moments and helps set the agenda by entering the debate from the start.

Precisely because we concur with Rome that revision is coming and that it will certainly be in a more radical spirit, we think it advisable to participate from the start in the movement leading toward it and in that way deny the radicals a monopoly when the decision falls.

§ 82   A GENERAL, NOT PARTIAL REVISION

Having thus called a revision of the Constitution advisable, the fact that we have abandoned the idea of a partial revision and declared ourselves in favor of a general one is merely a question of expediency.

If it appeared feasible to remove the worst hindrances from the Constitution by means of three or four amendments, we would be satisfied.

But a third of a century has gone by without advancing a single step.[9] And now that the general political situation seems to allow serious political action only through a combination of interests, we give priority to "the better part all at once."

Another reason is that there is an unmistakable link between the various partial changes that are desired. At every debate that digs below the surface one notices time and again that something is wrong about the

---

9. *Note by the author in later editions*: The revision of 1887 gave us virtually nothing.

very spirit of the Constitution and that this defect makes itself felt in virtually every important provision. Add to that the defective prose in which the Constitution is written, which repeatedly leaves a loophole for the grossest arbitrariness, and one will appreciate why in our opinion a drastic revision of the *entire* document is to be preferred.

No Coup d'État §83

That, in the second place, we do not ask for a revision of the Constitution except through legal avenues, is hardly a meaningless and therefore redundant addition.

First of all, *counterrevolutionaries*, with whom we are often confused, deem a coup d'état quite permissible. Moreover, it is true that to all appearance no revision of the Constitution is conceivable without a breach of the Constitution.

In response to the first point, we simply declare that we are not counterrevolutionary and abhor a breach of oath by the king at least as strongly as by his subjects. We do recognize, however, that the king's conscience is not bound to the partisan interpretation of the dominant coterie, and that he himself decides in what sense and to what extent his conscience is bound to what is questionable in the Constitution. But to the extent that the Constitution speaks clear, lucid, and unambiguous language, violating an oath sworn on it would simply be, also in our eyes, a crime.

The second point is a thornier question: will a revision that is in any way decisive prove possible without violating the Constitution? Is not the padlock that Thorbecke placed on the Constitution so firmly rusted that reopening it is impossible without using force?[10]

Our answer is that under normal circumstances, indeed it is. Anyone who expects to find two-thirds of both houses of parliament open to a revision is dreaming. A revision can only result in a reduction of power for those who currently have it.

We need not waste another word on that subject. It never happens in normal times.

But if you recall that in 1848 not two in ten who voted in favor of the revision were actually in favor of it; and if you allow yourself to be instructed by history that all nations experience convulsions every now and then that sweep everything before them; and how an external commotion

---

10. Johan Rudolph Thorbecke (1798–1872) was a law professor in Leiden, leader of the liberals, and chief architect of the Constitution of 1848.

can totally disorganize normal domestic relations (as it did in 1848) — then it will be clear to you, we think, that a constitutional revision can certainly occur along legal avenues even when it does not get there along normal channels.[11]

§ 84   Revision in a Christian-historical Sense

With the addition "in keeping with Christian-historical principles" we do not in any way imply a recasting of the Constitution in a sense that would give us a privileged position.

Political life is falsified to the core as soon as one party, no matter which, succeeds in stipulating privileges in its favor in the Constitution or having the country's fundamental law be a codification of its own political program.

One must distinguish carefully here.

The antirevolutionary party certainly has ideas about the kind of state it would like to see if all the citizens of this land were on its side, were of the same mind, and hence were spiritual children of Calvin. But our party also has its ideas about what a fair and equitable arrangement of the state has to be for a politically mixed population. Only the latter, not the former, do we wish to transfer to the Constitution. And we believe we may demand this with all the more confidence because we are convinced that it is precisely in Reformed countries that the only correct legal system has gradually developed that offers a lasting *modus vivendi* to a population of mixed character.

What we have in mind are no privileges of any kind and nothing but equal rights for all.

For the time being we make an exception only for the atheist. The case of atheists is like that of the blind and deaf: they are exceptions that the law cannot accommodate. Dutch statute laws are geared to normal people and lack even the slightest provision for compensating the deaf and the blind for their political handicap.

The same holds for the incurably sick, for cripples, and for the insane. The Constitution states that every Netherlander is eligible to hold public office. But could a blind person be a minister, and a cripple a cavalry officer?

---

11. In March 1848, popular disturbances in Paris, Berlin, and Vienna struck panic fear into members of the government in The Hague. A more liberal constitution was adopted soon after. See above, § 25n13.

Such, and worse, is the situation of the atheist, and there are far fewer atheists than there are blind and deaf people and people with a physical handicap. We would not even want to be as heartless as our legislation has been thus far and gladly create an optimal situation even for the atheist (as we showed above when discussing the oath), provided the rule follows those who believe in God and exceptions remain exceptions. Should atheists grow in number and cease to be exceptions, then, but only then, things could change. But we have not arrived at that stage as yet.

And if we were asked, finally, which provisions of the Constitution we would focus on if a revision were undertaken, then we would briefly list the following subjects: the composition of the States General; the relation between government and parliament; the organization of the municipalities; defense; the relation between church and state; and education.

The changes we would like to see in these areas will automatically become apparent as we continue our commentary on specific articles of our Program. Now that our discussion of the historical, dogmatic, and philosophical points have come to an end, we shall start with these specifics in the very next chapter, which deals with parliament.

CHAPTER NINE

POPULAR INFLUENCE

To this end it desires to see affirmed the legitimacy of popular influence that, in virtue of the moral bond between electors and elected and in keeping with our history, is exercised upon political authority by means of the States General.

ARTICLE 8

I. THE CONCENTRATED NATION

§ 85   STATE AND SOCIETY

In Article 8 the framers of our Program wrote that the antirevolutionary party desires to have it affirmed that the popular influence upon state authority, exercised by the States General, is legitimate, in keeping with our history, and in virtue of the moral bond that exists between the voters and those whom they elect.

This desire contains three ideas, each of which requires an explanation: (1) The States General is not the government, but the concentrated nation. (2) The States General should not consist of "men we trust," but of "men of principle." (3) The States General should work towards an extension of popular influence on political authority, rather than seek to establish parliamentary government.

Point 1 describes the antirevolutionary principle in contrast to the false constitutional principle entertained by both the conservatives and the liberals. Point 2 indicates our difference with the conservative party. Point 3 marks our difference with the liberals.

Our liberals and conservatives, like true children of the Revolution, both claim that the States General has the right to share in the power that belongs to the attributes of government. The power of the state, so they lecture us, is divided over legislative, executive, and judicial powers. A nation's government has exclusive rights only to the *executive* power, while the *legislative* power is shared equally between the government and the States General, and the *judicial* power is exercised, under certain conditions set by the government, through an independent body of jurists.

This scheme therefore delegates a portion of the legislative power, hence a portion of sovereignty, to the States General. In a certain sense the States General is given the character of *government*, and the sovereign power of government, instead of remaining unified, is split in two.

As we know, this capital error also crept into our current Constitution. In Article 104 we read: "The legislative power is jointly exercised by the King and the States General." It is a most fatal clause that we must attempt to rectify at the earliest possible opportunity and bring to the attention of the nation as forcefully as we can.

It is a falsehood, pure fiction, and a complete reversal of all sound concepts, to have the States General occupy the seat of government. Such an unnatural mix robs both government and people of their specific character and wrenches them from their proper relationship.

DUALISM OF SOVEREIGNTY AND NATION   § 86

To realize this is not difficult.

As soon as the States General is invested with governing power and consequently begins to act as the government, it becomes a member of the body whose actions it is meant to check. Instead of defending the rights of the people it will automatically be out to expand its own power at the expense of the people. And the end will be that a body that was installed in order to plead the people's cause to the king will gradually slip into a cause against both prince and people for the sake of its own parliamentary authority.

In consequence, nothing will be left but an all-powerful, despotic parliamentary government, ruling a people bereft of all rights to be *represented*, the difference being that earlier that government was the king but now is more and more a *party leader* who uses the king's name to cover his own arbitrary policy and party tyranny.

But, inversely, government authority too is weakened.

Subjects revere their king and citizens respect a sovereign body. They are willing to submit to them. They recognize their superiors and obey those who bear divine authority.

But when government becomes a mixture of the sovereign and the elected representatives, hence internally divided, and acts with a falsely assumed authority, then respect for such a falsified government cannot but wear away in the hearts of the people.

Worse, in the bosom of the nation thus deceived there arises an uncontrollable feeling of resentment and an irrepressible cry for vengeance against such double-crossers. While promising to stand up for the rights of the people, once in the seats of power they sacrifice those dearly won rights to a modern despotism and betray them in the interest of gaining more power for themselves.

If you had personally chosen a lawyer to plead your fair and honest case against the aggressive allegations of a public prosecutor, and he turned out to be colluding with the prosecutor in order to further his own interests, would you not stop listening to him and fire him the sooner the better?

This wrongheaded liberal conception of the States General corrupts our political situation in two ways: first, by depriving the people of its advocate with the government; and second, by depriving government of the people's respect which constitutes the foundation of its influence.

Thus we cannot emphasize enough that our allies in the antirevolutionary press and among the antirevolutionary members of parliament ought to do their part in clarifying this point to the public and making everyone realize that a States General that wants to play at government instead of defending the rights of the people forsakes its duty and forfeits all claims to our respect.

Our adherents ought to make clear that we are in no way amiss in paying due honor to the "authorities instituted by God" when we unsparingly and forthrightly demolish the credibility of a States General that forsakes its calling—and that for the simple reason that as little as a lawyer *you elected* has power over you, so little is the States General "an authority instituted by God."[1]

At the same time, after removing the fallacy, our adherents should have our people realize again what is the healthy and only proper conception of this relationship, in order that the antirevolutionary ideas may become more solidly rooted. The healthy, proper conception is to assign to the States General the character of *advocate of the rights of the people*, or if you will, the *concentrated nation*.

DEVELOPMENT OF CONSTITUTIONAL LIFE   § 87

According to antirevolutionary principles, the issue is as follows: there is a people, and over that people there is a government, appointed by a power outside that people, namely, God.

This government is sovereign, and its sovereignty is absolutely indivisible.

Since in our country the king is sovereign, it is the king, and he alone, who makes the law and administers justice and reigns as executive power.

If the king has this done by other persons, as his organs who substitute for him, this does not in the least detract from the principle at hand. He and he alone is and remains the sovereign who makes laws to be the *law* of the land, makes justice to be *justice* in the land, and can give orders and demand compliance throughout the land.

To be sure, this sovereign government's power, both in the physical and the moral sense, is bound to *the condition of the people over which it rules*.

It is in a similar position as a doctor treating a sick person.

If the doctor is called to the sickbed of a small child who cannot yet talk, it is out of the question that he has to consult this child. He may put his questions, but the child does not answer. He can speak, but his patient does not understand. So it follows from the condition of the object entrusted to his care that he can simply do what he thinks is right, on his own responsibility, without any consultation—like an absolute despot, if you will.

But if he is dealing with an adult, it would be the height of irresponsibility if the doctor did not ask him questions and took into consideration what his patient tells him about his perceptions, his symptoms, and the effect of the medicines he is taking.

---

1. Kuyper alludes to Rom 13:1.

And in a case where the doctor is treating an ill person who is not only a grown-up but who also knows a thing or two about the human body, about ailments and medicines, then he will naturally not only hear him out but in part turn the bedside visit into a mutual consultation.

Now then, this is exactly the case when looking at the relation between government and people. An immature people, without any national sense or political mind, can only be ruled by an absolute sovereign, and any toying with constitutional forms would be nothing but a reckless attempt to absolve oneself of part of one's responsibility.

But if a nation has progressed politically—if it is able to look at itself and give an account of what it is experiencing—then any despotism is absurd, and government is obliged to listen to the nation in order to get to know what it is able to bear and to tailor its measures accordingly.

And finally, if a government, as in our country, has to do with a people that has made still greater progress and is able to think about its condition and its illness, its past and its future, then it is only natural that to take such a people into account has to go further and turn into a consultation.

Now in order to be able to do this, the people must have an *organ*. A doctor does not put his questions to your leg or your arm, to your members one by one, but to *you*; and he listens to what your mouth tells him, as the speech organ of the whole body.

Similarly, the government does not inquire of its citizens one by one, but of the nation as a unity. And since that nation is too widely dispersed and too large to act itself, it is concentrated in its representatives—in its organ, the States General—for the purpose of informing the government what it perceives, what it thinks, and what it believes to be the most advisable.

To ensure that things are right, and normal, and in keeping with God's justice and the people's well-being, the composition of the States General should first of all be such that it can indeed faithfully give voice to the perceptions of the nation; and secondly, it ought to relate to the government in such a way that it can be the mouthpiece of both the people's respect for the king and the people's attachment to freedom.

Since we do not at present have such a States General, it is the duty of every antirevolutionary to be relentless in offering principled critique of our States General, woefully departed as it has from its essence and purpose, until at last it succumbs under the wrath of the national conscience, and a free arena opens up again where a proper States General of true historical mold can speak on behalf of the nation.

II. BEARERS OF PRINCIPLES

IMPERATIVE MANDATE; TRUSTED MEN   § 88

The States General is not the government, nor "the authorities instituted God," nor a part of the administration, but it is the advocate—*to* the administration, *next to* the ordained powers, *opposite* the government—of the rights and freedoms of the nation. So runs our first thesis.

Our second thesis reads: the members of the States General should not be chosen because they are "honorable persons" who inspire trust, but because they are "bearers of principles."

Every conservative-minded person in our country has always looked for trusted men—from Thorbecke to the most conservative newspaper editor. But the entire antirevolutionary party demands bearers of principles. Meanwhile a third possibility is conceivable: liberalism, as it spirals further downward, arrives at what is called an "imperative mandate."

To forestall any misunderstanding, we need to define what is meant by each of these three terms.

An imperative mandate is like an enforcement order. Here it means that a member of the States General speaks and votes as a mandatory of the people, not in order to express his own conviction but in keeping with what the voters have ordered and mandated him. An imperative mandate presupposes therefore that every issue to be decided is known to the voters *before* the elections and that they determine, in clubs or official assemblies, what the vote on their behalf shall be concerning this or that issue; only then do they proceed to choose a candidate who undertakes to honor this decision unconditionally. Presupposed as well is that if an issue arises that was *not* known to the voters at the time of the elections, the elected delegate will consult with his constituents, in order to be informed how he should vote. In fact, it even assumes that a delegate will vote in the spirit and according to the mandate of the people, if need be against his own conscience—not because it is so honorable to go against one's conscience, but because a member of the Chamber is nothing but an *organ*, a *machine*, and therefore has no conscience.

Directly opposite this approach is that of the "trusted men" favored by the conservatives, so perfectly sketched by Thorbecke in his clipped phrase: "without any tie to the voters." According to this system, what the voters have to do is to find, in their district or elsewhere, a candidate of independent means, respectable character, and recognized ability, of whom one in general does not yet know but may at least assume that his sympathies lean in the same direction as those of his voters. The voters are deemed not to have the slightest understanding of political matters; like good children they leave these high interests to the superior wisdom and insight of their patron. Thus it is absolutely unbecoming to ask someone before he is elected what he thinks or wants, let alone to try and elicit a statement from him about this or that point, or to force him, once elected, to stay in contact with his voters. "The serf agrees to what the lord decrees" is the old-fashioned motto for this outdated system. Not just consulting but even conversing with the voters is contraband in this system. For, rightly considered, all conversation that might have some influence is a contradiction in terms in the case of an electorate that, kept immature politically, must be deemed capable neither of forming an opinion nor of expressing it.

§ 89   BEARERS OF PRINCIPLES

Unable to go along with either of these two systems, the antirevolutionary party demands instead that a member of the Chamber be a bearer of a principle and have a moral bond with his voters.

The underlying premise here is that there are mutually exclusive political principles that contend with each other for control over the future of the country; further, that voters are conscious of the general nature of these principles and by means of conversations, public lectures, meetings, political writings, and the daily press form their opinion about where the country's affairs ought to be headed; and finally, that they give their trust only to a candidate of whom it is known in advance or during the election campaign that he will act as the mouthpiece of this opinion.

In what manner the opinion thus held can be incorporated in the laws of the land is up to him. That is a matter that lies outside the competence of his voters. The people have political instinct, not legislative expertise. And the delegate fully honors the moral bond with his voters if it is evident that he indeed aims at what the voters intend, and intends what is prescribed by the principle they hold dear.

However, if he found himself obliged by oath or conscience, as a result of a change of conviction since he was first elected, to vote differently in the Chamber from what he knew his voters expected, then he would have the duty, either to explain this change to the satisfaction of his voters, or to honor the sacred character of moral trust by resigning his seat.

On the advice of Groen van Prinsterer, the antirevolutionary party has persisted in strictly adhering to this system. It has insisted that the shaping of public opinion should occur not only in the Chamber but also among the people. At every election it has formed a clear idea of the main issue in which its sacred principle was being submitted to the decision of the ballot box. And it has demanded from those candidates it recommended that they declare themselves openly on this main issue.

Our party does not ask such a declaration from *known* candidates. Groen needed no test. A candidate whose views were widely known through publications or the press could pass muster without a test. And even a member of the Chamber who spoke little but showed his stance through his voting pattern, was accepted.

But when dealing with a new man, a candidate unknown to the people, one who had never spoken out clearly on the main issue in the political struggle and of whom one might assume good things yet would know nothing definite, then our party stood its ground. This was made clear as recently as 1877 in Delft, when an otherwise highly educated person refused to give an unambiguous declaration and our party refused to endorse him.[2]

It adhered so strictly to the moral bond between elected and electors that it did not hesitate for a moment in acknowledging, with Groen van Prinsterer, that to abandon this bond would be "to destroy the pith and marrow of political life in a constitutional state."[3]

THE MORAL BOND BETWEEN SOVEREIGN AND NATION　　　　　§ 90

What is our reason for taking this stand? Our reply, briefly and to the point, is this: without that moral bond, there is no connection whatever between

---

2. Kuyper refers here to O. W. Star Numan, doctor in law and secretary of the Second Chamber, who as a candidate of antirevolutionary sympathies in District Delft refused on principle to declare himself on any specific point prior to the elections of June 1877.
3. In several publications during the 1860s Groen argued against the liberal historian and publicist Robert Fruin (1823-1899) that the constitutional provision that members of parliament should sit "without instruction or consultation" did not preclude the right of voters during election time to ask of candidates what political program they promised to support if elected.

the political culture in government circles and the political concerns in the bosom of the nation.

There are situations, we readily admit, where no such connection exists or can exist. For example, it is up to our administrators of Achin[4] to determine what to do; it cannot bring to expression the national life of the Achin people. The same goes for the Russians in Poland, the Austrians in Bosnia, the Prussians in many regions of Alsace, and the French in Algeria. Aspirations do reside in the bosom of these conquered peoples, but these are so confused, so derailed, so disorderly, that the populations and their governments are circles that intersect but for the time being cannot overlap.

But what we cannot abide is that some want to apply this awkward, primitive, and extraordinary situation to constitutionally governed peoples whose privilege it should be to have a well-organized link between people and ruler. In these countries it will not do to leave the art of politics to a certain group of intellectuals as a kind of isolated monopoly and to demand of the people that it concern itself solely with its social and domestic affairs.

On the contrary, every developed and maturing people ought to have its politics derived from its firm principles which do not float in the air as so many abstractions but which have deep roots in the soil of national life. Our thinking mind, after all, is not some kind of pharmacist's cabinet with drawers and cubbyholes in which we have a separate compartment for politics and another for social affairs and a third for spiritual questions.

Everything in our minds is interconnected, and our deepest life-principle is nothing but the root from which the fullness of our thoughts shoots up, over whatever area of life they then spread themselves.

Your political ideas are connected with your social insights; your social insights with your thoughts on marriage and family; those thoughts with your views about the church; your views about the church with your spiritual convictions; and your spiritual convictions with the relation of your heart to God.

Precisely because of these undeniable interconnections, every system that severs politics from its roots in the nation's life-principle cannot but lead to a situation in which government and parliament turn into a coterie

---

4. For more on Achin, see below, § 275.

that rules apart from the people and over the people and simply leaves unfulfilled the primary condition for a healthy national life.

POLITICAL DEGENERATION   §91

This evil, if allowed to take root, carries its own punishment in all kinds of ways. Let me point out five harmful effects.

(1) A party that chooses trusted men instead of bearers of principles is incapable of arousing civic spirit. This can be seen in the conservatives, who have been reduced to an impotent group. It can be seen in the Thorbecke liberals, who shortly after the death of their leader have been reduced to only a few dozen in the Chamber, and outside the Chamber have long been outstripped everywhere in the press and in local clubs.

(2) By pushing trusted men to the foreground you fill the Chamber with members of a social class who are rich in earthly goods but mostly poor in intellectual knowledge, so that you deprive government of the fruits of scientific progress.

(3) Nominally clinging to the Constitution yet severing all ties between elected and electors leads to a complete demoralization of our politicians who during elections parade as bearers of principles but once elected vie with one another in skillfully purging themselves of this leaven of principles.

(4) In this system people play with the term "conscience," saying that they have to vote "according to their conscience" without consulting their constituents—as if it is possible to serve people's well-being in good conscience without paying attention to its most sacred wishes and therefore also without connecting with its life-principles.

(5) Finally, such a system was perhaps conceivable before the outbreak of the Revolution, when politics was a struggle over "degrees of more or less" while everybody held to the core values. But it became the height of absurdity after the Revolution tore apart the life of nation and family, of head and heart, and the struggle between the mutually hostile principles became a struggle of life and death.

III. OUR POPULAR LIBERTIES

§ 92   PARLIAMENTARY CABINETS

The question still remaining is this: In what sense does the antirevolutionary party want to see an extension of "the legitimate influence of the people"?

Let us first state for the benefit of friend and foe what we do *not* mean by this.

We protest, in a word, against the liberals' ongoing attempt to bless us unawares with the benefits of a *parliamentary cabinet*.

In our eyes a parliamentary cabinet is pure nonsense. It turns upside down the first principles of our constitutional law. And— just as bad—it is the very opposite of what is commonly understood by "affirming popular liberties."

As we know, the intention of a parliamentary ministry is to remove the government's center of gravity from the king's cabinet to the Second Chamber.

If such a ministry were to take hold, things would unroll as follows: The liberal coalition has the majority in the Second Chamber. This majority meets outside the Chamber in its club. This club has an executive. This executive, together with the members of the club, fixes the agenda. Next, in accordance with the agreed upon plan it enters the Chamber and dominates the floor as well as the committees. It speaks, or does not speak, as the coterie pleases, and introduces into the legislative bills all the changes that the club approves, on pain of destroying the minister who dares to resist the party leadership.

Now if a cabinet acquiesces in this dependency, all is well. For then there are really *two* ministries. The one is the hidden ministry; it is master of the situation, rules the country, and dictates its will. The other is the formal ministry; it does the work and serves as the instrument by which to coerce the king.

Should the cabinet oppose the club, however, then the club without delay signs the death warrant of the noncompliant ministry and terminates it on the spot.

When a cabinet crisis thus arises, the king is bound, so they insist, to request a consultation with the president of the liberal club, to learn from him who the club has decided should now become ministers.

His Majesty is then handed a prepared list. All he has to do is sign at the bottom. Should he dare to appoint someone else, he will be thwarted and forced to the wall by repeated defeats of the budget, until at last, at his wits' end, he puts his royal signature on the act of submission.

Such, and no other, was the intention of "submit or resign" that Gambetta boldly flung at Mac-Mahon, and that was first repeated on Dutch soil by Kappeyne van de Coppello under the thunderous applause of the entire liberal establishment.[5]

PARTY SOVEREIGNTY[6]   § 93

Antirevolutionaries oppose this whole system, not just in its most offensive manifestation but also in its more moderate form.

We oppose it because it contradicts the letter and the spirit of the Constitution; because it is at odds with the principles of our historic polity; because it is a slap in the face of both the government's sovereignty and the House of Orange, which has deserved better from the Dutch people.

We oppose it no less because it allows the lie to creep into the very core of our political institutions; because it turns everything into a fiction; because it appears to be one thing but is really another. It would be far

---

5. Joannes Kappeyne van de Coppello (1822–95) was the leader of the progressive wing of the liberals who chafed at the bit to replace the conservative government and its compromise school bill because it was "not in step with the modern worldview." On December 8, 1874, he stated in the Second Chamber of parliament that a religiously neutral public school should by rights have the monopoly in primary education. If the religious minority protests, he said, "I would almost say, Then that minority will have to be oppressed, because then that is the fly that spoils the ointment and has no right to exist in our society." To this Kuyper replied: "If ever the day should arrive, Mr. Speaker, that a minister of the Crown announced the honorable member's program as the program of the government, saying that if need be the minorities would have to be oppressed and the fly killed that spoiled the ointment, I would say to him: Then also remove the lion from the Dutch coat of arms, the proud symbol of liberty, and replace him with an eagle holding a lamb in its claw, the symbol of tyranny." Quoted in A. Kuyper, *Eenige Kameradviezen uit de jaren 1874 en 1875* [Selected speeches in the (Second) Chamber (of parliament) from the years 1874 and 1875] (Amsterdam: Wormser, 1890), 243–44. For Gambetta and Mac-Mahon, see notes above in § 14.

6. This section and the next appear to have been written (dated November 4, 1878) under the still fresh impression of the disappointing outcome of the People's Petition, July 1878, which failed to persuade the king to veto the Primary Education Act sponsored by the liberal government under Kappeyne.

preferable to drop the masks and in an openly revolutionary move to propose the abolition of the monarchy.

But we oppose this system above all because if that is the direction developments will take, the rights of the people will be left undefended and the nation's influence on state policy will be more and more paralyzed.

If this system gains the upper hand, things will come down to this: a liberal coterie that makes up a minority in the country and among the voters nevertheless manages to become the majority in the Chamber as a result of an unjust voting system and an even more culpable division of districts. Using this stolen majority, it makes the work of the States General serve no other purpose than to have this coterie dominate the nation, throttle the voice of the people, and deform this poor people at the cost of its own tax monies and reshape it according to a foreign, impractical model that is directly contrary both to its historic traditions and to its higher interests.

§ 94   EXTENSION OF POPULAR PRIVILEGES

So not that! But what then?

We believe we can summarize in three points what is required if the people are to make constitutional progress. To extend the legitimate influence of the people, the following must be done:

(1) Our representative assembly must increasingly become *the pure expression of national life*.

In the measure that the States General in this respect gains in national character, in that measure it will gain in moral influence.

The people itself has no respect for a States General of the kind we have at present. How could the king attribute moral authority to such a parliament and yield to it except under compulsion, unsupported by right?

But let all this change. Let the Chamber get the whole people behind it again, and its moral prestige will automatically, without any show of power, keep every cabinet from measures that militate against the character and consciousness of the nation.

The States General can achieve this only through a large-scale extension of the franchise and an accommodation of minorities in the composition of both Chambers. More about this when this series arrives at that chapter.[7]

(2) The government should decrease its intervention in affairs that are not necessarily political matters.

When a child is still in the crib, its mother does everything for it.

When it starts to walk, that task already decreases. When it can leave the house it automatically gets a larger share in deciding what to do in its own interest. And once it begins to earn its own money a healthy division arises between parental authority and the family rights of the child.

In the same way a government that rules a young nation must simply begin by doing everything, leaving nothing to the people. Once a people begins to develop, the government can gradually let go of this or that task that can easily be taken care of without it. And when this development enters a sufficiently mature stage a natural division arises between on the one hand social, ecclesiastical, domestic, and local interests, and on the other the rights of government, a division that can only end in lifting the former tasks from the shoulders of the government and having it act solely as sovereign.

Liberalism, by contrast, wants to have things exactly the other way around. It regards the people increasingly as immature minors and so keeps expanding the power of the state.

Since every gain in state power means a loss of influence for the people, it is clear how this throws into bold relief the difference between liberals and Christian liberals, that is, antirevolutionaries. Our aim is gradually to take away from government whatever does not by nature belong to its task. To repeat for a moment what we wrote earlier, our agenda has three points: extension of local and municipal autonomy; freedom of education; and freedom for the church.

(3) Taxation should be made increasingly more difficult for the government and not be possible except with the compliance of the people and under its supervision. It is up to the people to decide how to spend its money.

---

7. See chap. 12 below.

This is an area where the difference between justice and arbitrariness comes out most sharply. The boundary between despotism and popular government runs through the pocketbooks of the inhabitants. If a government can take from those pocketbooks whatever it deems desirable, freedom has become a fiction.

If justice is to be done and freedom is to be upheld, the national household should not be expected to part voluntarily with any of its possessions except upon request and after consent.

This was always the rule in constitutional states. From of old this was the rule also in our country.

And so it should remain, as a guarantee against a new encroachment of despotism.

And since it happens repeatedly today that taxes are voted which only a coterie has been consulted about and not the nation in its organic entirety, we therefore believe that the hour has come for the voice of the people, together with the voice of history and constitutionality, to be heard loud and clear, in order that by legal means this festering evil may be checked.

CHAPTER TEN

BUDGET REFUSAL

Except under exceptional circumstances, it condemns as abuse of power the rejection of budgets for reasons that lie outside those budgets.

ARTICLE 9

I. THE SYSTEM OF THE REVOLUTION

REJECTING BUDGETS FOR POLITICAL REASONS   § 95

The political question of our day revolves entirely around the issue of the budget.

If it is proper that the States General by simply voting down the budget has the right year after year to bend the king to its will, then—let's speak plainly—then we no longer have a monarchy except in name only. Factually we then live in a crowned republic. And it is a republic, note well, that is not like the one we used to have, but a republic of purely revolutionary origin, where the king is the agent of the popular assembly, accountable to its high and mighty representatives, standing under their legal power and factual control.

And yet, that is how the liberals want it. Not just here, but in every country. The right of budgeting is the sacred sheet anchor for the liberal vessel. They feel that constitutional government counts for nothing if it does not include the right to reject budgets at their discretion.

Remarkably, on this weighty point of constitutional law diehard conservatives present a common front with the liberals.

Leading spokesmen from the better periods of conservatism insisted already that this ingredient in particular must not be lacking in the recipe for popular liberties; and what is worse, they sealed their opinion about this in practice by in fact rejecting the budget.

We may not even hide the fact that among the older antirevolutionaries in our country Groen van Prinsterer stood quite alone in combating this theory. He had to experience more than once that his best friends fell for the tempting theory of our revolutionaries.

What was so tempting for those friends was that voting down budgets almost always struck at ministers of whom it was suspected that the king would be glad to replace them—thus that rejecting a budget, instead of being used against the king, often appeared to be an act of loyalty to the king.

But appearances concealed a perfidious principle!

§ 96   EXCEPTIONAL CASES

Our Program states in Article 9 that the party condemns the rejection of budgets for extraneous reasons, "except under exceptional circumstances."

The intent of this article is clear. The right to reject a budget is given with the right to accept it. But an act of either rejection or acceptance is legitimate only if it concerns a matter of administration, and hence is limited to control of finances.

The article presupposes therefore that whoever considers voting down a budget should specify to the minister which article he finds objectionable and so also indicate that he is prepared to vote in favor of the budget if the minister meets the objection.

It unconditionally condemns every other kind of negative vote on budgetary bills, except—and this proves the rule and does not cancel it—under exceptional circumstances.

A king may be tempted—there are examples of this—to stage a coup with the use of military force and so flagrantly violate the Constitution he swore to uphold. Prominent voices in our country have gone so far already that they have called upon our king to do so. The liberal party feels so insecure that recently in an official state document it cast aspersions on the leaders of our party for desiring a similar move.[1]

---

1. Upon receiving the People's Petition to quash the Primary Education Act in the interest of equal treatment for all his subjects, King William asked the minister responsible for advice. Kappeyne's report to the king, published in the official gazette, minced no words: by suggesting that public money should also go to private schools

But what is shocking above all is that the well-known Danish prelate Martensen writes in his *Ethics* that "under certain circumstances" a coup d'état is in principle legitimate.[2]

Thus we have no choice but to reckon with the possibility of a coup d'état, and in that case we think that to refuse all financial means, out of self-defense, is not at all out of place.

A bad king might allow an immoral person from among his favorites to play with the interests of the people like a tyrant.

Or a minister might treat the Chamber with such disdain that one wondered about his sanity while the king did not see it or want to see it.

Now then, in all such "exceptional circumstances," against which the people's representatives had no defense in terms of a motion in the Chamber or an address to the king or prosecution through the courts, rejection of the budget would in our opinion be a duty, not as a theoretical right but as means of self-preservation in a situation that would be tantamount to the abolition of justice.

BUDGET REJECTION STRIKES AT THE KING, NOT THE MINISTER §97

In normal circumstances, however, rejecting the budget strikes us as a fundamental violation of the rights of the king, and what is even more important, of the divine right of government.

If there is friction, the Chamber can pass a motion of nonconfidence in any minister of the Crown. If it does not like his legislative proposals, it can vote them down. It can also respectfully request the king to dismiss such a minister. In fact, if there are grounds for it, the Chamber can initiate legal proceedings against him. But it may never halt the machinery of government.

It may not do so for the simple reason that it does not then act against one or more ministers but against the king himself.

---

the Petition was advocating "the rankest communism," and that by asking the king to withhold his signature from a bill approved by both Chambers the Petition was attacking the very foundations of the Dutch constitutional order and inviting the king to commit a coup d'état. The report is reproduced verbatim in N. M. Feringa, ed., *Gedenkboek betreffende het Volkspetionnement* [Memorial volume regarding the People's Petition] (Amsterdam: J. H. Kruyt, 1878), 136–49.

2. See H. L. Martensen, *Den christelige Ethik*, 3 vols. (Kjøbenhavn: Gyldendal, 1871–78). ET: *Christian Ethics*, 3 vols. (Edinburgh: T&T Clark, 1873–82), 1:403–6; 3:228–31.

After all, if the king is on their side and it is merely a matter of removing a minister, then an address with the request to dismiss the unwanted person will not be displeasing to the king but instead be most welcome.

However, if the king deliberately refuses such a request and maintains the minister against the will of the Chamber, then the rejection of a budget by that token will take on the appearance of attempting to coerce, not the minister, but the king.

The liberal system is thus so little in harmony with even the most basic notions of our fundamental law that the Constitution deals with the budget, not under the heading of the political powers of the Chamber, but under a separate, administrative rubric (Art. 119–22).

Their revolutionary system is so at variance with even current rules that to escape the difficulty they have devised "credit bills," a kind of legislation that lacks all constitutional basis and serves only as a screen to hide from the eyes of the passersby the damage done to the front of our state edifice.[3]

In fact, the liberals themselves are so little at ease in using budget refusal that they have never yet dared to apply this weapon to its full extent, preferring instead to proceed slowly and finish ministers off one by one, until the cabinet lost its equilibrium, became top-heavy, and fell.

Meanwhile, one should not conclude from all this that we would want to deny that this false principle has in fact crept into our Constitution. On the contrary, precisely one of the many things that we have against our Constitution is that it muddled the whole budget question.

The only thing we wanted to show at this time was that the liberal theory has not yet been introduced entirely into our constitutional provisions and that in respect of this topic, too, we do not find in our fundamental law the embodiment of a principle but rather a patchwork of compromise.

In order to set out, clearly and briefly, the antirevolutionary standpoint in opposition to both the ambivalent nature of our Constitution and the revolutionary practice of liberals and conservatives, we shall do three things: first, contrast the evident intent of the French revolutionary system with the theory of British politicians; then, in connection with that theory, describe the ideal that most commends itself to us; and finally,

---

3. Kuyper refers here to "credit bills" [*crediet-wetten*], which seem to have originated earlier in the nineteenth century as temporary measures extending the power of governmental expenditure during times when the budget had not yet been formally approved. Thanks are due to Albert Gootjes for insight into this phenomenon.

indicate the relation between this antirevolutionary system and the system of our Constitution.

II. THE BRITISH PRACTICE

ORDINARY REVENUES   § 98

What is the British practice with respect to the budget? We raise this question because it is a common delusion that British practice is about the same as that of the constitutional states on the Continent.

To demonstrate how mistaken this view is, we shall briefly note the following six points.

FIXED EXPENDITURES   § 99

(1) The British Crown freely disposes of "ordinary revenue" and is dependent on Parliament only for "extraordinary revenue."

It is not even accountable to Parliament for its ordinary revenue. The king collects and spends those monies without anyone's supervision or advice.

Now we are well aware that in absolute figures those ordinary revenues have gradually come to lag far behind the extraordinary ones. Yet as a constitutional principle it remains highly remarkable that only the "*aides et benevolences*" (as the English call them with a French term) are voted on by Parliament.

(2) Parliament concerns itself with the Crown's financial administration in two ways: by means of provisions for an undefined period and by grants for one year only.

Thus there will be a double list of revenues as well as a double list of expenditures. The first list contains the revenues and expenditures that Parliament has granted once for all; the other list contains only those revenues and expenditures that end that year.

As far as revenues are concerned, approximately 75 percent belong to the first list and approximately 25 percent to the second list. As concerns expenditures, the government is authorized at all times to spend what is necessary to service the national debt, the civil list, the salaries of the judiciary, and all salaries and stipends fixed by acts of Parliament.

§ 100   Extraordinary budgets

(3) In Britain, the term "budget" does not refer to the entire budget but only to proposals by the minister[4] for the "extraordinary" means not yet granted.

The procedure is as follows: Parliament begins by having a "Committee of Supply" examine the proposals made by the Crown for that year, and the first things looked at are the estimates for army and navy. These estimates are usually explained to the committee of the whole by the secretaries of the departments in question and not by the ministers. Not until the war and naval estimates are established by the House of Commons does the Crown table its request for "*aides et benevolences*" in order to cover those expenditures.

This "Supply Act," as the British call it, or "an act toward making good the supply granted to Her Majesty," is placed in the hands of the standing committee known as the Committee of Ways and Means.

On the basis of the Report of this committee, the House of Commons then decides (a) how much of the approved expenditures shall be met from the "consolidated fund," and (b) how much of the remainder shall be met by raising existing taxes or by levying new taxes. (The consolidated fund represents the proceeds from all taxes granted earlier, which originally formed separate funds but are now amalgamated into a single fund; hence the name.)

By this law of supply a third bill stipulates the heads of expenditures for which the monies will be spent in each case, without permitting right of transfer. This bill, if passed, is called the Appropriation Act. Thus it designates the causes for which a given amount of money is earmarked.

These three acts then are passed from the House of Commons to the House of Lords. After this body has approved the supply, the means, and the appropriations, the Crown is authorized to levy and spend.

§ 101   The Appropriation Act

(4) It is clear from the above that on British soil the treatment of the budget in more than one respect differs markedly from the procedure in our country.

---

4. The "minister" here refers to the chancellor of the exchequer (the minister or secretary of finance).

For suppose that the British Parliament votes down the budget, in particular the Appropriation Act; then the Crown would nonetheless (a) continue to have at its disposal the "ordinary revenue"; (b) be able to collect those taxes that were approved by former laws; and (c) be able to spend whatever was required for national debt, civil list, and salaries.

To put it another way, if you will: the difference is that in our country the *entire* budget, covering both revenue and expenditures, is submitted *annually* to the vote of the Chambers, whereas in Britain no approval is needed each year, for those taxes that have already been approved by other laws.

And from this seemingly minor difference flows the enormous consequence that when a budget is defeated in Britain the machinery of administration can to some degree carry on, whereas in our country things immediately grind to a halt.

Add to that the custom of discussing the expenditures with the well-informed departmental secretaries. The result has been that in Britain a political conflict practically never arises when the estimates are presented and is seldom seen when the ways and means are set. Politics does not enter in until the Appropriation Act and therefore targets not a single minister but the cabinet as such, that is, the power of the Crown. Either this power has to be pushed back from seeking to transgress the legal limit, or else it has to be guided in another direction lest the nation's future be jeopardized.

THE MUTINY ACT § 102

(5) The compulsion that the British Parliament is able to impose on the Crown as a result of bloody conflicts in the past depends but little on the vote on the budget and must be sought mainly in a totally different bill, the so-called Mutiny Act.

In Britain the standing army, unlike ours, is not formed in part by drawing lots but consists exclusively of troops recruited by means of pay and press money. (There is also a militia, but militias only serve in the counties and cannot be employed for waging war except by a separate act of Parliament.)

The standing army, meanwhile, precisely because it stands outside the nation, might pose a threat to popular liberties. To fend this off, it has been established that Parliament never grants the army estimates for longer than a year. Thus if the year comes to an end without a new army bill having been approved granting the right to recruit men for the following year, the standing army by that token is disbanded and the Crown is disarmed.

(6) Finally, we should remember that the British Parliament, however much it may be jealous of its prerogatives, has only on rare occasions and in very exceptional circumstances defeated a budget for political reasons.

Westminster has always honored this powerful weapon as a weapon which no partisanship should lavishly and wantonly play with but which, in the hands of free and prudent men, should serve to prevent the inroads of political violence and tyranny.

There was more than levelheadedness in this sober handling of budgetary rights. It involved a principle—the principle that Parliament should remain the House of the Commoners, and that the authority and power of government can only radiate from the Palace of the Crown.

And, note well, the result of this totally different theory and even greater difference in practice has been no less than this: while in our country the Second Chamber more and more embarrasses itself, the British nation as a whole respects and applauds its Parliament; while our state grows ever more oppressive, across the sea the people's liberties are expanding all the time; as well, while our constitutional practice is more and more being perverted, in Britain it continues to develop in a consistent, historic, national spirit.

III. THE BEST ADVISABLE FOR THE NETHERLANDS

§ 103   NATIONAL CHARACTER

We do not hesitate for a moment, if we have to choose between the French and the British system of dealing with budgets, to opt for the latter—although we add at once that to slavishly copy the particulars of what time-honored custom has stamped on British constitutional practice would carry its own punishment.

Respect for a nation's historical development demands keeping an open eye for the peculiar characteristics of each nation and therefore barring all imitation among the nations in the area of law and legislation.

Dutch law, if things are well, should develop solely out of the past of the Dutch nation itself. When revolutionary activity has recklessly cut the thread of national development, as it has done here, it is quite acceptable to borrow general viewpoints from the example of kindred nations and to profit from their experience. But even then these general ideas ought to be poured into molds that suit the national character.

Keeping this in mind, we should urge no more than the following four points for our country.

BY LAW OR BY RESOLUTION?   § 104

The first point would be that the granting of financial means on the part of the States General should not come in the form of a law but in the form of a resolution.

We place this point in the foreground because it is extremely important. The system of budgetary laws is nothing but the embodiment of the wrong, unhistorical, and false concept of the States General that liberalism is forcing upon us.

In the footsteps of the French revolutionaries, our liberals magically transformed the old States of the Low Countries into a bicameral legislature: a system of two chambers which together constitute a component part of the legislative power.[5] Wrong on both counts.

Our States General, as Maurice has correctly observed, should not be "chambers"; if it must have a name it should be "a house."[6] It is to be a representation of the people, a tribune for their interests, an advocate of their rights over against the Crown.

To be all that, it must have independent status; and to occupy this status with honor and maintain it with show of character it must live apart, that is, it must "have its own house."

According to the French, revolutionary system, however, the States themselves are co-bearers of the power of government. They are co-workers with the government, performing the same task. Accordingly, they co-inhabit the same dwelling with the government—that is to say, they are assigned but two chambers in the state edifice.

In this way, says Maurice, the very names of "Chamber" and "House" accentuate the all-important difference between the authentic *Germanic* view of a parliament as the concentrated nation acting on its own, and the *French, revolutionary* conception that has sovereignty divided into

---

5. Kuyper here alludes to Art. 104 of the Constitution which reads: "The legislative power is exercised jointly by the Crown and the States General."
6. Kuyper is perhaps referring to the English author F. D. Maurice (1805–1872).

three pieces and assigns parliament a place among the bearers of sovereign power.

Of course we do not dream of introducing the British name of "house." But we do want to denounce the French, revolutionary name of "chambers." We want to make our parliament again what it always was and should have stayed according to Netherlandic traditions—a meeting of the States. The very name *States* expresses, in a beautiful way and in decent Dutch, the independent status of our representative body. The name is a standing rebuke, if revived and allowed to speak, of the false liberal concept. But the name is also closely bound up with the sphere of action to be assigned to the States.

In the French system of our liberals, our "Chamber" can do nothing except legislate. In the one big edifice of the state there are various floors and rooms. One room has been made ready for administration; another room for internal affairs; still another for defense issues; also one for the judiciary; and in the same vein a couple of chambers have been set apart for the making of laws.

Now then, these last chambers have been assigned to our States General. From this it follows that all it can do, really, is to make laws, and more laws, and to pour everything it does into the form of laws.

Some even doubt whether it is lawful to entertain a motion.[7]

Apart from the right to address the king, to set up an inquiry, to nominate members of the Supreme Court, and to impeach ministers, any freedom of movement that does not lead to legislative work is blocked. It is, after all, an imitation of France's "*chambre législative*" and therefore all its power and all its prestige must exhaust itself in the making of laws.

To what absurd situations this can lead became apparent only recently, when the States had to deal with the king's marriage. This concerned a situation in which king and chamber were not working in tandem but were at opposite ends.

---

7. Kuyper possibly makes an oblique reference to a motion of September 27, 1866, sponsored by the antirevolutionary member L. W. C. Keuchenius (1822–91), censuring the government for its recent conduct in the appointment of a governor for the colonies. The motion passed the Second Chamber but was branded by the sitting government as trespassing on the prerogative of the king and therefore providing a cause for dissolving the Chamber and having new elections. See S. L. van der Wal, *De motie-Keuchenius; een koloniaal-historische studie over de jaren 1854–1866* [The Keuchenius motion: a study in colonial history during the years 1854-66] (Groningen: Wolters, 1934).

The king wishes to marry and desires that his consort will have the title of Queen, that any possible offspring will enjoy dynastic rights, and that after his death his widow will be ensured a state pension. What the situation calls for is a declaration by the nation that it does not regard the proposed marriage as a threat to national interests.

The nation cannot make such a declaration except through the States General. The proper legal step ought to be that the king approach the States General to receive consent for his marriage.[8] However, at present this is impossible.

The States General is part of the "legislative power" and on that account can only "legislate." In this case, too, it saw itself obliged to cast its consent in the form of a law. The whole situation was absurd and led to the grotesque result that a law was passed which read: "We, William III, by the grace of God king of the Netherlands, the Council of State having been heard and the States General consulted, do hereby grant to William III, by the grace of God king of the Netherlands, permission to marry Princess Emma of Waldeck with retention of dynastic rights."

But this same absurdity, which was exposed to all who have eyes to see, falsifies almost the entire sphere of action of the States General, particularly its involvement with the budget.

A law, after all, as everyone senses, is a legal provision, whether it commands or forbids, by which an uncertain legal relationship in the land is permanently regulated.

But a law such as our budget laws for one year, or in the case of credit laws for twenty-five weeks, truly, what kind of "law" is that? What has that got to do with a "law"? What else can it be but the ridiculous caricature of a law?

Moreover, note well, for whom is that "law" then given as law, and who are the culpable people when the law is broken? Answer: just one man in the Netherlands—the minister involved.

And what is even more foolish and more absurd: in many instances that law comes to make into law again *what was already law*, or was even

---

8. After the death of Queen Sophie in 1877, the widowed King William III at the age of sixty-one married the twenty-year-old Emma of Waldeck-Pyrmont, partly in an effort to ensure the continuation of the Orange dynasty for the Netherlands, given that of the two princes still living, one was unfit and the other unwilling to succeed his father on the throne. Failing new offspring, the crown would go to the Grand Duke of Luxembourg.

contained in the Constitution, for example when the budgetary law once again grants the king 600,000 guilders[9] that were already guaranteed him by our first and fundamental law.

We do not hesitate for a moment, therefore, to state that our budgetary laws lack virtually every characteristic of what makes a "law" a law. They are nothing other than resolutions of the States General—but one unhappy hour, to keep up the false separation of powers, they were cast in the *form* of laws.

This fiction, too, ought to be removed. And it will be removed as soon as our constitutional practice acknowledges once again that the States General are not "legislative chambers" but "States for the representation of the people."

When once it has penetrated the minds that people and ruler are two entities, it will again be realized instinctively that next to, and if need be over against, the Palace of the Crown stands a House of the People; or if you like: "king" and "States" are not only distinct in origin but *to the very end* are also incapable of blending their power and their function.

And then—do we still need to point this out?—these States, in a word, will decide and transact everything that falls under their competence without allowing themselves to be bound by the fictional form of "law."

Then they will no longer, as now, speak only *through the mouth of the king* in the form of a law, but they will also speak their mind *to the king* in an independent resolution. And when the king asks, "States of my realm, does my proposed marriage oppose any national interests?" then the States themselves, and not the king, will say in the gazette: "No, Sire, it does not. May God Almighty bless your marriage!"

And similarly, when the king asks the States through his ministers, "States of my realm, for these and these expenditures can I be granted such and such amounts from the public treasury?" then the States themselves, and not the king to himself, will reply in the gazette and grant him his request in the name of the nation.

§ 105   Ordinary and Extraordinary Budgets

Our second point is this: Let the king lay down in the form of a *law*, after gaining consent from the States General, which revenues may be collected and which expenditures must be paid every year; and let him lay down

---

9. In 1880 this amount would have been the equivalent of between 5 to 7 million US dollars.

in the form of a *resolution*, again after gaining consent from the States General, what is still to be levied or spent for one year over and above what has been established by law.

Fixed taxes regulate on a permanent basis the financial relations between government and citizens, between citizens among each other, and between the nation and foreign countries. Nothing is more natural than that these relations are established by law, and equally, that they cannot be lawfully binding unless the nation, which will be taxed, has lawfully given its consent.

But the case is different if, for the extra needs in a single year, surcharges on existing taxes or a flexible right of raising capital or revenue have to be granted, or if treasury bonds have to be issued to create temporary fictional capital. For in that case it is not a question of fixed revenue but of temporary supply, and therefore a law is out of the question.

But even when in the case of extra supply the form of a resolution comes in the place of a law, still the dearly bought rights of the nation prescribe that such extra levies in particular can never be made without its consent. Prior approval of the States General should therefore be the inexorable condition for such a resolution to be lawful.

More or less the same holds for expenditures. There are fixed expenditures that ought to be permanently regulated by law, and there are other expenditures that constantly change in amount, or else are not strictly necessary, or can vary from year to year, and hence have to be decided upon each year.

We have deliberately kept silent about the Constitution, because in our opinion it can at most fix *minimums* for annual salaries, and even then only for members of the royal family and members of the States.

The Constitution, however you wish to view it, is a reciprocal statement of rights that king and States guarantee each other. Accordingly it is proper that the king knows exactly how much income at a minimum he can count on every year. And if you feel that members of the States General, too, should be paid from the national treasury (which we think is a wrong idea), then it is likewise proper that their minimums, too, are mentioned in the Constitution. But all other terms of salaries should be removed from the Constitution, since they do not concern a contract between parties. And even for those parties that are mentioned, the indicated amount should only fix the minimums, which may be exceeded but never diminished.

So-called organic laws should have the remaining task of establishing fixed sums as minimums for the various state officials, in a word, for everything that binds the king towards third parties, right down to the salaries of officers in army and navy.

Whatever is not a fixed expenditure, however, or an obligation to third parties or amounts that would exceed the minimums, should be determined each year by resolution.

Again, not without prior approval of the States General! For it is the right of the nation over against the king, not only *not to grant* except what is consented to, but also to know that what is consented to will be spent for the indicated purpose.

In separate sections we will discuss the two remaining points, dealing with (1) the refusal of monetary means, not to the minister but to the *Crown*, and (2) the merely *conditional* nature of such a refusal.

IV. THE BEST ADVISABLE FOR THE NETHERLANDS (CONTINUED)

§ 106   ACTION AGAINST THE MINISTERS OF THE CROWN

According to the ideas we have developed thus far, the government would be given the permanent right—that is, so long as the laws in question remained in force—to collect the fixed taxes and use the revenue to disburse as much as was needed to discharge the legal obligations to third parties. For everything else not established by law in the regular way, it would need the consent of the States General on a yearly basis for both the collection and the spending of monies.

Now suppose that under such a system it would seem that for sound political reasons the government had to be opposed. In that case such opposition (thus we concluded our previous section) would have to be opposition to the Crown and not the minister, and would have to remain of a conditional nature.

That brings us to our third point, and it is this: Opposition to the budget for political reasons is permitted against the king, but not against a minister.

In itself, of course, we have no objection to opposing a minister of the Crown. On the contrary, we demand that the States General, without prejudice to their person and office, closely supervise ministers of the Crown and should certainly have the courage to speak up if a minister pays homage to principles that are bad for the country or proposes measures that are harmful to the people.

But the instrument for such much-needed supervision, politically speaking, is not associated with the coffers of the state. The instruments given to the States General are (1) the right of interpellation; (2) the right to withhold consent from bills; (3) the right to pass a motion of censure; and (4) the right to request the king to dismiss a minister if he remains insensitive to the earlier measures; not to mention (5) the right to impeach that minister.

After all, there are only two possibilities when the States General opposes a minister: either the king is inclined to let go of the minister, or he is not.

If he is, a request to dismiss him is all that is needed. And if he is not, then it follows that the resistance encountered by the States General appears to come from the minister but in fact resides with the king himself. But if that is the case, let the struggle be waged openly, and let the States General and the people on the one hand, and the cabinet and the Crown on the other, realize clearly from the start that the struggle is not about a person but indeed about the limits of power.

To resist that power by refusing monies can therefore never be admissible or dutiful unless the struggle between the States General and the king has reached this very critical stage.

Smaller, less violent and less far-reaching means of resolving a difference are available for every other conflict that might arise. Who would not consider it folly, for example, if an officer, facing a rioting mob, gave the order to fire so long as there had as yet been no question whatever of resistance to arrest?

Thus not until the king says, *I stand behind my minister!* does the conflict turn into a struggle over power. Ordinary instruments having failed, it is then time to resort to a refusal of monies. If this is correct—and we can hardly imagine what might be objected to it—then it follows that rejecting a "budget for *expenditures*" can simply never take place (barring financial reasons) and that the political issue can never come to a head except when deciding on the *means*.

This proposal has nothing to do, of course, with the question of increasing or extending taxes. Even apart from occasions of crisis and conflict, it will at all times be the duty of good and faithful States General, whenever it is approached by the Crown with a new request for increasing taxes, to also impose new conditions, in the interest of the rights and liberties of the people. This is a duty, by the way, the very memory of which seems almost forgotten with our current Chambers.

But no, what we said about opposition refers only to those rare yet conceivable and sometimes unavoidable instances when the States General faces the question whether it may furnish the king any longer with the financial means to carry out what it knows to be harmful to the nation.

Among these conceivable circumstances is a coup d'état, as we have already pointed out. We now add: the intention to wage a ruinous war, or the permanent use of power to undermine the national principles.

§ 107   Only Conditional Opposition to the Crown

Nevertheless, and this leads to our fourth point: such opposition should always be conditional.

The kind of clash we are discussing should not, after all, happen as the result of accident or mischief. Rejecting budgets as a common practice, in vogue in our country for many years, discredits the States General and does not enhance its power to oppose the government if need be, but rather diminishes it.

We therefore demand as a first condition for such robust resistance to the Crown that men be sober-minded and give prior warning.

If the States General wants to confront the king with a budget refusal, it is only fair that the king be informed, in careful, well-defined wording, what it is that the States General desires from him.

Rejecting a budget therefore should be preceded by submitting a respectful address in which the demands are clearly formulated. And after such an address is submitted, the king ought to be given time to consider it. Also, if it is at last decided to draw the purse strings shut, it should not as a rule be done in peremptory fashion.

Much of a peremptory tone would vanish if, as our proposal implies, at least the obligations to third parties could be met without interruption and no sudden arrest of the machinery of State would force an immediate decision. The king would then not be deprived of the opportunity to go to the people with the formulated demands and so ascertain by means of new elections whether the demands of the States General are indeed supported by the electorate.

And should the king, after this sober-minded and respectful action, unexpectedly persist in his intention, then in our opinion the States General will have to investigate to what extent this resistance seems to them to stem from the king's *moral conviction* or whether it has no more noble origin than whim or bias.

That brings us automatically to the second condition we attach to budget refusal: namely, *that the king should never be compelled to act against his conscience*. Even in a constitutional State a king remains a human person. He is not an automaton, but a personal being. He is of like passions with us, but he also has a conscience, a conscience that asks to be respected.

To want to force a king to approve, hence to carry out, what he deems unjust and therefore unlawful before God is *immoral* and reprehensible in the extreme.

If therefore a king responds to the strictly formulated demands of the States General with a *non possumus*, "We cannot," for reasons of conscience, then the States should be allowed to refuse to consent to laws that would further regulate what they disapprove of; but they should never push the king with his back to the wall by the naked power of money.

Should anyone judge that this would smuggle into the hands of a wicked king the means to feign conscientious objections, or else to take for conscientious objections what are but the hallucinations of a sick mind, very well, then we see no problem whatsoever in meeting this objection by granting the States General in addition the quite exorbitant power to stop, at a given moment, the collection of all taxes.

Provided always—please note carefully—that the States General does not, half asleep, decide randomly every year or so to put to a vote whether to turn off the taps for a change. Such a measure should only be possible at the initiative of a fair number of members, with the requisite guarantees, after prior warning to the king and after, say, three votes at least three days apart.

We underscore these conditions all the more because our intention in no way aims at sacrificing the liberties of the people to authoritarian whims, but rather because serious matters ought to be treated in a serious way. Such a coup should not happen unless both king and nation are amply informed. Other, less risky avenues have to be explored first. Those who consider taking this step have to be clear about the gravity of the deed.

We admit that even under these conditions it is nevertheless possible that an injustice is done and that a king is misunderstood and pressured against his conscience. Yet we question whether that should condemn our system.

No system is perfect. And imagine for a moment that a king honestly resists the States for conscience's sake and yet it tries to force his hand — then abdicating the throne, we think, would truly not be too great a sacrifice for such a noble prince in order to preserve his integrity before God. The States would then have to decide in the presence of the same God whether forcing this supreme sacrifice can count on the blessing of the Almighty.

§ 108   OUR COURSE OF ACTION FOR THE PRESENT

The above shows clearly that the provisions in our Constitution for dealing with the budget are at odds with antirevolutionary politics because it confuses the powers and drives out gravity from the proceedings. Accordingly, the question what our course of conduct should be under the existing provisions can only be of secondary importance. It may perhaps be indicated in the following four features:

(1) be tireless in urging the inclusion in our Constitution of different provisions that better fit your principles;

(2) never exercise your opposition to the personal policy of a minister at the final vote on his budget, but at his other bills; and further by interpellation, motion, an address to the Crown, or impeachment;

(3) if resistance to the government is necessary, do not turn to force except in the direst of circumstances, after exhausting all other means, and never against the king's conscience; and

(4) if you must press, apply that pressure, when rejecting the law of the means, not on one or other minister but on all minister jointly, hence on the Crown.

CHAPTER ELEVEN

DECENTRALIZATION

It desires that regional and local autonomy be restored insofar as it does not conflict with the demands of national unity and does not leave the rights of individuals unprotected.

ARTICLE 10

I. THE SYSTEM OF CENTRALIZATION

HOW THE REVOLUTION ARRIVES AT DIVIDING THE COUNTRY   § 109

There are two ways to look at a nation. It all depends on how you view a people. Did it originate and grow, and thus come to be, by a dispensation of divine providence? Or do you think it is up to the majority of individuals at any given moment to make of their "nation" whatever they please?

The latter view was that of the majority of the wise men of the French Revolution and has in principle, *mutatis mutandi*, always been copied by our liberals.

In the eyes of the revolutionaries, France was nothing but a piece of the globe inhabited by living beings whom we are accustomed to call humans. The country was an undivided and unbroken tract of land, capable of being split up if so desired, and if it was to be split up, capable of being cut up into ten pieces just as well as into twenty, or into twenty just as well as into eighty. All that needed to be looked at was the number of acres and the number of souls. The pieces had to end up roughly equal, and to achieve this, customs and traditions could be ignored. The revolutionary scissors cut right across all historical partitions.

The result was *departments*, not provinces—sections, squares, pieces of the kingdom, parts without any semblance of independence, units that had a right to exist merely as means "to facilitate centralized administration."

And when those departments turned out to be still too large for direct administration, they were in the same manner cut up again into subparts that were then named *arrondissements* or *districts*. And wherever even these districts turned out to be too large, the scissors were employed a third time, splitting the districts into *communes* or *municipalities*, to arrive finally at the entity of the indivisible unit—the "individual."

Thus they first had a piece of the globe, cut this convex domain up into departments, divided these departments again into districts, and sometimes split even these districts into municipalities, while reserving the right of course to alter or abolish the whole scheme tomorrow or to carry it further, depending on the wishes of the agent of the majority of individuals.

The only feature that was sometimes taken into consideration was a high mountain ridge or a wide river. If some boundaries had to be drawn anyway, mountains and rivers accorded best with bureaucratic supervision.

Thus the only reason for dividing a country according to this system was that it was too large to be administered at a single stroke. If there had been a generation of immensely talented officials who could have imposed order on the whole in one move, that would have been far preferable. But since this type of wonder-working bureaucracy did not exist, the revolutionaries, in the spirit of "divide and conquer," had to cut the country down to size in order to stay in control. And so they split up the country in such large parts and such small pieces as could be suitably administered.

§ 110   THE TENDENCY TOWARD CENTRALIZATION

It follows from this system that there will be three types of administrative actions: (1) those that can be done for *the whole country* by a single measure; (2) those that can at most deal with a *section* of the whole; and (3) the smaller things that require daily supervision and so cannot cover more square miles than one person can survey in a day. In short, this system on the one hand allows for a series of actions that can be delivered in one stroke for the whole country, and on the other for a host of things that require a separate set of officials in each subdivision. Thus some things are taken care of from the center and some things are not. There are national affairs and regional and local affairs.

This division of administrative affairs automatically raises the question which things will be handled centrally and which will not. And depending on how much is placed on the shoulders of the central government or is unloaded on the non-central bodies, there will be centralized or decentralized government.

The rule is that whatever can be dealt with centrally *must* be dealt with centrally. Administration at the lower levels is a necessary evil. It would be better if the state could do without, and it makes do with it only because it cannot dispense with it for now. But the ideal—by far the best arrangement, the goal to be pursued—will always be to get rid of those subordinate centers of power and to manage everything from the center, stretching its power to every point on the periphery by means of a single action of the will for the whole country. The image that fits this ideal is the spider's web, with the spider at the node where all the threads come together.[1]

By virtue of its guiding principle, therefore, which our liberals follow in the main, this system of the Revolution impels to ever greater centralization as soon as the possibility for it arises.

Now that the railway, the improved mail service, and the telegraph are shrinking the community, the arms of the state can reach ever further. More and more matters can be transferred from municipal councils and regional offices to the departments of the central government.

Moreover, the art of imitating the spider becomes second nature. The bureaucrat grows in efficiency and the individual citizen learns to be ever more compliant. The necessary evil of regional and local administration is confined to increasingly narrower tasks. It cannot be done away with as yet, but it gradually loses its significance. Imperceptibly drawing closer is the vaunted ideal of a single "administered people" in a realm one and indivisible.[2]

---

1. The day did arrive when the minister of education in Paris would look at his watch and say: "In five minutes every child in France will open its arithmetic book."
2. On the idea of an "administered people," the French statesman and political philosopher Pierre Paul Royer-Collard (1763–1845) wrote, "Nous sommes un peuple d'administrés sous la main de fonctionnaires irresponsables centralisés eux-mêmes sous la main du pouvoir dont ils sont les ministres [We are an *administered people*

Boards and Administrative Divisions

In the nature of the case, applying this system has a twofold effect.

First, the heads of the lower governments are appointed by the central government. After all, lower administrators are nothing but temporary aids toward extending the power of the central government which would otherwise come to a stop; or if you will, they are instruments for lengthening the arm of the state which would otherwise prove too short. Hence the presiding officer of those administrations is simply a lieutenant of the king.

Actually, every regional assembly and every municipal council ought to be presided over by the central government itself; but since that is impossible, "The king multiplies himself "[3] by appointing governors and mayors. The secret of this administrative system is that the king can be everywhere at once.

Secondly, the natural upshot of applying this system will be that as much as possible a separate division is created for each branch of administration.

In historic nations, each region functions at one and the same time for both the administration and the judiciary as well as for defense, elections, education, and what not. In the system of the Revolution, however, this is absolutely forbidden—for three perfectly valid reasons.

(1) For military matters, for example, a much larger portion of the country can be dealt with, so that division on a much smaller scale will suffice. (2) The subordinate administrations must be kept as subordinate as possible, lest they become too powerful by having all these affairs together placed under their control. (3) The actual divisions must show clearly that they are but temporary, not essential, lest the indivisibility of the realm suffer damage.

That is how it happens that for matters pertaining to the military a completely different division into territories and commands is deliberately devised; for matters touching the judiciary a still different division is made, creating districts and cantons; and still another layout is adopted

---

governed by irresponsible, centralized functionaries who themselves are governed by him whose ministers they are]." See Prosper de Barante, ed., *La Vie Politique de M. Royer-Collard ses Discours et ses Écrits*, 2 vols. (Paris: Didier, 1861), 2:131.

3. *"Le roi se multiplie!"*

for each branch of government, one suited to the nature of the branch in question.

POPULAR LIBERTY §112

Evidently, except for the initial starting point there is no place anywhere in this system for self-rule or popular initiative. Nor could there be!

Only one act is reserved for the individual citizen: *he votes*. "Citizens" and "voters" are conflated in this system.

The individual citizens are proffered a *will*, and supreme sovereign power is put at their disposal. However—and this is the fatal weakness of this whole system—these same individuals can make use of this will only once every four years. And no other consequence follows upon the exercise of that will than that all the power proffered them suddenly passes to someone else and the voters themselves are reduced to the level of will-less beings, bound hand and foot, awarded the slavish name of "administrative units." A citizen is lord of the land, and therefore he may vote. But no sooner does his ballot drop into the ballot box than he is no longer lord, and the one elected has become the master of his fate.

Now we concede at once that except in the days of the initial flush of enthusiasm this system was never applied in all its rigor. Dutch liberals were forced to adjust their demands considerably before their plan was accepted. Yet that does not detract one whit from the principle of the thing. Adjustments to the model were not necessarily viewed as improvements but became unavoidable because it was impossible to work it. The model itself was impracticable; it broke down in the face of reality; attempts to implement it showed that its character was simply against nature. As well, liberal constitutions, even in their most moderate form, invariably exhibit the typical traits of this centralizing system. In the experience of every country in Europe, liberal constitutions have conspired to favor at a growing rate the centralization of all power—of the entire administration and all government action.

Our next chapter will show just how this whole system and the fatal consequences attendant upon it collide with the organic conception of constitutional law in the Christian-historical tradition. In order to bring out what would be the antirevolutionary position, we had first to sketch the system that we cannot endorse and that we therefore combat on principle.

II. THE SYSTEM OF DECENTRALIZATION

§ 113   THE ORGANIC FORMATION OF A STATE

The pattern of thought and the leading idea of the revolutionary system can be summed up as follows:

A country is a single tract of land. That land is populated by individual beings. These individuals should all be governed as much as possible in the same way from a single center. To the degree that this is not possible, the central government may be supported by temporary regional and local administration. For that support the country needs to be cut up, as the pencil-lines fall, into departments and arrondissements, districts and cantons, territories and jurisdictions.

The antirevolutionary system is diametrically opposed to such a system, so sharply opposed in fact that we have to flatly challenge this system at every point. To draw the lines of our own system accurately, it almost suffices simply to reverse this bizarre way of thinking.

According to the principles that we profess, it is simply not true (apart from cases of immigration, colonization, and land reclamation) that one could ever just come upon a country that one could cut up, find a people that one could construct, and conjure up for such a manufactured people an administration.

We contend, and all of history confirms our opinion, that at least among the non-nomadic nations one does not start with a people that can then be cut up into parts. On the contrary, the smaller parts come first, and those things of smaller dimensions form and make up the larger nation. So the parts do not arise from the nation, but the nation arises from the parts. Or if you will, the provinces do not arise from the nation, but the nation arises from the provinces as they grow together and intertwine.

And this remains true even when descending to a lower level. A province as a rule does not arise by occupying a strip of land and then dividing it. Instead, groups of people settle here and there and only afterwards, either voluntarily or by force, gradually enter into a political union. This means that municipalities, too, do not originate by randomly dividing a province into squares or circles, but inversely, provinces are born by the union of *already existing* manorial estates, territories, and communities.

In fact, if we descend still lower and go down to families, it is true even there that the village is composed of families and not that the families are cut from the village. The family was there first, and only then could the village take shape. Finally, if the village vanished there would still be families; but if the households were to disband the village too would come to an end.

Families and Individuals   § 114

At this level, however, we come to a stop.

Lower we do not go. Whoever were to use the same idea and descend from the family to the individual would be wide of the mark.

Once you arrive at the family you have reached the final link. Should you want to continue with this analysis down to the individual persons you would go wrong and end up at odds with the givens of nature.

Consider, when several persons live together they form a group home or a barrack or a lodging house, but never a family. To form a family, only a twosome of the opposite sex can enter this relationship. It is a relationship that is independent of their will and ordained by God. A family household must then be procreated out of these two persons by the creative power of the same God.

Thus the basic unit for us is not the individual, as with the men of the Revolution, but the family.

Our analysis goes no further. Nor are we permitted to do so, for the simple reason that it does not depend on an individual whether he will be part of a family: he belongs to a family, willy-nilly, *by birth*, by the fact that he exists. However weak that bond may be, everybody has a mother, and without that mother he would not exist.

In the transfer of the family to the individuals, therefore, we come into contact with a relationship that is entirely independent of people's will or doing and that is laid upon them, over them and around them, without their knowledge, as part of their very existence, hence ordained for them by God.

Likewise, when arriving at the circle of the family we are face to face with a sphere of life that did not arise from a combination of what was there already, but a sphere that was formed by new production, by new birth, by the appearance of what was not there before.

Thus the family, both as to the relationship and the related parts, places us directly before the living God. And it was precisely this undeniable encounter with a marvelous work of God that the men of the Revolution could not abide and why they leaped over the barrier of the family to find at last in the nondivisible "individual" the long sought glorification of humanity's vaunted, all-sovereign, truly *free* will.

The dual ordinance—the institution of marriage, and birth from a mother—is therefore the foundation on which antirevolutionary politics stands firm. And it is precisely against these two ordinances that the demonic force from the abyss shamefully reacts by the godless invention of open marriage and the even more godless invention of contraception.

§ 115   LIMITS OF STATE AUTHORITY

We need hardly indicate what this means for the nature of government. All you need to do is ask yourself three questions.

(1) Does the responsibility for good order in the family rest with the head of the family or with the head of the state? Does your calling as a father to keep order in your family extend only to the things that the state leaves unordered? Or, inversely, does government have a right to intervene in your family only if you scandalously neglect your calling with respect to your family? In the matter of ruling your household, do you supplement the state, or does the state supplement you?

(2) Did you receive the power to exercise authority in your household from the state, or do you have this power by the grace of God?

(3) Were you as a father given authority over your children because they charged you with this by majority vote; or did you possess this authority independently of their consent, long before they could tell you their mind or inclination? Did they appoint you as father, and therefore also have the right to depose you as father; or are you their father and remain their father by the fact itself of their birth, without even reckoning with their will?

To these questions your answers can only be the following.

(1) *Do you supplement the state, or does the state supplement you in your family?* Answer: the state may not intervene in my family unless I neglect my duty as natural head of the family.

(2) *Did you receive your authority over your family from the state or from God?* Answer: I would be sovereign of my family even if there were no state, and therefore I am head of the family by the grace of God.

(3) *Were you appointed by your children, or do you have authority over them independently of their consent?* Answer: As father I have the right to give orders to my children, for which I am not accountable to them but to God alone.

If we now relate these conclusions to what we saw earlier about the linking of the spheres of life from families to communities, from communities to regions, and from regions to a state, then we can only come to two further conclusions. They are obvious, and they overthrow the entire revolutionary system.

In the first place, the central government may only take on and carry out what is not (and for so long as it is not) properly taken care of in the smaller spheres of life.

If all were well in the state, if people were as they should be and things were normal, the task of the central government would consist exclusively of two things: (1) to take care of those things that flow directly from the connection of the provinces to the one state; and (2) to defend, whenever abuse of power crept in, the rights of individuals over against the family, of the family over against the municipality, and of the municipality over against the region.

However, if the subordinate spheres in many respects still evince a deplorable lack of energy, then the central government has the additional right and duty to intervene in family, municipality, or region and attend to whatever should never be left unprovided for yet continues to be neglected or poorly looked after.

But in that case—and this is decisive—the central government is a caretaker, a deputy, and therefore nothing but a temporary curator.

A *temporary* curator has the right to carry out what is absolutely necessary, but his duty is to withdraw again as soon as the energy for self-rule is sufficiently aroused. Thus he is to fulfill the role of caretaker in such a way that this energy does not weaken but rather gains in strength.

In the second place, the divisions to be reckoned with should not be made with compass and ruler but should be derived from history and reality and should serve to nourish the vitality that is appropriate to each life-sphere.

If there is first a family, then a town or village arising from families, then municipalities that combine to form regions, and a group of such regions that gradually give birth to the higher State unity, then the central government has no business making divisions and incisions in the land but must simply respect the divisions and groupings which it finds there.

The French Constitution reads, in typical revolutionary fashion: "*France is divided into* 86 departments." Our Constitution states, in an antirevolutionary spirit: "The Kingdom of the Netherlands *consists of* the following regions."

§ 116   LEANING TOWARD DECENTRALIZATION

There you have the whole difference: "is divided into" and "consists of." "Cutting up into atoms" or "respecting organic bonds" mark the totally different roots of the two mutually exclusive systems.

For if I accept these two ideas: *first*, that the central government supplements the governments of region, municipality, and family instead of the governments of region, municipality, and family supplementing the central government; and *second*, that a country cannot be cut up into arbitrary sectors but instead is composed organically of life-spheres that have their own right of existence and came to be connected with each other through the course of history—then for anyone who thinks for a moment, the matter is settled in favor of decentralization.

Then, surely, to centralize all power in the one central government is to violate the ordinances that God has given for nations and families. It destroys the natural divisions that give a nation vitality, and thus destroys the energy of the individual life-spheres and of the individual persons. Accordingly, it begets a slow process of dissolution that cannot but end in the demoralization of government and people alike.

Despite the sneers about "national pride," "narrow provincialism," "urban smugness," and the much dreaded "mediocrity," and despite all the noise about "love of humanity," the uplifting power of "cosmopolitanism," the inscrutable mystery of "state unity," and the broad outlook of "men of the world"—despite all that, we shall continue to love the old paths, since they are paths by divine dispensation. With all who are of the antirevolutionary persuasion we shall maintain, over against the fiction of the all-competent, all-inclusive, and all-corrupting state, the independence given by God himself to family and municipality and region as a wellspring of national vitality, according to the ancient law of the land.

III. NOMINATION OF THE HEADS OF LOWER GOVERNMENTS

§ 117   RULES FOR DECENTRALIZATION

In this sense, then, our Program desires that "regional and local autonomy be restored" by means of decentralization. But this cannot be achieved, I believe, without the application of the following four principles.

(1) the appointment of chief administrators in municipalities and provinces should be made from nominations;

(2) whatever transpires and ends within the orbit of a province or a municipality should be dealt with by the provincial or municipal government;

(3) the division into municipality or province should hold as much as feasible for all branches of government; and

(4) administrative justice should be given greater independence.[4]

Crown-appointed Governors and Mayors §118

As things stand, the mayor of a municipality and the head of a region is a royal superintendent. That this was the wish of Thorbecke is clearly evident from the un-Dutch title that he invented for the heads of provincial governments, namely, the *King's Commissioner*. A commissioner of the king is the same, in poor Dutch, as a prefect in France—a governor brought in from the outside and placed over a province to carry out the king's will and law.

Similarly, in the municipal domain we have, in good but misused Dutch, a mayor or "burgomaster," who is simply a commissioner of the king in the small, placed over a municipality to watch over the rights of the king.

These institutions were not created out of love for the monarch. The appointment of both a provincial governor and a mayor is actually made by the sitting minister of the interior, who in turn usually consults the political and personal interests of his party.

When vacancies for governor occur during a conservative ministry— which has happened quite frequently—the king appoints men who have deserved well of the conservative party. And inversely, if vacancies for mayor occur when it is the turn of the liberals to govern the country, we get the appointment—as happened recently in Zwolle and Leeuwarden—of men who are highly thought of among the leaders of the progressive party.

We do not condemn this, but merely record the fact lest anyone be deceived by the appearance of monarchical loyalty. The office of provincial governor is gradually becoming little more than an honorary post for deserving party members. And worse, the office of mayor in ninety out of a

---

4. Later editions read: "administrative justice should be organized separately and so be made independent."

hundred cases threatens to become a means to make propaganda for principles that enjoy little local sympathy.[5]

When you consider how the States Deputed dominate the Provincial States[6] and how they are in turn the close colleagues of the King's Commissioner, then surely no further evidence is required to establish that this whole show of regional government results in nothing more than a subdivision of the Ministry of the Interior, tied to the central government with ten firm cords and connected to the people of the province by a single thin thread.

By far most inhabitants of the province never get to know in their lifetime who the great man with the French title in the provincial capital is. They do not feel any connection to this titleholder and so he has no place in their affections. Who he is, or who his successor is, leaves them entirely cold. This indifference can descend to such a low level that no one could care less if an out-of-province person is installed as commissioner.

Add to this that this subdivision of the Interior Ministry, this branch office of the central government, can do almost nothing and cannot carry out what it may still do except with approval from above—then everyone can see that our Provincial Act not only fails to give autonomy its due, but leaves no room for autonomy at all. From the outset, apparently, the Act was designed to erase as much as possible the historic distinctions between the provinces and to convert regional governments into bureaus of information and implementation—and bureaus of inspection to keep *municipal* government under the Ministry's thumb.

§ 119   PROVINCIALISM

According to our principles, this design must be combated, since the unique character of a province should not be allowed to erode but should be developed in keeping with its distinctiveness.

We do not wish to trade in the pithy concept of a Zeelander or a Frisian for the vague and airy concept of a "Netherlander." To our mind, no one

---

5. When Kuyper became prime minister in 1901, he ordered a study which reported that in 88 percent of the municipalities "north of the rivers"—thus in predominantly Protestant provinces—previous liberal governments had arranged the appointment of mayors of liberal persuasion—many of whom were theological Modernists or agnostics. The same incongruity existed among government-appointed school superintendents.
6. The "States Deputed" refer to a province's executive council; the "Provincial States" refer to a province's elected assembly.

is a Netherlander except by being a Zeelander, a Frisian, a Hollander, and so on. And not even that except by knowing himself to be a resident of Middelburg or Leeuwarden or Amsterdam, or in whatever place his family is rooted and his life-work is found.

That kind of provincialism does not scare us at all. We welcome it, because vigorous life in the parts is the best guarantee of energy in the body as a whole. That is also why we do not want a mayor sent from elsewhere who will transform the "backward villagers" according to modern ideas; nor do we desire a French prefect who arrives to administer the province like some kind of colony. We desire regional and local government in which a region's inhabitants and a municipality's residents are personal stakeholders, so similar to what we still have in the water boards for our polders.

We point to our polder boards with some emphasis because the Netherlands with its water management has always been unique, an aspect for which it is still admired throughout Europe.

This is one area where we have not copied the French revolutionaries but have remained good Netherlanders. And is it not remarkable that precisely our water management has remained a badge of honor for our country? Indeed, everything about our water management has always attracted a great deal of interest.

GOVERNORS BY NOMINATION   § 120

But how to refresh the feature of autonomy in our regional and local spheres of life in such a way that everyone can see and touch it? There is only one effective means, and that is that the administrative heads in those spheres are nominated by the regional and local authorities.

Our provinces are no longer counties or duchies that fall directly under the personal rule of a prince, hence are not governed in his name by an actual lieutenant governor. Nor are they free states that are federally united and so appoint their own heads. But neither are they colonies over which a ruling commissioner is installed. On the contrary, our provinces are national components that have independence within their own orbit and are required to sacrifice their independent character only in cases of common national interests. Thus they exhibit that mixed character whereby the right to nominate is usually conferred upon the stakeholders and the right to appoint is reserved for the higher authority.

Accordingly, we would wish that both the provincial assemblies and the municipal councils were given the right to nominate two candidates, from whom His Majesty could then appoint the governor and the mayor of his choice.

If this were done, you can be sure that half our mayors would be gone, to make room for men from the municipality itself; and similarly, that no province will ever be headed by a governor who is not a son of the province and a resident of the province.

That is what we would wish.

But at present the families of the landed nobility and the well-to-do quit the provinces for The Hague, Rotterdam, Amsterdam, if not Brussels, because they feel less and less at home in their region. They have nothing to do there. Nothing ties them to the region. There is no future for their sons there. This promotes their collecting in the large population centers, inflating their lifestyle and little by little causing generation after generation to go under in opulence and ostentation.

But turn this situation around, give your provincials a provincial interest, invest the dignitaries of the region again with power and influence, guarantee that these high posts are in the gift of the province—and you shall see how our families will again take an interest in their region, will feel connected again with their social circle, will regain an appetite for administrative affairs, and thus will occupy again the honorable places that are naturally theirs.

§ 121   MAYORS BY NOMINATION

Equally valuable will be the influence of a mayor who, though not elected by the residents, at least will be nominated by them.

At present it happens time after time that a town or village is favored with an unknown young man, a stranger who knows nothing about the local people or local conditions and very little about real life. Equipped only with a bit of theoretical knowledge about administrative law, he comes to lord it over the simple folk, to join hands with the equally foreign notary public and justice of the peace, and so on, and to form a modernist club that sets itself the task of liberalizing the "colony."

This cannot but banish trust, silence the natural order of life, and kill civic spirit. When that is the way things are arranged, who still cares about how the municipality is run?

To be sure, the authorities know better than to appoint a person from The Hague to be mayor of Amsterdam, or appoint someone from Amsterdam to be mayor of Rotterdam. Those cities still have sensitivities to be taken into consideration. But a provincial town or a rural village—what could be lost there? They can be managed. They can be wrapped in the threads of the "higher authority," as the spider encircles the fly in its web.

But put an end to this evil and give the local people the right to let the king know whom they would like to see appointed, and you'll see how a "burgomaster" will again become a "burgher father" in the full sense of the word—not an agent of the central government for bending the people to its will but a man of the people, capable of representing the interests of the municipality before the higher authorities.

IV. AUTONOMY OF PROVINCE AND MUNICIPALITY

INCONSISTENCY OF OUR MUNICIPAL ACT $\qquad$ § 122

Before going on to discuss the three points that remain, we would like to add a brief remark to what we raised in connection with the appointment of mayors and governors. It touches on the inconsistency of the system currently in force.

As we recall, at present it is the king as head of state who appoints the heads of both the municipal and the provincial government. This also implies, of course, that the king (or if you will, the central government) should pay the salaries of these commissioners of his, and inversely that the king has the exclusive right to suspend or dismiss these servants of his.

And yet our Municipal Act stipulates, contrary to this, that a mayor's salary is the responsibility of the municipality, and that under certain circumstances Article 60 grants the States Deputed the competence to suspend a mayor from office.

Of course we have no objection against either of these provisions. On the contrary, we deem them excellent—provided it is acknowledged that they fit in with *our* system but directly contradict the intention of the liberals when they drafted these laws.

But what we do object to, and what cannot be defended in either system, is the clause in Article 95 of the Municipal Act that forbids a municipal council to discharge its secretary at its discretion if that secretary is the same person as the mayor. That is an utterly indefensible restriction on the rights of municipalities, typical of the centralizing tendency that has insinuated itself into all our legislation since 1848.

§ 123   Administration from the Bottom Up

Our second point was that whatever transpires and is completed within the orbit of a province or a municipality should be taken care of by the provincial or municipal government.

This proposal derives directly from the principles explained in article II above [about the system of decentralization]. It serves to take out of the hands of the state whatever does not concern the unity of the state.

We share the conviction that the unity of the state must be strictly maintained. We are absolutely averse to any return to federative conditions.[7] Thus whenever it is a matter of upholding sovereign authority or equality before the law or national unity, our support goes, sight unseen, to assigning these interests to the national government.

Not at issue therefore are almost the whole Departments of the Interior, Defense, Navy, and the Colonies. Nor the interest payments and ledgers of our national debt, the postal service, the national roadways, the trunk lines of the railway system. And equally, all regulatory boards and inspections that concern the kingdom as a whole.

But that about finishes the enumeration of what must necessarily fall directly under the central government. At almost every other branch of government the question arises whether we are not dealing with a mixed form of what is only in part a central concern and for another part could as easily be handled at the provincial or even the municipal level.

In saying this we do not just have in mind secondary interests— for example, burial regulations, poverty relief, mortgage companies, pawnshops, mental patient care, polder flooding, peat digging, land reclamation, maritime fisheries, mining concessions, the promotion of local industry and agriculture, and similar affairs. We include as well all government branches of broader scope.

Thus we reckon that municipal government should control tram lines and ring roads, provincial governments should control local railroad lines, while the central government should control interprovincial railroads.

Under municipal government should fall the smaller polders, the ordinary canals, drainage canals and harbors; under provincial government

---

7. Kuyper alludes here to a distinct political weakness of the Dutch Republic. See also note that follows.

the larger polders, dike watch committees, the minor rivers and channels; under the central government the flood control boards, coastal dikes, head channels, the major rivers and commercial harbors. Militia regiments should fall under the municipal government, the organization of these regiments into corps under provincial government, and the use of these provincial corps combined in time of war under the central government.

Primary education should fall under municipal governments; teacher's colleges, secondary schools, and gymnasia under provincial governments; and only universities under the central government. And so on and so forth. Divisions like these can be extended to other branches of government in a most natural way, without further definition.

Still, we would want to take decentralization even further.

We cannot see, for example, why the office of notary should be a national concern; why direct and indirect taxes cannot in part be collected by the municipality and the province; why the church rates cannot be a provincial matter; why the police cannot in the main be a provincial matter; why penal institutions cannot be administered municipally and provincially; why associations whose scope of activities is entirely local cannot suffice with a charter issued by local government. In fact, already here we would like to raise a question to which we shall return later: why can some of the work of administering justice, maintaining law and order, and resolving disputes and lawsuits not be left to lower levels of government?

It is well known that things are arranged that way particularly in the more Calvinist countries like Scotland, England, America, and Switzerland. Much of it still exists also in Germany and Austria. Only in the countries of the Latin race on which pagan Rome put its stamp, partly as a result of that ancient influence but especially through the fresh influence of that same power in the form of the French Revolution, these natural jurisdictions have become increasingly paralyzed, to leave nothing but activity that proceeds from the central government.

Accordingly, we are not at all deterred by the fact that a polity of decentralization in our country once caused affairs to grind to a halt and led to the most impossible political arrangement.[8] First of all, it is generally agreed that it was a mistake to grant the provisional constitution

---

8. Kuyper makes another reference to the highly decentralized Dutch Republic (1579–1795), which unhappily stood as a model for the American Articles of Confederation (1777–89).

of the Union of Utrecht [of 1579] an enduring character. According to the unimpeachable testimony of history, it was not the Orange party but the party of the Regents, in the interest of their class, that was responsible for resisting a unitary state.

Our system, in the second place, rather than deterring us, recommends itself to us by the fact that our fathers with their impossible contrivances were still able to work miracles, while the statesmen of '48 with their neatly assembled state machinery, after a quarter century of toiling and moiling, ran stuck on every side.

Moreover—and this should not be overlooked—our intention is to include the following safeguards: (1) Matters that are normally handled provincially or locally might, as a result of particular issues or persons, rights, or functions, have repercussions in the domain of another province; these matters would be regulated by the central government. (2) The central government would continue to send out inspectors to make sure regulations were followed and to force compliance if necessary. (3) The central government would be the court of last appeal to decide any disputes that could not be resolved amicably between one province and another.

Finally, although we concede at once that this decentralized polity far more than at present would give rise to disruptions and complications, still we admit just as frankly that we would be quite happy to put up with such less streamlined functioning if more civic spirit and energy could be aroused at that price.

Really, an *automaton* too speaks with a very even voice; but we for our part would rather be in the company of a sometimes stuttering *human being*.

§ 124   ADMINISTRATIVE DIVISIONS ACCORDING TO PROVINCE AND MUNICIPALITY

In the third place, for all branches of government the divisions of the country should coincide with the boundaries of province and municipality.

The French system went so far as to adapt even education, for example, to a cut-and-dried system that set up an entirely separate division of the country into *académies* (not to be confused with our "academy" but understood as *school districts*). Such exaggeration has not yet infiltrated our country, thanks to provincial pertinacity. In the main, the system of centralization has not carried the day except in connection with the national militia and elections for the Second Chamber.

The mistake of our politicians lies more in constantly changing the combination of regions that are too small and then again creating inspector posts for provinces where there is almost nothing to inspect.

The cause of this confusion was especially the province of Drenthe. Thinking it over carefully, one can only conclude that it would have been better in 1813 and 1848 if Drenthe had not been given provincial status. In fact, perhaps a reversal of that decision—with the approval of the people of Drenthe—ought still to be considered. It is not right, after all, to put up with the not so little costs of maintaining a provincial administration and inspection for a population that is smaller than that of a single city like Rotterdam. And what counts for more in our estimation, Drenthe even in the days of the Republic was not included among the Seven United Provinces of Holland, Zeeland, Guelders, Frisia, Utrecht, Overijssel, and Groningen. Drenthe was administered by the States General as an "annex," precisely because it was so small.

The smallness of Drenthe's population has led to its being assigned to Groningen and Frisia for the judiciary, to Groningen for water control, to Overijssel again for public hygiene, and so on. Evidently the authorities were at a loss of what to do with this small province, and so they joined it at one time to the North, at another time to the South, without rhyme or reason.

Now if it should turn out that the people of Drenthe were willing to foot the bill for looking after their own affairs, then of course to unite it with another province would not be advisable. All compulsion in this area should be banned—unless the national government has to take care of its lawful business in Drenthe *at the nation's expense*. In that case this region ought once for all to be merged either with Groningen or with Overijssel.

Furthermore, when creating our combinations of provinces we should avoid the constant unsteadiness we currently indulge in. At present we divide the justice system over five courts, water control over ten inspection districts, public hygiene over seven inspectorates, paymasters over twenty-four arrondissements, direct taxes over nine jurisdictions, crown lands over six directorates, postal service over five regions, and primary education over no less than eleven districts.

Is this order? Does this promote cohesion? And is this not in part responsible for the big mistake that all these inspectorates and directorates function without any ties to the regional governments?

We shall return later to the organization of the armed forces. Let us just note here that we cannot applaud the current system of assigning to one and the same regiment a mixture of Frisians, Zeelanders, Limburgers, and still others. Not just for the sake of organic political life but also for arousing a military spirit and facilitating mobilization, we would far prefer the formation of a Frisian regiment, a Groningen regiment, and so on, even at the risk of now and then causing irritations in a mixed garrison.

§ 125 ADMINISTRATIVE JUSTICE

In the fourth place, we believe that administrative justice should have autonomy and thus be made independent.

As things stand currently, in our administrative justice the government involved is both party and judge at the same time. This system ensures that town and village councils are almost entirely at the mercy of the appointed mayors. For if the councils oppose the mayor, the States Deputed will intervene; and since the latter mostly enjoy the support of both the King's Commissioner and the minister of the interior, it means that in questions of autonomy, that is, in the most vital issues that may present themselves, every lower body is virtually defenseless.

Suppose you still manage to salvage a certain measure of independence for the lawmaking powers of these bodies. When it comes to their implementation, however, each party will interpret regional and local laws in its favor. And whenever disputes arise over the interpretation of these laws the weaker party will lose.

The current system works well in the event of disputes between municipalities and between provinces. But as soon as one of the parties is a higher authority, there is no assurance of the kind that can inspire energy and a sense of duty, namely, the assurance of getting impartial and independent justice.

For that reason it seems to us imperative that at least in the case of disputes between higher and lower bodies there be the possibility of appeal to an independent judge, so that there be a halt somewhere in the fatal circle, a point where the centralist drive is compelled to let you have what the law grants you.[9]

There you have—too brief perhaps to be clear, yet also almost too detailed for a popular publication—what we deem essential for regaining

---

9. The third edition of 1892 adds: "This possibility will become available thanks to the revision of the Constitution that was completed in 1887."

autonomy for our regional and local governments.[10] And although none of us flatters himself that we shall ever reap such a generous measure of liberty so long as the liberals' tyranny is not put down, still it was our duty to show what consequences would ensue from the application of *our* principle. And if we were given back only a small trinket, that already would in our opinion reinforce a better principle and therefore be gain for our nation.

V. LEGAL PROTECTION AGAINST CORPORATIONS

THE RIGHT TO LEAVE A CORPORATION §126

Meanwhile, however strongly our Program may urge decentralization and therefore push for regional and local autonomy, it does not do so except under the explicit proviso "that it does not leave the rights of individuals unprotected."

This point is of the utmost importance, since true civic freedom stands or falls with the realization or evasion of this proviso.

Freedom, after all, is to be able to dispose of one's person, power, and property according to the dictates of one's conscience. Such freedom exists in name but never in truth if every life-sphere in which I have to move and work can ensnare me with the tyranny of superior force.

This does not hold for spheres of life that I enter voluntarily or that I can leave again at any given moment. For then my submission to that tyrannical force is an act of will and the result of personal choice, and I have myself to blame if the legal requirements or usages to which I must submit abridge my freedom.

When someone enters a guild it goes without saying that he arranges his labor and his product according to the rules of the guild. When someone becomes a member of a prohibition league it stands to reason that he cannot spend his money on liquor. Or again, when someone joins an abolition society it needs no argument that he may not profit from human trafficking.

This holds even for a church. To be sure, in no way is a church in this respect on a par with an ordinary association, and we well realize that a person belongs to a church already by birth, or at least by the sacraments of baptism or circumcision. But so long as one is free to leave the church at

---

10. The reader is reminded that the present work was first published in installments from April 1878 to February 1879 in Kuyper's daily newspaper *De Standaard*.

any time, then ecclesiastical compulsion, however far it extends, may never abridge the rights of conscience. After all, so long as I am free to leave and nevertheless decide to stay in my church, the compulsion inflicted upon my conscience is a compulsion that I put up with and am therefore partly responsible for.

The rights and freedoms of the individual with respect to corporations of this sort are therefore perfectly safe, so long as the government makes sure (1) that no one is forced against his will to join an association; (2) that anyone may withdraw from an association of which he is a member at any time he wishes; and (3) that he is not molested for his withdrawal by those who stay behind.

The latter holds even for an undertaking entered for life, for example, in the case of monastic vows. Not that a government should have to judge whether such permanent vows are desirable or not, but rather that it should reckon with the possibility that someone was persuaded to make such a vow more than he was compelled by his conscience—and thus leave the voluntary nature of such an undertaking open to question.

But it is especially in cases of immoral engagements that a government should unconditionally uphold the right to immediate withdrawal. The occurrence of instances where a prostitute was forced, for example, by her madam to stay in a house of ill repute against her will on the basis of promises she had made is one of the most grievous insults that can be inflicted on one's sense of justice. Even in civil lawsuits involving money, engagements of this kind should simply be declared nonexistent, and the judge should not even order a defendant to pay back any advances received.

§ 127   No Meddling in Internal Affairs

Uncompromising protection of freedom of association, however, ends the government's task with respect to the corporate bodies reviewed above.

It might perhaps be useful if such corporate bodies were obliged, when accepting new members, to hand them a clearly written description of the obligations they are letting themselves in for. But if the freedom to withdraw is assured at all times, even this precautionary measure seems to us to be superfluous, not to mention the impossibility for many an entrant to gauge the full import of a constitution or set of bylaws.

What might at most be done, to prevent abuse, is to introduce the requirement for institutions which shut their members off from the outside world that they allow an independent government official once a year to inform all inmates that their right to leave, then and there if they wish, is unabridged, and to ask them: "Do you wish to make use of this right?"

But government should not go any further.

Every attempt, for example, to enter within the walls of the church to restrict her free functioning is not to uphold her rights but to curtail them. That is not a government's right—not even in regard to a mighty organization like the church of Rome.

However, government must give uncompromising protection to freedom of association, also against Rome. It must keep under control, if need be by billeting a full battalion of troops in the village, any Catholics in the province of Brabant who are bent on harassing a person that has renounced his vows. If such a violation of public freedom should ever occur, the government must take strong action, even if a single instance would entail the cost of a ton of money.

The new Criminal Code[11] should prescribe severe sanctions for violations of this kind.

Once this one freedom is affirmed, however, a government's authority in this matter has reached its limit. If someone on account of his withdrawal loses clients or is forsaken by his friends, of even if perhaps his own wife withholds part of her love—such things, and so much else, are private consequences that a government is not able, and not allowed, to take into account. They are consequences that a person must be prepared to suffer if need be, if his conviction is to command respect.

PUBLIC-LEGAL CORPORATIONS OF A POLITICAL NATURE   § 128

The duty of government to protect the freedom of individual persons looks quite different the moment we consider not the spheres from which you may withdraw whenever you wish, but the spheres to which you belong because you exist.

A child for example cannot, if it so chooses, step outside its father's household. Similarly, no one can reside in the Netherlands unless he resides in a province; and again, no one can live in a province unless he lives as well in a municipality.

---

11. This code was in preparation at the time of writing; the statement was not adjusted in later editions. The Criminal Code was finished in 1881 and went into effect in 1886.

The family relationship we can leave out of the discussion, for one part because it binds only those under age, for another because it is not directly involved in regional or local autonomy.

But we do have to look at autonomy, because in the former Dutch Republic the autonomy of these spheres was extended so recklessly that the right to self-rule literally degenerated into an excessive right to domineer individual persons. Not intentionally evil, it came about without warning. Nevertheless it was unbearable.

Our country, too, was a free country. There was freedom even to the point of licentiousness. But it was a freedom for the corporate bodies, not for the individual citizen as a human being and head of a family. Citizens were free to do what they wanted; but to be able to do this as citizens, these corporations dealt with the *individual* citizen at their will and pleasure.

This led naturally to oligarchy and nepotism and gradually brought us to a situation that under the semblance of freedom kept the vast majority in an unworthy state of subjugation, almost of slavery. It destroyed the energy of the state and sowed bitterness into the hearts of the citizens.

§ 129   INTERMEDIATE DIVISIONS

A reaction to this unbearable situation erupted in the Revolution toward the end of the eighteenth century, and aside from the way it was carried out, it was perfectly justified, morally speaking.

This tyrannizing of the masses by a coterie of Regents was as little bearable in those days as the tyranny of a coterie of liberals is becoming in our day—particularly since the national character of the Hollanders has traditionally taken delight in forming small cliques for lording it over the masses.

It would have been most reasonable therefore if men, realizing this evil, had employed, without impairing the state's natural strength, prudent political institutions and wise laws for imposing limits on the operation of these corporations that are situated midway between the unitary state and the individual citizen.

To succeed in that would have required hard, painstaking work, and would only have achieved the desired situation through slow development. But once achieved it would have greatly benefited national life.

The natural spheres of family, municipality, and region would have been preserved in their full strength and function. At the same time it would have delivered the priceless benefits *at the top* of ensuring the cooperation of these spheres by the strong arm of the central government, and *at the bottom* of protecting the rights and liberties of individuals over against the corporations. The country—what is more, the nation—would have flourished.

But, shying away from that long and difficult road, the French Revolution decided it was much simpler to sweep away all these intermediate relations at one go and bring the individual citizen in direct contact with the central government—in effect, to change him from a citizen to a subject.

To this end the power of the corporations was crippled in such a way that they retained no more than a servile function, that is, utter dependence. And so, maimed on every side and robbed of their natural organs, they could not but lose every chance of developing vigorous life.

This robust measure did succeed in protecting the individual citizen against the corporations that, thus chained, could no longer harm him. Yet at the same time the nation suffered the double damage of seeing the finer organization of its national life blocked and its individual citizens, freed from the tyranny of the corporations, brought under the yoke of the much more oppressive tyranny of the parliamentary majority.

The distinction between the finer and the more coarsely equipped organisms, after all, consists precisely in this, that with the coarser ones, for example in starfishes, the main organ acts on the cells without almost any intermediate linkages, whereas in the finer organisms, for example in the human body, the very opposite is the case: every grouping of elements forms an independent organ of sorts that serves as an intermediate link between the brain and the individual cells; your brain has no power over the cells in the muscles of your arm except through the intermediate links of the nerves and blood vessels that control the muscles of your arm.

The Revolution has lowered our body politic from a finer to a coarser organism, and as a result the character of our political life is increasingly less human.

Legal Protection for Individuals and Lesser Corporations   § 130

To counteract this development, the antirevolutionary policy can be no other than the one indicated in our Program. We need to galvanize and inspire again the paralyzed organs that as regional and local spheres of life should function between the central government and individual families.

Freeing up these life-spheres, however, should be strictly bound to two conditions: (1) that the manner in which authority is established in these spheres be in conformity with the corresponding national law; and (2) that anyone at any time may seek redress of wrongful acts and abuse of power from an independent judge.

Heads of families must have these twin guarantees against local government, and so do local authorities against regional government.

But if these conditions are met, we need not worry about the outcome of the exercise of freedom. There will always be hitches in the smooth operation of the complicated machinery, but at least a natural, healthy interaction will arise between the various national organs. And freedom—if only people would realize this!—will be all the more proud and noble in the measure that it is no longer thrown in your lap as an act of charity but is won through your own exertions and, if need be, through your determined struggles with those in power.

CHAPTER TWELVE

OUR STATES AND COUNCILS

In order that the States General be rooted in the nation and not represent the people in name only nor any longer offend minority rights in their composition, the party demands the introduction of a new electoral system and in preparation of that a lowering of the census.

ARTICLE 11

I. THE OLD AND THE NEW "STATES"

THE HISTORICAL SIGNIFICANCE OF OUR PROVINCIAL STATES AND   § 131
MUNICIPAL COUNCILS

We are now ready to discuss the electoral system.

As we saw earlier, at all levels of government the people should get their say: the nation needs to be consulted, the people ought to be represented. The question is, how are we to attain this goal through our States and councils, and in what way are the elected men at the various levels to interact with one other?

To deal in a somewhat orderly fashion with the main issues that present themselves here, we begin by pointing to the concept and the historical significance of our States General.

The "States" are not persons, but groups of people who let themselves be represented by persons. Thus the elected members are not themselves the States but merely the representatives of the States; and those States are found, not in The Hague, but throughout the country.

States—also called estates or orders—were similar to our "classes." The term was used to refer to groups of citizens of similar background, profession, or livelihood who had common interests to defend.

This usage has survived in everyday speech. We talk of a peasant class, a business class, the class of tradesmen, and so on, names that indicate that we think of farmers, merchants, artisans, and so on, as groups who in public life wish to defend similar, common interests.

"State" and "estate" were synonyms, the only difference being that "State" was used only for those higher classes who had risen to political importance and could live in a grand style.

Factually, these higher classes resolved into three estates: the clergy, the nobility, and the third estate or burghers of a town. The peasant class was considered to be represented by the nobility, while merchants and artisans were counted among the third estate.

The three estates defended their rights over against a duke or count, not by head but *as a body*. The entire clergy met as a single body; the nobility formed a second body; the towns reported as a third body. Now, according to old Germanic custom, all the members of each State could show up in person. To obviate the inconvenience of large numbers, however, it became customary to authorize *delegates* to act on behalf of all, with the result that gradually the States came to be composed of three delegations: one each from the clergy, the nobility, and the towns.

§ 132   THEIR FORMER FUNCTION

Originally, therefore, "the States" stood for a meeting of three delegations, one from each of the estates that had risen to political prominence.

When in 1579 the States of seven of our provinces entered into a federation by the Union of Utrecht, it became necessary, of course, to create from these seven meetings of Provincial States one additional, central States to take care of the common interests of all the provinces. And since the whole of the united provinces were referred to as "the Generality," the central delegation was given the name States *General*, bringing into vogue the title of *Provincial* States for the meetings of the States in the duchies and counties.

The term "State" for a country or a political domain, which is the general term today, is of later date. It did not arise until people became conscious of the fact that every man of honor, besides the bond with the members of his class, also has a bond with his fellow countrymen. A man is not just a member of one of the estates or classes in which a nation is organically differentiated; he is also a member of the one State to which all belong by the mere fact that they are inhabitants of the kingdom.

Such in general was the history of "States" in the Low Countries. Similarly, France had its *Etats Généraux*, the German lands their *Stände*, Britain its *Lords* and *Commons*, and Spain its *Cortes*.

Everywhere in Europe, representative government arose from the organic body of the nation. And only from the differentiation of estates did representative government become aware of the one State to which all belong, namely, the kingdom.

We should add that moral considerations prevailed of old, so that minority rights were respected. Numerically, clergy and nobility were outnumbered by the third estate. If voting in their combined assemblies had been by head, the result would simply have been that the burghers could have their will all the time, the clergy and nobility never. To prevent this, it was laid down in Britain that clergy and nobility together should form a separate upper house, which could vote down whatever the other states of the realm, assembled in the lower house, wished to push through. In France the rule was established that each of the three estates would have only one vote. In Germany and Scandinavia, it was a division into *curia* that guarded against oppression of minorities.

The Three Political States of our Constitution   § 133

Under our present polity, the form of these institutions has been retained but the essence has been allowed to slip away.

Our Fundamental Law no longer reckons in any way with the social classes that even today exist in the country. Instead, it divides[1] the population quite arbitrarily into three other classes or groups, namely, (1) the highest taxpayers, (2) those who pay direct taxes in an amount between 20 to 160 guilders, and (3) those who fall beneath that amount.

Of these three estates, classes, or groups, the first numbers only 1,200 members, the second no more than about 100,000 members, and the third

---

1. Since the 1892 edition, the text reads: "Until 1887 it divided…"

1,500,000 members.[2] Nevertheless it has been thought fit to leave the third category without any political rights and to place all political influence in the hands of the first two, small categories, those of the higher and intermediate taxpayers.

Next, to prevent the 1,200 higher taxpayers from being outvoted by the intermediate taxpayers, an old model has been falsely mimicked by separating these two classes into two chambers, the former being assigned to the First Chamber and the latter to the Second Chamber, each with the right to vote down the other's decisions.

Compared to what was formerly the case, this situation evidently is no improvement.

Although it is undeniable that the former estates of "clergy, nobility, and towns" had ceased to be in harmony with the social conditions, having been gradually transformed into different groups within the bosom of the nation, nevertheless few will argue, let alone try to prove, that the current division of the people into "States" has improved the situation.

The current division, based on tax assessments, uses a false and immoral financial criterion, resulting in the fiction of "States" instead of the real classes that do exist. And what is worse, we make do with "States" that can no longer act as a body and on close inspection are not true "States" at all, even though they are adorned with the honorary title of States General.

It is obvious that this false system works even less well in the case of the Provincial States, since in that assembly only the class of taxpayers has a say. And in the case of municipal councils, finally, any notion of organic relationship is lost entirely; given the absence even of electoral districts, nothing but an aggregate of individuals, called "voters," is left to tend to local political interests.[3]

§ 134   CONSEQUENCES OF THE REVOLUTIONARY PRINCIPLE

Our representative system is ambiguous through and through. It halts between two opinions. Its ambivalence leaves us without energy to elevate ourselves politically. It more or less stays with the *forms* of the old, sound, historical representative system that we are accustomed to calling the

---

2. The total population of The Netherlands at the time of writing (1878) was just under 4 million.

3. The following sentence was added as a new paragraph in the 1892 edition: "Although it must be admitted that the new Electoral Act of 1887 has mitigated this evil, still the system remains what it was—always the three 'States.'"

organic system, but into that old form it slips the newfangled, revolutionary idea of the *atomistic* state that is an aggregate of individuals and comes to expression in *universal suffrage*.

The revolutionary system does not recognize states or classes or groups in the nation. It sees in the nation nothing but a large mass of isolated individuals who have no other political connection or social ties than the single, vaunted bond of "the state."

This system does not attain its purest expression until each of these individuals, one by one, by head count, with complete equality of rights, is allowed to have a say in the administration of the country's affairs—in other words, through universal suffrage. This system, acknowledged or not, is the inevitable consequence of every atomistic conception of the state.

That these individuals are still divided over districts is done for convenience's sake, but that really makes for an improper refraction of the pure light that ought to fall on the common interest from the collective vote of the individuals.

The ideal would be, in the words of Napoleon: "one plebiscite, by all Frenchmen, undivided and unbroken, throughout the country, on a single day!"

To which one should add that on this standpoint the bicameral system is totally senseless and absurd, and that France's National Assembly made sure no Senate arose next to it.

The doctrinaires demand that the system should everywhere be as Bismarck stated recently in the German Empire: "One Reichstag, elected by all German individuals"—a system that ill suits both a bicameral setup and representation based on annual taxes paid.[4]

And since this system, too, contains a logic that will have its way, resistance won't help. On this question the "wholehearted" will prevail over the "half-hearted." Sooner or later the popular cry, "One Chamber and universal suffrage!" can no longer be silenced.

Meanwhile the liberals in our small country, not as yet daring to risk so much consistency, fancied they were giving a specimen of commendable wisdom by tentatively pouring this new wine into old wineskins. Thus they entered the path of deluding themselves and the public through

---

4. The form of government representing voters who annually paid a minimum amount of direct taxes came to be known by the name *census democracy*.

reprehensible double-mindedness. Factually and essentially, they opted for the theory of the Revolution but held on to the form of the old organic law.

That was the lie in their system.

And, as always, so in this case, punishment came hard on the heels of that lie. No blessing could be expected. Our liberals reaped years of struggle and years of bungling and harvested nothing but derision and impotence.

Our present States, let's admit it, have neither the respect of the people nor any ascendancy over the nation.

II. CORPORATIVE STATES

§ 135   ORGANIC REPRESENTATION

Clearly, our current system of representation is of two minds. Basically it wants to embody the French revolutionary conception that wishes to see in a people nothing more than "a heap of people on a hunk of soil,"[5] yet formally it still honors the old traditions of organic representation by dividing the country into three estates. Clear as well is the fact that this system from inner necessity must gradually discard the old form and is on its way to universal suffrage. And equally clear is the fact that the Provincial States and the municipal councils are already dominated by the atomism of individuals.

Seeing this phenomenon, antirevolutionaries judge that this disorganization of the nation should stop, the sooner the better. Our representative system should again do justice to the organic relationships in the nation, and while eliminating the attendant flaws that used to taint it, it should go back to its natural and gradual development.

Antirevolutionaries base this demand on the fact that the nation is in fact an organism and can only exist organically. The more a nation unfolds, the finer the threads and tissues it weaves. Or, if you prefer to express this in a more practical way: antirevolutionaries base this demand on the undeniable fact that, socially and politically, not just individuals but also *groups* of people have interests to defend which they share as a group.

Human society, at least in civilized countries, is made up of classes, groups, and communities of people. Individuals cannot be equal, for the

---

5. The original *"een hoop zielen op een stuk gronds"* is an expression attributed to the poet Isaäc da Costa (1798–1860).

simple fact that they differ in background, aptitude, upbringing, occupation, property, and basic convictions. And if inequality is the rule, it is only natural that in the midst of all these general inequalities groups should arise that have a common outlook or share common interests and are therefore motivated to band together against other groups and defend what is common to them.

These groups, not *made* by contract or whim but *born* from the bosom of the nation, constitute as it were the "joints" and "members" of that great "body" that people call a "nation." And since a body does not exist except in its joints and members and cannot express itself except through its joints and members, so every popular representation is to be rejected as false if it prevents the nation from declaring itself in a regular way through its joints and members, that is, organically.

Thus, if the nation is again to properly manifest its will and inclinations as an organic whole, a proper States General ought to be chosen by the Provincial States, those Provincial States by the municipal councils, and finally those municipal councils by the local corporations.

Guilds   § 136

Those local corporations, however—and this is the greatest stumbling block on the road to realizing our idea—have been shattered by the French Revolution. These prime members of the national organism can grow back again only very slowly.

We have especially in mind, of course, the guilds, a kind of corporation that had the same function for the municipal governments as the States had for the central government: they were the organized groups in the towns who in defense of their common interests gradually also acquired political power.

It falls outside the scope of these articles to sketch, even in broad outline, the origin and significance of those guilds. However, we do call to mind that the guilds were in no way intended just for crafts and industries. As the far-reaching influence of the well-known *guilds of civic guards* shows, for example, a "guild" referred in general to "a body of citizens united for a common purpose."

Little by little the guilds succeeded in obtaining a share in government, not just in affairs touching their interests but also in a more general sense. Especially in the free cities of Germany and the still mightier towns of Flanders and Brabant the power of the guilds rose so high that for all intents and purposes they had the municipal authorities under their control. It was taken very ill of burgomaster Van der Werff during the siege of Leiden [1573/74] that he negotiated with the [Spanish] enemy without first consulting the assemblies of the guilds.

We do not deny that the jealousy of these guilds, the pressure they put on people, and the way they frustrated municipal government gradually led to confusion and intolerable situations. We do not deny this, provided you also keep in mind on the other hand that thanks to the activity of the guilds and in spite of these troubles, the times saw the development of a vibrant civic life and the flourishing of a public spirit that our age is so nostalgic about.

To be sure, we concede at once that at the end of the eighteenth century, guilds and local government could not remain what they were. As the ludicrous and annoying caricatures of a glorious past, they could not but succumb under the wrath of the outraged citizenry. Nevertheless, we deplore most deeply that men at that time simply swept away the guilds and sold them for scrap, instead of improving and reforming them. For in that way they created the disorganized situation that takes such bitter revenge today in a decline of civic spirit, a growing indifference to public affairs, and an increasing alienation between the richer and poorer classes of society.

We are not suggesting that even these evils could not be remedied. On the contrary, even now we see in the Chambers of Commerce and in the Workingmen's Associations the nation's organic life-force at work for restoring and nourishing its shattered members.

But this takes time. This will not come to an end without tremendous convulsions. And it is especially true—our children know all about it—that to undergo growth spurts is painful.

Yet even as it hurts, the organic fabric is growing little by little. And if our present Chambers in The Hague will one day be retired and a Labor Code (more about that later) comes to promote the development of the lower classes instead of frustrating it, there is hope for our cities and towns to regain their former vibrancy. All the more so, as the changing status of the estates and manors of our nobility enables our rural villages and hamlets to enter this development as well. As a result of that very significant change, the importance of the municipalities can now rise to a much higher level than they ever enjoyed in their best days.

The new organization will have to fit the changing situation. To that end, municipal councils—under strict conditions and in wisely chosen proportions—ought to be opened up to influence from every group of persons that can demonstrate that it represents a common interest. Each group should have its say and not squeeze to death any other groups, but complement their activity and keep it within bounds.

It should be made possible that corporations like that can be formed if their constituent elements are present in a municipality in sufficient numbers: members of noble birth, educated people, freehold landowners, religious societies, or educators. And similarly farmers or producers, manufacturers who prepare and process what is produced, and merchants and small business people who market what is produced. To which should be added, finally, chambers of labor, the multitude of workers and journeymen, clerks and domestics, and perhaps the officers of large garrisons.

Under strict conditions and in wisely regulated proportions, with the approval of the Provincial States and if need be with the right of appeal to the central government (to exclude any suppression of minorities), these corporations ought to have the right to make appointments to the municipal council, with freedom to elect members from among their own or from outside their circle. The only exception would be religious bodies and military garrisons, for whom it would obviously have to be law that they elect councilors from *outside* the clergy and uniformed personnel.[6]

In this way a municipal council would reflect the organic life of the citizenry. In the simple village context this organic relationship would be extremely simple; in the highly diversified life of the city it would be extremely complex. But every interest group or profession, every rank or class would have its advocates in every municipality, be it a village, town or city; and deadly competition would be replaced by the constructive element of cooperation.

Next, these organically elected municipal councils could then send delegates to the Provincial States, in numbers proportional to their size, such that the more important municipalities had greater influence in the assembly of the States.

---

6. Clergy and military were forbidden by law to hold political office.

There are compelling reasons for this direct transition from councils to States. The assembly of nobles was dissolved in 1795,[7] the clergy lost all direct say in the country's affairs already in the sixteenth century, and the wage-earning class of society cannot be included at the provincial level with the best will in the world. Moreover, to revert to this partial result of history would be neither desirable nor feasible.

As well, the nobility and the manorial landowners have lost virtually all importance and might be brought back to a weak political existence at most in the provinces of Guelders, Utrecht, and Limburg. But especially if the members of this order in those towns and villages where their influence is sufficiently far-reaching—for example in The Hague and in some rural municipalities—were given the right to elect members of the municipal council, it would be a needless repristination of what is irrevocably past if they were still allowed to function as an order in the Provincial States.

And as for the clergy, the influence of the prelates was once great, especially in provinces like Utrecht and Zeeland. But, first of all, it has been a rule in this country ever since the Reformation that ecclesial office and political involvement cannot be combined. Moreover, in the second place, the public rights of the denominations are sufficiently upheld, we believe, if the religious bodies of a certain numerical strength can delegate to council as their spokesman an expert in political matters.

§ 138   STATES GENERAL

Finally, the Provincial States, thus composed, would then, likewise in organic fashion, have to send their delegates to the States General. This too should be done in proportion to their relative importance, which could be ascertained in part from the size of the population, in part from the tax rolls.

These delegations would then have to be elected by secret ballot, so that the States would be beholden neither to the highest nor to the intermediate taxpayers. Those chosen would only have to be residents of the province and, once elected, remain so.

This procedure would give birth to a States General whose lifeblood had traversed all the arteries of national life. It could truly be said to represent the people as it exists in reality as a "living, thinking, and working nation."

---

7. The "ridderschap" was restored in 1815 but permanently abolished by the Provincial Act of 1850.

There would therefore be three tiers of elections. First, every member of a corporation would participate directly in the election of the person that would represent that corporation in the town or village council. Second, every member of the municipal council would have the right to help elect the person that would represent council in the Provincial States. Third, every member of the Provincial States would participate in electing the delegates who would sit in the States General.

Meanwhile, we will need a separate article to examine the reason why next to this organic body for the diverse interests (which can best be compared to our present First Chamber) there should be still another body of national States, one of a more political character (which is more reminiscent of our Second Chamber).

III. POLITICAL STATES

SOCIAL AND POLITICAL GROUPINGS   § 139

We are not there yet if our States and councils are composed as indicated thus far.

If we were to look only at the organic relationships in our nation, we for our part would fall into the same one-sidedness that has led liberalism astray and we would overlook the fact that there is also another relationship among people.

An image may illustrate what I mean. A steamship has a propeller at the rear that the captain can only control by means of the entire intricate wheelwork that connects the steam to the pistons, from there to the levers, and so to the shaft that turns the propeller. But a steamship also has a rudder that the helmsman can directly cause to turn left or right as his fingers move about the spokes of the steering wheel. That is also the way things are in the organism of the state.

The thrust whereby the people can be propelled on the path of genuine development does not work except through the composite organism of corporations, municipalities, and regions. But the direction in which that thrust will move the "ship of state" is determined more immediately by the life-principle and outlook that are nurtured in the family household.

Let us take an example: When a proposal is made to introduce, expand, or abolish a tax on licenses, an interest is at stake that will give rise to a contest between the various corporations and groups in society. Catholic farmers will unite with atheist farmers against atheistic or even Catholic city folk to keep licenses out of agriculture. And inversely, equally orthodox urban dwellers will then join their Modernist fellows to break the coalition that wants to perpetuate agriculture's privileged position. In this case organic ties are operative and corporative interests and local or regional relations must tip the scales.

But when, for example, the schools issue is at stake, all those class ties of rural and city folk evaporate, and you will see the orthodox farmer work together with the orthodox townsman, the baker with the pensioner, the merchant with the professor—all in order to break the presumption of liberalism.[8] That is to say, you will then notice nothing of corporative ties, but instead discover that the decision will be directly influenced by the spirit that animates heart and home. This is so much a fact in the case of the schools issue that the "education corporation"—the "guild" of school-teachers—will burst apart and the orthodox teacher will sooner sacrifice a salary raise for his profession than reinforce a false principle.

§ 140   TWOFOLD STATES

This fact, which could be reinforced with numerous other examples, shows that governments make decisions of two types: decisions that concern the nation in its *corporative* relations, and decisions that concern the *spiritual* direction in which the nation will be led by its government.

By ignoring this distinction, the prerevolutionary polity in these lands detracted from the idealist nature that must belong to all politics worthy of the name: by wishing to be solely corporative it denied the nation a legitimate organ for expressing its spiritual unity. Our current Constitution, by contrast, fell into the no less disturbing error of giving our States General an exclusively political character and assigning even questions of detail to men elected for an exclusively political mandate.

This caused steam propeller and steering wheel to work at cross purposes and so gave our Chambers an increasingly hybrid character—on the one hand too political to tend to corporative interests, on the other too interest-driven to have a heart for a politics of principles.

The results were predictable. Thanks to a flaw in the Constitution, the country's politics and its corporative interests alike were neglected. Without realizing it, and without being able to do anything about it, we drove up a dead-end street where our polity proved a lame horse and

---

8. Kuyper alludes to the People's Petition of July 1878, signed by people from all walks of life.

the nation's interests, here as well as in the Indies, were gambled away through mismanagement and bad policy.

There is only one means to reverse this evil: give a nation that tries to serve two goals (namely, the triumph of its life-principle and the advancement of its interests) and that therefore, to attain these two goals, expresses itself in two ways (namely, corporatively when its interest, and directly when its life-principle is at stake)—give such a nation, we say, a twofold representation, the one chosen corporatively and the other directly.

No one can deny that our nation, to the extent that it divides into classes and corporations, resolves into groups that are quite different from when it divides into its liberal, Calvinist, and Catholic elements. Likewise, no one can deny that the boundaries of these three elements cut right across the boundaries of the classes and corporations. No one can possibly conceive of a type of representation that simultaneously mirrors both groupings.

But if this is so, the conclusion must be one of two things: either you create a popular representation that does justice to only one of the two groupings (the political or the corporative) and treats the other simply as nonexistent; or you create a twofold representation that reflects the twofold grouping that exists in the nation. In the latter case you would divide the States General into two branches: next to the *corporative* States discussed in the previous article you would place an assembly of States with a *political* mandate, elected directly by the people.

Such political States should therefore not be chosen by a class of experts, nor by a group of taxpayers, nor yet by a class of prominent men or by this or that corporation, but by the nation as a unity, the country as a whole, the people itself.

Suffrage for Heads of Families § 141

For a moment the question might arise whether universal suffrage, that is, the right to vote for all adult males, might not be the natural instrument for the nation to express itself. But only for a moment.

For if you stop to think about it you sense immediately that a form of suffrage such as that in France, which gives the vote to some eight million inhabitants and yet denies the vote to twenty-eight million other inhabitants, may call itself "universal" but is anything but.

A system of universal suffrage that begins by excluding all women, that is, a little more than half the community—this already sends an odd message about your "universality." And if you then again shove aside the bigger part of the smaller half that is left, to leave the decision to *a very small quarter*—or actually to the *majority* of men in this small quarter, that is, to just *an eighth*—then, seriously, this highly praised "universal" suffrage becomes so inexplicably exclusive and limited that you can save yourself the trouble of combating it.

No, suffrage can only be truly universal if it is given to heads of households or those who are declared equal to them, that is to say, to the heads, the spokesmen, the natural mouthpieces of those small cells or spheres that make a nation *a nation*. After all, not the lonely brooders in their rented rooms but the people in their family circles nurture the thinking that rules the spirit of a people. A solitary philosopher may order that thinking afterwards; a poet may interpret it in song; a statesman may express it in a constitutional theory—but just as "language is the soul of a people," a language that is not taught to the people by the professor but is overheard by him from the lips of the people, so it is with the political spirit that animates a people.

Unconsciously and imperceptibly, a people as a whole gives shape to that spirit at its hearth and home, and only after this domestic life has delivered the result of that world of thought does the expert's task begin of translating into legal forms what has ripened in the bosom of the nation.

We, too, therefore demand national suffrage, "universal" suffrage, but then placed on the only footing on which it can become truly universal, namely, by assigning it to all heads of households, without restrictions.

§ 142 WITHOUT RESTRICTIONS

The emphasis falls on this last condition.

The restrictions that some add to it, that one must be at least of such and such an age and should be able to read and write, and so on, seem to us to be perfectly superfluous.

If the state deems someone old and wise enough to allow him to marry and rule a household and rear children, then this same state does not have the right at a later stage to deem this same man too young and too unwise to have a voice in determining the spiritual direction in which he desires that the nation should be moving.

As for reading and writing, these skills are certainly priceless (and our antirevolutionary folk—just ask our booksellers—do considerably more reading than the supporters of the liberals), but they offer absolutely no guarantee for nobility of mind and spirit. Literacy in fact has so little to do with the direction of a person's life that we can point to thousands of people who are proficient in reading and writing yet lack all firm spiritual direction, while we are acquainted with many men and women who are bunglers at reading and writing yet who excel at judging whether the way one wants to go is good or bad.

All these additional qualifications, however well meant, originate from the liberal marketplace and can never be binding in our system, for the simple reason that they do not touch the basic premise: the quality of the family head as factor in the formation of the national spirit.

We would, however, want to make an exception for all those who run a disgraceful business such as a bordello or a bar; also, all family heads who have been found guilty of unpaid debts and thus have proved incapable of running a proper household; and finally, all such who have been convicted of a crime by an independent judge.

Weighted Voting §143

To conclude, and to make such a popular election indeed an expression of the life of the nation, one could add, if so desired, that someone who possessed still other qualities, associated with the quality of being a family head, should be given the right to cast more than one vote.

This has a lot to say for it, because that's how things are in civilian life as well. A professor, for example, exerts a much stronger influence on the formation of the national spirit than a wage earner, a factory owner than a workman, a pastor than a bricklayer, a judge than a dockhand.

Thus, if someone, aside from being the head of a household, in addition is a director of a philanthropic organization, a full-time unsalaried caregiver in a poorhouse, a scholar with a university degree, a superintendent of a workhouse, an owner of real estate, a minister of a church, an elder in a congregation, a teacher in a school, or a judge in a court—then it seems to us perfectly legitimate and as it were demanded by our principle that at least these measurable influences should count for something at the polls.

We are well aware that there are still other influences, sometimes very strong ones, that fall outside every rubric and are tied to talent or character. But these cannot be classified and therefore cannot be measured. Those that are definitely measurable, however, may not be left out of account just because others cannot be classified. They ought to be included, provided the system gives priority to moral qualities and does not just favor college and university graduates, as is the tendency in our intellec-tualistic age. Those graduates, after all, include some very lazy and stupid people who have not the slightest moral influence and carry no weight in comparison with men of moral standing who work in charities and serve Christ in our nation.

To the extent, therefore, that someone who in addition to being a family head is also the bearer of one of these measurable qualities, he might be eligible to receive one, two, three, or four extra votes. This would also avert the danger that the most numerous class could outvote the more educated class of society, an evil that we too do not desire.

And if such a directly elected *political* States could then be coordinated with the *corporative* States sketched earlier, such that each were given power in accordance with their makeup, then uniting the two would create a States General that would have roots in the nation itself. It would reflect the way the nation actually exists and would have sufficient moral prestige to inspire the people to trust it and the government to respect it.

IV. ELECTORAL SYSTEM

§ 144   ELECTION OF THE CORPORATIVE STATES

Having now come to the topic of rules for electing the two branches of the States General, we can be brief about the corporative States. Just three comments will do:

(1) Each guild or corporation should set its own election rules. A higher body, however, would have to approve such rules and be able to disallow them if they violate the general provisions for guild elections that are to be established by law and that should aim only to prevent the abridgment of the rights of single individuals or minorities by the majority group in that corporation or guild.

The rule will have to be that all who possess the capacity for which that guild or corporation exists shall be able to vote on a footing of equality. Thus the vote should be given, in a society of scholars, to anyone who has earned a degree or has earned his spurs through recognized publications; similarly, in an association of realtors, to anyone who has a license and is active in the profession; and again, in an order of the nobility, to anyone who can verify his family tree. And so on. Other rules should be that voting is done by secret ballot and that a simple majority is enough to declare a winner. And, finally, it should be a rule that an appeals committee is installed to hear complaints about any irregularities.

(2) Corporations and guilds that are spread over different municipalities, as is conceivable, for example, in the case of shipbuilders along our major rivers, should have the opportunity, according to strict criteria, to exert their influence directly in the Provincial States.

(3) While the elected deputies should vote "without consultation, according to their oath and their conscience," the corporations, councils, or States that they represent should retain the right to revoke their deputy's mandate whenever they deem this expedient.[9] They should also have the right to temporarily replace their deputy with a specialist when special interests need to be defended.

CRITICISM OF THE EXISTING ELECTORAL SYSTEM §145

We need to say more in connection with elections for the political States. The chief aim of this Chamber should be, of course, to mirror as faithfully as possible the spiritual disposition of the nation, its outlook on life and its world of thought, its principle and direction.

That is precisely the reason why in regard to this Chamber it should never happen that the minority is outvoted by the majority other than in this Chamber itself.

For—and this is our insuperable objection to the current election rules—by the way things are arranged at present the majority trumps the minority twice in a row: first in each electoral district, where the votes of the minority are lost; and then in the Chamber itself, when in turn the majority of those elected again sideline the minority.

This should not be allowed. This is manifest injustice.

If in a representative system you allow the majority to outvote the minority twice over, you are simply eliminating the minority. Suppose, for example, that there are three districts with a minority of 9,000 antirevolutionary and 10,000 liberal votes in total, then it is conceivable that in district A, 3,500 liberals wipe out 3,000 of the minority vote, that in district B, 3,600 liberals reduce the remaining 3,000 to zero, and that only in district C, 3,000 antirevolutionaries defeat the 2,900 liberals who share the district with them. Thus already at this stage the ratio of 10:9 is reduced to a ratio of 2:1.

---

9. Kuyper is quoting Art. 82 of the Constitution.

But when that majority has the power in the States to trump the minority a second time, the minority ends up being dropped completely. In two stages, a ratio of 2:0 displaces what was 10:9 in the country.

This scenario, and primarily this scenario, masks the real lie, the cardinal sin, the palpable injustice of every system that makes the minority bow to the majority even before it enters the political Chamber. It is this keenly felt (albeit not always clearly understood) injustice that at present enervates our political life and paralyzes any impact of the middle classes on the governance of the country.

A majority should prevail over a minority once—this cannot be arranged otherwise. But to have one defeat follow upon another, twice in a row, blow upon blow, that is to open the door to domination and tyranny in the very heart of political life, an evil that will come home to roost, once election results are in, by stirring up rancor and disgust.

§ 146   ELECTING THE POLITICAL STATES

Abandoning this system altogether, we would by far prefer a system that gave every group of like-minded voters, in accordance with a fixed criterion laid down in the Constitution, the right and the power to delegate one or more of their people. The method of election would be as follows.

Suppose that the number of votes cast (including the cumulative votes described above) would turn out to be 500,000, then we want to see the Constitution stipulate that every candidate who garnered 5,000 votes would be declared elected. Initially we would then have a States General of at most one hundred members, and in the measure that the population grew and the number of voters expanded, the number of members could then rise proportionately.

Since of the 500,000 voters the turnout would probably never exceed 450,000 voters, the factual outcome would be that those who stayed home would not be represented (which would be perfectly fair), and in the measure that the elections were hotly contested or tame, the States would be composed of seventy, seventy-five, eighty, eighty-five, or ninety members.

This method would work very well, and would be eminently fair.

No one, after all, has a particular interest in knowing in advance whether the States will be composed of eighty or eighty-five members; but everyone does have an interest in sending as many as possible of his own like-minded candidates to parliament. And if there happens to be a portion of the people who do not trouble themselves about the public cause, who do not give it any thought and have no heart for it, then why in the world should the system be required to count these stay-at-home voters among the number required for being declared elected?

In our proposal the Constitution would not contain an annoying stipulation but only lay down a benchmark; and that benchmark, as elastic as life itself, could never stand in the way of the States being an accurate mirror of the life of the nation.

And what would definitely settle the matter: no minority would ever be suppressed. As the population grew there would be no opportunity for party intrigue by means of gerrymandering;[10] and people's interest in elections would never flag because of the certainty that their candidate could never win anyway.

Elections of this kind would have to take place simultaneously throughout the country for a term of, say, five years; and every elected member would have to have the right, in case of forced absence or resignation or death, to personally designate a replacement.

This step might be avoided, for example, by having the voters appoint an alternate at the time of the election, but this seems to us too cumbersome and perfectly redundant to boot.

In the assembly of the political States, after all, it is first of all someone's political creed that counts, hence a person can be either "not my man" or else the person whom I deem best able to name the kindred mind who can take his place as the situation may require.

This procedure would eliminate the need for by-elections and forestall vacant seats during important votes. It would reserve the energy of political involvement for those single great ballot questions that keep the entire nation abuzz for up to three months. It would not ask the nation to speak its mind until it was sufficiently animated for a vital issue by the enthusiasm of the moment.

To make things more convenient for voters, they could at the same time be granted the right (1) to paste a printed ballot on their official ballot, and (2) to write in as many names as they wished, on the understanding that only one name from each ballot would count, in this order that, counting from the top, that name would be removed who had already been chosen by others.

---

10. Kuyper refers to tinkering with district boundaries to give special advantages to the party in power.

Providing these conveniences would make it possible to complete a nationwide election involving 500,000 ballots within twenty-four hours and to compute the result no later than the next morning. The list of candidates of the different groups would be known beforehand and a central bureau, set up in The Hague or, better yet, in Amsterdam, would only need to receive telegrams reporting the figures from each local polling station in order to tally the votes cast and publish the outcome that same evening.

The only objection that might be lodged against it would be that from the 1,200 municipalities combined, some forty or fifty thousand votes could be left over, cast in favor of various candidates who each did receive one, two, three, or four thousand votes but too few to warrant a mandate.

Yet this objection too is only apparent. If groups, expecting to make it, yet in the end failing to get a candidate elected, had simply been allowed to write below the name of their own candidate the party of their second choice should they lose, their total vote would [go to that other party and so would] still count in its full strength.

§ 147   BENEFITS OF THIS SYSTEM

Thus a very simple way of voting would ensure the following benefits.

(1) The rights of minorities would be fully guaranteed. (2) All political intrigue as the population grew, by means of redrawing district boundaries or other unethical combinations, would end. (3) Men would be elected who expressed most purely the principles that the nation wanted to see prevail. (4) All by-elections would be eliminated. (5) The malaise of never being able to have one's candidate elected would no longer drain voters' energy. (6) Elections would take place at a time when people's enthusiasm and inspiration for the exercise were at their peak.

For the sake of completeness we add just one more comment. Our principle demands that parliament, not the government, should be in control of the elections.

If, as we have seen, parliament is not part of the government but stands next to, and if need be, over against it to defend the rights and liberties of the people, then it follows as well that it must be made impossible for the sitting government to influence the elections in any way.

Neither the minister of the interior nor any central bureaucrat should have any say whatsoever in the election process.

Verifying the election results belongs to the elected body. Hearing disputes about possible illegalities falls under the independent courts.

Finally, managing the election process should be the task of a committee from the States or councils. This committee should be appointed annually by lot and maintained even after the session is over, to be discharged only after new States or councils can act legally and proceed to appoint a new committee to oversee elections.

The right of dissolution, finally, should of course fall to the king, both for the corporative States and the political States. In the case of the corporative body, he should have the even more important right to order new elections for the Provincial States and the municipal councils.

We would like to see the king resort to such dissolutions not only—we make no secret of it—when government and States clash, but also whenever the government considers a bill or any other matter in parliament that could on principle be decisive for the nation's future yet was not known to the public at the time the elections for the States were held.

V. INTERIM PROVISIONS

Lowering the Census §148

There remains the question, so long as the Constitution is not revised, what can be done for the time being to mitigate the existing injustice.

The First Chamber has to be left out of consideration, alas. Nothing can be done about it so long as its members are elected by the Provincial States from among the highest taxpayers. The only change that might be made in the composition of this rigid body would have to be realized by changing the way the Provincial States are elected, which could then in the second instance change the face of the First Chamber.

For this reason our Program seeks to recover the political significance as well as the constitutional rights of the minorities by first of all achieving a lowering of the census. [According to Article 139 of the Constitution] the census has to fall between 20 to 160 guilders [a year] in direct taxes. However, it may be lowered, if so desired, to 20 guilders for the whole country.

Nevertheless, we would not recommend the latter option.

A careful reading of the Article in question shows unmistakably that its intention, if not its letter, excludes a uniform census for the entire country.

We would therefore prefer a classification that assigned a census of f20 for all municipalities where the cost of living was "normal"; for the more affluent provinces, in particular Holland, Frisia, and Groningen, that figure could rise to f21, and for municipalities over twenty thousand souls the figure could rise again, according to a fixed criterion, to end in *f*40 for Amsterdam.

There is no reason, however, that on that account the census figure for municipal councils would have to be lowered to *f*10, *f*19, *f*20, and so on. When Article 139 stipulates that the census figure for municipal elections is to be reduced by half, it does not at all refer to the figure quoted in the Electoral Act but rather in Article 76 of the Constitution. And Article 76 stipulates that the census for the Second Chamber and the Provincial States must range between *f*20 and *f*160. The logical conclusion can be no other than this: the census for municipal elections must fall between *f*10 and *f*80. Suppose, therefore, that in a given province the census for local elections of the Second Chamber was *f*20, then the municipal census, as far as the Constitution is concerned, could perfectly well be put at *f*15, or even be left at a figure of *f*20, and still stay strictly within the prescribed limits.

Thus we leave entirely undecided to what extent it would prove proper and wise to also have a proportional reduction of the census for municipal voters. That depends on local conditions and must be judged for each municipality separately. We ask just one thing: that for these elections, too, there actually be a reduction, and a reduction in more than appearance. As Groen van Prinsterer famously declared: "Once placed on the false terrain of individual suffrage, I would not be afraid to bid one guilder lower than Thorbecke."[11] That is our view as well.

§ 149   IMMORAL BUSINESSES

Nevertheless, lowering the census is not the end of our wishes that could already be met. Another three could be added: (1) that the privilege currently granted to immoral businesses be revoked; (2) that men of measurable learning be given a better chance at gaining the vote; and (3) that the division into districts be amended.

---

11. Stated in a speech of December 11, 1849, in a comment on voter qualifications for the direct elections that had recently been introduced by the new Constitution of 1848. Cf. G. Groen van Prinsterer, *Adviezen in de Tweede Kamer der Staten-Generaal, zitting van 1849–1850* [Speeches in the Second Chamber of the States General, session of 1849–50], 2 vols. (Amsterdam: Johannes Müller, 1850–51), 1:42.

(1) The Immoral Businesses

In itself—we concede at once—the sale of alcohol, pure or diluted, is to be judged immoral as little as it might occur to someone to stigmatize a pharmacy for dispensing opium.

But just as an opium den definitely *becomes* immoral because of the abuse to which it owes its existence and which it promotes, so the bars and taverns are certainly to be stigmatized because of the social sin to which they owe their origin and the moral evil for which they afford the opportunity.

No question, therefore, that it is wrong, unseemly, and reprehensible that the more than ten thousand bar owners in our country, who live off people's misery, receive as a bonus the right to participate in governing the country.

The liberal coterie, which has the support of most of these votes, ought to be ashamed of itself for benefitting politically from this social misery. And yet, there is no doubt in our mind that the neutral public school would long ago have been defeated and the liberal party, even under the present suffrage, would not lord it over the country if the bar and tavern licenses were gone. Do not forget, the total liberal vote was never higher than 33,000; at such a low number, a corps of barkeepers, even if you estimate it at no more than 5,000 votes, makes a big difference.

On that ground we therefore demand that the liberals take the moral high ground and assist us in putting an end to the unbearable situation that operating a bar in the Netherlands gives a person, whoever he may be, the right to vote in national elections.

The desired result could be achieved in two ways: Either by converting the tax on licenses into a municipal tax for all businesses and occupations of a fixed address, enabling a reduction in staff by four-fifths (a reduction that would immediately benefit national revenue); or else by having Article 3.f in the Licensing Act, which reads: "with the exception of magicians, street musicians, acrobats, etc.," followed by a clause 3.g, worded as follows: "as well as all who maintain establishments, large or small, for the purpose of preparing or selling distilled beverages containing alcoholic ingredients."[12]

If this were done, separate permits could be issued, as is done elsewhere, for the preparation and sale of these beverages, which would, on

---

12. This clause would effectively deprive bar owners of the right to vote.

condition of payment in advance, yield significantly more revenue than the current Licensing Act and at the same time bear a moral stamp and contribute to the curtailment of this evil.

§ 150   PEOPLE WITH ACADEMIC DEGREES

(2) Educated Persons

It is also not right, in our opinion, that an ironmonger or a ragman has the vote while it has happened that a member of the Council of State fell outside the census. This is intolerable. To mitigate this injustice as much as possible, we would want a law on "the right to bear titles." You may call this a tax on vanity, but in addition to providing welcome revenue for the national coffers it would also give every man of social status, rank, or professional degree the opportunity to become a voter if he so desired. All that would be required is to levy a tax equal to a municipality's census figure in the Electoral Act (reduced, in all fairness, by any additional direct taxes paid into the national treasury).

If such an ad hoc piece of legislation is objectionable, then strike Article 3 in the Licensing Act that exempts lawyers, doctors, and so on, thus forcing them to pay for a license to practice their profession— although the drawback here would be that this duty would also be imposed on those who cannot pay for it or who do not think the privilege is worth it, nor would it give such a person a reduction for other direct taxes paid.

The first expedient would therefore have our preference. But whichever is chosen, we will be satisfied if the goal is achieved of giving the vote to persons of influence by having them fall within the census.

§ 151   DIVISION INTO DISTRICTS

(3) Amending the Division into Districts

We want to see this change not only for the Second Chamber but also for the Provincial States.

Now, one of two things: either one creates very small or else very large districts. But whichever is chosen, the mixed system must be eradicated root and branch. The offensive and irresponsible partisan activity of the liberals is simply scandalous and indefensible. They have made Sneek, for example, into a district with three seats in order to nullify the antirevolutionary strength in the city's south and west ends by votes from the east end. Inversely, they have created a single-seat district of Zevenbergen in order to stop the election of a Catholic candidate.

If single districts are proposed, that would be fine with us as an interim measure, provided they are created everywhere, to the point of adopting the Paris system for Amsterdam, Rotterdam, and The Hague by dividing these cities into smaller precincts.

Or else, if plural districts are proposed, we would say that is even better, provided the single districts are abolished once and for all and a division is made that precludes all party intrigue. Such a scheme would be well served by the brilliant proposal of former minister Heemskerk Azn[13] to turn the present arrondissements into permanent electoral districts, with the proviso that it not follow a contemplated redistribution of judiciary districts and that it grant as many members to each arrondissement as indicated by the population figure divided by 45,000. Then it need only to be laid down that excess votes under 30,000 would not count, while those over 30,000 would count for full. That would cut out all party intrigue and fanaticism for all time and enable us to contemplate growth in our population, at least from this viewpoint, without worry.

Of course we are not forgetting about a change in our tax system, either by converting indirect into direct taxes, or by expanding the latter, or by transferring the same tax to other categories of people. That too would indirectly bring about a considerable change in the number of voters. But unless we are mistaken, it would be a corruption of our economy if a tax reform were misused as the welcome mother of as yet unborn voters. Extending the franchise, after all, should not be the guide or goal when considering the best regulation of our taxation system.[14]

---

13. Jan Heemskerk Azn (1818–97) was a pragmatic statesman of conservative leanings who served as prime minister from 1874 to 1877 and again from 1883 to 1888. The extension Azn stands for "Abrahamszoon" or "son of Abraham," distinguishing him from his cousin Jan Heemskerk Bzn (son of Bysterus Heemskerk) (1811–80), who was a member of the Second Chamber for most of the period 1849–72.

14. A final paragraph was added in later editions: "Fortunately, with the 1887 revision of the Constitution almost all restrictions have been removed. What is stated in the additional articles is not permanently binding. One may safely predict that before long a second, substantial extension of the franchise is coming. May it be thoroughgoing enough that the electoral question will once for all be put to rest!" A bill for sweeping electoral reform was considered in 1894, but it split the Anti-Revolutionary Party into a progressive wing under Kuyper and a conservative wing under Lohman.

CHAPTER THIRTEEN

EDUCATION

It desires that the state (unless compelled by lack of vitality among the citizens) abandon the premise that government is called upon to provide education; that it prevent government schools, if need be, from being misused for propaganda for religious or antireligious ideas; and so extend to all citizens, irrespective of their religious or pedagogical views, equal rights also in the matter of education.

ARTICLE 12

I. THE SCHOOL A COUNTER-CHURCH

§ 152   CHIEF PURPOSE OF SCHOOLS

Antirevolutionaries have explained the schools question so often, in such detail, and from so many angles, that it seems almost superfluous to spend a separate chapter on the topic of education.

Still, it may be profitable to discuss this topic briefly in connection with our principle, apart from all current politics. That is why we decided without hesitation not to omit commenting on Article 12 in our Program.

Let it be stated at the outset, then, that a country's schools must have as their goal to transmit to the next generation the level of education attained thus far and gradually to improve upon it to the extent that this relies on classroom instruction. All schools—tertiary, secondary, and primary schools, military and art academies, music and trade schools—all should further this goal. A school that lacks this goal or ignores it forfeits every right to exist.

This alone shows that the evaluation of schools, on their own or in comparison with others, usually fails to grasp what really matters.

For although we are increasingly being told that the future of the nation depends first and foremost on the public school, that is, on primary education, the future of a people is governed much more by its academies.

Three factors account for this.

(1) The education suited to most of the population can be furthered without classroom instruction if need be, for example, in the home or the shop.

(2) A nation's intellectual superiority comes out chiefly in its more cultured members.

(3) The influence of educated people in a nation as a whole preponderates.

This analysis is confirmed by history. History shows that the flowering of universities always precedes that of primary schools. In our country, for example, the peak of national vigor was reached when primary schooling was still very primitive while our academies shone with inextinguishable brilliance. What is more, in those very days, when the ordinary citizen lived in seemingly less favorable circumstances, the trades and business, commerce and industry flourished more robustly than today.

Exaggerating the Usefulness of the Primary School   § 153

It would seem, therefore, that the value of primary education is overrated. It cannot possibly provide what the spirit of the age demands of it. The primary school is supposed to raise the level of popular education and the level of national vigor. It would put an end, so men prophesied, to the follies, prejudices, and sins of our people. If every child could just receive an "adequate primary education," so people dreamed, every future man or woman would be sounder of mind, quicker of hand, and purer of heart. The blessings of cultural refinement, now limited to a few circles, would flow down to the broad masses. And instead of growing degenerate, debauched and brutish, the masses would move ever higher toward that most desirable ideal!

Bitter disappointment at the outcome has shattered that dream. Shattered it, perhaps not so much among the parrots who don't know the first thing about it and who simply follow the political boasts and toasts. But certainly among those who can think—think and reflect because they are informed.

Toasts nor boasts can hide any longer that the exaggerated praise of the primary school has come to nothing but failure. It is generally recognized, even at this early date, that despite our far too expensive public schools we are failing intellectually, are gradually losing vigor, and are regressing morally.

And although this fact tempts utopians to jump to conclusions and wager that if only the medicine is applied in larger doses for longer periods and if only the schools are given more money—if only education is valued more highly and school days are made even longer—the outcome will be different. But more practical and levelheaded people are beginning to realize that to follow that recipe would ultimately succeed in getting all the young people in school but would give these young people swelled heads while making them clever in facts but bunglers on the job.

§ 154 Yet of Greater Value Than in the Past

Nevertheless we should guard against inferring from this that therefore the primary school is of minor importance.

On the contrary, much of our future depends on its well-being. This is true on its own merits alone. Every child ought to acquire facility at reading, writing, and arithmetic—especially reading. Furthermore, every child ought to be at home in history—what happened in our country and what God did for the salvation of sinners. And finally, every child ought to become accustomed to those forms of morality and discipline that the classroom setting provides better than the nurture at home.

To value this behooves especially the Calvinist, who wants God's Word to be read also by the common people, who wants the history of his church and his country to be known also by the lower classes, and who wants to reinforce the bonds of discipline and orderliness.

Our fathers therefore, in their better days, did not fail to provide for schools, both "public" and "private." And even now, if you look at our concern for schooling and that of our opponents, you will find (provided you focus on the main point and take the available resources into account) that any comparison will beyond any doubt turn out in our favor.

But there are more reasons today why the primary school deserves to be rated higher than under normal circumstances. We would like to point out three of these reasons.

First, the busy lives we lead in our day and age leave almost no time for deeper, lasting impressions. The quiet, contemplative, retentive element is disappearing from our meetings, our conversations, even from our correspondence and private confidences. In its place has come an element of distraction. And in the measure that all impressions come more quickly and are therefore more fleeting, we are forced all the more to use our eyes rather than our ears, because the ear can only catch what is momentarily there whereas the eye has the capacity whenever it wishes to absorb written and printed—hence lasting—impressions.

Second, the education at home and the influence (at least for Protestants) of the church on this education increasingly falls short. The weaving loom has moved from people's living quarters to the mill and thus has moved father out of the house for as long as it is day—during the very hours that the children are up. In more affluent families the nursery is beginning to play the role again that it once had in heathen cultures and still has under Islam. And the apparent need for parents to go out is becoming so common that home education has been reduced by at least half. That, added to the powerlessness and listlessness of the church, refers the child for a far greater portion of its education than formerly to the school.

Third, now that genius appears to have departed from our nation, nothing remains but to copy foreigners if we are not to lag too far behind in the competition among the nations. Thus we cannot do without the school as the most profitable means to help our children make progress in this copying.

Although we maintain that the public school is overrated today, still for now we would be the first to protest any dismantling of this overpriced vehicle. Not, mind you, out of enthusiasm for the fanatical zeal of those who set the tone today, but because the child can do with nothing less, and because home and church for the time being lack the energy to make up for the deficiency.

AREA OF COOPERATION   § 155

Considered in this context, the public school need not at all be a bone of contention in the country. Even Dutch Catholics, although they can rely more on their church, never openly opposed a school of the dimensions we described above. On the contrary, liberals, antirevolutionaries, Catholics, and conservatives will all agree that in the given circumstances (and surely these deserve to be considered first of all) the facilities of classroom instruction that we possess in our primary public schools should be organized and managed on a rather large scale for raising the level of popular enlightenment. Accordingly, if nothing else came into play there would indeed be room, precisely in the area of education more than anywhere else, for a common endeavor to benefit our people and our country.

The goal of such an endeavor, taking into account the available financial and intellectual wherewithal, would have to be to have the public schools function as much as possible in harmony with the other means that are indicated for the education and formation of the child by the nature of things, that is, by divine ordinance. The school should also operate in harmony with the workplace where the child will eventually earn a living or develop its talents. It ought also to work in harmony, finally, with the person of the child itself that as a spiritual being will have to live (to state it for once in very inadequate yet telling figures) at most eighty to ninety years here and at least eighty to ninety centuries elsewhere.

The chief feature, after all, of the primary school—let's not forget—is classroom instruction, which is hardly all there is to education. It is at most a relatively small part of it. Besides and beyond the school, the task of education—the most important part—is assigned to the parents or guardians and to hired caregivers. Another part is the responsibility of the church. Still other parts fall to siblings and friends; to the ways and customs of society; to a nation's history; and in the final analysis, let us especially not forget, to the effectual workings that travel directly to the child's soul from the living God himself.

The school, therefore, is a part of the instrument, not the instrument itself. And it will not be good, and it will not answer its purpose, until in harmony with all these other parts it stops stretching or warping the springs of the child's heart and instead has them working regularly along the lines laid out for the eternal personhood, that is, for the human being in the child.

§ 156   Sectarian School of the Modernists

Meanwhile, we see nothing of that cooperation and of making the school work in harmony with the other parts of nurture and education. On the contrary, everyone is working at cross-purposes and would rather leave each part on its own than consider bringing them into harmony.

People go so far in this that they prefer to cover up the wretched consequences reaped thus far for public decency, alcohol consumption, industry, the trades, commerce, and even our maritime shipping, and to act as if they do not see them, rather than negotiate and compromise with others in order to improve the schools.

This fact shows clearly that behind the schools question something else is at work. The real motive behind the interest in the primary school is not just to educate the people, but to educate them in a specific direction. In promoting the public school, its supporters do not see that school as an end but as a means to an end.

This is the real situation.

The men who went to work after 1789 to remove the Christian stamp from society and change its face completely in keeping with the principles of the Revolution gradually came to the realization that they could not move forward or make any progress so long as people's hearts were not cut loose from the living God who has revealed himself in his Word, that is, in the Bible.

Now then, those hearts are chiefly shaped by the home, the church, and the school.

Accordingly, the revolutionary party successively tried, first to secularize the spirit of the home, then to make the church look irrelevant, and finally to ban the Bible from the school.

But now that it has become more and more apparent that most homes do not yet want to go the way of "emancipation," and that the churches, to stay alive, always go back to being either strictly Roman Catholic or strictly Reformed, the revolutionary party quite naturally has decided to focus all its available forces for combating Christianity on the school and to use six years in the lives of the country's young children[1] for the purpose of erasing those inconvenient ideas from the heart of every child.

And so the public school has become a counter-church.

It is a powerful institution for the purpose of squeezing out of our children the worldview of the Bible and saturating them with the worldview of Pelagius, Rousseau, or whoever. The school where the Bible is banned has become a weapon of defense as well as of offense for the spirit that *resists* God's Word against the spirit that *embraces* that Word.

Hence the panic that seized their hearts when the slogan "The School *with* the Bible" was recently raised again throughout our towns and villages. That slogan captured the whole conflict. It arose from the hearts of

---

1. The primary school encompassed grades 1–6.

the people and reverberated throughout the land like the "sound of many waters."[2]

II. THE MONEY ISSUE

§ 157 REVENUE AND EXPENDITURES

Our first grievance was: "You do not just want to educate the people, but you want to educate them in a specific direction." A second point of complaint that we would add is this: "You want to have it all your way, not through fair competition but through the leverage of money."

The situation is as follows.

There is in the nation a stream of intellectual development, but there is also a stream of financial power; and each has a level gauge.

Normally, the number on the gauge that will be covered by the water should be about the same on both gauges, and should stay that way—on the understanding that if a nation's financial capacity goes down, the expenditures for its schools should also go down; and inversely, if the costs of its schools go up, the money stream should also go up. Thus the levels should move up and down on both gauges, in tandem.

If the levels differ, the natural link between revenue and expenditures has broken down. The course of events becomes abnormal, and a false situation arises that can (and will) be abused with a minimum of skill for a maximum of injustice and party tyranny.

For let us assume for a moment that the little man (we exclude those on relief) is unable to pay school tuition that exceeds 5 guilders per child, that the middle classes can go no higher than 25 guilders, that the more affluent can go up to 100 guilders, while the well-to-do, taken as a class, can go as high as 250 guilders a year for university tuition—then it would follow from this that a primary school of about two hundred children may not cost more than 1,000, a secondary school of about one hundred pupils no more than 2,500, a gymnasium of about fifty pupils no more than 5,000, and an academy or military college of about five hundred students no more than a good 100,000 guilders.

On these assumptions, maintaining an education system would pose no difficulty, and church or private benevolence would need to provide

---

2. See Rev 1:15, the quoted words of which serve as another reference to the People's Petition of 1878.

only for the needy (except in very small municipalities, where a deficit might arise due to a shortage of tuition-paying pupils).

By "the needy" we would have to understand—as we used to in former times—(1) in the case of primary schools, the poor widows and low-paid laborers, for whom schools would have to be set up funded by church deacons or private donors; (2) in the case of secondary schools, the lower middle classes who desire a little more than primary education for their children yet cannot pay more than can skilled laborers; and (3) in the case of the academies, the low-salaried civil servants, pastors, and so on, whose needs could be met by means of bursaries and scholarships.[3]

The deficits that resulted from a shortage of tuition-paying pupils used to be covered by donations from the lord for the small village schools, by subsidies voted by town councils for the Latin schools, and by provincial grants for the low-attendance academies of Deventer, Harderwijk, and Franeker.

Even then, we admit, the question might still arise whether all that extra money provided directly by the governments to the educational institutions did not in fact come down to providing relief for the rich and might not better be left to private endowment. But this issue aside, general relations in our educational system, when so organized, would indeed have to be considered normal, and the economic situation therefore healthy.

DEFICIT   § 158

Such fairly equal levels of revenue and expenditures, however, are nowhere to be seen. The academic standards for our schools have gradually gone up to the same degree as the level of funding has gone down. There is simply no question of a normal relation between the two. Particularly in the last few years the idea that the financial capacity of the parents ought to have at least some relation to the acceptable expenditure for school attendance by the children has quite eroded among the leading voices of our contemporaries.

Hard figures have led to this with irresistible force.

Take the increasing costs of education. They have been forced up so high that to make up for all the expenditures the primary school would have to charge 25, the secondary school 100, the gymnasia 500, and the academies at least 3,000 guilders. Most parents cannot pay those amounts.

---

3. Note that Kuyper assumes at this time that the different levels of education are meant for the different social classes.

If such fees were imposed, the primary schools would see three times one hundred thousand pupils drop out again, the secondary schools would dwindle to half, the gymnasia would be depopulated, and our universities would be reduced to miniature gentlemen's clubs—all the more so, don't forget, since this shrinkage in attendance would automatically bring about a considerable rise in the cost per child and per student and leave Leiden University, for example, only to the sons of millionaires.

There is no question, therefore, that if we want to maintain our educational system we will have to add money, much more money, to all three levels. Without relief, the system, even on the present footing, cannot keep its head above water. It will have to get used to "living on relief" permanently if academic standards are raised once more, this time to the maximum level that brain capacity can bear.

§ 159   State Coercion or Voluntarism

The extra monies needed can be acquired in two ways: by state coercion or voluntary giving. Faced with this choice, our best advice would be: follow the same rule in education that you follow for every other form of relief—private benevolence should have priority and government relief should follow only if duties are neglected or private aid does not suffice.

There are two arguments in favor of this.

First, the money, whether coerced or voluntary, has to come from the people's pocketbook. If the Dutch state, as in America, owned tracts of land that were quite worthless for a time but would rise in value if schools were built on them, then grants of such land to a school would surely be regarded, also by us, as permissible and commendable.

Or if tax revenues were ample enough that after providing for all the normal government expenditures a surplus would be left in the government coffers, then too we would say: "Spend it on the schools first of all."

But as we all know, our nation is not in that enviable position. Just to cover the ordinary expenditures of the state, our citizenry has to open its pocketbooks and hand over money that, if it could stay there, would certainly find other destinations.

So whether you have the tax receiver or the private fund-raiser collect the ten or twelve million that needs to be added to the education budget, it makes no difference in the end. *The people pay for it!*

In the second place, having to pay the receiver has the moral drawback that comes with any coercion. He who gives voluntarily gives out of principle, makes a sacrifice, donates from love; whereas he who is forced to give does not ask why he should, but why he must. He grumbles as he hands it over, and so does not soften his soul but hardens it.

This drawback in turn is avenged on society by blunting initiative, blighting people's energy, and eroding the spirit of liberty.

At the same time, however, we would strain the truth if we fed the notion that if the government were to close the purse strings, those ten or twelve millions would be raised through voluntary contributions.

That is an illusion, at least for the present time.

Now that the Revolution principle has been at work for almost a century to sap the nation's sense of duty and moral energy, a miracle, literally, would have to happen if this people, unaccustomed to standing on its own feet, were suddenly to drop its crutches and rise to the challenge. That is not about to happen.

It does happen among those who belong to a tiny "Gideon's band": trained in voluntary giving thanks to the schools struggle, it has developed a capacity to step up its efforts.[4] But it will not happen among the sluggish masses who, intoxicated and drugged by liberal and conservative fallacies, have lost the strength to rely on their own resources.

If the government were suddenly to withdraw, the result would be that (1) the parochial schools of the Roman Catholics would continue to flourish; (2) the schools of the orthodox Protestants would survive; (3) the schools of the rich would remain what they are; but (4) almost all the young people of the liberals (with the exception of the children of the rich), in the absence of an affordable school, would end up on the streets.[5]

GOVERNMENT SCHOOLS, SUBSIDIES, OR SUBVENTION TO THE PARENTS   § 160

Notice, however, that our analysis offers no excuse for the current behavior of the government. On the contrary, we denounce its behavior unconditionally. And here is why: The government can provide in two different ways for the shortage: making it up to the school or making it up to the parents. The first choice is the practice today; the second is the only ethical choice. The following reason clinches it. When the government subsidizes the expenditures of the school board, the board lowers tuition fees for all parents. This means that this form of public relief benefits not only

---

4. An allusion to the judge Gideon, who led 300 men against Israel's enemies as recounted in Jdg 7–8.
5. School attendance was not made compulsory until 1900.

the needy, who have a right to it, but also the rich, who enjoy large incomes. Every honest person will deem this reprehensible. It evokes deep aversion and cannot be justified under any circumstances.

If on the other hand the government were to supplement the parents' share of tuition, it would yield three relative benefits: (1) The government could contribute a portion, the greater part, or all of the tuition, depending on whether the parents are poor, poorer, or very poor. (2) The parents who could afford the tuition would receive nothing. (3) It would come to light who was willing to sacrifice for their children's education and who was too ashamed to beg, at least for his own child.

A subvention system of this sort, progressively decreasing according to fixed rules and ultimately ending, would help stimulate people's energy, quicken parents' sense of duty, and so cause the only true, voluntary principle to take root so deeply that it would overshadow our entire nation with its shade.[6]

§ 161   UNFAIR COMPETITION

A system with that outcome is exactly what the revolutionaries do not want. At the end of the road they are traveling lies a school that is totally paid for by the state and made available to all without charge. Consequently, they will not hear of any directed subsidies for education and insist instead that public money earmarked for education shall benefit "education taken as a whole."

This policy destroys people's spirit of liberty, their sense of justice and sense of pride, and so surrenders to the coterie that is in power a docile populace with whom one can do as one pleases.

This policy expands the area of *coercion*, that is, of heathendom, and shrinks the area of *love*, that is, of Christianity, and so damages the Christian church (their main target).

This policy automatically leads to the notion that since the government pays almost the whole bill it might as well run the school, and so the school becomes the apple of discord for the politicians.

---

6. *Note by the author in later editions:* Of course it is regrettable that the [1889] Education Act of the Mackay ministry shied away from a subvention system. The cause of this lay in the deplorable condition of our tax system that made it impracticable to have tax assessments determine a classification of parents that would work for the whole country. That is why the Act followed a system of subsidies, though with moderation and in such a way that the dangerous feature of every subsidy system was neutralized as much as was feasible.

And last but not least, this policy smuggles into their hands the thoroughly unjust means to drive the private schools on the road to bankruptcy. They simply raise the academic standards a few notches, drive up the corresponding costs, and do not rest until the private school is defeated.

Every guilder thus spent by the government on primary, secondary, and tertiary schools is therefore a tax levied for the benefit of the intellectualist party at the expense of the nation's moral energy, its sense of justice, and spirit of liberty.

The difference between the revolutionary and the antirevolutionary principle regarding this issue can therefore be summarized in this formula: the antirevolutionary disapproves of every form of state subsidy and demands, if subsidies cannot be avoided, that they always be granted on the basis of Article 195 in the Constitution (on poor relief) and never on the basis of Article 194 (on education).

III. FATHER, CHURCH, TEACHER, AND GOVERNMENT

FATHER AND CHURCH

§ 162

The third question is: Who has the right to control the school? Who is to set it up? Who is to run it? In short: keeping school—whose business is it?

Involved in the school, apart from the pupils (who of course do not count in this context), are the father, the church, the teacher, and the government.

(1) *The father* (or in his absence, the mother, temporary caregiver, or guardian) is charged by God with the task of rearing his child so that it fears God, respects the law, develops its potential, and is prepared for its life's task, initially here below, to be continued hereafter.

(2) *The church* does what the father cannot do. She admits the child into—or recognizes its membership in—a life-sphere that lives *in* the world yet is not *of* this world and is animated by a distinctive spirit all its own.

Through holy baptism the church has brought the child in a mystical way into communion with the living God (not in a generic sense but in the specific sense of "God Triune according to the Scriptures").

To be able and authorized to do this, the church obligates the father by means of very positive, clearly defined promises, made in the presence of witnesses, that he will raise the child, to her satisfaction, in her doctrine, thus in her whole approach to life and the world.[7]

We must certainly concede, to ease the conscience, that such promises are binding only for as long as the father remains a member of that church, hence is absolved of them as soon as he removes the child from the church communion by leaving it himself. But the possibility of a lawful breach of promises only emphasizes that, so long as the father does not withdraw from the church, that church rightfully has a say in the education of the child. She can make sure that such a child is being raised in keeping with the baptismal promises and is being introduced to the mind and spirit of the church.

If it were the case that the Christian church at holy baptism only required the father to promise that the child would be taught, besides ordinary knowledge, also a certain set of formulas, facts, and songs, then the church could surely be left out of the school if the school authorities merely ensured that a certain time be left for this special religious instruction.

But this is not the case. The situation is altogether different, in fact quite the opposite. The promises made at holy baptism entail conditions that bind the *whole* of education in *all* its parts and for its *entire* duration. Accordingly, the father is bound, by law and by honor, to acknowledge the church's part in the education of his child.

§ 163   THE TEACHER

(3) The *teacher* likewise, whether at a primary, secondary, or tertiary school, can lay claim to independent rights in education.

He represents academic scholarship—not just at the universities, where the ore is dug up from the mine, but also at the secondary school, where the raw material is worked up, and even at the primary school,

---

7. Kuyper alludes here to the Reformed liturgical form for the baptism of infants, which asks the parents "Whether you promise and intend to see these children, when come to the years of discretion, (whereof thou are either parent or witness) instructed and brought up in the aforesaid doctrine [contained in the Old and New Testament and taught in this church], or help or cause them to be instructed therein, to the utmost of your power?" See *The Catechism, Articles of Faith, Canons of the Synod of Dordrecht, and Liturgy of the Reformed Dutch Church*, 61, in *The Psalms and Hymns: With the Catechism, Confession of Faith, and Canons, of the Synod of Dort, and Liturgy of the Reformed Protestant Dutch Church in North America* (Philadelphia: Mentz & Rovoudt, 1847).

where pupils are taught how to apply what has been worked up. At all three levels, too, both the method and the content are transmitted.

Since human thought, linked to what has been thought and consciously experienced by earlier generations, creates a separate world that lives according to its own laws and its own principle, it stands to reason that the men of academic learning—in this case the teachers, instructors, and professors—ought to be assured a position in which they will not be used as hired hands but can do their work in accordance with academic standards.

To be sure, such a position does not, as people conceive of it today, give them a permit to entertain any heresy or grant them a license to follow every pedagogical fad.

On the contrary, teachers, instructors, and professors are bound by the task they have accepted. The father asks: are there people who will take my child into their classroom and teach it *in my spirit*? What that spirit is will be defined by him. And as an honest man he will add what the conditions are that he has promised the church to observe.

Informed of this, the teacher, instructor, or professor then has to judge whether or not his professional conscience allows him, and whether his art enables him, to teach *in that spirit*. If he decides that this cannot be, well, then he is free as an academic to continue to work in his profession, but then he does not belong in our schools. If he decides that he can see his way clear, then he will declare as an honest man that he will strictly fulfill that one condition but must also insist for his part that he will not be bound by the father in his professional choice of pedagogical method and curriculum material.

The Government   § 164

Finally (4) the *government* rightfully has a say in education. It has the life of the nation as a whole within its purview and must take care that the nation's intellectual development does not lag behind that of other nations. Furthermore, it has to see to it that the history of the nation continues to remind people of its ethical mission as a nation. Finally, it must intervene, through regulations or in the courts, whenever disputes arise between often conflicting interests between father and child, or between church and academy.

The government is the organ of the legal order and the bearer of national unity. To the extent, therefore, that questions about justice or national interests turn up at any of the three educational levels, it is indisputable in our opinion that the government should have a say in the educational system.

Recall as well that when we discussed the task of government we found that it has to function at times as "emergency aid" and do whatever society leaves undone that cannot be left undone.[8] In that light, the government is permitted, in fact obligated, to intervene under three rubrics: (1) protection of the interests of the nation; (2) upholding the legal order; and (3) substituting for whoever defaults in his task.

Analyzing these three functions more closely, we conclude that the first rubric entails that the government ensures, first of all, that the rising generation is inspired by the heroic spirit of the country's history; secondly, that the population speaks one and the same language throughout the country; thirdly, that the level of people's intellectual development remains sound; fourthly, that civil servants, physicians, and jurists are well trained; and fifthly, that museums and laboratories are furnished with the scientific wherewithal, since they must serve not just one generation or sphere but the whole nation in its successive generations.

The second rubric implies that the government should first of all create some general rules for the organization of education; secondly, that it open up the possibility for the father, the church, and the academy to fulfill their tasks and so preserve among the people the blessings of family life, godliness, and morality as well as sound knowledge; and thirdly, that it establish procedures for settling any disputes that may arise.

The third rubric entails only that the government ought to maintain schools and teachers' colleges as a substitute or emergency measure, hence under the following two conditions: first, that the government as closely as possible fulfill the obligations normally incumbent on the father toward God, his child, and the church; and secondly, that the government do all it can to have the defaulting party resume his proper task as soon as possible.

§ 165   INTERRELATIONSHIPS

If we now try to put the above in an organic relationship and ask how the right and the duty to operate schools should be regulated if each of the four participants (father, church, teacher, and government) is to be

---

8. See above, § 60.

capable of fulfilling its task within its own sphere, then it is obvious that on the main point the decision lies with the *father*.

The father, after all, has authority over the child. The father is responsible for the child. The father is obligated to pay for its nurture and education. And the father has agreed to certain conditions set by the church.

In addition, when you walk you don't just wander, but you always walk *towards* something. Thus to raise a child is to permeate it with a certain spirit, to impress upon it certain ideas, and to inspire it with a sense of duty that will contribute to setting the direction of its life.

Thus, if it is in the nature of the case and the outcome of natural law that every child should be raised, apart from godliness and morality, in the spirit of the father, then it also follows that the father is the only lawful person, called by nature and called to this task, to determine the choice of school for his child.

To this we must hold fast. This is the prime truth in the whole schools issue. If there is any axiom in the area of education, this is it.

Now the father can always, under his personal responsibility, delegate the operation of a school to others. The most natural way is, either that he personally take up contact with a free school after taking due cognizance of the program and the spirit of that school, or, if he does not find what he is looking for, that he consult with other parents to establish a school of their own.

But this does not in any way exclude the possibility that he can also let others do this on his behalf, either because he does not trust his own insight or because he lacks the means or because there are no like-minded others to work together with. The father can delegate this task to a private association, or to the church, or to the local authorities.

We shall not waste any words on private associations. About the church we shall only say that, provided she has not deteriorated, she can quite properly act for the children of the poor, representing the spiritual unity of the parents and the agent of organized charity. But a little more needs to be said about the government.

In municipalities, regions, or countries with a state church that is unopposed and where all parents are working in the same direction as regards basic principles, there would be no objection to having parents delegate the obligation to operate a school to the government as their agent—provided always that the act of delegation remain true delegation, so that if controversy should arise, the father's primordial right would again go into effect.

But now that the spirits in our country are so hopelessly divided that every man is turning against his neighbor rather than working in the same direction, it is conceivable that to have the government operate schools could be done, or might morally be done, at most in one or two villages in Brabant, Limburg, or the Veluwe.[9]

We repeat, now that such a unity of spirit is absent and every conceivable opinion already exists or is on the point of clamoring to be heard, to want to enact in law, *despite loud protests from the parents*, the government's claim to a delegation that never took place and that is said to be irrevocable—that, dear reader, however you look at it, is tantamount to violating a father's sovereignty, willfully breaching promises made to the church, and undermining the independent rights of science and scholarship. As a consequence of this triple transgression it loosens the bonds of godliness and family morals, weakens the parental sense of duty, fans the fire of discord in the bosom of the nation, and destroys the nurture and education of the nation by mocking every concept of unity and harmony.

§ 166   STATE ABSOLUTISM UNDERMINES PRIVATE INITIATIVE

Whether one has the government operate schools as an "emergency measure" or as an "agent of the parents," in either case the system introduced by our Education Acts is as indefensible as it is unjust. For when a government runs schools as an emergency measure it should go home as soon as the parents themselves step forward; and when a government acts as the agent of the parents, it should cut back its involvement at their discretion.

But by doing neither the one nor the other, our government can be regarded in no other way than as an organ of state absolutism that forcefully draws everything to itself and takes everything under its wings. Trampling every other right, it judges nothing sacred except its own show of power and prestige.

---

9. Brabant and Limburg were and still are predominantly Roman Catholic provinces. See above, § 9n8. The Veluwe was a region in the province of Guelders known for its largely orthodox Protestant population. These regions had local pockets where government schools were not necessarily obliged to observe religious neutrality since most if not all parents would approve of instruction according to their religious beliefs during school hours.

The quasi-freedom that it grants to private schools is fraudulent and hypocritical. The public thinks this "freedom" is a corrective to creeping absolutism, yet consider: (1) The authorities do nothing to promote the rise of parental initiative, but instead thwart it in the most spiteful manner.[10] (2) The government, in operating the schools, takes no account whatever of the spirit and intentions of the parents, but on the contrary offends them and tries to ban them. (3) The private school, which in effect leaves the rights of rich parents intact but counts the rights of poor parents as nothing, is an income-based privilege for the class of well-to-do voters.

INTELLECTUALISM THE CORRUPTION OF THE SCHOOL   § 167

Proponents of government schools are often called *intellectualists*.

With what right is obvious. There is a general complaint that throughout our school system *multum* (great) has dissolved into *multa* (many). Quality has been swallowed up by quantity. Familiarity with factoids has replaced genuine knowledge and mature wisdom for life.

That brings us automatically to our last point, namely, the independent right of choice that belongs also to the teachers in our schools, men of academic learning that they are.

The father decides in what *spirit* his child will be educated. The church determines the *principle* by which that spirit can be safely preserved in the school. The government decides the *level* to which our public education shall aspire. But the *manner* in which the child shall be taught in that spirit, according to that principle and up to that level, is at the personal discretion of the teachers, instructors, and professors themselves.

Formally they have to decide this in accordance with the science of pedagogy; *materially* they have to decide this in proportion to the formative power of the various branches of knowledge, the time required for acquainting oneself with their results, and their usefulness for life.

---

10. On the first anniversary of the date when Kappeyne's education bill became law, door-to-door collections were held throughout the country for "Schools with the Bible." The mayor of the town of Gorinchem refused to grant a permit to hold such a collection. When Kuyper complained about this arbitrary act to The Hague, the minister of the interior, Kappeyne himself, citing orders-in-council of 1823 and 1841, ordered the mayor to cease his obstruction. See Kappeyne to Kuyper, August 16, 1879, Kuyper-archief, #1720, Historisch Documentatiecentrum, VU University Amsterdam.

If this rule had been observed, the teaching profession would never have committed the folly of continually adding new ingredients to the mishmash of subjects to be taught and so corrupting education and pupils alike. Almost every teacher complains, and every informed observer admits, that superficial polymaths are steadily increasing among the boys, but among the men "in robes and togas" spinelessness and dullness are rampant. Whatever shoots up too quickly fades quickly if it has no deep roots.

It is altogether just that we hold the supporters of government schools responsible for this intellectualistic corruption of our schools and our youth. In the interest of its cultural agenda the government has given teaching licenses to a lot of young men who lack every aptitude, talent, and calling for the office of teacher. Further, the government's neutrality policy has foisted a straitjacket onto those young men who are cut out for teaching and in so doing has made them unnatural. And by making pupils ever more "intelligent" (that is, know-it-alls)—under the delusion that whoever is intelligent will probably also turn out liberal—the liberal government believes it has created an effective means of propaganda for the triumph of its principles.

The result has been that the teachers without pedagogical talent have created a void in the schools that is now simply being filled by mechanical drill and rote learning. Talented teachers, on the other hand, have tended to concentrate on those subjects that are less restricted by the straitjacket of neutrality. Superintendents, inspectors, members of parliament, and ministers keep raising their demands for expanding the school curriculum. In this way, along a threefold path, as the bitter fruit of a false principle, a cancer has insinuated itself into our educational system that we have branded with the not too strong label of *intellectualism*.

IV. CONTOURS OF A SKETCH

§ 168   GENERAL RULES

From the above four considerations no other conclusion can be drawn than that the entire school system (primary, secondary, and tertiary) as it has been regulated under Article 194 of the Constitution is incompatible with the antirevolutionary principle and that by virtue of that principle a protest must be entered alike against Kappeyne's Primary Education Act,

Thorbecke's Secondary Education Act, and Heemskerk's Higher Education Act.[11]

We are anything but content with these laws. We are opposed to all three, especially the fatal article in the Constitution that, formally useful perhaps, but precisely because of its warped and twisted clauses, has become a license for the systematic corruption of our national education.

Our opposition is directly rooted in this sevenfold conviction:

(1) that the father is responsible for the education of his child;
(2) that the church has a right to see performed what she has been promised;
(3) that pedagogy must be able to make independent decisions;
(4) that nurture and education are inseparable;
(5) that money donated is better than money extorted;
(6) that free initiatives by citizens ennobles a nation, but state meddling debases it; and
(7) that a school that makes it difficult for the mind to submit to God's ordinances and so sets itself against the Christian religion must be deemed a curse and not a blessing for the nation.

And since each of these seven convictions expresses either an incontrovertible fact or a direct consequence of our antirevolutionary principle, therefore the school that offends all seven is for us not just sick, but simply reprehensible.

HIGHER EDUCATION §169

If now at last we are asked what kind of school system in our view would fulfill the claims of God's Word, the well-being of the nation, and the demands of a sound education, then we take the liberty of drawing a brief sketch, albeit perhaps in all too coarse an outline.

For higher education the government should enact only some very general rules. It ought to set the conditions on which schools for this purpose may be erected, furnish excellent libraries, and take no action itself unless private initiative fails or if the number of students, despite private aid, dips too low.

Should the government have to take action, then it ought to do so only for the training of civil servants, doctors, and university instructors, and

---

11. Legislation of 1878, 1863, and 1876, respectively.

for providing bursaries for young men, to be awarded after competitive examinations to the brightest, regardless at what university they enroll.

For the rest, the government should confine itself to making the accreditation of academic degrees for holding public office depend on an official examination, followed if so desired by a probationary period supervised by superiors.

Provinces and municipalities ought to be denied the right to establish a school for higher education. There can be no objection to the city of Amsterdam having a university, but then one rooted in free soil, the fruit of private initiative.[12]

§ 170   SECONDARY EDUCATION

For secondary education, taken in the widest sense (thus including maritime academies, agricultural colleges, normal schools, and so on), the principle should hold that the provincial government occupies the place that the central government has with respect to the universities.

This principle rests on the following two grounds: (1) the requirements for this type of school are quite different in a maritime province than in an inland region, and different again in a border province; (2) secondary education, as it gradually develops, will, as in Switzerland, have to consolidate several small municipalities into one school. Whatever can embrace several municipalities and yet differ from region to region is provincial in nature.

We emphasize this especially because the organization of secondary education (as well as the gymnasia) is the thorniest problem of all, given a population that is spiritually divided.

Separation as a rule for primary education is feasible. Likewise for higher education, since a university assembles young men from the whole country; thus every party in the nation—Calvinist, Catholic, liberal, or Erasmian[13]—can easily maintain its own distinctive university.

In the case of secondary education and the gymnasia, however, that would be utterly impossible.

In Amsterdam and Rotterdam, perhaps in The Hague and Utrecht as well, separate schools might be conceivable. All other towns and villages,

---

12. This article was being written as talks were underway in a small circle of Kuyper's friends and associates about founding a "free" university. The Free University (*Vrije Universiteit*) would open its doors in Amsterdam the following year in 1880.

13. To Kuyper, Erasmianism stands for Christian humanism.

however, could jointly afford at most one school of this type, and then only with difficulty.

On this level, therefore, it will never be possible to follow through on the principle that every party in the land should have its own schools. As a rule, secondary schools will always be mixed schools.

But for that very reason we insist all the more that the provinces themselves regulate this level of education, since that would already make it possible to largely meet this unavoidable difficulty in, for example, the provinces of Brabant, Utrecht, Limburg, and Guelders.[14]

As for diplomas and other general rules, an arrangement like the above would have to accord with a law to be introduced by the central government, and for the rest would have to leave it to the initiative of private citizens or municipalities to determine the content of the adopted framework.

Only if such initiatives were lacking should the provinces be allowed to take action.

Scholarships and bursaries, to the extent that private charity fell short, could be awarded to the best graduates after competitive examinations. The entire costs of the secondary schools, thanks to such scholarships and bursaries, could be apportioned over those parents whose children benefit from these schools.

PRIMARY EDUCATION   § 171

Finally, as concerns primary education, we would like to see its organization left entirely to the municipalities, under compliance with state and provincial laws, provided both state and provincial laws offer guarantees against the corruption of education as well as the violation of minority rights.

The principle to be adopted for this level would be that the operation of private schools funded by the parents should be left to teachers or to charitable school associations, while operating a school by the municipal authorities should enter the picture only if a given number of parents, being unable to establish a school themselves, were left without an educational institution for their children.

Furthermore, the financial needs of the lower middle class, the working class, and the poor could be met by financial assistance from private charity, by schools operated by the church's diaconate, or if financial aid

---

14. See above, § 165n9.

were even then still needed, by supplementary aid from the municipal coffers upon proof of enrollment of the children at a school of the parents' choice.

The teachers at all these schools, provided they had equal accreditation, would have to be treated by the government on a completely equal footing.

To these general ideas, three remarks may be added:

(1) No education[15] should take place in government schools that went beyond order and discipline, love of truth and sense of justice, hard work and cleanliness—and to complement this very incomplete offering, every child should have at least one whole free day a week; in such a way, however, that parents, if they agreed among each other, could demand a form of religious instruction for their children approved by their church.

(2) The inspection of institutions of higher education should emanate from the central government, that of secondary education from the province, and that of primary schools from the municipality, on the understanding that the central and provincial governments could at any time appoint a special commission to inspect any school under their respective jurisdiction on the point of compliance with the law.

(3) The common courts should have the right to hear all disputes that might arise between stakeholders, of whatever title, involving existing laws, statutes, or bylaws.

If this is more or less the system that we ought to pursue, then it follows at once that the stance to be taken for the time being can scarcely be restricted any further than within these two guidelines: "Build your own schools, as many as you can, including a university!" and also: "Resist the agitation of your adversaries with all lawful means!"

What those means ought to be cannot be spelled out in a permanent program or a fixed formula. That will depend each time on the situation facing us and will have to be devised each time with tact and prudence—provided, let this be highlighted, such temporary maneuvering (which will increasingly become less significant anyway) never cause us to lose sight of the great end goal of the struggle, namely, "the triumph of the voluntary principle and thereby the recovery of the public school of baptized children for Christ our Lord!"

---

15. That is to say, no education other than instruction in the normal school subjects.

CHAPTER FOURTEEN

THE JUSTICE SYSTEM

[It desires from the sovereign that by means of an independent judiciary, acces-
sible to all and in keeping with the moral sense of justice in the nation and in
accordance with laws founded on the eternal principles of justice, first, that it
decide all disputes between parties, both of civil and administrative law; second,
that it pronounce sentence against anyone who offends against the public order;
and third, that it execute punishment on the convicted, not just to protect society
or to improve the offender, but in the first place to restore violated justice, if need
be by the death penalty which government in principle has the right to impose.]

ARTICLE 13

I. JUDICIAL CONSTRUCTION

UPHOLDING JUSTICE   § 172

The highest and most sacred attribute of the sovereign is that he upholds justice.

The fact that justice in any given case is the judgment that God himself,
if he were to speak, would pass in regard to a case in point, implies that he
who maintains justice acts on God's behalf.

Even then, it is God himself who upholds justice. He does so in three
respects without involving people and in just one respect through the

intermediary of people. The Almighty upholds justice in people's conscience, through trials and tribulations, and at the last judgment.

In people's *conscience*. God does not allow offenders peace of mind. Moreover, he will cause public opinion, both of contemporaries and of posterity, to testify against everything that offended his inviolable right.

Through *trials and tribulations*. As for individuals, they will reap the bitter fruit that injustice usually bears for the unjust. Also, God will visit adversity, plagues, and illness upon them. As for families, whole regions, and nations, they will experience a decline in prosperity, or destruction brought on by the forces of nature and the virus of pestilence.

At the last *judgment*. God has appointed a day when all nations and peoples will appear before his judgment seat, and he will repay everyone according to what he has done in the body, whether it be good, or whether it be evil.[1]

A fourth respect in which justice is upheld is not immediate. Here divine authority is mediated through people—through people who are each invested with supreme power in their respective life-sphere. In this sense justice is upheld on earth, relatively by the father in his family, temporarily by the captain on his ship, and absolutely by the king or whoever else is the sovereign in the land.

No one should think, therefore, that the sovereign can uphold justice in the strict sense of the word. He cannot do so as to content, and the very scope forbids it.

As to scope, the sovereign has to respect, for example, the father as the one who upholds justice in the domain of the family. He must keep his hands off people's conscience, which God himself watches over. And he cannot intervene in more personal settings where people may be victims of greed, pride, and so on.

As to content, the sovereign lacks the means to always know exactly what would be just. Nor can he always have the courts determine beyond a shadow of a doubt that the accused is guilty or innocent. He cannot guarantee the timely discovery of the guilty if he is hiding somewhere. Nor can he assure the injured parties of full redress of the wrong done to them.

---

1. See Eccl 12:14.

THE SOVEREIGN §173

Three demands are made on the sovereign to uphold justice in this more restricted sense. First, he is to make just rules and have them recorded in written laws. Second, he is to determine in any given case whether and to what extent the written law has been transgressed. Third, he is to repel the transgression and so "reward the just and punish the unjust." To say it more concretely: (1) there has to be a law that prescribes in what cases someone must be imprisoned; (2) there has to be a judge who decides whether someone falls under such a case; (3) there has to be an armed officer who can conduct the convicted person to prison and keep him there.

Differentiating between these three conditions is indispensable for acquiring a proper view of the judiciary. One would be incorrect, however, to conclude from this that such legislative, judiciary, or executive institutions constitute a power *next to* the sovereign. On the contrary, the law is promulgated in the name of the king, justice is pronounced in the name of the king, and the guilty is imprisoned or executed in the name of the king.[2]

In miniature states like Monaco, San Marino, and Andorra, it is in fact conceivable that he who holds the supreme power personally records a law, hears a case, and passes judgment on a transgressor, and himself puts the shackles on one convicted. Especially aboard a ship and in the family circle this scenario is far from unusual.

Since it is impossible, however, for a sovereign to be personally present in each and every case, given the multitude of his subjects and the vastness of his realm, he "multiplies himself" by powers that indeed replace him, but never take his place in any other sense than that the sovereign is deemed to act *through them* and that they therefore *speak in his name*.

Thus the sovereign uses councilors, scholars, and civil servants for drafting and promulgating laws; he uses justices and jurists for administering justice; and he uses the police, the national guard, the militia, and the military (or else the prison warden and the executioner) for dealing with those convicted. Yet this never leads to a division of sovereignty into separate and independent powers. In all these functions the sovereign is the one who is and remains ultimately accountable to God.

---

2. Or in Britain, the Crown; and in the United States of America, the People or the State.

§ 174   Judicial Construction

Being accountable to God, the sovereign obviously is not a "free man" when making laws and administering justice. He is not free to stamp as law what amounts to an arbitrary choice, nor is he free to declare any of his subjects guilty before the law according to his whim and fancy.

The sovereign is not to please his will but to uphold justice. He does not have to invent law or establish right, because law and right were there before he started. It exists even now *outside* of him. It is so little subject to him that the sovereign himself is under the law—unconditionally.

Hence the beautiful expression, still heard today, that the first task of the sovereign is to *find* the law. It is there, but it is hidden. He has to search for it, and keep on searching until he has found it. He has to search for it in the divine ordinances of the Word, in people's sense of justice, morals, and customs, in the legislation of other nations, and in the findings of the science of law.[3]

That is also why the law codes that are to indicate what shall be called right and just in the land must not be promulgated until after seeking the advice of jurists, consulting the nation, and testing them against the eternal principles of justice.

Ministry staff or ad hoc committees ought to be appointed for gaining the advice of legal scholars. For consulting the nation we have the States General, whose importance we won't repeat here. But a brief word is in order about testing laws against the eternal principles of justice.

§ 175   According to Eternal Principles

We think we are assured of unanimous agreement when we place in the foreground the thesis that a law that, say, declares theft to be lawful is an unjust law; that is, a law that is far from helping to uphold justice is a most dangerous violation of justice.

Nevertheless, such a law is far from inconceivable.

We are told that some non-Christian nations in the past had laws that looked very much like licenses to steal. And what speaks louder: the main article in the sociopolitical program of the Communards of Paris and the social democrats of Berlin is the slogan: "Property is theft, so to punish theft is unlawful!"

---

3. The point is more readily made in Dutch, where the equivalent of "judicial construction" is *rechtsvinding* (the finding of law or right).

We cannot escape the question: Why are property owners right and social democrats wrong? How do we know for sure that we are not the dupes of a colossal illusion but instead are letting right be right when our laws offer protection of private property and threaten thieves with sanctions? Who decides? And on what grounds?

Surely not the majority. Suppose the social democrats in Saxony could push ahead and by majority vote expunge punishment for theft from their law books. This would not be to uphold justice but to violate it.

Where principles are involved, right is right, or it is not. And if it is right and just, then so it remains, anywhere on earth. If a majority of votes decides, then what is called just in one region may be branded unjust elsewhere. All certainty about justice would be lost.

But on what basis, then, do we want to found justice?

On people's sense of justice? But even that fails, because the Communard replies: "My sense is exactly the opposite!" And the social democrat disagrees flatly with renowned jurists like Rudolf von Gneist and Eduard Lasker.[4]

Is justice then to be based on the science of law? Since when does science invent its own object of study? And was Karl Marx, the leader of the International,[5] ignorant of the science of law?

However you look at it, you cannot find in any of these three instances the immutable and unshakable basis of justice. And why not? Because absolute justice must be in conformity with the *will of God*, whereas none of the three sources of law can interpret God's will for you.

Not people's sense of justice, for though it is still operative it is impure, because people are sinful. Nor the majority, since it changes and can turn into its opposite, a fact that militates against all concept of justice. Nor yet science, since it can indeed draw logical conclusions from given principles, but legal scholarship is anything but clear about the principles of justice.

For this reason we deliberately referred in chapter 3 to the "ordinances of God" and tried to show that sinful people can have firm and incontestable certainty about the eternal, unchangeable principles of justice only by means of *special revelation*.

---

4. Heinrich Rudolf Hermann Friedrich von Gneist (1816–95) was a prominent German jurist, politician, and scholar of constitutional law and history. Eduard Lasker (1829–84) was a leading German liberal politician, civil servant, and jurist.

5. Karl Marx (1818–83) was the leader of the First (Communist) International, also known as the International Workingman's Association.

If it is true, as we firmly believe, that on Mount Sinai the Almighty himself condemned murder, theft, adultery, and perjury as decidedly unrighteous acts, and furthermore that through his prophets God pronounced his divine verdict on all the great questions of justice, then I possess in this source, and in this source alone, a sure communication of God's will, and therefore also (since his will is identical with it) of justice itself.

Granted, this certainly does not enable us to be sure in every given case. It is not permitted us, even with that revelation in hand, to claim that the laws we make are simply identical with justice.

But there is a world of difference between the uncertainty that thus remains and the utter uncertainty that leaves one groping otherwise.

On our standpoint, one at least has a series of fixed points that indicate quite clearly the direction in which the various guidelines for justice are to be drawn. There is a whole series of distortions and miscarriages of justice that one can reject with full certainty as *unjust*. And what should clinch the matter for us: repelling the vagaries of conventional laws and resorting to the universally accessible principles of justice for testing what is just and unjust are the only means that nurture, in the conscience of ruler and subjects alike, that deep awe for justice that upholds its majesty before which all creatures must bow.

II. JURISPRUDENCE

§ 176   INDEPENDENT JURISPRUDENCE

After judicial construction comes jurisprudence, that is, the obligation of the sovereign to settle disputes in the courts and convict the transgressor of the public order in accordance with established laws.

All parties agree that jurisprudence should be independent, and the antirevolutionary too does not hesitate for one moment to subscribe to this demand—though on different grounds.

Usually men speak of the judicial power with almost the same intent with which they curtail the sovereign's legislative power in order to place the larger and more important part of it with the States General.

Against this we protest.

To be sure, the judiciary is the organ through which the sovereign works, but it is not an independent power next to him. "Independence" here means only that the judiciary ought to be so organized that it truly serves justice and precludes all possibility of ever becoming a tool of tyranny or injustice.

Its task is to determine whether any violation of justice has occurred and of what nature it is. No more; no less. Just as your eye, the organ that helps you see what is there and what is not there, functions entirely independently of your will, that is to say, transfers the images of things onto your retina according to the laws of optics, so too must the judicial eye, by which the sovereign is to see whether there is guilt or not, function according to the strict laws of *justitia*. Completely free of sovereign whims, it must convince the sovereign of guilt or innocence and of a punishment that fits the crime.

All of us, including the sovereign, must accord the same independence to anyone who is to serve us as an organ for our own sphere of life. Thus a father can hire a mathematics tutor for his child, but he cannot force him to teach anything other than that two times five equals ten. The father hires, sets the hours, and the salary, but the rules of mathematics are beyond his will. On that score, not the father but the tutor—better: mathematics itself—is independent, absolutely independent. Similarly, government can appoint, say, a professor of logic, but only on condition that such a "master of rhetoric" shall be free and independent in teaching the unchangeable axioms and laws of thought. Or, to give one more example, a king can have an observatory built and telescopes installed, but only on condition that he leave the astronomers free to let the heavenly bodies move, not as he would like, but as they do in fact.

In the same way, a country's sovereign can appoint judges who on his behalf in any given case will decide "whether there is guilt and how grave it is," but only on condition that he allow these judges to judge in complete freedom, in order that justice is served in accordance with the laws of justice. Never should the God-given "rules for guilt or innocence" be exposed, against one's better knowledge, to the danger of being violated for the sake of pleasing the sovereign.

Guarantees for Independence   § 177

Accordingly, the courts are not independent in the sense that they can do what they like and operate apart from the sovereign. On the contrary, it is the sovereign who installs them, the sovereign who tells them how to conduct trials, the sovereign who allows their verdicts to be appealed, and the sovereign, finally, who can apply amnesty or pardon, or both in combination, to stop their sentences from being carried out.

Thus the independence of judges comes down to this, that once they are installed they need concern themselves only with the laws and simply judge cases as honest men according to the dictates of their conscience, without asking for the sovereign's preference, whim, or fancy. It is an independence that to a certain extent is enjoyed by every servant of the country who is employed for a specific purpose and with specific instructions, and who needs only to adhere strictly to these conditions of employment to do his job. After all, the sovereign as legislator retains the right to alter the laws, including the law governing the judiciary, after which judges are obligated to conduct themselves according to the requirements of the newly created situation.

The only thing to keep in mind, however, is that the sovereign himself can become party to a dispute, be it through political misdemeanors or through acts against the state. For this reason the courts, to remain free and to inspire respect, must have more guarantees than other bodies in order to guard the sacred honor of the judiciary against possible violation by the authorities. That is why it is customary to establish that at the higher levels of judicial power a judge cannot be deposed and that the courts themselves can make nominations for the filling of vacancies. These two guarantees we deem rather too weak than too strong, and their partial cancellation in Van Lynden van Sandenburg's act for the reorganization of the judiciary[6] is to be considered one of the most deplorable phenomena to affect our political life since 1848.

This curtailment of judicial independence is all the more intolerable for an antirevolutionary since, in Stahl's choice remark, "the transfer of judgment by the Father on the Son of Man" is for every Christian the fundamental consecration of the holy ordinance that it must be a different hand that writes down "guilty" and a different hand that punishes the guilty.[7]

§ 178   ACCESSIBLE TO ALL

The question how the judiciary ought to be organized and what guidelines it ought to follow touches the antirevolutionary principle only very

---

6. Theodoor Baron van Lynden van Sandenburg (1826–85), a politician who passed for a "conservative antirevolutionary," was minister of justice from 1874 to 1877.

7. Friedrich Julius Stahl (1802–61) was a German jurist, politician, and political philosopher whose work was particularly influential on the antirevolutionary thought of Groen van Prinsterer.

indirectly and can therefore be passed over in this series of popular articles. Let me just repeat briefly what was discussed at length in the chapter on decentralization: the organization of the judiciary should coincide with the provincial boundaries. I now add, with the Program, that the justice system should be *accessible to all*.

At present this is often not the case because the proceedings are either too costly or too complicated. As things are, a citizen of meager income shrinks back from the court system. He would rather swallow the injustice than venture into that mysterious maze that everyone knows how to enter but no one knows how to exit. To start litigation is a scary thing for the average person.

To be sure, solicitors and attorneys are available to help the average person find his way; but such a one looks upon these fancy gentlemen as clever fellows, the kind you have to watch out for, rather than as fatherly protectors of his rights. Moreover, there are lawyers and lawyers, and the best ones usually charge the highest fees. The effect is that a person from the lower classes involved in a lawsuit with someone from a higher class, almost always, despite the unimpeachable honesty of the judges, is fighting a duel with highly unequal weapons.

This faulty system harbors a double evil to which every antirevolutionary ought to be fundamentally opposed. First, certain people and their partners, lured by those expensive and complicated legal proceedings, all too often milk the system and step by step make use of the common citizen's predicament to contest his rightful demands. Second, nothing wipes out respect for authority and calls up resentment in a person so much as pent-up anger about an injustice done to him that he dare not bring an action against from fear of worse damages.

THE NATION'S SENSE OF JUSTICE § 179

That brings us to the third demand mentioned in the Program: that justice be administered in keeping with the moral sense of justice in the nation. This alludes to the contrast between "scientific knowledge" and "practical sense," in two ways.

What develops from practical sense, if trained and sanctified, is what Scripture calls *chokmah*, a kind of wisdom that has clear insight into things and intuitively grasps the nettle of relationships and sets right what is unjust in them.

Unforgettable examples of pronouncing justice that is rooted in *chokmah* are Nathan's condemnation of David and the judgment of Solomon. And although we must concede that the nature of Easterners lends itself better for that kind of intuition than the Western character, this hardly decides the question whether this practical wisdom is not often superior to legal studies for weighing evidence and establishing guilt.

Its fourfold advantage is that it combines insight and conscience in a single grasp, is able to make adjustments to fit persons and occasions, always remains connected to ordinary life, and decides a matter then and there.

Moreover, one should not forget that this sort of justice is still meted out in family life, has an official voice in Britain, practically dominates American jurisprudence, and has its spokesmen in *alcaldes*.[8] It once obtained in our own country as well, and it is still loosely used in judging petty cases in our police courts.

Accordingly, we fail to see why this precious element of ripened wisdom cannot in part be revived in our judicial system. Every municipality (or in larger cities, every urban precinct) could appoint a distinguished, respected and wise person from among the people who could sit on fixed days and hear petty cases on the spot; and he could, if both parties agreed to it, render "quick justice" even in the more important cases.

At present, countless small cases—trifling affairs to most people, but sometimes critical and with fatal outcomes in the neighborhoods and alleys where they arise—remain unresolved or are settled with the fist. And what is worse, in the bosom of families— between husband and wife, parents and children, a mistress and her maids—such unresolved disputes often remain a wellspring of anger and bitterness that otherwise would have stopped flowing without delay.

An additional benefit would be that the "little man," who is afraid of complicated proceedings and who cannot afford expensive litigation, would have a very simple and inexpensive way of getting his mind off the hurt in his heart.

---

8. An *alcalde* was a judge in late medieval Spain, elected for a limited term by members of the town council. By extension, the title came to refer to a variety of "citizen" judges.

JURY §180

The above would not, however, give full satisfaction to the moral sense of justice. Jurisprudence in the courts will not come into direct contact with the life of the nation until our ancient *schepenen* or *gezworenen*,[9] mostly called by the brief title of *jury*, were somehow picked up again.

In no way are we suggesting that on the basis of so-called popular sovereignty, jurisprudence should be in the hands of the people themselves; even less, that a jury should have the right, as a political instrument against established authority, to acquit a political felon; nor yet, that a jury system should replace the order of learned jurists that our nation enjoys today.

Our real objectives are: (1) that the citizenry itself participate in the battle between justice and injustice, to stimulate its sense of justice; (2) that learned jurisprudence be constantly brought into contact with the nation's instinct for justice; (3) furthermore, that the possibility be created for paying greater attention to the moral factor of *intent*; (4) as well, that treatment of widely different persons in the selfsame way be prevented, lest *summum jus* turn into *summa injuria*;[10] (5) and finally, that in weighing guilt or innocence the altogether realistic standard of public opinion be taken into consideration.

To work this out falls outside the scope of these articles. Yet the following facts are recommended for consideration. (1) Germanic law among all nations insisted that the subjects participate in the judiciary. (2) Roman law and canon law is chiefly responsible for ousting this lay element from the legal system. (3) The lay element was honored again particularly in Reformed countries, in line with their Presbyterian leanings in the ecclesiastical domain. (4) Almost everywhere juries are used, notably in Britain, Germany, France, and Russia, not to mention many smaller countries. (5) Eminent jurists such as Gneist, far from wishing to reduce the rights of juries, recommend extending them from criminal to civil cases.

This does not mean that we deem the introduction of a jury system indispensable for the Netherlands. We definitely reject a jury for political crimes, and a political construct such as the French jury would never appeal to us. In fact, we would initially be quite satisfied if the element of

---

9. The terms *schepenen* and *gezworenen* refer respectively to urban aldermen and common burghers placed under oath who were involved in criminal law proceedings during the old Dutch Republic.

10. This Latin phrase means the height of law is the height of wrong, or a literal and inflexible interpretation of the law can produce the greatest injustice.

our old *schepenen*—that is, of local, nonprofessional jurisprudence—were but allowed to revive and that at least some counterweight were offered to the exclusive jurisprudence by men of abstract science.

As things are, lay influence is confined to nominations by the Second Chamber for justices of the Supreme Court, and a vestige of *pares a paribus*[11] remains in the special immunity enjoyed, for example, by ministers of the Crown and members of parliament. Although we appreciate these small privileges, in no way do they satisfy the nation's conscience, especially not given the well-deserved unpopularity of our States General and the falsification of its composition by Constitution and census suffrage. Thus these privileges have no conscious link whatever with the nation's sense of justice.

This particular link must simply be emphasized by every person in possession of Christian-historical sense. He knows from the sacred history of Scripture and the profane history of his country that this critical link is sacrosanct. And what is more, he cannot overlook the divine intention in the apostles' prophecy that not Christ alone will judge the world, but the children of the resurrection will judge along with him![12]

III. SPECIAL LAW, ADMINISTRATIVE LAW, AND CRIMINAL LAW

§ 181   Special Jurisprudence

Our all too brief scope does not allow us to treat of special jurisprudence other than in passing. It is well known that special jurisprudence exists on merchant ships and ships of war, in the army, and in part also in consulates abroad. Special courts are also being proposed for trade and labor disputes in our country, and they have already been introduced in other countries. We can therefore confine ourselves to touching lightly on two points: (1) it is desirable to have a legal method for composing an *honor tribunal*; (2) it is imperative to improve the definition of *church law*.

Duels fortunately are no longer indigenous and only very seldom do we hear of duels with sabers or pistols in our garrisons and university towns. Yet we all know that estrangement, injury to reputations, and flaming rows between seemingly peaceable citizens occur quite frequently. Since these personal quarrels are no longer thrashed out and seldom resolved,

11. The term *pares a paribus* refers to peer judgment, or the right to trial by one's equals.
12. See 1 Cor 6:2–3; Rev 3:21; 20:4.

and since they even less often die out, the woeful result is that in every town and village a heap of anger and bitterness, of hatred and resentment, all too often poisons social life and even infects the next generation. In France and Italy, duels keep resentment from lingering and in most cases promote the quick restoration of good relations, sometimes of even more intimate relations. This gives us the right to ask in all seriousness: why can't an honor tribunal not have the same happy effect here as duels elsewhere? If an offended party had the right, under the law and under certain conditions, to demand an honor tribunal, and if a permanent organization guaranteed the soundness of its verdicts, there would an opportunity and a prospect, once a feud arose, to dispel it without delay and so prevent parties from brooding on revenge.

As for *church law*, unless we are mistaken the right of the church to her own law and her own courts should be recognized by the government much more explicitly than is the case thus far. Every church, on the other hand, should then offer guarantees (and the state should ensure the continued enforcement of such guarantees) that no one who has come to the years of discretion can be compelled to remain a member of a church for even one moment longer than he cares to.

CIVIL PROCEEDINGS   § 182

Coming back to ordinary jurisprudence, we ought to deal separately with civil law and criminal law. The distinction, though not identical to the distinction between private and public law, is nevertheless closely connected to it.

Private law for the most part regulates the rights and duties pertaining only to individuals or private corporations, whereas public law refers to the rights and obligations of legal authorities *vis-à-vis* those who fall under their authority, and vice versa. Still, one must not assume that the boundary between the two can be drawn with any precision. The boundary fluctuates. A legal authority, even "the State of the Netherlands," can acquire property on the basis of private law; inversely, the last will and testament of the lowest commoner can be of a public-legal nature. To compound the confusion, crimes like fraud, deception, swindling, and so much more can involve, on the one hand, the private right of an individual citizen, and on the other, the public right for which the authorities are responsible. Thus we ought not allow ourselves to be daunted so speedily by the glib appeal to the distinction between private and public law that lawyers are quick to trot out (as they did recently in the schools question). No distinction is less open to a uniform interpretation and is therefore less decisive and less capable in thorny cases of determining the difference in law between what is private and what is public.

On that account we strongly support the far-reaching notion in our Program to also transfer a portion of administrative law to the ordinary civil courts. In the chapter on decentralization we already suggested how important it would be to reform our administrative law on this point. Unless we are mistaken only a short exposition will be required here to bring to light the eminently antirevolutionary character of this notion.

If the liberals are right in proceeding from the false premise that the state represents the *plenitude* of power—which accounts for their view that a province, a municipality, a church, and a family have only as much power as the state hands over to them as a conditional grant—then of course it is entirely appropriate that the state itself controls these subordinate spheres and coerces them to interpret the law in such a way as to always please the sovereign. When all is said and done, administrative law deals only with disputes between municipalities and municipalities, provinces and provinces; but none of these bodies can ever obtain their rights over against the state.

If on the other hand we antirevolutionaries are right in proceeding from the belief that the family, the church, the municipality, and the province are spheres of life that exist by the grace of God and function in their own right and which therefore have all the power and all the rights that have not been reserved for the sovereign in the interest of state unity and for the sake of supreme authority—then of course it is utterly absurd that a type of administrative law obtains in which the state is at one and the same time party and judge. The most elementary concept of justice demands that every family, but also every municipality, every province, and every church, should be able to appeal to an independent judge, at least as regards the application of the law, against abuse of power by the higher or the highest authorities.

It is nevertheless quite conceivable that administrative law as a rule could continue on its normal course if this idea were realized. After all, to uphold justice does not in any way require that the ordinary judge decide each and every case of this type, only that when a plaintiff just cannot get justice, the possibility should be there to break through the administrative fences and appeal to an independent court.

Whether the attempt will be successful, as our Constitution would like, to regulate administrative law on a footing of autonomy to such a degree that the ordinary civil judge can stay out of all lawsuits, remains to be seen; but we doubt it very much.

CRIMINAL PROCEEDINGS   § 183

As for criminal proceedings, finally, brevity constrains us again to stay strictly within the limits of the Program and to discuss only those two points that are directly related to the antirevolutionary principle, namely, the *purpose* of punishment in general, and retention of the *death penalty*.

The purpose of punishment has to be, first and foremost also according to us, to strengthen justice or, if you will, to avenge violated justice.

God's justice, insofar as it can come to expression in the country's laws, must be honored unconditionally. No one should dare to violate it, and whoever does violate it may not be spared but must resolutely be seized by the avenging arm of justice. The obligation to do so rests on the sovereign. He is to hunt down the criminal with all the means at his disposal, cause him to be sentenced, and have him undergo the pain that the law requires for upholding the honor of justice.

The sovereign needs to take care of only two things: (1) that he punish only the truly guilty; and (2) that he weigh the punishment in proportion to the crime committed. And since in his zeal for justice he may perhaps push too hard and make mistakes, a bulwark for innocence is thrown up in the independence of the judiciary, which makes it virtually impossible for the sovereign to sentence any others than the guilty or to sentence the guilty in any other way than in accordance with the law.

By means of the public prosecutor the sovereign can therefore accuse freely, present the case in the severest terms, and demand the maximum penalty, without imperiling innocence. His first organ, the public prosecutor, guards the rights of justice; his second organ, the independent judge, guards the equally sacred rights of innocence. And only after an honest trial has convicted the transgressor does his third organ come into play, the strong arm, to carry out the sentence and impose the punishment.

In no way would we deny that this whole procedure at the same time protects society. But it should be borne in mind that what protects society is justice, not the police; and what the sovereign is to protect is not society, but justice.

The result of a conviction seldom leads to improvement of the criminal. In fact it may well happen that justice demands a penalty that makes the transgressor worse rather than better, as is almost always the outcome in case of lengthy prison sentences. But this should not deter the sovereign. He is not a pedagogue, but a judge. Although he should not deny freedom to churches or private societies to work for the rehabilitation of the criminal, the sovereign himself must first of all be mindful of punishment, discipline, retribution, and make the prisoner understand that he has brought this miserable existence upon himself through his own guilt and sin.

§ 184   THE DEATH PENALTY

The above argument alone vitiates the only compelling argument against the death penalty. For if the sovereign is to be mindful, not of bettering the criminal but only of carrying out punishment in the interest of upholding justice, then the state of the convict's soul can never be an impediment to having him executed. The only question that remains is this: does government *as such* have the right to take someone's life?

That question, we think, is decided and settled for believers and unbelievers alike by the fact that a government sends soldiers into the line of fire in time of war or has them shoot into crowds in times of mutiny or revolt. But for believers the question is decided more stringently by the pronouncements given by God both after the flood and in the laws of Israel, or if you will, in the cross of Golgotha and in the unimpeachable word of the apostle (Romans 13). The objection that then the innocent too may perish runs inexorably aground (1) on the same objection to firing into a rioting crowd; (2) on the same objection in time of war; (3) on the conscientious procedures of the courts; (4) on the right to grant pardon; and (5) on the very cross of Golgotha, which, even when the strictest demand of justice requires the sacrifice of the innocent one, could reconcile us to that most horrible death penalty even if it applied to ourselves.

Premeditated murder, without the slightest circumstance that might extenuate it, has therefore always and inexorably had to be punished—we do not hesitate to say this—with the death of him who shed the blood. Not even the severity of such punishment has ever resulted in pardon becoming the rule. Justice and equity always meant pardon to be an exception.

CHAPTER FIFTEEN

PUBLIC DECENCY

[It is of the view that government is obliged to watch over public decency on public roads and in public spaces; to restrict the consumption of alcoholic beverages; to ban the display of indecent books, posters, and other printed materials; to make the luring of minors into indecent acts a criminal offense; and not to regulate prostitution in any other way, neither by prevention nor protection, than by discouraging it; on the understanding, however, that with every measure flowing from this obligation it stay strictly out of that which belongs to the domain of domestic life.]

ARTICLE 14

I. THE HONOR OF THE PUBLIC DOMAIN

DECENCY, NOT MORALITY   § 185

The Program speaks of public *decency*, not public *morality*. Correctly, it seems to us.

In the past, after all, an overactive police force and a meddlesome government have done considerable harm in this area. The area is a veritable minefield. Whoever wants to set forth his views about it had better define his terms carefully, otherwise he runs the danger, when offended by sinful behavior in public, of today putting the whole of society under police surveillance and tomorrow, out of reaction to all that irksome meddling, to open wide the floodgates and allow the stream of scandal to flow unhindered over the public domain.

In our opinion, nothing has contributed more to this harmful unsteadiness of views and leanings than the thoughtless exchange of *honestas* and *mores*, what we call *honor* and *morality*.

Morality touches the heart. It refers to intentionality and is directly related to the inner prompts of the hidden life of the soul, an area where police cannot see and government is blind.

To get out of this difficulty, people have been quick to argue that "public morality" refers only to appropriate conduct and decent demeanor. But this is playing with words. We protest against playing fast and loose with the most tender interests, turning everything into anything.

The word *morality* is too good, the concept too sacred for that. You are assisting both government and people in getting used to a very low and false view of this lofty concept. No, be in truth what you call yourself; or if you admit that you cannot be what you say you are, then drop a name that does not suit you and be content with a more humble title.

We emphasize this all the more since government will from time to time still be seduced by that false title to venture outside its natural hunting ground and embark on highly questionable raids, even as harmful wildlife is multiplying on its own preserve.

The fact of the matter is that government as such lacks the instruments, the talent, the ability, and thus also the calling, to insert a moral or spiritual good into people's hearts. That typically is the work of upbringing and national customs, or it is wrought by the Holy Spirit, who achieves that mainly through the administration of the Word, hence the church.

§ 186   ON THE BASIS OF MORALITY

Are we implying that government can contribute nothing to the moral well-being of the nation?

By no means! By its very laws, government, whether it likes it or not, exercises influence on the moral development of the nation. What is more, as God's servant government is called to check *bestiality*, to posit *the human* in humans as norm, and so to pave the way for the manifestation of still higher—that is, divine—forces in the conscience of the nation and in the consciences of individuals. This is an argument that is all the more firm since without it all lawful distinction between good and evil would fall away, not even leaving room for the administration of justice.

It must therefore be acknowledged that government has to pay attention to the moral development of the nation. But government at the same time must be required to carry this out in its own way and according to God's ordinances. This comes down to the following: (1) Laws concerning these tender matters should only forbid, not command, and should only concern what is capable of proof. (2) Government should leave to home, church, and school what belongs to those spheres. (3) When the nation has to choose between two options, government may not abuse its power to force it to go left or right.

Clearly, this extremely delicate task of the legislator cannot be left to the police, and no town councilor and no chief of police can be deemed high enough to deal with such extremely sensitive matters. It is for this reason that in the area of policing we much prefer the expression "public decency" over "public morality."

Decency does belong to the domain of morality, but it does not relate there to what is not seen, but to what is seen. It refers to the form, to the external phenomenon, to what everybody can see. Thus it does not judge the motives and prompts of the heart.

Just as one maintains the honor of one's name by not divulging the misdemeanors of one's children, and the honor of one's home by not giving the visitors in the drawing room any inkling of what is going on in the kitchen or the family room, thus maintaining the reputation of one's drawing rooms by outwardly maintaining polite decorum—in the same way the police has to maintain the reputation of the community by not allowing to appear in public what it may suspect (or even know) is going on in secret, behind closed doors.

Thus the idea of decency gives expression to people's sense of shame. This explains attempts at forcing one another, in the domain exposed to the public eye, to observe more stringent rules and to assume a higher norm than the one that in many ways obtains in private life.

People rightly desire such decency in the public domain, first, because if everybody were allowed to do their thing the bad would soon force their lifestyle on the good; and also because the streets are walked by people for whom mere seeing of what is offensive corrupts them.

A respectable patrician does not receive his guests in the drawing room half-dressed, nor does he tolerate that the guests arrive half-dressed; he does not want games to be played or business to be conducted there that are considered in bad taste, nor does he allow sick or drunk persons to enter the room and cause a nuisance; neither will he put up with coarse and profane language or the handing out of indecent prints. Similarly, the police, guarding the reputation of the community on behalf of all, make sure that in the one great drawing room we call the public domain, anything that is offensive from the standpoint of decency is banned or removed.

§ 187   The Public Domain

Placing ourselves on this standpoint, we realize at once that the police must extend its operations to every open place or enclosed space that is accessible to the public and secure under the shield of the government— in particular to the public roadways, public buildings, churches and public schools, theaters and places of amusement, and shops and department stores.

Theaters are included for the simple reason that these venues operate with government licenses under government protection, and so government shares responsibility for the performances they stage in public.

Accordingly, local government must see to it, in the first place, that on public roadways, in streets and squares and along canals, but also in laneways and alleys (usually neglected by the police) no one appear outside (or before open doors or windows, which amounts to the same thing) other than properly dressed. Also, no one may offend others through loud profanity, rough language, or vile songs; and no one, through drunkenness or wantonness, may disturb the law-abiding citizen in his free use of the road.

The police do not have to pay heed to quiet, unnoticed conversations. But if someone likes to vent, in a loud voice so that every passerby can't help but hear it, the most brazen curses and the most vulgar language, then the police must certainly put a stop to it, whether the speakers are atheists or not. Everyone agrees that such actions are indecent, and to guard against indecency is the task of the police.

Similarly, in the second place, government must see to it that theaters and various places of amusement that are licensed to entertain the public do not present anything that is improper or indecent. This could be achieved by having a trio of respectable men censor any presentations, and if the trio condemns them, by having the police declare the license terminated and prohibiting the establishment from reopening for a whole year except under a temporary permit. That is to say that any establishment found guilty of the infraction pays five times the normal fee, is subject to preventive oversight, and forfeits all rights to public posting or advertising.

Thirdly, government must be vigilant about publications on billboards and in print. Whatever offends decency, invites vulgarity, or offers filth must never—so also not on board or in print—find cover under the shield of government. In particular the scandal should not be tolerated that some papers contain entire columns with advertisements that are literally nothing but exploitation of the "spirit from the abyss."

In the fourth place, no store owner should be allowed to display a smutty book or a suggestive photograph in the window or on the counter. The police may not forbid the sale of such items; that would exceed its competence. Nevertheless, it should see to it that only he who looks for them can find them, and not conversely, that he who is not looking for them is exposed to them against his will. Stores that are guilty of this should likewise have their license immediately revoked and replaced by a temporary permit. Their wares should be taken from the rooms facing the public roadways and moved to backrooms not visible from the street. In the same vein, authorities ought to shut down public libraries that make books available that corrupt morals.

GAMING   § 188

In the fifth place, the police ought to ensure that in the public domain the demands of decency are not violated by providing opportunities for lottery and gambling, excessive drinking, or prostitution.

Pursuant to the puritan spirit of God's Word, we for our part condemn all gambling for money. Calvinist authors on ethics, Danaeus[1] first of all, have explained the reasons for this so often that we are excused from repeating them. To be sure, anyone should be free to decide whether or not he wants to lower himself, his family, and his guests to such gaming in the privacy of his home. That is no concern of the police; the question lies outside its jurisdiction, hence does not fall under its responsibility. But as soon as an establishment starts to misuse its license in order to seduce or incite the masses to play for money—big money—and deludes them with false hopes of high gains, inflames their passions, and ruins their families, then—experience in Germany has passed a verdict on it—then this

---

1. Lambertus Danaeus (1530-95), a Calvinist theologian who taught successively in Geneva, Leyden, Ghent, and several French academies, was the author of *Ethices Christianae* (1577).

misuse of the license becomes so thoroughly scandalous that the police have the imperative duty to put a stop to it immediately.

The swindle with bogus transactions, practiced by unfunded companies at the exchange, as well as all money lotteries, fall under the same rubric. For indeed, it is not enough to insist that the state lottery ought to be abolished. Our protest also needs to be directed against the practice of local governments (in Amsterdam and Rotterdam, for example) to operate so-called lottery loans, as well as against the indulgence shown by our central government toward foreign lotteries that take advantage of our simple folk.

Drawing lots for a painting or for consumables and the like, where most of the revenue is spent on the prizes or given away to the needy, is of a totally different character and should not be mentioned in the same breath with money lotteries. This is not a police matter, because there is nothing indecent about it.

But what all men of good will still view as indecent, what clashes with God's ordinances, and what political economists condemn outright as a social evil—let this ill, this playing with money for money, be banned from the public domain by our guardians of public honor and decency.

II. ALCOHOL ABUSE AND PROSTITUTION

§ 189   Drunkards

To what extent alcohol abuse and prostitution can be severely restricted and ultimately eradicated from the domain of morality, hence by moral means, is a question we shall leave for another time.

Public decency requires that we concern ourselves with just two things: (1) that the abomination of these two sins be prevented from manifesting itself in the public domain; and (2) that the public domain not be misused to promote the festering of these sins.

These two concerns, and these two alone, determine the *honestas publica*, that is, the honor of civil society, or if you will, the decency of public life.

As for background causes or contributing factors, these are either a direct concern for Christian works of mercy by the church or by private individuals, or they fall indirectly under the scope of the laws of the land, which through the administration of justice, the civil code, the system of taxation, and the police affect the temper of society. These factors, however, do not concern public decency.

Staying within these boundaries, we wish to spend a few words on al-cohol abuse and deal at greater length with prostitution. There is affinity between these two sins, but the difference is that imbibing alcohol only becomes a sin after abusing it, whereas prostitution is absolutely, and un-der every conceivable form, sinful.

Now as for alcohol abuse, in our opinion it goes without saying that every person who is found in a state of drunkenness in the streets, even if he is not harming anyone, should be placed under arrest by the police, not in the interest of public safety but for the sake of public decency—and not, as happens today, to be released again after "sleeping off his liquor," but to make him pay for his taunt at public decency with a jail term of three days. If such a person is arrested a second time for the same offense, the jail term should be doubled. And it might be useful, should similar instances keep recurring, to inform the public of such an intractable drunkard, to take away his political rights, and if nothing worked, to cut him off from the public domain altogether.

ALCOHOL ABUSE   § 190

A much more difficult question is, what should be done to keep people from using the public domain to promote alcohol abuse?

We believe it is absolutely imperative that licenses to sell alcoholic bev-erages should only be issued to persons who can give sufficient guarantees that they will only sell alcohol on medical prescription—in other words, only to pharmacists. Such prescriptions would give complete control, and in the law regulating the medical profession a clause could be inserted that stipulated in what manner a doctor or pharmacist who abused this right could have it permanently and irrevocably rescinded.

The right of vendors to sell all other spirits should be transferred from a license to a permit, that is to say, to the category of things that the police do not promote and protect as being socially beneficial and therefore hon-orable, but which instead they seek to contain within the strictest limits as being harmful and dishonorable.

Pursuant to such regulation, the inventory of these vendors ought to be subject to police inspection, on pain of permanent closure for any distiller, wholesaler, retailer, or tavern that evades the law even once. At regular intervals, a certain percentage—say 30 percent—of the excise value of the inventory ought to be paid in advance as a payment fee. Only a limited fixed number of permits ought to be issued per one thousand inhabitants. No tavern ought to be established in the slums. No women or minors ought to be allowed entry to a pub. And not only should the rooms for the sale or consumption of liquor not be visible from the street, but the police must satisfy itself that the very houses in which these rooms are located ought to be unidentifiable to the public eye.

We have already mentioned that the keepers of pubs and taverns ought to forfeit their political rights. Here we merely add that their permits ought to exclude all Sunday sales, and also that clubs or resorts with closed membership that wish to serve alcoholic beverages—including the clubs of the highest nobility—ought to be subject, without a trace of weakening, to the same strict sanctions if they exceeded a fixed quantity per member per year.

§ 191   Prostitution in the Streets and on the Roads

Following the same division for the issue of prostitution, the first question to address is: how can the manifestation of this sin in the public domain be prevented? Here, too, we gradually arrive at a threefold conclusion.

First, in our streets and roadways, open courtyards or public squares, woods or parks, the police should not, openly or on the sly, tolerate any prostitutes, under whatever name or pretext. Even less should policemen allow any solicitation of prostitution, whether by a man or a woman, or any exploitation of bawdy houses.

Second, no prostitution or invitation thereto should be allowed in any house, theater, resort, or any other place that operates under a government license.

Third, there should be a strict ban on lewd advertisements and enticements posted on doors and windows that open onto the public roadway.

The streets themselves, all licensed establishments, and whatever opens onto the streets—all belong to that great public domain that is concerned with the honor and decency of civil society and should therefore be kept free of everything that is shameful or infamous.

However, and here we come to the second, much more complicated question: to what extent can the police also prevent people from misusing the public domain and their civil rights for the promotion of prostitution?

And then we thrust to the forefront the inexorable demand that the entire personnel of the police, from high to low, should consist of men who are personally uncompromising foes of all prostitution. After all, without a morally impeccable police force you cannot make any progress with respect to prostitution. A police officer who chats up a prostitute in the street should be fired on the spot as a rogue, and inspectors or police chiefs who in one way or another turn a blind eye to prostitution should be prosecuted for abuse of office.

This is one of those key points on which everything hinges. A smuggler cannot be your border guard; a poacher cannot be your gamekeeper. In the same way a policeman whose moral character is not known to be above even the possibility of suspicion will not be a blessing but a curse.

Prostitution Can Be Combated § 192

Conversely, a great deal, if not everything, can be accomplished with a morally upright police force.

It should be remembered, when dealing with this issue, that among the greater portion of our population, in the countryside and the smaller towns, the incidence of prostitution never reached even a third of the scandalous proportions it managed to assume in our large urban centers. Granted, we know that the goings-on in our villages are far from holy, but prostitution—selling your body to one and all—is almost unheard of there; and it may safely be said that most of our soldiers and students, when they arrive at their garrison or university, have no inkling of the magnitude to which the abomination of prostitution has grown in those places.

This is true in particular of those regions that lie at some distance from market towns or urban carnivals.

And yet all this only underscores the fact that the abuse can be combated, provided men have the courage to take a strong line and push back the sin of prostitution by half even in the larger centers and in our garrison towns and river and coastal ports.

To achieve this, only one thing is needed, namely, that government should never allow itself (or the rights it grants, or the domain entrusted to it, or its civil service) to be used in any way whatsoever for the recognition, protection, or promotion of prostitution.

Once the government pronounces, *Prostitution is dishonorable!* and opposes it as the upholder of our common decency, then, if done consistently, half the evil will be curbed—the half that would not be there if the government did not indirectly support prostitution.

That the authorities are in fact doing this very thing is precisely the grave but undeniable allegation that we bring against them.

Any form of trade and commerce will flourish if it has free access to the public domain. If the authorities were to prohibit access it would suddenly be reduced by at least half. Now then, it is our contention that government must never open the public domain except for honorable transactions, and must shut it forthwith to indecent activities like prostitution.

And that is what it is not doing today. Rather, it offers every advantage of public life to this traffic, promotes it in the grossest manner, and so is responsible, before God and all decent men, for at least half of its expansion.

§ 193　　HOW TO COMBAT PROSTITUTION

If the government were prepared to discontinue its indirect support of prostitution, as is its duty as a servant of God, we believe the following measures would have to be taken:

(1) permanent abolition of issuing licenses for bawdy houses or health check cards to street or escort prostitutes;

(2) permanent abolition of health inspection of prostitutes;

(3) permanent abolition, as Van der Brugghen observed so correctly,[2] of the use of euphemisms in official documents, and reinstatement of former terms of contempt such as *whore, whorehouse, whoremonger,* and so on;

(4) suspension, upon evidence of prostitution, of all rights, granted by the Civil Code or by license or permit, against theft or robbery in connection with sale and resale, lease and sublease, advances or mortgages.

This in turn would result in the following: (a) no pimp or madam could set up shop in a house or part of a house without the owners or renters losing all claims to rental income; (b) whoever put part of his house at the disposal of a madam would lose all claims to charges for the renting or subletting of the house in question; (c) whoever kept a brothel would lose his license or permit as owner of lodgings or as innkeeper; (d) whoever opened a brothel in his own house would not be able to register his property with a notary and so could never sell it; (e) whoever operated a brothel in a rented house while operating no other business there, would have no remedy against defaults in rent

---

2. J. J. L. van der Brugghen (1804–63) was a justice in the regional court of Nymegen, board member (1852–60) of a rehabilitation center for "fallen women" (*Asyl Steenbeek*), and opponent of the legalization of prostitution.

for the rest of the house; (f) any theft or robbery committed in such a house against whores or whoremongers could not be prosecuted in the courts; (g) no agreements or advance payments, of whatever nature, transacted outdoors for the purpose of procuring the services of a prostitute, would be actionable for any man or woman in such a house or brothel, or could oblige the person in question to stay one minute longer than they chose in such a house of ill repute;

(5) no houses where prostitution was carried on, or where opportunity was provided for prostitution in designated rooms, would be recognizable by any signs whatever to the passerby, and the police would be given unrestricted authority to demand, on pain of immediate closure, the removal of any sign, audible or visible, by which the licensee tried to evade the law of public decency;

(6) persons would be severely punished if they were caught in the act of openly calling the attention of strangers to the presence of such houses by word of mouth or advertisement or poster, however covert and nearly imperceptible;

(7) no minors of either sex would be tolerated in such houses;

(8) incarceration of children caught in prostitution would be made available free of charge to any parent or guardian who so requested;

(9) every salaried civil servant would be suspended forthwith if spotted in such houses or brothels, other than on government orders;

(10) no pimp or keeper of a brothel could obtain a liquor license;

(11) similarly, both would be regarded as having waved the rights of guardianship, affidavits, and political elections for a period of at least ten years;

(12) anyone found to have delivered, directly or indirectly, a woman or girl into the hands of a pimp, or any pimp found to have lured a woman or girl not on her own initiative, would be charged with the crime of committing or abetting "unlawful confinement" (Criminal Code, sec. 341). To which should be added, of course,

(13) that the police should have unrestricted freedom to satisfy itself, by day or by night, whether in any house where prostitution is carried on,

any sale of liquor, gambling, or unlawful confinement has occurred. And, finally,

(14) that governments in the respective jurisdictions should establish the *legal presumptions* for all these regulations and should act upon these presumptions.

In this manner, public decency, which at present lies prostrate in the mire of our Voltairian method of policing,[3] would be able to raise its head again, and yet in such a way that, even with these rather severe measures in place, the sphere of domestic life would be left to the responsibility of personal conscience and the domain of morality would be left to the nurture and education in home and school.

The government would merely guard the decency of its own domain and the honor of its officials. Adults who at their own risk insisted on sinning would be left the full responsibility, and therefore also the freedom, to engage in such acts.

The government would merely make sure that nothing that belongs to government should be misused and that what is evil in the sight of God could never be committed under the seal of its license.

This is also a standpoint on which the police would at last attain what it has so far pursued in vain and what is so essential to its invaluable work, namely, the helpful assistance and the moral esteem of the entire citizenry.

---

3. This "Voltairian method of policing" probably refers to a libertine, live-and-let-live approach to public policing.

CHAPTER SIXTEEN

PUBLIC HYGIENE

[It is of the view that government has the duty in the interest of public health to guard against adulteration of foods, pollution of public roads, and poisoning of air and water; it is to provide for cleanliness in its own premises and for decent interment of bodies; and furthermore, at the manifestation of contagious diseases (excepting the right of everyone to make decisions about his own body and his own conscience) it is to take all such measures as may be conducive to and are indispensable for preventing anyone without their will or consent from being dangerously exposed to the viruses of these diseases.]

ARTICLE 15

I. THE TASK OF GOVERNMENT

CONFLICT §194

The transition from decency runs over neatness and cleanliness to hygiene.

However, neither decency nor hygiene should be looked after by the government (in this case the health authorities) apart from the living God. The honor of God's name certainly does depend on the decency of our public life in our public spaces, and an abomination perpetrated in the full light of day is far more blasphemous than an iniquity committed in private.

When discussing public decency we constantly urged that our honor as a people be safeguarded. If we were silent about the Almighty it was only because this point was definitively dealt with in chapter 4 on government.

On our standpoint there can be so little disagreement about the honor of God and the decency of our public spaces that on the contrary anything that can dignify *us* in public spaces is but a dignity derived from honoring God's name.

The case is different when dealing with public hygiene. Here, disagreement is not just conceivable but has already occurred.

Just think of the battle over cowpox inoculation, or of the shameful idea of some heartless magistrates to close the churches during epidemics in the interest of public hygiene. Think also of the outrageous attempts in a Christian nation to discourage burials and to bring into vogue the pagan practice of cremation.

Thus it is essential to be very circumspect about choosing one's point of departure and to give our doctors (many of whom are philosophical materialists) not one tittle more than they, strictly speaking, can demand.

Many take public hygiene to mean health care that turns not only the public spaces but also our bodies into the private hunting ground of our medical colleges. And since our bodies are inexplicably and marvelously bound up with our spiritual being—a spiritual being that these gentlemen hygienists for the most part concern themselves very little about—it goes without saying that our physical needs can come into conflict with our psychical needs. And in that case we must fight tooth and nail against the materialistic conclusion that in all such cases body takes precedence over soul!

§ 195   CALVINISM

Two points should therefore be placed in the foreground when discussing hygiene. (1) Sickness does not come "by chance, but by [God's] fatherly hand."[1] (2) A Reformed person, who confesses "that I, with *body* and soul, both in life and in death, am not my own, but belong to my faithful Savior Jesus Christ," knows that caring for the body is interwoven with the very core of his faith.[2]

The first point speaks for itself. As for the second point, we briefly note that cleanliness is the mother of all sound hygiene, that in God's Word cleanliness was laid upon the people in great detail, and that the Reformed

---

1. See Heidelberg Catechism, Q&A 27. See also Prov 16:33; Matt 10:29.
2. Heidelberg Catechism Q&A 1 (author's emph.). See 1 Cor 6:19-20; Rom. 14:7-9; 1 Cor. 3:23; Titus 2:1.

people, whose confession is the purest expression of that Word, outstrip all other nations in their reputation for "supercleanliness."

To be reminded of this from God's Word, recall the whole series of laws on purification of the body, clothing, eating vessels, and dwellings, and especially of the law on leprosy. And then, to honor the Calvinists on this point, merely compare a Dutchman with a German or a Scot with an Englishman, and we can rest our case.

From this fact our health authorities can draw three conclusions: (1) particularly among Calvinist nations, public hygiene is above all served by strengthening people's propensity for cleanliness; (2) in case of conflict, the health authorities must not let the soul suffer for the sake of the body; (3) for that reason they must keep their hands off our bodies, our churches, and our conscience.

Under these conditions, the task of the health authorities may be defined roughly as follows: to ensure that people's health is molested as little as possible by the public domain itself or by what is found in that domain.

The phrase "as little as possible" is the most that can be achieved, a proviso that should not be overlooked. As long as the air cannot be locked up and the waters of our streams and canals cannot be filtered; as long as the processes of our soil elude us; as long as people can deceive you unawares; as long as blood circulation cannot be arrested; and, last but not least, as long as the viruses of not a single disease have been isolated, analyzed, and measured—so long no quarantine measures, however severe, and no bylaws, however strict, will ever be able to prevent harmful elements from simply making a mockery of every doctor who is still blind to the limits of his knowledge.

But given those conditions, what *can* be done *ought* to be done— not by way of tolerance, but on the basis of calling and duty. Following the order in the Program, we will discuss (1) adulteration of foods; (2) pollution of air, water, and soil; (3) uncleanliness of the government itself; (4) cremation; and (5) contagious diseases.

(1) Adulteration of Foods   § 196

Our bakers, grocers, milkmen, wine merchants, and so on, operate under a license. This means that their establishments for a part occupy public space—which amounts to saying that they have placed themselves under the shield of the government in order to make their business flourish by making use of what is entrusted to the safekeeping of government, namely, the public domain in the broadest sense of the word.

That is precisely the reason why they have the public's trust, the responsibility for which is therefore shared by the government. Now then, for the simple reason that it can happen—as happened once in Brighton, where a baker had mixed poison in a batch of pastry of which he sold some to a dozen families before it leaked out, with the result that some ten families were plunged into mourning[3]—it is the unquestionable duty of the government to subject to severe punishment any licensed merchant who is caught selling food or drink in which toxic substances have been mixed.

If a vendor wants to cheat people by diluting his milk or wine, or supplementing his tea with willow leaves—that and so much more is not a matter for the police. In such cases our alert housewives themselves will have to keep their eyes open and have a galactometer[4] in the kitchen.

But if greed and recklessness go so far that people can be so unscrupulous as to sacrifice the health and lives of their customers for the filthy lucre of a few pennies by mixing harmful substances in their wares, then the government in our opinion must intervene, in two ways: (1) by random testing of merchandise; and (2) by opening a consultation office where anyone (the poor free of charge) can have his purchases tested.

The inexorable penalty for the evil deed, once detected, ought to be suspension of the license for at least five years.

§ 197   (2) POLLUTION OF AIR, SOIL, AND WATER

A paint factory can poison the atmosphere; a cesspool or open drain can make the soil toxic; water can be contaminated by a sewer—and all this can take place without the ordinary citizen, who breathes this air, treads that soil, or drinks that water, being aware of it or able to do anything about it.

Thus my health can be molested by a form of deterioration which others have introduced into the public domain and against which I, as a private citizen, am powerless. Accordingly, this is another area where the public health authorities have an appropriate sphere of action.

---

3. The notorious Brighton poisoning case that involved chocolates and caused the death of a child took place in 1871. Kuyper appears to be quoting from memory.
4. A galactometer is an instrument for measuring the relative density of a liquid such as milk, thus determining the milk's fat content.

They are to investigate how many harmful substances are released from a given factory's smokestacks and how far these harmful effects reach. On this basis they are to make sure that such a factory is set up at a considerable distance from residential areas.

Similarly, they must see to it that the effluents from factories, the feces from houses and asylums, and the sewage from cesspools do not sink into the soil in greater quantities than the soil can absorb to the point of saturation, or flow into canals of mostly stagnant water, at least not in any water that is used for drinking, or flow into any brooks or streams that have no direct outlet and simply run on from one municipality to the next.

Finally, they must take care that no trash or garbage, dumped in crannies and alleys, under bridges or on quays, is allowed to generate noxious gases that can have harmful consequences for the surrounding residents or passersby.

To the same category belongs the care that no trash heap, manure pile, or outhouse that belongs to a citizen is a nuisance to his neighbor. This may seem to relate only to the transfer of impure fumes from one private domain to another private domain, yet the vehicle that conveys the fumes from one area to another is the open air, which is the public domain.

We insist on very strict controls against this sloppy and filthy custom inasmuch as it is not only an attack on our health but even more an affront to our human dignity. Environmental conditions in courtyards and farmyards are deemed tolerable for humans—free citizens, indeed, baptized Christians—that would not even be tolerated in a horse stable and are customary only in a pigsty.

(3) UNCLEAN PRACTICES OF THE GOVERNMENT   § 198

"Either teach not, or teach by example!" This Greek saying contains a truth that our government ought to put into practice when it comes to public hygiene but which it all too often sins against. In its public buildings, after all, a government of a Dutch nation should be a model of tidiness and cleanliness to residents and visitors alike.

Applying that criterion, look about you in our towns and villages and, to begin with, at the offices and buildings in The Hague, and ask yourself which are less clean—which fronts look more unsightly from lack of paint, which windows look grimier, which curtains behind those windows look dirtier, and which premises, when you enter them, can confront you with a dingier sight and often staler air? They are the government buildings for administration, judiciary, public works, and so on. It is hard to resist the impression that reminding the government of its duty in this regard is far from superfluous.

II. INTERMENT AND EPIDEMICS

§ 199   (4) INTERMENT

Bodies of the deceased must be rendered harmless for the living, but this should be done in such a way as comports with both respect for the deceased and the sentiments of the living.

This means that the authorities have the duty to make it mandatory before all else that it be established with absolute certainty that a person has indeed died and does not just appear dead. To have buried a body that merely appeared dead is tantamount to judicial murder, and to neglect what can give certainty on this score is loveless. Thus our current Burial Act sins against the sixth commandment.

This in no way precludes fixing a term within which a body ought to be taken from the home. Cemeteries can have mortuaries, neatly and fittingly furnished, where a body that does not show any signs of decomposition can remain until such signs should appear. Especially in times of severe epidemics, when medical attention is scarce and when the family of the presumed deceased often urge removal of the body, one cannot be too scrupulous in taking these precautions.

In the second place, the authorities ought to take care, wherever burials are a public service, that they can take place in such a way, particularly in our raw climate, that it is possible to bare one's head and remember God the Lord at the grave that swallows its dead. The most suitable means would be a temporary tent or canopy that, stretched over the open grave and its surroundings, can offer shelter against wind and driving rain.

And, thirdly, in our opinion the authorities ought not to issue a permit for cremating a body unless it is clearly evident that the person wishing it wishes it for himself and not in order to make propaganda for pagan customs that assail Christian burial.

§ 200   CREMATION

Under those conditions we would not be opposed to the option of cremation. At present, when those conditions are in no way being met, we are opposed to it.

As we have argued extensively in the past with citations from the writings of cremators themselves: cremation is mostly recommended because the burial of bodies is considered harmful to health. And once you accept this premise you can only come to the logical conclusion that this harmful practice must be combated without letup until it loses its support in public opinion, after which burial can be prohibited by law.

We are aware that the cremators in our country, at least for now, are opposed to any such prohibition; and none of us questions their subjective sincerity. But looking at it objectively, one could ask: "How now? If you appeal to *our* defense of freedom in the case of *your* advocacy of cremation, then why do you not help us in our opposition to cowpox inoculation and the still worse inoculation of religious neutrality in the minds of our schoolchildren?"

For these reasons we will continue for the time being to support the resistance to cremation.[5]

Moreover, in the villages and towns with a population below fifty thousand, proper burial causes none but imaginary problems for hygiene, since the soil (at least in not too low-lying regions), without becoming oversaturated, can absorb and sanitize in these moderate proportions the chemicals released by decomposition. If soil levels are too low, they can be raised. And finally, as for the great centers of population, both for Rotterdam and The Hague the immediate proximity of dunes provides an obvious location for a cemetery; and a railway line from Amsterdam to Het Gooi can easily connect that city with a "city of the dead in the sand," to avert all hazards to public health.

All the same, there is no disguising the fact that the appalling accumulation of people, such as is more and more the case in Paris, London, Berlin, and Vienna, is itself a symptom of a pagan development of life and an expression of the spirit that once tried to build Babel. It is driven by unchristian motives that are gradually coming into conflict with both natural conditions and Christian customs.

In any case, the clearing of burial plots as is sometimes done these days—dumping skulls and bones, soft tissue still attached, into the

---

5. A loophole in the Burial Act of 1869 made it possible for sporadic cremations to take place in the Netherlands, but cremation was not formally legalized until an act of 1955.

charnel house—is simply a disgrace and ought never to be tolerated by law. Every grave should be allowed to rest for at least thirty years.

§ 201   (5) Contagious Diseases

Finally, more difficult than the question of burial is the question of contagious diseases.

It is not that one need hesitate for a moment to dissect that piece of existing legislation. Unless we are mistaken, laymen and specialists are in complete agreement that no law could be more ineffective, sloppy, and unenforceable than our Contagious Diseases Act.

Yet leaving that act for what it is, no one should make a secret of it that we are confronted here with an extremely difficult issue, one that every legislator will probably continue to stumble over.

An effective law, after all, would require knowing (1) which diseases are contagious; (2) whether they are contagious in their incubation period, through physical contact, or through the air; (3) whether the virus is spread by clothing, bed linen, furniture, feces, and so on; (4) whether a third person can be a carrier of such a disease; (5) whether they can be transmitted over a distance by letters and such.

Next, if all this were known, one would have to have the power, depending on how the data turned out, to consign the ill person and his housemates to complete isolation.

At present, neither is possible.

Medical science has not advanced very far in discovering the laws that govern communicable diseases. It is known that measles are contagious already when a person has it without his knowledge. About cholera we still have nothing that can pass for knowledge. About typhus we know that not the patient himself but his excretions are contagious. About the plague it is believed that everything causes the disease to be transmitted in the most horrendous manner. That mere touch transmits leprosy. That syphilis, too, spreads horribly even by a single breath. And that in the most common epidemics, diphtheria, scarlet fever, and smallpox are believed to communicate their viruses also through third parties or inanimate objects.

As to the second point—complete isolation—the main difficulty resides first of all with our doctors themselves who are daily in very close contact with the infected patient and yet immediately thereafter visit other families again to touch a patient with the same hand that a short while ago touched the infected patient. But the difficulty extends further: it is impossible, for the sake of one ill person in a large family, to keep all the other family members away from their workplace, and it is unthinkable to bar all of them from the streets and shops and to cut them off from all contact with others.

Truly efficacious measures, it should be kept in mind, will never be available in the case of contagious diseases.

It is not the case that an infected person may not be restricted in his movements. Everyone who believes in the divine origin of the Mosaic law knows otherwise from the law on leprosy (see Leviticus 13 and following). But restriction of movement is not always warranted, inasmuch as most infectious diseases are of quite a different nature than scabies or leprosy and can therefore not be controlled in the same manner.

What Can Be Done   § 202

The little that government can do will probably come down to this.

(1) Whenever deadly epidemics are spreading like wildfire, the authorities should open sick bays where sufferers can be taken who are not being looked after and where they can receive proper nursing care, free of charge or for payment. Also, the authorities can publish what is the best advisable lifestyle; what is recommended by way of preventative measures, and what should immediately be done at the outbreak of the dreaded symptoms. Medicines ought to be made available to the needy free of charge (if private initiative is not forthcoming). The authorities should issue ordinances to regulate the use of cabs, order the burning of feces in infected houses, have houses disinfected from which a patient was removed ill or dead, and set the time at twenty-four hours within which bodies have to be taken to the mortuary.

(2) During calmer epidemics, though still of a very serious nature, such as smallpox, typhus, diphtheria, and scarlet fever, the authorities should require doctors to register cases and order destruction of any feces, followed by disinfection. Anyone entering such houses has to be warned. Anyone leaving such houses to step onto the street or enter a shop or a church, must be made to wear a white armband, and any children of such a family should be prohibited from attending school.

(3) During minor epidemics, such as measles, the authorities should refrain from taking any measures. First of all, there is no way to fight a disease that is mostly transmitted during the incubation phase. Moreover,

minor epidemics scarcely warrant such an infringement of personal freedom and would only rouse the repugnance (which is not negligible) of all respectable mothers and eager schoolchildren.

§ 203   ALWAYS RELATIVE

The reason why we do not recommend posting warning signs on houses is that this only causes alarm, works unequally for shops and private homes, and gives doctors occasion to turn a blind eye. We agree that licensed shopkeepers should be subject to stricter regulations than private persons, but this should be expressly stated in the law; and persons who leave the sick room and enter the shop to help customers should have to undergo a prescribed method of disinfection. But whatever is tried in this matter, the best measures will always be frustrated by the nature of the illness, the demands of daily life, and the unwillingness of the imprudent.

And if the government does not wish to stiffen this resistance but cause it to diminish, then as a servant of God it should demonstrate in such critical days that it has a heart. Then it should not, like a violent accomplice of unbelieving science, turn against the nation's religious beliefs that only intensify in times of epidemics. Rather, when God's judgments break out the government ought to share in the spirit of awe that stirs the souls before the majesty of God. Rather than prohibiting prayer services it should itself proclaim a day of prayer. In this way its solemn decisions and actions will underscore the impression that as a government it is powerless to ward off the plague that is visiting the nation and that it knows no better refuge for deliverance that to humble itself before almighty God.

§ 204   VACCINATION

For this reason alone, compulsory cowpox vaccination should be out of the question. Our physicians may be mistaken and government may never stamp a particular medical opinion as orthodox and therefore binding. Moreover, compulsion can never be justified until the illness manifests itself and may therefore never be prescribed as a preventative. A third reason is that government should keep its hands off our bodies. Fourthly, government must respect conscientious objections. In the fifth place, it is one or the other: either it does not itself believe in vaccination, or if it does, it will do redundant work by proceeding to protect once more those already safeguarded against an evil that will no longer have a hold on them anyway.

Vaccination certificates will therefore have to go—and will be gone at least from our free schools. The form of tyranny hidden in these vaccination certificates is just as real a threat to the nation's spiritual resources as a smallpox epidemic itself.

Syphilis

And now, in conclusion, a brief comment about syphilis, the worst and the only shameful one among all communicable diseases. Syphilis undermines our society like a hidden enemy and lurks beneath it like a traitor. And yet our health legislation has given up on fighting it. In fact, it has given license for it by obligating doctors never to divulge the names of patients who have secret diseases. We call this more than scandalous, an abomination to God, an insult to society, and unacceptable for the future.

It is not that we fail to appreciate the intention to shield innocent women from undeserved shame when they have become infected, or to protect those who are victims of this horrible germ as a result of hereditary factors. But we fail to see why the culpable corrupters of public health should have the benefit of this fair-minded provision.

On the contrary, in the two different cases mentioned we would like to see regulations in approximately the following vein: (1) the right to instant annulment of a marriage if it became apparent within a fortnight after the wedding that without prior warning the person one married was exposed to the risk of contracting this disease; (2) registration by the doctor of all unmarried persons and married men who are being treated by him for nonhereditary syphilis; (3) removal from their home, until cured, to a designated building, of all married men who are found to be infected through adultery; and (4) notification of registered unmarried persons, mailed under seal, to their parents, keepers of boarding houses, employers, or superiors.

CHAPTER SEVENTEEN

FINANCE

It desires that in the financial governance of the state the relationship between government and citizens not be one of contract but a moral, organic relationship; that the equilibrium between revenues and expenditures be arranged, not by oppressive increase in the burden of the nation, nor by cutting down on what is necessary, but by cutting back on state interference; and furthermore, that our system of taxation be so reformed that the development of the nation suffer less harm, high revenue not be the only criterion, the tax burden be less unequal, and the cost of collecting taxes be reduced.

ARTICLE 16

I. THE RIGHT TO LEVY TAXES

§ 206   THE CONTRACT SYSTEM

On what basis does government have the right to levy taxes?

Does government collect and spend monies by virtue of a contract with its subjects? Do tax revenues represent wages for work done or fees for services rendered? Or is it that government collects and spends only because it is necessary and cannot be otherwise, hence by virtue of the law of necessity?

Each of these systems has been defended.

Conservatives and classic liberals are passionate defenders, for as long as they can, of the contract system. This system comes down to this, that government serves as a contractor and an insurance company.

For example, it is necessary to administer justice for the citizenry. The government assumes this role and installs courts of law, builds jails with solid walls, and pays for guards to secure them—in return for which it charges the citizens so and so much per capita per annum. Or, to take another example, these citizens have possessions that need to be protected—by troops against a possible foreign invader, and by a police force against thieves. Very well, this role too is assumed by government. It guarantees citizens the undisturbed possession and unhampered enjoyment of their property. But for this benefit they pay the government a commensurate insurance premium. Whoever owns little needs little coverage and so pays a premium of a few pennies; whoever is rich needs much protection and so pays a premium of several hundred guilders.

THE SYSTEM OF PAID EMPLOYMENT   § 207

Still more consistently revolutionary is the system of the young liberals. They define the nature of the state's financial governance in terms of wages for work done or fees for services rendered.

This notion fits the idea of popular sovereignty. The sovereign people no longer acts individual by individual, to have each one draw up his personal account with the insurance company called "Government." It now acts as a whole, as a unit, as the majority of the nation. And since this nation has borders to guard, court cases to hear, roads to maintain, and so on, the sovereign people hires a bevy of civil servants to take care of all these jobs. Depending on their terms of employment, these civil servants can charge wages and demand advances. Government is then regarded as having power to serve rather than power to rule. This is a system of "employees," with the king as the first footman of the sovereign people seated on a throne sans majesty. And whoever still harbors some respect for government may refer to the system as a system of paying fees, similar to paying fees charged by a doctor, a governor, or a lawyer. Whoever is a more consistent revolutionary, however, shakes off all respect for government, refuses any longer to honor that form of relative respect, and calls such professional fees simply ordinary wages, whether paid to John Doe for paving a road or to William of Orange for signing a government bill.

THE SYSTEM OF THE ABSOLUTISTS   § 208

And yet, even worse, finally, is the system of our absolutists. They justify the state's entire financial administration as simply a matter of *coercion*. Those who push this idea are the men of state omnipotence. They trifle with justice and bend the knee only to the right of the strongest. They are the *politiques* who teach that we cannot do without government, whatever its origin, and that this government, the partisan product of a party, a coterie, or a faction, must manage to stay in the saddle through talent and energy, to get things moving and force the unwilling to yield.[1] And since this costs money, lots of money, and simply cannot be done without money, they hold that government, under certain legal forms, has no choice but to take the money where it can be found and spend it as it sees fit.

So say the fanatics for Caesarism! Both Augustus and Nero in ancient Rome belonged to this school. It is a system that was used by Napoleon, who was great, and by Napoleon III, who called himself great. It has been used by Bismarck in the period that was [almost] terminated just recently by the would-be assassin Hödel.[2] And it is increasingly propagated by a certain influential political club in the government circles of The Hague.

If you now investigate what happens to our constitutional liberty in each of these three systems, then it goes without saying (1) that the men of the insurance system place public finance exclusively in the hands of those who have something to be insured, that is, they place it in the hands of the propertied class; (2) that the demagogues of the wage system will not rest until a quasi-universal suffrage has made the king accountable even to the poorest beggar; while (3) the partisans of revolutionary absolutism turn your entire parliamentary instrument into a sham, in order to legitimize— in name of the people, as a mere formality—what in fact is done without the people and against the people.

§ 209   A MORAL, ORGANIC SYSTEM

These three systems are all equally revolutionary. We antirevolutionaries counter them with a totally different system, given our fundamental principles concerning government and the essence of the nation. Our system is one of a *moral, organic bond*. According to this system, government (1) has a God-given right to levy taxes; (2) does not tax the property of individuals but draws its revenue from the organic property of the nation; and (3) collects its revenue neither on its own authority, nor by permission of the

---

1. The *politiques* were those in France in the sixteenth and seventeenth centuries who advocated the success of the political regime as the greatest good.
2. In May 1878 the anarchist Max Hödel made an unsuccessful attempt at assassinating the German emperor William I. Chancellor Bismarck responded by having thousands of radicals of every description arrested and imprisoned.

owners, nor yet by permission of the masses taken head for head; rather, it imposes taxes with the free consent of the nation, which on this issue, too, speaks organically with the voice of the whole.

"For because of this you also pay taxes, for the authorities are ministers of God, attending to this very thing. Pay to all what is owed to them: taxes to whom taxes are owed, revenue to whom revenue is owed, respect to whom respect is owed, honor to whom honor is owed."[3] Thus reads the word of the apostle of Jesus Christ, a word that still today sanctions and hallows the government's right to administer finances. A government does what it does, not because you ask it to, nor because it wants to, but because God so ordained it. Its duty is "attending to this very thing," that is, to defend the good and punish the evildoers, a task that incurs great costs. Thus taxes are a nation's sacred offering, rendered to God in order that God should rule the nation by means of the authorities he has ordained.

Accordingly, the obligation to pay taxes, tolls, and tribute does not fall on individual people personally, but on the members of the nation as a national community. For through the civil authorities God rules only the nation as such; he has not handed over to government the rule over individual persons but has reserved this for himself, via people's conscience. The nation, meanwhile, is in constant flux. Every day it changes, since on a daily basis members depart from it through death and other subjects are added to it by birth. And keeping in mind that the nation is and remains the nation, not just for many years but for centuries, and that therefore the financial administration of the government affects not just the people living in the present but the nation of yesterday, today, and tomorrow, then it stands to reason that seizing a portion of what individuals possess does not advance us one whit but for the sake of the nation revenue has to be taken from the property of the nation as a whole.

Finally, the nation alone knows what it possesses, and in what form; and it alone knows how it can continue to possess it. Therefore the natural and just system of financial administration, as well as the only system worthy of mankind, is only realized when the nation, organically, consents to the levying of taxes by the government. In this way its submission to authority at the same time becomes a national offering, and its payment of tribute becomes, via the government, an offering to God. As the apostle

---

3. Rom 13:6–7.

writes in the same context, "Therefore one must be in subjection, not only to avoid God's wrath but also for the sake of conscience."[4]

§ 210   THE PRICE OF NATIONAL INDEPENDENCE

Proceeding from these principles, one has to distinguish first of all between the expenses that the government incurs as government and the monies it spends as an agent of the people. The postal service, harbor pilots, telegraphy, schools, the verification of gold and silver, and so much more are concerns that do not belong directly to the essence of government. Even if the government left these to the care of the citizens, it would not thereby be any less the government, or have less honor and dignity. By contrast, the judiciary, the police, maintaining a navy and army, relations with foreign powers, and so on, cannot be left to others. These are the government's affairs, else it ceases to be a government.

Strictly speaking, therefore, only the last rubric of expenditures ought to be charged by the government to the taxpayers, and everything else should be settled between public officials and the private parties concerned. And since this is done as a rule in the case of the mail, the telegraph, and so on (and only in the case of education, for the time being, has this rule been infringed upon, for partisan reasons) we shall therefore leave out of consideration the first rubric and deal only with the direct government expenditures as such.

The first of these, and rightly so, are expenditures for the national debt and national defense. The two belong together since by far the greater portion of the debt was incurred to cover the cost of past wars. Thus they are expenditures for the preservation of our national independence. A nation, too, must *struggle* for its existence. Its independence does not come free but has to be conquered or defended, and reconquered after losing it. These painful, bloody struggles serve to make the nation aware of its latent forces, so that it can develop those forces to the highest degree they are susceptible of. In the present dispensation, the eradication of war is so unlikely that the only choice we have is between inspired and energetic nations filled with spirit and enthusiasm and ever vigilant because of the threat of war, or a category of peoples that are half asleep, without pith or spirit, a kind of pantomime of nations with shadowy movements, carrying on a phantomlike existence without inspiration or power.

---

4. Rom 13:5.

The *struggle for life*[5] among the nations is a condition of their higher development, the only safeguard they have against withering away. Periods of peace alternate with times of trouble in which they must prove they still have the will to exist and are worthy of their independent existence. But that independence comes at a great cost.

Think of what navy and army cost at present—and of the even greater costs they brought in the past, in proportions that threaten to increase constantly because as the nations get older they have to pay increasingly more for their past and they incur increasing costs in their present life. The only positive aspect about this enormous price for defending national independence is that it checks luxury and fosters a readiness to make sacrifices.

On our national budget today (omitting Colonial Affairs) these two departments account for ƒ65 million, which means (calculating per capita) that each person (not every family or household) has to put down 18 guilders a year just so that we can exist as a nation.

THE PRICE OF KEEPING THE NATION UNITED   § 211

Qualifying in the second place are the costs of administration, the justice system, and the police, since the nation, to manifest its unity, had to be given an authority that lays down the law, delivers justice, and so maintains law and order in the land. At present these costs amount to a total of about 7 million guilders a year for the central government.

In the third place, the government has to look after foreign relations, to the tune of just half a million.

In the fourth place, another ƒ18 million have to be spent on the government's care to keep our country from flooding and to maintain an infrastructure (by land and water) that can express the unity of the nation in its internal communication.

This completes the state's proper budget. All the rest are either expenditures for what government would do better to leave to others, or expenditures that are offset by at least equal revenues, such as the postal service. They may also cover the cost of paying for nationalized goods, for example, to the churches; or, finally, indirect costs for administering accounts payable and receivable.

---

5. This expression appears in English in the original. It was popularized in Kuyper's time by Charles Darwin (1809-82) and referred to the competitive struggle for survival between living things.

All things considered, therefore, the state's budget (if foreign affairs is counted with defense) could be reduced, strictly speaking, to the following three categories:

(1) the costs of maintaining the independence of the nation over against foreign nations—of former and present days—to the tune of upwards of 65 million guilders;

(2) the costs of maintaining the unity of the nation as a state through administration, the justice system, and the police, in the amount of ƒ6 to ƒ7 million; and

(3) the costs of maintaining a domestic infrastructure, to the tune of approximately ƒ18 million.

Thus the nation deals with a differential of 65 to live and just 25 to live well!

This certainly shows, it seems to us, that it is to turn things upside down and to mock the nation's moral capacity if its zeal to live as an independent nation is extinguished and the illusion is created that "to live well" is the only thing of real value.

II. ORGANIC ADMINISTRATION

§ 212   ORIGIN OF TAXATION

In its simplest form the problem of administration occurs only in the case of a newly established colony.

Suppose a colony makes landfall in a coastal region that is far from safe. At once, every able-bodied man will be expected to wield a sword should the colony be attacked. Furthermore, every man fit for service will be required to help build roads and canals. As buildings and storehouses are erected, people will be conscripted, depending on their skills, to do carpentry, lay bricks, or work as blacksmiths—all of them personal contributions because there simply is no money to be earned, and if it could be raised would in that first phase be metal without any value.

Gradually, however, this primitive situation would take on firmer lines and sharper contours. As a result of population growth, contact with neighboring tribes, and a beginning of overseas trade, the original patriarchal system would change into relationships based on civil rights. The duty to serve in case of war would remain, but it would be regulated. Contributing to the building of roads and canals would be replaced with some prescribed form of community obligations. Labor on communal lands would be limited to designated days. A tithe would be levied on breeding animals and on the produce of the land. Trade would contribute through tolls. Gifts to the chieftains, half voluntary, half compulsory, would assure their well-being. And tribute would be demanded, if possible, from a neighboring tribe that had been subjugated by force of arms.

While still advancing in development, a colony would sooner or later proceed to distribute the communal land, on condition that a considerable portion would remain public property in order to use the revenue to defray part of the cost of government. And as industry made its appearance, as commerce at home and abroad expanded, and as law and order put down firmer roots, such a colony would little by little approach the critical moment when it became the rule for colonials and hence for their government "to convert everything into money." Inevitably, all personal services adhering to a piece of land or to residency would be made redeemable for a sum of money. No carpenter or blacksmith would work except for payment. And for waging a war, troops would not be brought into readiness until expenditures had been made for building forts, purchasing arms, and training officers.

TAXATION IN MONEY   § 213

Once the money phase (if we may call it that) has set in, the tendency automatically arises to convert every right and every revenue of the state into money, until at last men fancy the ideal situation to be one in which nothing but hard cash flows towards the government—through a single channel in fact. In that situation the national, regional, and local authorities will vie with each other in selling off every bit of territory or its equivalent, making the tithe redeemable, maintaining only a mercenary army, selling the toll booths for firewood, and preferably removing the last customs officer from the national borders and turning every approachable inlet along the coast into a free port, preferably with free entry of goods and gratis pilot services.

At the same time, in this situation all income *in natura* for the government is done away with, all so-called emoluments are abolished, legal fees are cancelled, and the whole of the government's revenue is preferably paid in four fixed money payments. It is a system that, walking in the leading strings of our revolutionaries, must lead with inner necessity—by two opposite avenues, those of revenue and expenditure—to one single, supremely simple financial settlement, namely, to a single tax, to be paid to the receiver general, and a uniform salary, to be paid out by the general paymaster.

From this brief—and, we trust, not too unclear—sketch of the historical progress of a nation's financial affairs, the following is clear: (1) That it is in no way unfair to have "the people of little means" contribute toward the cost of government. After all, the conversion of personal services into a "money tax" has benefitted them too—in fact mainly them. It leaves them free to dispose of their time and relieves them of a bond that restricted their independence. (2) That the original contributions to the government, in the measure that they were organically present among the people, would also be demanded from them within an organic framework. (3) That these services would be divided and arranged in such a way that everyone saw the necessity of them in their own life-sphere and exercised supervision over them. And (4) that our revolutionaries have misused "payment in money" to destroy the organic concept of property, hence of administration and taxation alike. In the place of an organic system of contributing services within one's own life-sphere, such that a person could see them for himself and realize the need for them, they have substituted an abstract, lifeless concept of fiscal affairs for which the nation has no heart, nor ever can have.

§ 214   LIMITING STATE MEDDLING

Over against the liberal practice we would like to see improvements in accordance with the demands of our principles, as indicated by the following four points: (1) limit your meddling by the state, and (2) decentralize your administration; and also (3) raise your money from the organic property of the nation, and (4) decentralize your levy.

(1) Limit your meddling by the state

Reduce the sum of what the government needs to the smallest size possible by leaving to private persons and corporations whatever they are at all willing to take in hand.

This principle clearly commends itself as the starting point for all financial administration. For by meddling with what does not strictly belong to the task of government you diminish the respect your high office should inspire. By carrying on in such a meddlesome fashion you will inevitably come into conflict with people's love of freedom. Worse, by getting your subjects accustomed to the idea that government does everything for them you frustrate the release of their energy, you arrest their development, and your own foolish practice is the cause of their physical and moral decline.

It is only right to point out that the peoples of Switzerland, Scotland, Holland, and America became noted above all for their resilience and civic spirit. Their incredible initiative was inspired by the spirit of John Calvin. Always zealous for "do it yourself," they more than other nations resisted government encroachment on civil society.

DECENTRALIZING THE ADMINISTRATION §215

(2) Decentralize your administration

That is to say, split what you will then have to pay yourself in such a way, organically, that the municipality gets to administer the biggest portion, the province a considerable portion, and the national government as little as possible.

This basic rule, too, strongly recommends itself.

Especially if you take note of the fact that an unreliable, centralist path, once taken, has led to more than a doubling of your budget.

To convince you of this, just put side by side the main estimates [in guilders] for the various departments as they were presented to parliament in 1850 and today, a quarter century later.

	1850	1878	Difference
Royal House	800,000	950,000	150,000
Superior Boards	550,000	600,000	50,000
Foreign Affairs	500,000	600,000	100,000
Justice	2,300,000	4,500,000	2,200,000
Interior Affairs	4,000,000	29,000,000	25,000,000
Navy	5,500,000	14,000,000	8,500,000
National Debt	36,500,000	27,000,000	−9,500,000
Finance	8,000,000	17,500,000	9,500,000
War	11,000,000	22,500,000	11,500,000
Colonies	100,000	2,000,000	1,900,000
Total	69,250,000	118,650,000	49,400,000

Next, you ought to abolish all subsidies to municipalities by the central government and leave to the local government every service that possibly lends itself to it. The latter will carry out its task under its own oversight, in the presence and so under the direct supervision of the taxpayers. This continuous supervision will automatically enforce savings, people will know where their money goes, and their willingness to pay will come easier.

At present, however, you have played hide and seek with the three government treasuries. The invisible central government took over almost everything, and so year after year it submitted ever higher—and ever less verifiable—estimates. To withdraw still more from direct scrutiny, you then invented the unconscionable means of having the long arm of the state collect from the pocketbooks of the inhabitants large sums of money not just for itself but at the same time for the provinces and the municipalities. These sums were then later quietly returned to the local treasuries in the form of transfer payments, eighty percent of salaries and endless subsidies. At the same time these subsidized local authorities, totally forgetting what the citizens had already contributed indirectly to their needs, in their turn took to big budgets and sought to swell their coffers in part through loans, in part through high assessments.

Now, this is exactly the opposite of what it ought to be. A citizen can be the best judge of a municipal assessment, less so of a provincial levy, but hardly of a tax by the central government. Thus a citizen is in a position to imagine that payments by the municipalities to the central government could be just and fair; but never the reverse, regular payments by the central government to the municipalities. That is tantamount to introducing corruption into our financial affairs, and worse, into our national community, which is shaped as well by financial affairs.

If only the example of our water boards were followed! They do internally what needs doing. They raise the money themselves. They pay their own bills. In looking after their affairs (excepting for a moment the great rivers and their coastal outlets) they expend around ƒ10 million from their own resources, assisted respectively with ƒ1.5 million from the provinces and some ƒ3 million from the national government.

In other matters, too, the administrative center of gravity ought to lie with the municipalities, and in the second place with the provinces, leaving only what is left over to the central government. Then our administration would again be broadly based where it should be, at the level of the people, tapering upwards to the highest state offices. This is still the case in England, in America, even in Switzerland. Why can it not be so in our country?

CENTRAL GOVERNMENT, PROVINCE, AND MUNICIPALITY   § 216

Leaving aside defense and the national debt, state expenditures could then be considerably reduced if the expenses of the States General were paid for by their principals; if the expenses of justices of the peace, district courts, and prisons were removed to the provincial and municipal budgets; if the costs of provincial administration were transferred from Interior Affairs to the provinces; if every municipality were to pay for the costs of the standing army and elementary education and every province for the costs of secondary education, normal schools, gymnasia, and various inspections; if the historic debt were once for all settled with the churches; if the costs of Navy and Colonies were assigned to their own respective budgets; and if the cost of collecting taxes were considerably reduced by as much as possible having *local* government levy them.

Altogether the Dutch people are paying for the cost of government and administration (not counting the colonies) approximately ƒ180 million, or upwards of 50 guilders per capita per annum—to wit: for the national budget ƒ120 million, for provincial budgets circa ƒ5 million, for municipal budgets ƒ45 million,[6] and for the water boards circa ƒ10 million.[7] Subtracting the expenditures for debt and defense as of a unique kind, as well as ƒ3 million for savings, you would then end up with a total of circa ƒ115 million for government and administration in the narrower sense, of which sum the central government, if a transition to more expedient decentralization were made, would get to manage at most circa ƒ30 million,[8]

---

6. *Note by the author:* After subtracting 80 percent of personnel costs.
7. *Note by the author:* These estimates are based on figures provided by a qualified, accurate source.
8. *Note by the author:* The costs that would then have to pass from the central government to other government bodies would be a good ƒ22 million and mainly amount to: States General 300,000, Courts 750,000, Justices of the Peace 400,000, Prisons 700,000, court houses 150,000, unemployment pay in the justice system 100,000, provincial administration 650,000, Health Inspection 700,000, Education 2,000,000, Arts and Science 500,000, Navy 3,000,000, financial administration 1,500,000, Industry and Agriculture 250,000, Colonies 1,700,000, transfer payments to municipalities 8,000,000, closing of offices 300,000. Savings of the remaining ƒ3 million

the provinces circa ƒ10 million, the municipalities a good ƒ60 million, and the water boards the remaining ƒ10 million.

A redistribution of this kind would make for an arrangement that would finally enable the organic nation to express itself in financial affairs. People would then do for themselves what they have been able to do in private civil affairs: take care of the greater part of what remained by means of natural associations of local communities. What pertained to those municipalities combined would be administered by the provincial authorities. And only what turned out to be left undone would become the responsibility of the central government.

Also keep in mind that the ƒ30 million which the government would then spend apart from defense and debt, include the postal and telegraph services, publicly owned railways, pilot services, and so much more. In a few years' time, these services might not only pay their own way but even yield a profit. Thus the actual costs of the national government would come down to some ƒ25 million at most. This amount could easily be covered by indirect taxes. Debt and defense, which together require ƒ65 million, could be covered (assuming the present tax system is continued) by a small adjustment in the land tax (circa ƒ15 million), the yield of excise taxes (ƒ10 million), a slight increase in import duties (ƒ10 million), and the remaining smaller revenues (ƒ5 million). The municipality would then have to manage to cover its own expenditures, which is only just, by leaving to it the entire tax on staff salaries and fees for licenses, supplemented by a head tax if so desired. Municipalities would then be responsible for contributions to the provinces, while the national government should have the flexible means of balancing its annual budget by levying a certain amount of surcharges on the municipal head tax.

Furthermore, the rule should be adopted that large capital projects that serve more than one generation are to be financed through loans, and inversely, that any net proceeds from the Indies are to be used exclusively for paying off the debt. This would complete an organic approach to every item on the budget and on that very account achieve the steadiness and prudence which, instead of being furthered by the much-vaunted "non-complicated" French system currently in force today, is frustrated by the

---

could easily be found in the budgets of the municipalities if local finances were taken more seriously by cutting out luxuries. Besides, it would be only 6 percent of their current budgets.

system, precluding any adequate understanding of the country's finances for the ordinary citizen.

Economies

The organic distribution of financial administration over municipality, province, and central government, outlined in the previous section, had to be laid out, for the sake of clarity, within the framework of revenues and expenditures as they were in 1878.

It would be a mistake, however, to infer that this framework is not in conflict with our principles.

If things were done as we would wish it, then education, for example, which will soon cost ƒ15 million, would be privately funded almost entirely. The payment of ƒ2 million to the churches would cease within a decade through settlement by means of an annuity. Going to court for the first time would be free of charge. Many a high political office would henceforth be honorary.

Through such reforms alone, the total of the ƒ110 million (excluding debt and defense) that would be left annually for administration and governance could definitely drop in the next period to far below ƒ100 million, even when reckoning with future increases. Of that amount, about ƒ56 million would devolve on the municipalities, ƒ10 million on the water boards, ƒ10 million on the provinces, and no more than about ƒ20 million on the central government.

That this estimate for the central government is not too low is shown, for example, by a comparison with British conditions. Great Britain, which can easily match its pound sterling with our guilder in proportion to its population and wealth, spends £59 million on debt and defense and for ordinary administration between £22 million and £23 million. Denmark, with a population of 2 million souls, spends 22 million kroner for debt and defense and for the entire remaining administration 19 million kroner (a krone equals 0.66 guilders). Sweden, with a population of 4 million, spends 36 kronor for debt and defense and an almost equal amount for the remainder.

In Portugal, finally, to name no more, debt and defense cost a good 17 million milreis and the rest of the administration only 11 million milreis (a milreis equals 2.95 guilders), for a similar population of 4.5 million souls.[9]

---

9. In comparison to Portugal, Holland's population at this time was just under 4 million. See above, § 133.

In addition, if one followed the rule that large public works, which are meant to last at least a century, are financed with loans that mature in a century, the Department of Roads and Waterways would save a considerable sum. Despite an inevitable rise in salaries, our central government could then conduct its business with a good 20 million guilders without skimping on necessities or carrying economies too far.

This would have the great advantage that the oppressive preponderance of power that currently rests with the central government and that more and more paralyzes the nation's freedom of movement would for a considerable portion be relocated to the lower spheres of national life, to energize the people and swell their civic pride.

This much must be granted by now, that for all that paternal care for preserving the country's unity and developing national life, stimulating agriculture, industry, commerce, and shipping, the only result thus far has been that more than ever we are a divided people, that we are falling behind all our neighboring countries, and that—think of the Paris Exhibition of 1878 and the government's policy—virtually every source of national wealth can no longer flow generously.

III. ORGANIC LEVIES

§ 218   GOVERNMENT AS CONTRIBUTOR TO VALUE

(3) Raise your money from the organic property of the nation.

We now come to the question: In what way ought government to acquire the means to defray its administrative expenses in order not to short-change the requirements of the organic national community?

The first principle to be honored here is that the government ought to be *self-paying*[10] and more than that. That is to say, the government should draw its means from the increase in value that it adds to the properties of the nation by its mere presence. Compare for example the best land in Venezuela with our slightest moors: the latter are still higher in value simply because the national community and a government that guarantees law and order, builds roads, and links you up with the outside world, triples, at a minimum, the value of your land. Other examples: a house in Amsterdam with six rooms is worth three times as much as a house in Purmerend with twelve; a trading company in Rotterdam makes twice as

---

10. This word appears in English in the original.

much of its capital than a similar firm in Assen; and to name no more, a store in the Kalverstraat of our capital is worth five times an equally large store in Culemborg or Tiel.[11]

From this it is evident that the value of a property does not depend on one but on three factors: its intrinsic worth, its location in the country in which it finds itself, and the government under whose care it resides.

If now government has the power to act so as to increase the value of your property by, say, a third—or, to put it differently, if government by disappearing caused the value of your property to decrease by one-third—then government clearly is a contributor of value. If you wish to have it expressed in numbers: government is financially worth, say, one-third of your property, and it would not be guilty of communism if it took half of that added value, for it would still leave you with one-sixth pure profit. To stay with financial terms, this could be expressed by saying that in order to raise the value of your property by one-sixth net, you have to get it to rise one-third in value and surrender the other one-sixth to the government that gave you this gross increase in value.[12]

NATIONAL COMMUNITY   § 219

The second factor, too, represents a portion of value. The national community does not directly belong to you, yet it is present in your property. The thoroughly false concept, mostly borrowed from Roman law, as though what we have is our absolute property about which we alone have any say and with which we can do as we please, militates directly against the idea of an organically cohesive people.

Such a false concept gets us nowhere in the Christian domain. The Christian knows that God is the owner of everything and that he may only have the use of it in order to give glory to God, to benefit his people, and to provide for his needs. On this standpoint, therefore, to pay taxes is simply to pay what one has received from God to the government placed over us by God. And taxation entails this great mercy that precisely by paying taxes we have something of a bridle that can be put on political power. "*Pas*

---

11. Purmerend was a small market town just north of Amsterdam. Assen was and still is the modest capital of the eastern, inland province of Drenthe. Kalverstraat was and still is one of the finer shopping streets in Amsterdam. Culemborg and Tiel were and still are two small provincial towns in the Betuwe district wedged between two rivers, not far from the village of Beesd where Kuyper had his first charge as pastor.

12. The English term for this is *unearned increment*.

de griefs, pas de Suisses"[13] is a deeply religious motto, the mother of constitutional thought!

But quite apart from this check on power, the pagan Roman concept of property, on which our laws are based today, is untenable in and of itself as soon as you take the national community into account. If it is undeniably true that your country house is no longer worth a lease when its surrounding area is in decline; that the profits from your store diminish when the main route through your town is relocated; that your warehouses may as well be sold for demolition when a railway is built that makes putting into storage superfluous—then this alone proves beyond a doubt that living together with your fellow countrymen in the same national community represents real value, a value that adheres to your property yet does not depend on that property but on your surroundings.

Thus, since every property contains both a private portion and a national, communal portion, it goes without saying that the national community that adds this value to your property should be worth something to you, and that when the nation demands a share of this added value it in no way snatches at your property rights but still always gives you more than it takes away.

§ 220   DECENTRALIZING TAX LEVIES

(4) Decentralize your levy

If you ask yourself, given this purer concept of property, what system of levying taxes is preferable, then it is obvious that municipality, province, and central government should each go about it in a way commensurate with their nature.

To the national government belongs, first of all, the tax on every tract or portion of the national soil. The soil, after all, like the sea, the rivers, the mines, and the hunting grounds, is the natural productive power that affords the nation its first and foremost physical basis of existence. The government could have kept a large domain for itself or have work duties attached to it. It neglected to do so; it allowed its domain to dwindle to almost nothing, and it relinquished all forms of personal service (except for the army, militia, firefighting, and dike reinforcement). In that light,

---

13. Literally, "No grievances, no Swiss"; that is, if our grievances are not satisfied, we will not approve taxes to hire soldiers.

however, it is only right that it now regards a portion of landed property as national property and collects the revenue of that national portion.

Similarly, the central government collects import and export duties. These duties, after all, would be canceled if the nation lost its national independence. They are paid at the border and for the sake of the border and so belong typically to the national government.

In the third place, the central government has the right to impose a tax on mortgages and deeds and to collect registration and succession duties. These instruments guarantee the security of property, its legal transfer, and all other public actions.

Fourthly, the central government has a claim on the general excise tax that is not collected from the consumer but from the manufacturer, processor, and transporter. The cost of collecting it would therefore be squandered if it were regulated at the municipal level.

In the fifth place, it has a claim on all revenue that is due to the nation as a whole from any branch of public service, from national domains, from tribute by other nations, or otherwise.

TAX COLLECTION FOR THE CENTRAL GOVERNMENT   § 221

To prevent misunderstanding, let me add a brief word about each of these five categories.[14]

The land tax needs to be revised four ways: (1) it should not be based on a value long since surpassed but on its present value; (2) the increase should absorb at least 80 percent of transfer taxes and registration fees; (3) exemptions should be abolished; and (4) on properties of a very extensive nature the tax should be a progressive one.

The first point speaks for itself. There are lands that today are worth ten times their value of fifty years ago.

With respect to the second point it should be noted that the owner of a small piece of land, which has changed hands ten times during a century, still at present pays the full 100 percent of land tax, while a powerful family, which passes its land from father to son, pays nothing for registration. This strikes one as most unfair. The law ought to be changed in such a way that 80 percent of the normal proceeds of these transfer costs should be credited toward the land tax, leaving only a small amount for registration.

---

14. The published text deals with only three of the five categories.

About the exemptions, only this, for now: even properties bequeathed in perpetuity grow so out of proportion in value as a result of tax immunity that a foundation that was intended to be spiritual gradually turns unspiritual as a result of affluence. Simply recall the ecclesiastical property of the Roman Catholics in Hungary and of the Protestants in Ireland.

As for the progressive tax on land, it stands to reason that a person of this rank who owns, say, 500, 800, or 1,000 hectares,[15] profits more from the greater wealth he already owns precisely through that enormous combination, so that it would be only fair if the country took a larger portion of it.

Our import and export duties, too, are lower than is necessary. Five million [guilders] in total from nearly *f*600 million in imports and *f*500 million in exports is a trifle. They need to be raised appreciably, if only by way of reprisal if France and Germany continue their policy of protectionism. But even apart from that, we have entered more than one trade agreement in which we allowed our hands to be tied even for our excise taxes; in retrospect we can see that, sadly, our industry has suffered as a result of it. Our treaty with France especially is deplorable. Our private commercial houses are supplied from Paris. Now if we could only say that this overgenerous system had profited us! Unfortunately it has become apparent that our profit was only relative and that others profited still more than we did. Both from a financial point of view and from a national standpoint, a doubling of our import duties would seem highly desirable, without in any way jeopardizing our commitment to free trade. This would result in going from 0.5 to 1 percent of the total value of imports and exports.

The excise on sugar should eventually be abolished. That on wine and slaughtered meat should be raised, and spirits should be pushed up so high that the net revenue would stay the same while consumption would be reduced by a third. In that way, fiscal responsibility and ethical policy would work in tandem, something we think is our duty given such a serious subject as the sin of alcoholism. Tax on items like soap and salt could be left to the municipalities; they could choose either not to tax them or to tax the consumer.

---

15. That is, approx. 1,250, 1,400, and 2,500 acres, moderately large for the Netherlands.

Next to these levies for the central government we would like to see the municipalities have the right to tax noninterest-bearing capital, houses, consumption, and luxuries, as well as incorporation charters, business licenses and permits, and the head tax.

What is commonly called "domestic staff" should never have been subject to a national tax. After all, your home does not put you in any relationship with the national government but with your neighbors, hence with the residents of your domicile. Thus the municipality and not the national government should have the right to tax it. Only then will the expense of hired personnel be more equitable by having the payroll tax accommodated to the various conditions in towns and villages. At the same time the foolish tax on chimneys and windows can be abolished. As well, the progressive nature of the tax can be graduated more realistically by having it reflect the reality of local conditions.

Furthermore, if it were decided, as is entailed by our system, that municipal councils are appointed by guilds or corporations,[16] then it is only proper that each of these corporations, to show that it is not a fly-by-night organization, makes an annual payment to the municipality for its charter.

Licenses in the vast majority of cases function only at the local level, and so for the sake of assessing the scope and integrity of a business such licenses are best administered by the municipal authorities. The same goes for permits.

We must say that we fail to see why a municipality should not be allowed to levy consumption taxes if it so wishes. Our previous article gave ample arguments for having the common man contribute to the public treasury like any others. He too is a fellow countryman. He too is interested in the public cause and so should consider it an honor to contribute to its cost. However, he cannot pay an amount of any importance in any single transaction. But every day, say, half a cent per person: that would be feasible. And if that half cent were incorporated in the price of two or three consumer goods, the tax would be so little noticed that normal relations would be preserved without any problem. At least—and this must be mentioned in the same breath—at least if workingmen are allowed to form their own corporation and so have a voice in the conduct of affairs. *No taxation without representation* should also be the rule in our municipalities.

---

16. See above, § 138.

And to put the finger on one last item, no tax on capital or property, unless it consists of real estate, should ever go to the central government but should stay undivided and unsplit with the municipalities. Only in the place of one's domicile, surely, is a person sufficiently known to be fairly assessed financially. A head tax of some kind has been in vogue from the earliest times, throughout the ages, in villages, market towns, hamlets, or communities (or whatever name has been invented for places where people live together), and that for the natural and simple reason that only in that narrow circle of living together can people be gauged somewhat fairly. In the nature of the case, municipalities exceeding fifty thousand souls would have to be subdivided and have separate committees of assessment for each class; and everybody would have to have the freedom to appeal an assessment that he felt was too high by opening his books to an arbitration committee whose members would be sworn to secrecy and chosen from another class.

But a national income tax, however tempered and bridled, will always be unusable.

After all, a fair and equitable assessment of what you will have to pay has to take into consideration: (1) your income; (2) your family situation; (3) your rank and standing in the community; (4) any illness or adversity; (5) your provision for the future; (6) your external relations; and so many other details that do not fit any rubric and are not covered by any tax category. Only a jury of members of your class, with the possibility of appeal to a committee not of your class, can guarantee that each of these moral and social factors about your life will be taken into consideration.

§ 223   Contributions to Province and Central Government

The municipal revenues, thus reorganized, should also be encumbered with the twin burden of contributions to the province and surcharges for the national budget to cover any deficit.

In the case of the province, such contributions follow from its very nature. A province is not in touch with people themselves, nor with their houses, but only with municipalities. As a result, it lacks all fixed means of taxation. It can create revenue for itself through land reclamation and the like, which is always advisable. But any expenditures not covered in that way have to be prorated over the municipalities in proportion to their own budgets.

Finally, as for surcharges for the central government, it stands to reason that the state must have a flexible means to balance its budget every year.

With an organic system that looks for its center of gravity in the nation itself, this can be realized in no other way than by assessing the provinces—or what amounts to the same thing, the municipalities—for a percentage of the surcharges required. A national deficit of ƒ3 million would then raise the head tax in the municipality by about five cents. This would have the added advantage that the whole nation would immediately become aware that The Hague was running short again; and The Hague would find in this another incentive to guard against a repeat of such an unpopular deficit.

CHAPTER EIGHTEEN

NATIONAL DEFENSE

It seeks to promote a vigorous defense of our national independence by reinforcing the sense of justice, fostering knowledge of our history, affirming our popular liberties, practicing a skilled diplomacy, and by legislating an organization of the standing armed forces and the reserves on land and sea that, after improving life in the barracks and aboard ship and after abolishing the replacement system, relies for its strength above all on the morale of the soldier.

ARTICLE 17

I. NATIONALITY AND INTERNATIONAL LAW

§ 224   SENSE OF NATIONALITY

In a program of antirevolutionary principles, defense is no appendix but a major element—in three respects: as a protest against cosmopolitanism, as a protest against the supremacy of physical force, and no less as a protest against ignoring God in history.

Ever since the principles of the Revolution gained ground, this most serious subject, too, has seen views take hold of the mind of nations and the thinking of national leaders that are almost diametrically opposite to the views of former times.

In former times, the highest devotion a man could offer was to lay down his life for home and altar. A man loved his country and his soil. He was proud of his tribe and people and felt one with his fellow nationals. Granted, this could stem from a primitive instinct, an inherited passion if you will, which sometimes degenerated into contempt for the stranger, nationalistic boasting, and narrow-mindedness. Nevertheless, in pith and essence it had pluck and could animate and inspire heroes and in times of danger melt everybody together into one mighty whole.

In this way a centripetal force operated in every nation that threw into sharp relief the diversity of nations and the differences between peoples. It made men aware that things were different abroad, that people differed in intentions and feelings, in identity.

This focus on the distinguishing marks of national life proved conducive to a deepening of character that arises when the national conscience wakes up to its own calling and destiny.

Such growing awareness was not guided by any desire to imitate what foreigners modeled, but by a zeal to be original and to be oneself and therefore to be different from others. That is how the nations came to display their distinctiveness. Each loved its soil, its art, its labor. Everywhere you witnessed that rich splendor of multiformity that speaks to you and that embodies an idea and that proves to you that your nation has a right to an independent existence.

In those days people knew what homesickness meant. They understood the soul-stirring laments of the exile.

The sentiment "East, west, home best!" would fill the breasts of all who returned to our shores, and an "Amen!" would resound from the hearts of all people in the land.

INTERNATIONAL LAW §225

It was this concept of nationality that led naturally to the awareness that there is a "law of nations."

For if every nation is a distinctive organism, guided by a distinctive idea, energized by a distinctive blood, and called by God to a distinctive task, then it is only natural that the nations came to see that a single divine dispensation is common to them all and that they are, however different in character and essence, parts of a mightier whole, taken up in a higher community of nations, and therefore mutually bound to a higher law shared by all. Next to a special national mission, they came to realize that there is another, common human mission to fulfill, a mission in which the nations are to be led by the ordinances of the holy, Triune God acknowledged by all.

Hence the conviction that, just as every nation is a moral organism of which provinces and municipalities are the articulations, so also the nations of our continent in their turn together constitute one large organic whole of which each people is a living member and each nation, large or small, is one of the component parts.

This conviction in its deeper meaning did not yet exist in the pagan period of world empires; it remained foreign to the age of the Caesars and even now is but sparingly found in heathen lands. It did not take root until it was nourished by Christianity, and on that account it is Christian in origin and content. Consequently it can be further defined as a realization pervading the nations throughout Europe that the baptized nations together constitute one great "family of nations" that finds the strength for its higher unity precisely in the meaningful plurality of national distinctiveness.

Not until this was realized did international law acquire a genuine basis. It made for a moral foundation for international relations and based Europe's community of law not exclusively on cunning and armed force but first and foremost on the certainty of written treaties, invariably consecrated by the classic words of their preamble still used today: "In the Name of the Holy Trinity."

§ 226   GOD OF THE NETHERLANDS

Given this deepened mental state in people's consciousness and their sense of a higher law guarding the nations, it was ultimately only a matter of course that, when war broke out, confidence in the outcome could only rest, more than in force of arms, in the belief that the God who created the nations would also protect them against destruction and that the Judge of all the earth would do right by one's nation.

In this sense alone, and in no other, people spoke of a "God of our fathers" and a "God of the Netherlands." A common objection was that in that case two warring nations would be living with the same illusion and that at least one of them would always end up being disappointed. The proper response was, first of all, that nations too can be guilty before God and then cannot expect their prayers to be heard; and secondly, that a temporary defeat may hide a blessing while the most glorious victories, upon deeper understanding— just recall what happened to France and Germany—can conceal a curse.

This was the very motive behind—and we hasten to add, the perfectly reasonable ground for—our national days of penance, thanksgiving, and prayer. On those days of glorious memory our entire nation came together in its deeper unity and raised itself to the highest strains of its vital strength by humbly entering again into communion with its God.

EUROPE'S CHRISTIAN FAMILY OF NATIONS   § 227

Today, however, all this has changed.

That poetic world of old was, after all, as we are told, nothing but illusion and self-delusion. You can hear it every day in the talk of our liberalized citizens.[1] The wise people of this wiser age amuse themselves with the various innocent practices that our simpleminded ancestors were once upon a time fond of.

First they laughed at those days of prayer, and then they abolished them. Diplomacy, which was to maintain the bonds between the nations, they held up for ridicule, and then they condemned it as a useless luxury and degraded it to a polite exchange of courtesies and harmless communiqués. Respect for treaties they systematically undermined, and then they opposed and mocked them as childish naïveté.

To continue to speak of a "Christian family of nations" became more and more a thorn in the side of our secularized political philosophers and Jewish-liberal power cliques.

And if international law did in fact make progress in terms of splendid victories for humanitarianism, neither should we shut our eyes to the unnatural sentimentalism that crept in, and even less to the highly questionable effort to celebrate the triumph of international law on the ruins of the right of nations.

For if anything has stood out in the exploits of our century, then it is the endeavor to erase the boundaries between the nations, to erode the distinctiveness of each nation, and to recast all life among every people, in every town and village and every social class, according to a single artificial, uniform model.

This causes international law to cease being what it was originally and what it is intended to be, and to degenerate more and more into a system of highly dangerous arguments that flow with logical necessity from the revolutionary principle.

The purpose of international law in former days was to guarantee the right of existence—of existence with honor—to all nations, large and small. This guarantee rested on having the nations together submit to a

---

1. For "citizens," Kuyper uses the French *citoyens*, indicating a cosmopolitan, Revolutionary understanding of a person's identity.

higher law. Nowadays the purpose of international law is taken to mean the opposite. It demands sacrificing the nations' right of independent existence to a certain imaginary right of Europe's peoples to form large agglomerates and to eliminate every barrier and every obstacle that still prevent the merger and blending of the life of the nations.

This has already been affirmed boldly and forcefully by the apostles of the one great world republic, and even more brazenly by Communards and Socialists. Yet it was also affirmed factually by Napoleon, who swallowed up nation after nation; by Victor Emmanuel II, who annexed state after state;[2] by Bismarck, who dared to play with princes and kings as if they were toys.[3] And it has been affirmed once again by Britain in the Transvaal and in Afghanistan.[4] And, alas, even worse, by all European powers combined, when they had their way in the Balkans, not asking for what would be right and just, but for what fitted in with their system of utility.[5]

Hence international law in this modern view increasingly causes the smaller nations to vanish from the scene and to be robbed not just of certain incidental rights but of their very primordial right to exist. People no longer recognize that in organisms, and so also in Europe's family of nations, the smaller ones are usually the finer members, of the choicest value for the nobler blossoming of the whole. In every country, consequently, relying on one's rights counts for little, and living by the sword is again practiced in this century of the most refined culture.

§ 228   Internal Demoralization

The worst consequence is that as international law is violated, as treaties are torn up and the security of the smaller nations is gone, the same fatal Revolutionary principle is at work in the hearts of the smaller nations

---

2. Between 1860 and 1861, the king of Sardinia conquered Lombardy and annexed a number of other independent kingdoms and republics to create a unified Italy.

3. In 1866, Bismarck's Prussia defeated Austria and proceeded to annex the kingdom of Hanover, the principalities of Hesse-Homburg and Hesse-Kassel, the duchies of Nassau and Schleswig, and the Free City of Frankfurt.

4. During the late 1870s, Britain annexed the Transvaal Republic (until 1902 known as the South African Republic, not to be confused with the present-day Republic of South Africa) and expanded its sphere of influence in Afghanistan.

5. At the Congress of Berlin in 1878, Britain, France, Austria, Prussia, and Russia divided the Balkan Peninsula into a number of separate countries with borders advantageous to the short- and long-term interests of these powers.

themselves so as to undermine what still had the promise of tenacious defense and indomitable resistance.

Instead of burning with hot indignation at the traitor who dares to mock national honor and love of country, it has become the rule among our young men of social status and intelligence to laugh cynically at this "old-fashioned patriotism." Among the discontented lower classes there has been a steady erosion of every higher aspiration that might still have kindled deeds of heroic valor. Even in Christian circles sometimes—we can't help but note—men talk of being absorbed by a more powerful nation in a tone of voice that betrays an absolute lack of faith in a divine mission that still rests on our Netherlands.

And of course, if people, once swept away by that antinational current, still want to argue about Krupp cannon versus Armstrong artillery, of forts along the rivers or batteries along the coast—it is not even worth listening to.[6] On that standpoint our death warrant as a nation has been signed. Then we ourselves have forfeited the right to remain free. Then every guilder spent on navy or army is nothing but pointless squander, theft from the national treasury, a pure waste of money.

Reflecting on this, we wholeheartedly endorse what our Program has in mind when it insists that you cannot address the question of military defense until your right to defend yourself is assured and until you have the courage once again to trust in your people and to trust in your God.

II. MORAL DEFENSE

HISTORY OF THE COUNTRY §229

Moral defense, in distinction from military defense, consists of four heads: (1) the history of our country; (2) the sense of justice; (3) civic spirit; and (4) diplomacy. The significance of these four points is as follows.

(1) *Knowledge of the country's history.* This history is the story of the birth and evolution of our nation. It is a photograph, if you like, of the fibrous network of roots that lie hidden beneath the surface and that is now being examined by a later generation that has sprouted forth as leaf and blossom high up on the trunk, at a good distance from the root-ball. It is not just a story, therefore, of what was done in former centuries by hoary, long-forgotten ancestors, but it is the continued vibration of that

---

6. The Krupp cannon is of Prussian origin, while the Amstrong artillery is of British provenance.

selfsame life that comes to expression in today's Netherlanders but which expressed itself in the same breath in the generation then living. River channels are always filled with different drops, yet century after century it is always the same "monarch of streams from Alpine brow"[7] that discharges its wealth of water to our low-lying lands. Similarly, the one nation is continually made up of different people—other specks of dust on the scales, other drops in the bucket—yet it is always the same ethnic group, the same linkage of families, the same old blood, however rejuvenated, that courses from father to son and enters our veins as through a never-ending stream. And inside all the individual spirits whose fortitude once tingled or still tingles in that blood, at the end of the day there is and remains but one spirit of the nation. Never extinguished but passed on from one generation to the next, this spirit once suffered, lived, and gloried in our forefathers ten, eight, three centuries ago, and even now, in our own generation, rather than glorying, still suffers, lives, and grieves in us.

Hence a wondrous mystery cleaves to the history of one's country, the kind of mystery that is inseparable from all inspired and struggling life. It is a mystery that cannot be dissected in dates or exhausted in names and documents. Nor can it be unveiled by the most meticulous and pedantic description of what this or that historical figure thought and did and struggled through. Rather, behind those dates and names and individual exploits lies a mystery in what the nation collectively endured in days of anxiety, sinned in years of opulence, and gave thanks in the hour of deliverance before the face of its God. The mystery of the life of the nation—it is invisible and ineffable; it is that which redoubles the courage of the standard-bearer in the field of honor when he senses that the flag he clutches will decide the honor of a whole nation. It is elusive and indescribable. In moments of tension it stirs a people from its slumber into righteous anger. It is the mysterious drive which, though not exhausted by the Orange name, yet had the power to create heroes of the unforgettable princes of that house and to give that people a heart to love those heroes and their offspring with undying loyalty.

Precisely the history of one's country harbors that epic quality that can inspire fresh deeds through remembering the past. It harbors that sense

---

7. Kuyper here quotes an elegy by Leiden professor Elias Annes Borger (1784–1820), "*Aan den Rijn*" ("To the Rhine").

of unity that can in moments of peril take us out of our provincialism to face the foe arm in arm as one man. No less does it harbor those sublime signs indicating that with a very small force the greatest things can often be accomplished and that the most surprising results can be attained if, against all hope, one nevertheless ventures to rely on his God.

It is therefore essential for our people of all ranks and classes to be baptized once again with that holy enthusiasm for the history of our country. Not in memorizing tables and genealogies and reading dry chronicles, which never contained life to begin with and are therefore incapable of awakening life. Why not spare our simple folk all *that* baggage? It is a rare mother who knows how many ribs and how many vertebrae her child has, but she thinks, "The doctor will know that," and she just loves her child and shares its pranks over the fence with her neighbor. In the same way it makes no difference in the world to a child from the working classes if it is confused by a century or three and thinks that Orange lies in Frisia and William III was a son of Frederick Henry.[8] What matters for that child are the tableaus, the imaginary pictures in full color, the heroic figures, and even the legends of miraculous events. For without those legends your history, which is always a fallible narrative anyway, will no longer be real history; it will be without its truest, most inspiring element, that mysterious breath of life.

Let the supporters of the Education Act take heed. It is a fact that in the interest of their partisan intentions they have taken the soul out of our history and robbed it of warmth and life. Knowledge of our history has already dwindled considerably in the country. Under their system we will never again see a time when that history will have the power to inspire. They will have to answer to God and our people for allowing this breach in our moral defense for the sake of pushing their political agenda.

SENSE OF JUSTICE   § 230

(2) What takes hold of our conscience, far more deeply than our everyday awareness, is the *sense of justice*. This even comes out in animals. Watch the little dog as he attacks the trespassing hoodlum. The same instinct speaks incomparably more nobly, more inspired, more powerfully among humans.

---

8. The principality of Orange lies in southern France, and the king-stadtholder William III (1650–1702) was a grandson of Prince Frederick Henry (1584–1647).

Send the most powerful army into war, and however fine its weapons, polished its gear, and excellent its commanders, that army will remain a lumbering mass that may be able to maneuver but will not strike fear into a foe and will carry on its mindless task in silence. On the other hand, field a small army that, poorly equipped and barely trained, sees itself forced to lay down its arms straightway, but then inject into the souls of these armed men the awareness that their rights have been offended, violated, trodden underfoot, and you will see these same clumsy fighters at first stand their ground with great valor and then fly off in all directions—not to save their hides in flight but to operate in small guerilla bands to harass the enemy until such time as help arrives in the form of storms or floods, disease or pestilence, aid from men or from God.

Moreover, if we foster that sense of justice in ourselves we will also hold it high in our surroundings and so increase our chances of gaining sympathy for our cause, perhaps even assistance, if our national independence were ever threatened unfairly and unjustly.

Justice has invincible strength, provided we hold it sacred ourselves. In our own day, Christian nations have been wrested free from Turkish power after they seemed to have shed their best blood in a vain struggle for three, four centuries.[9] Their newfound freedom is an encouragement to every people that still dares to stand up for its rights, and it prophesies to nations that have temporarily gone under that they may yet revive and flourish again.

In particular with a view to this fact, we lodged a serious protest five years ago against Nieuwenhuyzen's conduct on the coasts of Achin.[10] It led to a war for which our people have had no heart or enthusiasm and which in part has even violated our own sense of justice. We fought this war without prayer. At the outbreak of hostilities our Keuchenius,[11] sooner

---

9. The Balkans were overrun around 1400 by the Ottoman Empire, which was gradually forced to retreat from the peninsula beginning in the 1860s.

10. In March 1873, F. N. Nieuwenhuyzen (1819–92), representing the Dutch colonial government, declared war on Achin (modern Aceh) in northern Sumatra, after failing to negotiate its cooperation in putting a stop to piracy in the Strait of Malacca, a strategic shipping route for trade in spices and opium.

11. L. W. C. Keuchenius (1822–93), one of Kuyper's correspondents, was a former vice-chairman of the Council of the East Indies and then a member of the Dutch parliament from 1866 to 1868, when he returned to Java and became a newspaper editor. In 1874 he authored a book protesting censorship of the press regarding the Achin war.

than many a government official, saw further and deeper, sensing at once that expedience had trumped justice and fear had trumped faith and that the wrong being committed against Achin would morally avenge itself on us.

And even if it should turn out with hindsight, which may just be possible, that as far as the question of right goes, Keuchenius was mistaken and Loudon[12] was correct, even then it is still an unforgivable error not to have provided the national conscience with information to be able to judge whether or not the war was just.

CIVIC SPIRIT   § 231

(3) In the hour of peril, the government needs the people.

If a government through wise rule and prudent administration has won people's trust in its intention to promote their happiness, it will succeed in creating a sense of satisfaction and concord, making a nation happy about conditions and growing in love for national independence. This fosters a situation in which unity provides strength and mutual appreciation promotes harmony and understanding. Now then, in such a case, as history shows, a government can count on its people when it matters: it will be met with compliance rather than resistance, and be carried by the citizens' readiness.

Wise governments have therefore always striven to gain the love and trust of their peoples and to promote a spirit of mutual attachment among the citizens, a spirit that arises of itself when authorities are not afraid of freedom and avoid provoking the citizenry to kick against the pricks.

Our government, however, seems to regard this as outdated wisdom. At least, it has been working literally for years to undermine every confidence in the government's power to rule. By almost every measure it has contributed to evoking discontent and bitterness. It has turned a deaf ear to the most urgent and justified complaints that came its way. It has lapsed into the worst state that a government can fall into—namely, into party tyranny—or if you will, in abusing the central authority, which is meant to serve all, by suppressing what more than half the nation desires.[13]

---

12. After Dutch forces suffered military setbacks in Achin (see above, n8), the governor-general in Batavia (modern Jakarta), James Loudon (1824–1900), decided to step up efforts to subjugate Achin.

13. Kuyper makes another oblique reference to the Primary Education Act of 1877, against which half a million people had petitioned.

This cannot be emphasized enough in a discussion of our *moral* defense.

If the present government continues its practice of offending our popular liberties instead of enhancing them, civic spirit cannot but dwindle in the measure that partisan spirit gains ground. In the hour of peril the government, as a party instrument, will find itself incapable of mustering energy and will find the nation incapable of united action. And the natural punishment for not *ruling* but merely *administering* will be that sooner or later (God grant, for only a few years) a foreign commander will occupy the royal palace and show us with a few hard facts what it means to *rule* the country if governance is to have any weight.[14]

§ 232   DIPLOMACY

(4) As concerns diplomacy, finally, we protest strongly against the bad repute in which our Foreign Affairs[15] has been held the last quarter century, but also against the insignificant and indefensible role that our Foreign Ministry has played in European affairs.

On the Christian-historical standpoint, a sound, competent, and energetic diplomatic service is far from a luxury. It is an absolutely indispensable instrument for guaranteeing our independence; for maintaining our organic connection with other nations and governments; and for having each nation contribute to the communal goal that rests on Christian Europe, namely, to uphold the sanctity of justice, to combat paganism[16] and Islam, to respect the human element in human society, and to hold high the honor of God.

To institute and maintain such a diplomatic service, however, takes an incredible amount of effort, especially given the inconstancy of cabinets and no less the breakdown of the European balance of power—as a result of which just about every calculation that is made of the outcome of events, even in the short term, can only fail.

What the diplomatic service needs, today more than ever, is a body of civil servants who can provide the intelligence for carrying out its almost impossible task. These servants of the state need to be quick

---

14. The Netherlands was ruled by King Louis Bonaparte from 1806 to 1810 and by his brother Emperor Napoleon from 1810 to 1813 (the Kingdom of Holland was dissolved in 1810 after which the Netherlands was annexed by France until 1813).

15. "Foreign Affairs" here translates the original "*het Buitenhof*," which is short for the Department of Foreign Affairs in The Hague.

16. Kuyper's main target in mentioning "paganism" here is Indonesian animism.

learners—men of solid training, wide knowledge, and creative and flexible minds. Their task is nothing less than to keep track of any incipient movements that might potentially turn against the interests or the security of the state. It includes using tact to extend the country's influence, to promote our reputation among foreign governments and peoples, and to intervene at any moment when to do nothing would be to lose our honor or to harm our interests for the future.

Those needs are not being met today. At this moment, we have almost no diplomat of sufficient influence at any foreign court. If such a one has any influence, it is more of social than political significance—regard for the person, not for our country.

What is lacking is competent personnel, unity of vision, and willpower in the department, and the appreciation of parliament.

At present it turns out repeatedly that even the Belgian diplomats beat us at our game. At many negotiations we are the dupes of the other party's cunning. We are treated as a nonentity, no longer as a nation that matters. Reliable documents have revealed that there was talk of the annexation of our country before Foreign Affairs knew anything about it.[17]

This fate pursues us even in our colonies. English settlers have outwitted us, and just recently we were shrewdly taken in by Spain when it accepted the sovereignty of the Sulu Islands[18] and sent us an almost comical notification after the fact.

And when you recall as well what unbelievable damage was done to us both on the Gold Coast[19] of Africa and the north coast of Sumatra by our clumsy and ill-advised negotiations with Britain, while we are already falling behind even on Decima,[20] then surely we have put enough on the table to support our serious indictment.

SELF-EFFACEMENT   § 233

In the interest of our calling within the European family of nations, we cannot end our indictment here but must go on to register a strong protest

---

17. Secret annexation designs were rumored during 1866–70 involving France and Prussia.
18. The Sulu Archipelago is a chain of over five hundred tiny islands lying between the Spanish Philippines and the Dutch East Indies.
19. The "Gold Coast" of Africa was the former name of (the south coast of) Ghana, where the Dutch had maintained a trading post since the days of the slave trade.
20. The island of Decima in Nagasaki Bay was reserved for Western trade with Japan and was an exclusively Dutch trading post from 1641 to 1853.

against the cowardly and disgraceful practice of countries, whenever a conflict breaks out, to fall silent and do nothing and eschew any alliance for future action.

In the Transvaal Question,[21] in fact even earlier, when half of Denmark and all of Nassau was broken up,[22] our government should have spoken up. Just recently, when the question of Islam was settled,[23] the world's second colonial power[24] should have got itself introduced to the power brokers. And what speaks even louder, now that it has become evident from the facts and from secret diplomatic archives that the existence of states of the second rank is actually at risk, our Dutch diplomacy should long since have taken the initiative to enter upon a policy of alliances that would have given notice that we are still here. A little slumber and a little folding of the hands, as the prophet says,[25] won't get you very far.

Among the smaller nations in particular, courage counts for more than life.

However, to arrive at a more active diplomacy, and thereby to stronger diplomatic action, four demands would have to be met at once: (1) The Ministry of Foreign Affairs should always be headed by a true minister, not just a titled individual. (2) To Foreign Affairs should be added a college of capable and experienced men who can maintain continuity with the past as cabinets succeed one another. (3) Our embassies should be sufficiently financed to enable a talented person of little means to afford an appointment there. (4) Every embassy of some importance should be sufficiently staffed to enable the envoy to be an *envoy*.

Recall what Venice once did! Recall our own diplomats in the days when not all of them were of the nobility. What men we had among them!

---

21. Kuyper refers here to Britain's annexation in 1877 of the Boer republic north of the Vaal River, ostensibly to protect the rights of British participants in the gold rush there. The annexation was undone after the British were defeated in the battle of Majuba Hill in 1881. See above, § 227n3.

22. This was the outcome of the Austro-Prussian War of 1866, when the duchies of Sleswig and Holstein were permanently separated from Denmark and incorporated into Prussia. The duchy of Nassau was annexed by Prussia for having backed Austria during the late war.

23. Kuyper makes a possible reference here to Turkey's pledge, given at the 1878 Congress of Berlin, to grant religious liberty to Christians in its territories in the Balkans.

24. Reference to the Netherlands.

25. See Prov 6:10–11; 24:33–4.

Recall Switzerland, whose excellent consulates surpass even those of great empires.

III. MILITARY DEFENSE

DEFENSE MUST BE ATTEMPTED§ 234

Our *moral* defense, if carried through to the schools for the sake of our national history, will save the state an appreciable sum of money. But our *military* defense, even at the current annual cost of nearly ƒ40 million, is inadequate.

Every ten, nay every five years, military science persuades the officer corps of the most belligerent nations to make both navy and army larger, faster, and more destructive. Britain attends to this cruel task in sea power; Prussia does the same for armed forces on land; and France is once again making these two powers nervous by slaving away in its arsenals and shipyards to uphold its military honor.

Of course this compels the other rival powers to follow suit by copying the expensive and destructive example of these three without any hesitation or second thoughts. When all the bigger states thus try to outstrip each other with ever bigger war budgets, states of the second rank would have to be extremely naïve if they did not realize that the course of events leaves them no other choice than to inflate their own war budgets or to withdraw from the arms race altogether.

In particular a country like ours, whose colonies might so easily titillate the insatiable acquisitiveness of the first power on the seas, and the location of whose harbors might so naturally excite the covetousness of the first power on land—this country has to keep an eye on the offensive strength of Britain and Prussia. We would have to conclude in advance that we are in a bad way if we shrink from expanding the war budget.

Every citizen in the land, people in every region of the country, in particular our parliament and government, will have to consider coolly and soberly what we want to do given this situation.

Do we want to forego defending ourselves and just knuckle under, seeing how Britain's sea power and Prussia's land power are rising like a swelling stream that we could never stand up against anyway? Or do we, if fall we must should it come to that, want to fall with honor?

Faced with that choice, we, and every antirevolutionary with us, would choose unconditionally for the latter. No nation of character may ever give up its God-given existence. Moreover, our people are of a type that could never thrive if annexed. Above all, it would be cowardly, dishonorable, and scornful of the memory of our forefathers if our patrimony, for whose freedom they once offered their finest blood, were surrendered without putting up a fight against a would-be conqueror.

§ 235   Firm Plans

Once this choice is calmly and solemnly made, however, there will be no need to argue about the big budgets of Navy and War. We will simply have to practice making sacrifices in order to put our precious patrimony in an adequate state of defense and for this defense to pledge our blood and that of our sons.

Our people of every rank and status will have to know that our military defense cannot be mounted except on an expensive—very expensive— footing. The only thing the nation can insist upon with the government is that for this great expense it provides an *adequate* defense.

With this in mind, therefore, our Program demands a fixed, that is, legislated organization of the entire military defense on land and sea, in order once for all to deliver us from this unheard-of and unbearable situation that we got ourselves into in spite of ourselves.

After all, to spend ƒ40 million a year and still be quite certain that the British can occupy the seat of government in The Hague within twenty-four hours, and that the Prussians can be in the central square in Amsterdam within twice twenty-four hours, is enough for a tiny nation to become furious with its military authorities and to lose all courage for the future.

The kind of situation in which we find ourselves at this moment is, simply put, shameful for the government and irresponsible for the nation.

This cannot go on. The first thing that has to be done is to stop all ongoing work for some six months, give the Departments of Navy and War a definitive organization, and bring the general staff up to snuff. Departments and staff should then establish, in connection with data to be furnished by Finance and Water Board, a brilliantly conceived, well-thought out, sound and coherent plan of overall defense. This plan should be considered in the committee of the whole, with the request that the Chambers cooperate in fixing by law those points in the plan that should not be in jeopardy every time a budget is debated or a cabinet changes.

Once we have gotten through this stage, a comprehensive plan of defense should immediately be drawn up for the three most likely attacks that will have to be repulsed. The duties of each army unit under each of these three plans will have to be established down to the smallest detail and communicated to the commanding officers. Everything should be arranged in such a way, finally, that any surprise attack on our eastern frontiers or on our seacoast will henceforth be impossible.

Only in this way will the army regain its self-confidence and our officer corps know why it exists. Guided by a fixed plan, the work required will be to the purpose, and the nation will not resent and begrudge a big defense budget but will pay for it with love and devotion.

THE SOLDIER'S MORALE   § 236

This outcome will be all the more assured if the War Department draws back somewhat from its focus on military hardware and attaches greater value than has hitherto been attached, also in wartime, to the *morale* of the soldier.

This, in fact, is the main issue for the future of our armed forces. Today the entire countryside curses an institution that literally demoralizes many of its young people, who then take back to the quiet life of the village the poison they themselves have first absorbed. Today the lower classes curse a military institution that, necessitating a replacement system, preferably chooses to sacrifice *their* sons. Every person of noble mind can only utter words of indignation and disapproval for an organization of our standing army that manipulates men without respecting them as human beings.

This can no longer be tolerated.

By virtue of the antirevolutionary principle, we, following the example of Groen van Prinsterer, abhor all traffic in human beings, also in its weakest forms. We join the demand that an end be put to the system of replacements[26] and that the cancer be cut out that has thus far tainted our army.

What follows from this, of course, is that the government ought to (1) provide livable barracks for our servicemen; (2) prevent the abuse of alcohol; (3) make visits to bawdy houses subject to severe penalties; (4) forbid

---

26. Conscription took place by lot. A young man who drew an "unlucky number" could hire a replacement to serve in his stead, usually at a steep price. The result was that members of the lower classes, who could ill afford to pay for a replacement, preponderated in the armed forces, while members of well-to-do families rarely served.

officers, sergeants, and corporals from swearing at our conscripts; (5) encourage the establishment of military homes; (6) open the possibility of more advanced education for some of the more advanced units; and (7) congregate the men in larger garrisons so as to make possible the appointment of chaplains and thus restore the religious character of the way our armed forces are organized.

The tone, the perceptions of the general public, the thinking in our army about what honors and elevates a soldier and makes him into a man of character, need to be thoroughly reversed. The soldier has to be reminded that military morals do not differ from civilian morals, since morality in the civil and military domain alike is bound immutably to God's ordinances.

We are not demanding the impossible.

We realize full well that armies like those of Gustavus Adolphus and Oliver Cromwell will always be the exception and that as a rule the military will not be able to conduct itself on a higher plane than the average level of morality in civil society.[27]

As long as it does not sink below that level! This we urge as strongly as we can. Life in the barracks must not inevitably cause the general level of morality, not high as it is, to sink even lower for the best among these average men.

§ 237   MILITIA AND MERCENARIES

Finally, as for military defense as such, it stands to reason that in a program of principles only those few points can come up for discussion that are more immediately related to those principles.

We restrict ourselves to five.

(1) All mingling of *conscripts* and *volunteers* should end. As is well known, this was the basic maxim of defense for all our kindred Calvinistic nations that were introduced by the spirit of Calvin to a deeper understanding of popular liberties. Switzerland, England, Scotland, America, and our own

---

27. Kuyper refers here to the reputation and military accomplishments of two famed Protestant figures. The Lutheran Gustavus Adolphus (1594–1632) was a Swedish king who led armies in the Thirty Years War. The English military and political leader Oliver Cromwell (1599–1658) supported Parliament by commanding forces in the English Civil War and was Lord Protector of the Commonwealth of England from 1653 until his death.

country originally had a sharply divided organization of the armed forces: one part consisted of paid soldiers, the other of the civic guard or militia.

This division was made inevitable by a political sensitivity to the nature of civic spirit as well as by a profound awareness that the morality of mercenary soldiers does not suit a society of peaceable burghers.

And although developments in our country have led to a considerable reduction of paid soldiers, which still form the bulk of the army in Britain and America, we still insist that, despite these smaller dimensions, the old division be reinstated. We do so on the following grounds: (a) the morale of the militia would gain immeasurably; (b) having a body of well-trained soldiers at the ready can offer security against surprise attack; (c) such a professional corps would be the obvious force for maintaining law and order; and (d) in Achin, for example, there would have been no such bungling and none of those casualties among our officer corps and that of our native army if an experienced body of troops had landed at Kota Raja[28] within eight weeks.

PROVINCIAL ARMY FORMATION   § 238

(2) The formation of the army should be provincial.

This is demanded by the organic nature of the national community.

At present each regiment has provincials of all kinds mixed through each other. The wretched results are that our regiments have no historical character, bear no inspiring name, and are distinguished only by a meaningless number. Conscripts are needlessly removed far away from home, large-scale joint exercises with the reserves are made more cumbersome, and mobilization of the army is costly and slow.

This ought not to be so. It goes against our Netherlandic character. Our military authorities were wrong to imitate the French generals, who are now themselves abandoning it.

If, instead, provincial formation were restored in our country, as in Prussia, Russia, Austria, and so on, so that we would have Frisian, Groningen, Brabant, Zeeland, Holland regiments, and so on, then the army, too, would mirror the organic nature of our national community. Every regiment would be filled with a competitive spirit, a sense of honor and pride of character; conscripts would stay closer to home; concentration

---

28. Kota Raja ("City of the King") was formerly the name of the capital city of Achin, located on the northernmost tip of Sumatra. The name was later changed to Banda Aceh.

would be facilitated; mobilization could be completed more quickly; and every provincial command center could have at its beck and call whatever is required for an immediate fielding of troops.

§ 239   CONCENTRATED DEFENSE

(3) The system of concentrating our defense[29] should not be exaggerated.

As things stand today, a flying Prussian corps could invade along the northern coast and permanently cut us off from the rich resources of Frisia, Groningen, Drenthe, and Overijsel provinces, while another corps could cross the Meuse river in the south and permanently leave us without Limburg, Brabant, and Zeeland provinces. We are not even mentioning the possibility that the Prussian marines, which are getting stronger every year, could attack the Water Line in the rear by making a surprise landing along the North Sea coast.

As things are organized at present, none of our regiments would be at full strength, our army would be reduced by one-third, and we would risk financial bankruptcy.

Moreover, the cold-blooded plan to leave these valuable provinces to the enemy without any attempt at resistance can only be detrimental to any patriotic zeal in those provinces. Their people would think "Holland is all that matters anyway," and they would resign themselves to their lot much sooner than we would like to see.

Obviously, a provincial formation would form a powerful counterweight against this, provided the active forces on duty were increased by some 60 percent and our militia were better coordinated.

§ 240   THE CIVIC GUARD

(4) The civic guard should be coordinated again with the army.

In former centuries the name of civic guards, at present mostly the target of ridicule, was a title of honor in these lands. It can become that again if we simply scrap the French revolutionary idea of a *garde nationale* as a

---

29. This system allowed for the northern and southern provinces to be left undefended in favor of defending only the three provinces of Utrecht, North Holland, and South Holland, as part of the strategic reliance on the old but modernized "Water Line" defense works, where inundations had held up Louis XIV in 1672 and the French revolutionary armies in 1794. (The Water Line proved largely irrelevant in 1940 when the German invasion deployed airborne troops and resorted to aerial bombardment of cities such as Rotterdam.)

power over against the army and invest it with what it meant of old and still means today: *arming the people.*

That would cancel all differences between the regular army and the civic guard except that the army would consist of the soldiers on active duty and the militia or civic guards would be those consigned to the reserves. Conscripts that had served their tour of duty, and they alone, would join the militia, and thanks to the provincial formation would remain posted to the same regiments and under the same command structure that they had served in former years. This would at the same time give the militia a firm formation, a solid training, and an efficient command structure, three qualities that would restore what it has completely lost: namely, military significance.

Consequently, we would gain a standing army that, provincially posted and directly linked to the militia, could within a fortnight field a well-trained force of 100,000 men and free up another 25,000 men for the fortified posts. We could then also choose to have the concentrated defense system serve as the fallback position after first protecting our name, heightening army morale, and paying the debt of sympathy to our northern and southern brothers by means of field operations ultimately converging on the Water Line.

THE NAVY § 241

(5) The navy is crucial.

One may be glad to note that to judge from events in 1854 in the Baltic Sea, near Lissa in 1866, with the French fleet in 1870, and now again with the Turkish fleet in 1878, coastal defenses are much stronger than any attacks.[30]

This fact yields the incalculable advantage that we may consider ourselves able to withstand any attacks from the sea. Provided, that is, that we take care that our sea batteries are of the heaviest and best caliber, that our torpedo branch is impeccably organized, and that at every station a certain number of heavily armed monitors of shallow draft ride at anchor, ready to come out and inflict damage on the attacker.

---

30. In 1854, an Anglo-French naval operation proved incapable of taking a Russian fortress during the Crimean War; in 1866, the Austrian fleet defeated Italian forces near Lissa Island in the Adriatic; in 1870, French marines tried unsuccessfully to land on the Baltic coasts of Prussia; and in 1878, Turkish warships in the Black Sea could not dislodge Russians from Bulgaria.

This undeniable fact means that our navy need not be fitted for battles on the open seas. Thus we can forgo purchasing battleships like the
Devastation.[31] We have no choice but to leave the colonies to their own defenses and limit our navy, apart from coastal defense, to a sizeable flotilla
of large ships to show our flag on a regular basis, and to a squadron of fast
torpedo boats that, fully equipped and preferably cruising at every point
on the globe, in case of war can keep open the lines of communication
with the colonies and above all are able to serve as raiders.

---

31. The British battleship *Devastation* of the 1870s was the first type to do without rig-
ging for sails.

CHAPTER NINETEEN

OVERSEAS POSSESSIONS

As to the colonial question, it affirms that the selfish tendency of our policy to exploit the colonies for public revenue or private profit ought to be replaced by a policy of moral obligation in pursuance of which (as repeatedly pointed out by antirevolutionary politicians who have studied the matter) all hindrances to the free proclamation of the gospel ought to be removed, private initiatives for primary education by the European population ought to be supported, and the Christian character of the nation ought not to be disowned in the face of Islam, to the end that political as well as social and economic relations are brought into line with the demands of Christian-historical principles.

ARTICLE 18

I. MOTHER COUNTRY AND COLONIES

DISSENTING SYMPATHIZERS
§ 242

In discussing the colonial question we want to proceed with the greatest caution, in view of the question itself as well as the dissenting opinions that to this day are being advocated in the lower house of parliament by influential and valued sympathizers with our movement.

However, we may not, out of respect for their dissenting views, be silent about what is demanded by our principle.

For us to remain silent, our dissenting supporters would have to do one of two things: either demonstrate how their ideas flow logically from the antirevolutionary principle, or else show that the ideas we hold do not square with this principle. So long as neither of the two is attempted and these popular tribunes, highly esteemed in many other areas, continue to confine themselves, as regards the political and social system for the colonies, to urging and reinforcing the arguments of their conservative colleagues, all will grant that we would be guilty of neglecting our duty if we lacked the courage to state forthrightly what the distinctiveness of our principle entails.

No one should conclude from this, however, that we therefore bracket with the conservative leaders those men within our circle who advocate for colonial affairs what we deem untenable from an antirevolutionary point of view. That would be unfair, because the gentlemen we have in mind boldly champion what we, too, consider the main demand: free proclamation of the gospel. They introduced this friendly amendment with such courage that for this alone they have an unconditional claim on our gratitude. This single amendment to the conservative program in fact kills and destroys it.

§ 243   WE POSSESS COLONIES BUT DO NOT OWN THEM

Moving on to discuss the question itself, we confine ourselves in this first article to those points of colonial policy that touch on the right of sovereignty or, to put it differently, that touch on the relation between motherland and colonies.

The Constitution takes as starting point the view as though motherland and colonies together constitute one kingdom. Article 2 states: *"The Kingdom of the Netherlands consists in Europe of the present provinces of North Brabant, ..."* and so on. Clearly, this wording presumes that the Kingdom of the Netherlands, in addition to Europe, also has constituent parts elsewhere, on other continents. Thus it assumes the fiction that our Netherlandic provinces form one single state, one undivided whole, with Java, Sumatra, Borneo, Celebes, Suriname, Curaçao, and so on, and that they all fall under the same sovereignty.

We antirevolutionaries cannot assent to this viewpoint. It is based on the pagan politics of ancient Rome. It is also the wish of the revolutionaries, aspiring as it does to what has already been realized in France. France has not just literally incorporated its colonies, but has also been serious about its intentions by granting each of its colonies a number of seats in the French parliament.

Indeed, if you adopt the false, unhistorical, and godless standpoint that humanity has the power to form a state by arbitrarily combining disparate parts, and in that state to form a nation, then of course you cannot come up with a compelling objection against equating motherland and colonies.

But if you condemn such human tinkering, as every antirevolutionary should, and if you hold that a nation is a product of a divine dispensation in history and that therefore every state is delimited by the natural radius of the national life thus shaped—then of course any idea falls away that you can embrace a Javanese and a Frisian, an Achin and a Hollander as fellow citizens of one and the same state, as members of a single organic community.

We Possess Colonies but Do Not Own Them (Continued) §244

Over against the revolutionary doctrine that the Kingdom of the Netherlands *owns* the colonies, we posit the organic idea that the colonies are *held* by the kingdom and for that reason are separated from them by origin and history, that is, by divine ordinance, each component part forming its own distinctive organism.

Rightly viewed, therefore, we have to do with a self-standing, closed realm called The Kingdom of the Netherlands that, partly through conquest but mainly through transfer from the Dutch East India Company[1] *came into possession of* extensive regions overseas, where different peoples with distinct histories and characteristics all their own live their lives distinct and different from ours.

Pagan Rome could bind together peoples from three continents because Rome was neither a country nor a nation but merely a city that conquered territories and then linked them together.

Similarly, Bonaparte could stamp as fellow citizens Neapolitans and Amsterdammers as belonging to one and the same empire, since mixing and melting was the godless pretension of revolutionary France, which in a flush of liberty pounced upon the peoples of Europe.

That is how even today a Constitution based on the political principle of the revolutionary system can make bold to maintain the fiction that

---

1. This took place in 1798, upon the bankruptcy of the company.

territories without any national or organic ties, territories that do not even touch, can be knit together into a single state.

But such an ahistoric, utterly revolutionary notion in defiance of nature will never take root among men of our principle, the less so because it concerns regions that do not abut on our national borders and that, like Curaçao and Celebes for example, lack all geographical and ethnic affinity with us.

Thus this absurd idea in the first article of the Constitution was never anything more than a dead letter. In our parliament there are no Dayak[2] delegates sitting next to the delegates from The Hague. Our laws here do not hold over there. They have their own government, their own courts, their own regulations. And the only fruits this untenable fiction has borne thus far can be seen in the political and fiscal harm that the constant skirmishes between Plein and Buitenzorg[3] and the tug of war between subsidies and credit balances have caused us these thirty years.

§ 245   THE TRUE SOVEREIGN OVER THE COLONIES

If the Netherlands has possession of colonies without owning them, the next question is: Who is sovereign over the colonies?

To answer that question we do not join those who simply say: the king. No, not the king but the state of the Netherlands possesses the overseas territories. They are not Crown domains but domains of the state.

In 1798 the combined holdings of the former Dutch East India Company were not taken over by a sovereign as such, but by the state, and declared to be possessions of the state. Rightly so, since they did not originate in victories achieved by the Sovereign of the Netherlands but much rather by conquests made by a trading company that had arisen from the bosom of the nation, that is, from society and thus from the nation itself.

Our king does not have Crown domains the way Queen Victoria has one in Ceylon.[4] The most one can say about our king's authority on historical grounds is that the king is sovereign over a state that possesses these territories as colonies. Thus the sovereignty over the Netherlandic state that belongs to the king is similar to the sovereignty over the colonies that

---

2. The Dayaks are a native people of the island of Borneo and were still given to head-hunting at this time.

3. *Plein* was shorthand for the Colonial Office in The Hague; *Buitenzorg* was the residence of the governor-general in the Dutch East Indies.

4. Modern-day Sri Lanka.

belongs to the Netherlandic state (since sovereignty in this case flows from the right of possession).

Decisions about the colonies may therefore only be made by king and parliament jointly, and nothing has been more immoral than the system, long insisted upon by old conservatives, as though the colonies in the final analysis were fully on a par with a "royal domain" with which parliament had absolutely nothing to do as regards sovereignty and supervision.

Even so, the conservatives were perfectly correct over against the liberal opposition at the time, which committed the absurdity of defending parliamentary involvement in colonial affairs on the same ground as parliamentary involvement with the affairs of the mother country. That was an absolutely untenable theory.

In the case of the mother country, after all, all constitutional involvement with government policy is rooted in the right of every nation to refuse or grant money to its ruler. But this basic right in the mother country was of course of little help the moment the liberals dropped their masks and tried to apply it to the colonies.

Frisians and Zeelanders, after all, have a say about the taxes Frisians and Zeelanders are expected to contribute. But as for the contributions to be made by the Balinese or the Javanese no other conclusion can be drawn, if you want to be logical about it, than that the Javanese and the Balinese should have a say in the matter.

To demand in a high tone, over against the king, control of the colonial budget to which one does not contribute and even profits from is to play with words, is to violate justice, and deliberately sow conceptual confusion.

That is the reason why the right and duty of parliament to be involved in the colonies is in no way deduced by us from a bogus and false right of control over colonial budgets, but based solely on the irrefutable historical fact that the colonies are not a possession of the Crown but of the state.

THE STATE'S SOVEREIGN RIGHTS §246

For our colonial policy in general, these considerations imply at once that the state should set up the administration of the colonies in such a way that, completely separate from the national finances of the mother country, it is rooted in its own soil, obeys its own laws, relies on its own moral responsibility, and lives by its own strength.

This can of course be further specified in a separate administration for each group of colonies as dictated by location, significance, and character. It is worth considering, for example, whether the very important island of Sumatra should not gradually be placed on its own.[5] But for the general question that concerns us at present such a separation can be left aside. What is important here is the principle that the political economy of the mother country stands on its own and that the overseas possessions, under the sovereignty of the state, receive an organization that suits their interests.

This is to be understood in the sense that laws are enacted, justice is administered, and regulations are passed in name of the state alone, but then in such a way that internal matters of the colonies are not decided at the Ministry for the Colonies in The Hague but in Batavia and Paramaribo.[6]

The Dutch state has the right to appoint governors and high courts to represent its sovereignty in the colonies. It has the right to enact without colonial involvement any laws for matters that embody its sovereignty. It also has the right to make conditional on its approval any legal regulations covering the internal affairs of the colonies. It has the right, furthermore, to commit the colonies to third parties by way of treaties. And finally, it has the right and the duty to hold the colonial government accountable, hence responsible, socially and politically as well as financially and fiscally.

§ 247   SOVEREIGN RIGHTS OF THE DUTCH STATE

The following affairs, separated from the colonial administration because they touch on the state's sovereign rights, should be the only ones to fall directly under the governor or else a special agent: (1) foreign policy; (2) military and naval forces; and (3) control of unimproved lands and other domains.

Foreign policy is included because it involves the sovereign—in this case the state—and can never be dealt with otherwise than by the lawful sovereign.

Included as well are the military and naval forces, insofar as they do not serve to combat piracy or maintain law and order, but exist and are employed to guarantee the possession of the colonies against a foreign enemy or against any possible internal tendency to mutiny and revolt.

---

5. That is, separate from Java and the other islands in the Indonesian Archipelago.
6. That is, in the capitals of the Dutch East Indies and West Indies, respectively.

Thus at least half of the military and naval costs should in fairness be borne, not by the colonies themselves, but by the mother country, for the simple reason that these expenditures are made not for the sake of the colonies but for our sake, to defend our honor and to serve exclusively for maintaining our sovereignty.

To possess colonies is an honor. It enhances our prestige, affords us a different place in Europe than we would otherwise have, and causes the splendor of a glorious past to shine over the weakness of our current life as a nation. Having colonies is a privilege that others envy. To defend the colonies should be worth something to us.

But any defense costs are offset, in the third place, by the state's right to enjoy what every sovereign enjoys, namely, to control the *regalia* and the *bona vacantia*, that is, the government plantations and the unimproved lands, from which the monies can be raised for all administrative costs related to its sovereignty, for defense and the maintenance of law and order, and for paying off the national debt since that debt included debts of colonial origin.

No Sharing of Responsibility   § 248

The question whether islands and regions that are very sparsely populated, without much activity or distinctive life, should eventually be put under direct rule can remain undecided here. Where no distinctive national life has taken root, hence no organic folk community exists, there the antirevolutionary principle has no particular demands to make. That principle requires only that we shall respect the shape and form of peoples and nations as they have come to be in their independence and distinctiveness under the providential rule of the Creator. So let us stop trying to melt together what by nature cannot be melted together. The antirevolutionary principle simply opposes the pretension that human beings have the right to take the future of nations out of the hands of God. Except for defending and guaranteeing our sovereign rights, our principle is met if we relinquish any false mingling with our own state so that our financial interest never ever stands in the way of the moral interest of these peoples.

If that requires advances, or what comes down to the same thing, loans guaranteed by the state, then there would in principle be no objection to that, provided such aid never cause a return to the disastrous policy of *shared* responsibility. For experience shows that such sharing always amounts to destroying all responsibility and turns out to be fatal and pernicious for motherland and colonies alike.

II. EXPLOITATION, COLONIZATION, OR TRUSTEESHIP

§ 249   THREE SYSTEMS

Our first article dealt exclusively with the formal question of the reciprocal relationship between motherland and colonies by virtue of the rights of sovereignty. We shall now address this question: *What is the Netherlands supposed to do with its overseas possessions?*

One can think of three possibilities: Such possessions can be exploited, colonized, or put under trusteeship.

In former times the first was the most common: a people would be conquered by arms and then made tributary. But as our own century has shown, a people can also be exploited indirectly—and quite profitably too: force it to live at its own expense and yet exist for the benefit of its conqueror by sweetening the bitter pill and wrapping the hand that pillages in a framework of social and economic regulations.

Next, colonizing such a possession can only be done if the conquering people finds a soil and a climate that suit its own character and if it has a surplus population driven by a spirit of adventure. So Britain, America, and Australia. So we in former days at the Cape.[7]

Finally, trusteeship over a nonkindred people is not possible until a moral sense of duty and responsibility to the Judge of the nations is aroused and then furnishes the means without which such a burdensome and often vexatious task is virtually impossible.

§ 250   NOT EXPLOITATION, NOR COLONIZATION, BUT TRUSTEESHIP

Of these three systems, the first condemns itself, the second is unfit for most of our colonies, and in our opinion only the third can be squared with the calling of a Christian nation.

Our country may no more exploit another people than I have the right to live off the field of my neighbor. That is a sin against the eighth commandment, according to the fine explanation of the Heidelberg Catechism: "God forbids not only such theft and robbery as are punished

---

7. The Cape of Good Hope in southern Africa was colonized by the Dutch starting in 1652.

by the government, but God views as theft also all wicked tricks and devices, whereby we seek to get our neighbor's goods."[8]

An even heavier judgment falls on exploiting another people indirectly by restricting its economic institutions. To do that is to commit a sin against *a nation as a whole*—the sin that is called slavery when applied to individual persons by taking away their freedom and compelling them to surrender the proceeds of their labor. If slavery is a sin against the eighth commandment when applied to single persons, as all will agree, how much more sinful is enslaving whole groups of people, not as a means of defense or reprisal, but purely for the sake of profit.

We are able, finally, to colonize, but not very much. We have no surplus population, and what is surplus has neither pith nor spirit. Moreover, the tablelands on Java, as a result of imprudent government measures, have not been connected by rail to the coast, and conditions on Sumatra are too unsettled for the planting of a Dutch colony. There can be no question of colonization as a general policy for our vast possessions.

Thus the only sound, lawful, and honorable system for us as a Christian nation is the system of trusteeship.

We do not have in mind, please note, to keep these peoples under tutelage forever, but rather to take them for what they are, minors, and to accept the threefold moral obligation that binds a guardian to his foster child: (1) to give it a moral education; (2) to manage its estate wisely; and (3) to enable it, if it please God, to advance to greater independence.

This brief argument alone is so compelling and transparent that if no other motives came into play, every moralist would be convinced by it and the conscience of every person who honors God's commandments would unconditionally subscribe to it. Accordingly, we do not for a moment hesitate to say that anyone who has learned in Christ to see the nations in a higher light can only adopt a lower standpoint if blinded by prejudice or bereft of logic.

---

8. Q&A 110. See Exod 22:1; 1 Cor 6:10; Mic 6:11; Luke 3:14; Jas 5:4–6.

§ 251   Origin of the Cultivation System[9]

Our conclusion can be no other than that the Christian-historical movement can adopt neither the conservative nor the so-called liberal colonial policy.

Not the conservative policy; it is embodied in the cultivation system and mixes paternalistic meddling with an unlawful desire to exploit. We do not claim that the cultivation system has not done some good, only that this good in no way outweighs the many evils it has caused. Even if the scales were to tip the other way, the cultivation system would stand condemned because of the wrong principle in which it is rooted and the immoral motive from which it arose.

There is no longer any disagreement about the motive. It has been established that Count van den Bosch contrived this intricate interlocking system upon arriving on Java with the instruction, not to help the natives improve their lot, but to increase the flow of money to the motherland. We needed money, a great deal of money;[10] and once you take this as the point of departure you must admit that the cultivation system was a stroke of genius—if you acquiesce in the maxim that a laudable end can sanctify a questionable means.

We do not deny that at first there was at least some intention, provided money was made, to ease the burden of Java's population as much as possible, yet in such a way that whenever the financial need of the mother country clashed with the social or moral interests of the Javanese, the latter were sacrificed as a unavoidable consequence of the system. For twenty years on end this became increasingly the guideline for action. Irrefutable evidence for our allegation is found in the advice of G. L. Baud,[11]

---

9. The *"cultuurstelsel"* was set up on Java by commissioner Johannes van den Bosch (1780–1840) in 1830. It provided for natives to reserve 20 percent of their land for growing cash crops for the European market (such as coffee, sugar, and indigo) in exchange for a reduction by half of the land tax. The cultivation system was supervised by government officials who set the monetary value of the harvest each year. Often they also assigned the better plots for growing the crops. The system was open to corruption and occasionally caused famine.

10. The need for money grew increasingly as a result of countering the Belgian Revolt and its aftermath.

11. Guillaume Louis Baud (1801–91) spent twenty years as a civil servant in the East Indies where he strongly favored the introduction of the cultivation system. He was briefly minister of the colonies in the short-lived Dutch cabinet of 1848/49. His older cousin Jean Chrétien Baud (1789–1859) had a very similar career, succeeding

recently brought to mind, that whatever it is about the cultivation system that undermined the morals of the Javanese and caused them to gamble away their economic future must, if necessary, be continued and maintained for the sake of the financial interest of the Netherlands.

This *original sin*[12] alone brands this whole system as contraband, a system that must be strictly banned from the Christian terrain.

THE PRINCIPLE BENEATH THE CULTIVATION SYSTEM   § 252

Wrong as well was the principle in which the cultivation system is rooted.

It was this: that the produce grown by forced labor on public land was bought from the growers at a mandatory price. The native tenants, in exchange for having to pay higher taxes, and even for a partial reduction of the already oppressive tax (two-fifths of the crop), would perform cultivation service on public land and surrender the produce into the hands of public officials for a price that usually was not a third of its real value and that also for a long time was paid in copper coins that were not worth a third of its monetary value.

In the case of the coffee culture (by far the most important component to this day) it came down to this: every family involved had to plant and take care of 600 to 650 coffee trees, sometimes at a distance of 10 to 12 *palen*[13] from their home, then harvest the fruit and process it. The labor involved amounted to at least 160 to 170 days a year and was paid with ƒ11.90 to ƒ19.60 (at an average yield of 140 *katties*[14] per 600 trees and a planting wage of ƒ8.50 to ƒ14 per *picol*[15]), despite the fact that, at a commensurate wage of thirty to fifty cents a day, the amount owed for that labor would have been no less than ƒ48 to ƒ80. Meanwhile at auction these 140 *katties* not infrequently netted the government far in excess of ƒ85, which would have left room for far more generous wages.

After all, even if it is averred—which would itself be exorbitant—that in fairness the product surrendered at ƒ11.90 to ƒ19.60 included (1) a tax *in natura* equal to an amount of ƒ15 per family, and (2) another ƒ15 for the rental value of the soil, even then there remained a profit of ƒ35 to ƒ40.

Van den Bosch as governor-general of the East Indies (1833–36) and after his repatriation serving as minister of the colonies (1840–48). The latter Baud is credited with the saying, "Java is the cork on which the Netherlands floats."

12. Latin, *vitium originis*.
13. A little over 9 to 11 miles (approx. 15 to 18 km).
14. 190 lbs. (approx. 86 kg).
15. 137 lbs. (approx. 62 kg).

This profit flowed from labor that remained unpaid. It was extorted from the Javanese so that we could restore order to our disordered finances, make tax hikes here at home superfluous, and allow the state to indulge in the luxury that corrupted our political system.

§ 253   CONSEQUENCES OF THE CULTIVATION SYSTEM

On the basis of our principle alone, this system ought to be condemned even if it yielded nothing but beneficial results for both the mother country and the colonies. It was intended as a forcible inversion of the social conditions of a nation, something no person has a right to do, no matter what authority he is invested with. Anyone who has the nerve to withdraw the entire organism of national life from the innate law for its existence inverts the axle on which the national cogwheels run and so commits an act of grave and consequential revolution that antirevolutionaries have no other duty but to protest against.

Thus the conservatives in subsequent debates were absolutely right in contesting the right of liberals to thrust Western concepts on an Eastern people. But they forgot that they themselves were guilty of the same fault, an evil of even greater magnitude, insofar as the introduction of the cultivation system had been an equally violent imposition on Java to meet the demands of interests utterly foreign to its economic life.

And the system evokes still deeper aversion when one looks at the evil it brewed. To what extent Java's population actually doubled while this system was in force or only achieved a double figure if a better count were taken can remain undecided here; let us accept for a moment that Java's population indeed grew, and what is more, that it grew in work habits and for a time gained in prosperity. Yet even then we ask whether the same phenomenon was not observed in, for example, Britain's factory districts and whether anyone would have the nerve to praise the factory system as a blessing for the population. We deny the conservatives the right to use this argument all the more since their best and wisest men made a point of instilling in the natives the adage "Easy come, easy go," even as their meager wages went up in smoke.[16]

§ 254   CONSEQUENCES OF THE CULTIVATION SYSTEM (CONTINUED)

The much-vaunted advantages of the cultivation system seem highly questionable to us and in any case are offset by the following factors.

---

16. Kuyper alludes to the widespread consumption of opium.

(1) It has thwarted indigenous developments in the colonies.

(2) It has encouraged and abetted extortion of the lower classes by their superiors and chiefs.

(3) It has charged the colonial civil service with the unnatural task of exercising authority on the one hand and supervising a commercial enterprise on the other, a most destructive way to undermine the sense of duty and to cause lust for money and egoism to creep into our Europeans on site.

(4) It has utterly unhinged our colonial administration by debasing it into a commercial enterprise.

(5) It has caused our national finances, after an artificial boom, to slide into hopeless disarray.

(6) Worst of all, it has caused the national conscience to grow callous rather than ennobling it: gold fever has gradually eroded the awareness before God that we have a calling to fulfill toward our colonies.

AMBIGUITY OF THE LIBERAL SYSTEM § 255

No one should conclude from this that the liberal practices must therefore be in agreement with the principles we profess.

We do not hesitate to offer liberals the homage of our sympathy for removing many offensive features and introducing improvements; but they have not brought us where we need to be.

Nor could they, given their standpoint that from the outset to the present day has halted between two opinions and laid itself open to the criticism of having fine-sounding but at bottom impure intentions.

A system like that of compulsory cultivation, after all, is either acceptable or not acceptable. If it is acceptable, don't tinker with it, for it runs like a charm. It has in its favor that it already exists, and it has proved its genuine profitability. But if it is unacceptable, which the liberals maintained in theory, then don't work with it but have the courage to throw it out and prove thereby that your moral indignation is sincere.

Our liberals, however, did neither the one nor the other. They had the authorities spoil the cultures and next to those they initiated private agriculture with European capital, agriculture that simply could not flourish precisely because the compulsory system was carried forward.

Private and government agriculture are each other's natural enemies because both compete on the labor market and both presuppose and help shape totally different social conditions.

Moreover, this anticonservative colonial policy could not succeed because it was accompanied by the endeavor to graft the concepts of our modern liberalized society onto the trunk of social conditions that are entirely different. The absurdity of this endeavor could not have been illustrated more clearly than when a sympathizer with the religiously neutral school—installed in the Netherlands by the Education Act of 1857—was assigned the task of drafting a school law for the Indies: this clever bureaucrat as good as copied the clauses of that Act!

§ 256   Fiasco of the System

This explains why the brilliant parliamentary struggle by the liberals against the conservatives ended in cruel disappointment.

True, the offensive features of the cultivation system have been done away with, but not the main idea of compulsory delivery of crops, and with that the warp that this system bestowed on Javanese life.

In many respects, extortion by the village chiefs has been bridled; but the principal cancer of an administrative system that enables district heads and large landowners alike to oppress the people continues to fester. Meanwhile the civil service, still finding itself in a false position, could not regain its dignity as representatives of the government. And the net result of the patchwork of reforms is that all those half measures have dislodged everything and settled nothing, leaving us groping in a bewildering chaos.

Hence the liberal colonial policy, which once flared up with such noble enthusiasm against tyranny and greed, has had its day and now hides in its tent, barely showing a sign of life and leaving us with a situation that is certainly not painted in too dark colors when we speak of malaise in the Netherlands and worse than malaise in the Indies.

Precisely because of this shipwreck of the liberal colonial policy we can say that no other options remain except to re-embrace the cultivation system or else to adopt a system that excludes all forms of compulsory cultivation or delivery of crops. And since becoming reconciled to the cultivation system is impossible for a strict antirevolutionary, for reasons outlined above, and since moreover no one any longer contemplates restoring the system in its former bloom, nothing remains for us but to abolish this tyrannical scheme and calmly choose for the system of freedom, not asking *What can Java give us?* but only *What would God have us be for Java?*

III. CHRISTIANIZATION OF THE INDIES

MORAL EDUCATION OF THE NATIVE §257

If our country is to fulfill its obligations as a trustee toward its possessions, and if trusteeship includes above all the duty to give one's foster child a moral education, then a colonial policy on the part of the antirevolutionaries is unthinkable in which the Christianization of the Indies is not the point of departure.

We therefore protest emphatically against the offensive view that the Christian-historical principle could be satisfied, politically speaking, if we simply became conservative or liberal colonialists and then went in for missions as well. No, the leaven has to be mixed in with the dough; it may never be meted out as an additive to the unleavened bread. And so in our colonial program the Christianization of the Indies cannot be some extra ingredient but must be the chief inspiration for all who also honor in the Christ of God the Savior of the Gentiles.

Meanwhile, the manner in which the church or her members arrive at this conviction is different from the consideration that leads the government to become conscious of that duty.

The church and her members stand in the spiritual realm and so confess that all power in heaven and on earth has been given to Christ. Therefore they honor him as king of all people and every nation. Accordingly, they know they are duty-bound to proclaim the Word also to the peoples overseas. Three motives guide them: (1) we are to obey the word, *Go into all the world, and preach the gospel to every creature*; (2) King Jesus must come into his glory also among the peoples of the Indian Archipelago; and (3) the salvation of souls ought to evoke our compassion.

The government judges differently. As government it knows only that it is called to honor the only true God, also in educating peoples entrusted to its care. Thus it must not honor or support either the heathen or the Islamic idolatries. On the contrary, according to the unimpeachable testimony of history, only a turning to the Christian principle of life can open up for these peoples the prospect of a higher level of development.

This last statement means that factually only the Christian nations in Europe and America have attained that purer disclosure of nobler strength that has created human society as we know it, a society to which the former—and in part still present—heathen civilizations in China and British India can in no way be compared. The Islamic way of life in disintegrating

Turkey, meanwhile, and the barbaric customs of the West Asian tribes stand self-condemned.

When these two, that is, this sure conviction on the part of the government and this sense of duty on the part of the church and her members, come together, the desired whole is automatically born. The government will then know: "The Indies must be Christianized, but we have no competence there!" while the church and her members simply wait for the government to open the highroads along which the gospel can be brought to these peoples.

§ 258   THE CRESCENT AND THE CROSS

The above standpoint alone can support a policy of moral obligation toward our overseas possessions. Should the government shrink from this avowed preference for the Christian principle of life, then it can do no better, in our opinion, then to vacate these possessions tomorrow. For then none of its fine plans for reform will take us any further and result only in turning these peoples' economy upside down and worsening instead of improving their lot. The goal, after all, is not to put a layer of varnish on the moldered trunk but to have that trunk permeated with new saps of life.

It is also true that this permeation is impossible unless it draws its motive power from the root, or if you will, from the most central and comprehensive element of a people's life, namely, its religion. It is no less true, as is attested by both history and the tragic picture of present-day Muslims, that Islam, even in its noblest form, can never yield anything other or better than either fanaticism or petrifaction.

However much you tamper with the peoples of our overseas possessions or experiment with them or spend on them, so long as they continue to wander in the shadow of the crescent moon you will not make any progress. You can take to them whatever you like, but it will not last. You may prick them or perhaps polish them, but you will never inspire them or make them thrive.

Thus the Christianization of the Indies must be our first priority. Only then can we look forward to a happier future. And if this "one thing needful"[17] is not embraced, then we think there is more common sense in a cultivation system, which at least yields some profit, than in the unprincipled

---

17. An allusion to Luke 10:42.

game of the liberals. They want to clothe Java's bare walls with green ivy by sending the felled trunk with its branches overseas but leaving its roots in the soil here. They will never get beyond dressing those walls with wood that suffers from dry rot and with leaves that wither on the vine.

PAGANISM AND ISLAM § 259

How then is our country to acquit itself of this weighty obligation toward the Indies? Four problem areas need to be pointed out: (1) idolatries; (2) the church; (3) missions; and (4) education.

(1) What should be the attitude with respect to the idolatries that exist over there?

With respect to the pagan and Islamic idolatries that are still honored there, our governor-general and his staff of civil servants, representing a Christian-European nation, ought not only to refrain from every semblance of complicity or approval but even from the impression of neutrality.

It ought to be a known fact among the Papuans and Madurese, the Achinese and Moluccans, that their sovereign ruler is a Christian state, that therefore all idolatry is condemned as sin, and that the only reason idolatry is not forcibly eradicated is that it would insult the honor of Christ to want to establish his rule by any other means than spiritual influences. Psychological Darwinism, which sucks all moral energy from your marrow by telling you that all these idolatries are not really idolatries but, rather, beautiful, albeit inferior, forms of "religious consciousness"—this must be resisted with all your might. And what you must especially resist is the utterly false notion as though the Muslim is not a worshiper of idols but that he worships with us the only true God, merely interpreted by Mohammed in the Qur'an instead of by Jesus in Holy Scripture.

It needs to be professed and acknowledged that "Allah" is a god invented by man himself, a god who has not even the name in common with the Triune God of the Christians. For this reason every state subsidy in support of this Allah worship must be stopped at once; all attendance by high officials at Allah festivities must be strictly forbidden; any form of accommodation to Allah worship (such as General Van Swieten[18] allowed himself to be charged with) must not remain uncensured; and anyone

---

18. Jan van Swieten (1807–88) was a distinguished military official and politician and was variously involved in expeditions to and government in Java.

who participates in an idolatrous comedy of sacrificing a buffalo in order to drive out a demon from a locomotive (such as an official recently took the liberty to do) must be summarily dismissed.

It must be brought home to the peoples of the Archipelago that we leave them free to practice their idolatries—not from appreciation, absolutely not; nor from fear of an explosion of fanaticism; but solely in virtue of the demand of the Christian principle itself, which desires to triumph in no other way that through persuasion.

By any other posture, be it of secret accommodation or of overt respect, the government betrays the character of our nation. It sins against the God who avenges the betrayal of his honor especially in his governments. It is simply transplanting onto Indian soil the fungus of *neutrality*, which among us has never gotten any further than producing a mere wisp of a plant and which in the climate of the Far East will simply wilt from mold.

§ 260   Church Denominations

(2) The current policy regarding church denominations in our Archipelago stands condemned as far as the Protestant churches are concerned.

The Roman Catholics have what they need. They enjoy freedom and are served by a corps of confessing, capable, and educated clergy. Through the titular bishop in Batavia they are in official yet independent contact with the government. They cannot complain about lack of interest on the part of Catholic civil servants. At almost every mission station they organize a parish. Thus they are firmly planted, are gaining every day and enjoying general respect.

The Protestants by contrast are their own worst enemy in their church organization. They find themselves organized in the preposterous and impossible body of a general Protestant state church. Those among them who are sincere believers are considered offensive. To the outside they are a laughingstock. Their congregations are not free and are spiritually impoverished and run-down. Their pastors are brought in from the outside by the government, and to their own embarrassment they are mostly without creed or confession. Besides this threefold shame the Protestants are disgraced even more by the undeniable fact that the European Christians among them have lost all faith and follow a frivolous lifestyle.

Plein and Buitenzorg should have realized long ago that this situation had become intolerable.[19] And the problem posed by the fact that both church and state had bound themselves to the existing arrangement in a bilateral agreement cannot for one moment be adduced as an excuse for their utter lack of resilience. A lifeless body like the church government in the Indies needed but the briefest arousal to be stirred into action according to holier guidelines.

What needs to happen is that this impossible and both spiritually and constitutionally reprehensible state church vanishes. That would stop it from putting the honor of Christ in our colonies under a shroud. The Reformed churches should regain their confessional and Presbyterian character. Congregations that have no substance, hence lack viability, should simply be disbanded, to revive elsewhere in mission stations that, once they have grown to, say, a hundred members, should immediately be transferred to the organized church.

Missions §261

(3) The government of the Indies should make it a point of honor to host thriving and successful Christian missions.

In order to fulfill its moral calling toward the peoples of the Indies, as we have just seen, it has to rely on their Christianization; and yet as a government it is incompetent to carry on missions. Given this dilemma, what can be more convenient for a colonial government than private initiative in the mother country directing a flood of activity toward the colonies for this enormous task, not from economic or political calculation but nevertheless with enthusiasm and dedication?

The aim of our trusteeship over the Indies is to share with its peoples the blessings that society enjoys in this country. Thus a way has to be found by which a Christian society from Europe can get into contact with the Islamic region of Asia, to transform it more or less into a Christian society. In so doing it would at the same time create the conditions required by the government's trusteeship to fulfill its obligation.

For this reason we demand that the government let both societies know that it will no longer, as it has thus far, put up with missions as a necessary evil, but from now on accepts it and wills it, with all its consequences. Such consequences would include that the government take

---

19. For notes on *Plein* and *Buitenzorg*, see above, § 244n3.

up official contact with those denominations that wish it—or when they decline, with missionary societies from their midst, provided they base themselves on a recognized church confession. The government can then regulate missions more or less on the following terms: (a) for the time being every denomination confines its activity on Java to a single residency;[20] (b) ordained missionaries have the same rank as pastors; (c) an inspector, appointed by a denomination, maintains correspondence with the government; (d) the denominations guarantee that they will send capable personnel; (e) each denomination is granted an adequate parcel of land in freehold, be it in government plantations or in unimproved land; and (f) the government undertakes to keep under control any disturbances that might result from honest attempts at proselytizing that are purely spiritual in nature.

There are three reasons why such a system requires confinement to a single residency: (i) it is the only way to prove that a durable order can be guaranteed; (ii) it is the only way to provide missions with the support of civil servants that are sympathetic to it; and (iii) it is the only way to prevent harmful competition between denominations, something that is entirely unnecessary so long as there is plenty of space.

§ 262   EDUCATION

(4) Just as with missions, the guideline in the area of education, finally, should be the principle that Christian Europe is free to bless Islamic Asia.

Fear of resistance should not deter us, since at stake is the honor of the mother country in demonstrating that it is and remains master in its domain. Nor ought the government to shrink back from such a policy as a consequence of motives derived from the system of the "religiously neutral" school.[21] The fatal impact of that disastrous system in the mother country is hardly a reason for subjecting the colonies to a similar experiment.

Primary schools established in the colonies, where teachers accredited in the mother country might want to serve, should therefore not just

---

20. The residency referred to here was a large administrative region headed by a Dutch official.

21. "'Religiously neutral' school" here translates the original *"moderne secteschool,"* that is, the school of the sect of Modernism—a term of contempt for the public school in the Netherlands as per the Primary Education Acts of 1857 and 1878. See also above, § 156.

be tolerated by the authorities in the Indies, but in our opinion should be financially assisted, if not fully supported. Here too a systematic approach ought to be followed—not a school here and a class there, resulting in squandered money and discouraged people; but consolidation of all available forces within a single residency, preferably in close contact with denominational missions.

If such education also aimed at Christianizing the natives, then that would, far from raising objections, much rather recommend it. The government should grant such a school a parcel of land as an endowment, provided the school guarantees sound instruction, is subject to proper inspection, and does not drop below a specified number of pupils.

In such a residency, thanks to the *vis unita fortior*,[22] Christianity would automatically become a force that would, over time, shoulder the burden of providing more advanced education to serve the Javanese nobility, and in this way gradually prepare the way for what Java should have had fifty years ago: *a free university*.

IV. SYSTEM OF ADMINISTRATION

TAKE IT OR LEAVE IT   § 263

The conclusion we are reaching is this: the Netherlands is in possession of colonies for the purpose of acquitting itself towards them of the moral obligation to be their trustee. To embrace this grand task can serve to enhance the nation's energy. It can inspire national unity and direct it toward a higher goal. And it can considerably enlarge the nation's all too narrow scope of activity. Apart from that, having colonies enhances our prestige through the aftereffect of a glorious past, and it more than strengthens our position on the political chessboard as a result of the factual significance attached to it.

It is up to the Netherlands, meanwhile, to decide whether it wants to take on this burden, and whether it can.

Nothing less is required, after all, than the following: (1) to maintain a standing army and an active fleet strong enough to defend our sovereignty over the peoples of those colonies; (2) to surrender a not inconsiderable portion of the best elements of our society for the administrative, educational, and economic needs of those territories; and (3) to dare to take the risk of any complications such colonial possessions may saddle us with.

---

22. "United strength is stronger."

These requirements are offset by the fact that the Netherlands, through its sovereignty, in addition to its enhanced prestige, (1) has at its disposal the *regalia* and the public land of the colonies; (2) creates jobs for any population surplus; and (3) indirectly opens up material resources for the benefit of its own economy.

Should our nation nevertheless judge that the burdens outweigh the advantages, and should it no longer have a heart, not even temporarily, for risking its peace and its assets for so elevated a goal, then such a soulless generation would no longer merit the honor of possessing colonies. It had then better withdraw quickly from such a precious trust, one that would only be harmful for its own moral development and shameful for its former reputation.

But if this is not the conclusion people want to draw—and who of our countrymen would, without blushing with shame?—then we must seize the opportunity, seize it with levelheadedness and holy intentions, to arrest a course of events that is turning the colonies into a social ruin as well as demoralizing us at home.

§ 264   FIVE CONDITIONS

As things stand at present, the Indies do us no good and we are no good to them.

The treasurer's books are balanced each year, and any surplus [from the colonies] is used to pay down the national debt [of the mother country]. People fail to take notice and the government closes its eyes to it. Nevertheless it is seen by the all-knowing God and cries out against us to the Judge of the nations.

To escape this judgment, our previous article indicated how the Christianization of the colonies ought to be attempted by the home front and supported by the government. Christianization, straightway and forthwith, is so much the principal aim and point of departure for us that without it we consider every measure we might undertake as trustee fruitless and idle.

Not that nothing more can be said.

Our country, precisely to show its moral superiority, should also see to it that its governance of the colonies is wise and prudent, that its administration of justice is strictly and inexorably applied to all parties, that the collection of taxes is efficient and evenhanded, that the conditions for economic development are fostered, and that the intellectually weaker native is protected against the wiles of the unscrupulous intruder by the shield of our authority.

ADMINISTRATION § 265

For the governance of our colonies we should not seek our strength in the quantity but in the instruction, quality, and effective deployment of our civil servants.

As for instruction, it should be firmly established that officials who are invested with authority have no other business than to exercise that authority. Officials should never be involved in commercial enterprise or government agriculture. Nor should they ever hold the offices of governor and judge simultaneously—always a fatal combination. They should be involved solely in acts of governing, to uphold our sovereignty and protect our moral reputation.

No less would we emphasize the quality of our civil servants, of whom, much more than here in Europe, the highest demands are made. Nothing is more precarious than the mistaken notion that the Indies can do with less than we can. On the contrary, since the power of public opinion in the Indies is so much weaker and since the task is so much broader and the temptation for abuse so much easier, every person who is to represent us there should be possessed of a moral integrity and gravity that is not found in the ordinary run of people, either here or elsewhere. What counts in such exceptional circumstances are knowledge, but even more prudence and mature judgment. A government that does nothing more than our Department of the Colonies has done thus far for recruiting such invaluable men and, once gained, for keeping them, is certainly guilty of neglecting its duty.

And then there is the matter of effective deployment. It would be an illusion to think that the Netherlands always has more than enough of such quality personnel to gradually fill all the government posts in the Indies. In lieu of the practice of staffing a branch of administration with Europeans, we propose taking only the brightest and the best of the mother country's civil servants and having the actual governing be carried out under them by properly prepared and disciplined sons of the inland aristocracy.

But then our approach should extend even to the ordinary village chiefs. In other words, these leaders must not remain what they have been thus far, namely, our sheepdogs for keeping the flock in check. They have to become persons who, under supervision, carry out a well-defined level of authority and are paid for their services on a regular basis.

§ 266   LEGAL SECURITY

For any people anywhere, the primary and indispensable condition for ennobling their character and growing in strength and vigor is legal security.

When that is lacking, the powerful are tempted to practice extortion and the weaker begin to nurture a resentment that breeds a kind of envy that either makes men grovel or brutalizes them. Hence one should keep in mind that when it comes to legal security, the question is not just whether one can go to bed with or without a revolver, but much more whether one can take the warp that entered the national character as a result of arbitrary treatment and abuse of power and replace it with more noble traits.

To that end the Indies require three things, namely: precise formulation of the law, strictly impartial and competent courts, and a well-disciplined police force that knows how to act decisively.

It will be important not to import our laws but to purify and codify the laws obtaining in the Indies. For only the latter are rooted in their histories and embedded in the conscience of their peoples.

Similarly, we should not try to introduce a judicial hierarchy based entirely on the European model. What do those junior officials, fresh off the boat, know about the local language, customs, and relationships? Our aim should be to install an indigenous judicial hierarchy, staffed by those educated in a university on Java. Their impartiality could then be guaranteed by reliable appellate courts staffed by Europeans.

Finally, a court system ought to be organized in such a way as to defend the rights of the natives against unjust civil servants and the rights of the lower classes against their economic oppressors. This must be insisted upon, not just to procure justice for plaintiffs, but also as a regulator of the civil service, since every other means to rein in the native officials would only humiliate them at the price of their authority, or at best would never raise it beyond mere show.

V. FINANCIAL MANAGEMENT

§ 267   TAXATION SYSTEM

It will be more difficult to devise an efficient taxation system for our colonies.

This difficulty is made worse by the regrettable fact that morally speaking we have forfeited the four best sources of revenue, namely, the export crops, the land rent, the road duties, and the opium licenses.

This loss is offset by the fact that the pseudo-wealth to which the political economy of the Indies has grown accustomed thanks to the cultivation system can and must be shrunk, and that the expense of supervising these industries will one day come to an end. But after deducting this expense, and even after deducting what the mother country in our opinion ought to contribute for navy, army, and senior administration, still the domestic budget of the colonies will always be in the millions. This is a sum that cannot be raised from the colonies' internal revenue except with the greatest of effort.

In §§ 249–56 we have shown why the cultivation system cannot permanently be used for this, while the land rent, the road duties, and the opium licenses fall under the same irrefutable condemnation.

THE LAND RENT   § 268

Take the land rent, for instance. A village as a whole is assessed based on land use, and the village chief is responsible for prompt payment. Experience has shown that this has led to situations in which village chiefs apportion the assessment most arbitrarily and unevenly. They exempt their friends, force the little man to make up the difference, and usually collect fifty percent more than the government receives. It is a scandalous state of affairs, needing no further comment than is found in the memorandum of resident Van der Poel: "There would be no end to describing the vexations, caprices, oppressions, and extortions that the peasant classes suffer every year at the hands of their village chiefs in connection with the collection of a tax that to this day is calculated and assessed by the resident and other officials according to their pleasure."[23] This statement is corroborated, to name no more witnesses, by Blommestein in his pamphlet *Java en de Javanen*, where he writes: "The land rent cries out to heaven! It is safe to assume that millions more are levied from the peasant than the actual assessment for Java."[24]

---

23. *Note by the author:* See *Koloniaal Verslag 1877* [Colonial Report 1877], appendix N, p. 20.
24. H. van Blommestein (1791–1864), *Java en de Javanen* [Java and the Javanese] (Zaltbommel: Noman, 1851), 27.

§ 269   ROAD DUTIES

Just as condemnable is the payment in labor. To be sure, the road du-ties[25] have been restricted and have had their wildest offshoots clipped. Nevertheless they remain a cancer that eats away at the well-being of the native people.

Given the dearth of money in circulation in the economies of the Far East, road duties are a necessary evil, but at least they are a partial cor-rection to that situation. However, they degenerate into a plague, often little different from a curse, the moment such an economy incorporates Western elements, resulting in disproportionate expansion and thus los-ing their [function as a] corrective by breaking up the social equilibrium. Where these duties can be bought off and replaced by hired men, road du-ties are a waste of energy: they produce poor work, encourage arbitrary practices, and debase the worker. The inherent evil has been condemned to a man, even by Messrs. Smissaert and De Sturler,[26] whose testimony will not easily be challenged by members opposite. The first, a resident on Java, writes, "In particular it is imperative that the extortions, often per-petrated under the guise of road duties, be severely checked." The other, a man of very conservative views, writes, "People complain that the road duties are abused. I acknowledge those complaints as justified."

§ 270   OPIUM LICENSES

The opium licenses, finally, cannot stand up against the twin objection that all such licenses, of whatever substance, can also lead to abuse, and that licenses to sell opium (thus making money from sin) render the gov-ernment an accessory to the moral undermining of Java's populace. For the evil attached to any license for the Indies, suffice it to quote Minister Baud: "The intention shall be to abolish, for the greater part or in their entirety, the licensed substances that are so onerous and give occasion to so many vexations, dismissals, and sanctions."[27] And for the special evil attendant upon the sale of opium licenses, allow us to refer to what we said in one of the earlier chapters about the government's tolerance of

---

25. Road duties consisted of compulsory, unpaid labor constructing and maintaining public roadways (much like manorial duties under the feudal system).

26. J. W. H. Smissaert (1802–74) was a senior official on Java during the 1840s; W. L. de Sturler (1802–79) was an expert on Java's agriculture.

27. G. L. Baud (1801–91), speech to the Second Chamber, March 14, 1849.

prostitution: cases of this kind, given the moral character of government, deserve to be roundly condemned.[28]

CONVERTING GOVERNMENT ENTERPRISES INTO PUBLIC-LEGAL BURDENS § 271

To combat these four abuses we should restore justice by proceeding from the basic premise that the government be guaranteed a similar level of revenue from Java's natural resources and its people as it enjoys at present, but that these resources be converted into forms that are more genuinely public-legal and less blameworthy from an ethical viewpoint.

We are not convinced that the tax burden is too heavy for the Indies, but that it impacts in the wrong way.

When we advocate shrinking the cultivation system we do not have in mind to exempt the Javanese from all burdens, but rather to convert government enterprises into public-legal burdens. Do not forget that in the revenue from the forced cultivation are included (1) rent for the acreage under cultivation; (2) wages; (3) the cost of processing and transportation; (4) interest on investment capital; and (5) taxes on soil, business, and product.

This tissue should be disentangled. Let the tax be collected as tax. Let wages be paid out at their full value. Let the land yield its rent value. Let the processing industry establish the price of its product in the world market. Let capital investments find their own returns via purchase, lease, or mortgage.

These measures can have the following results, as has been demonstrated on Ceylon. (1) More intensive agriculture, when replacing practices leading to soil depletion, almost doubles the yield with the same amount of effort. (2) More careful processing so improves the quality of the product that its price rises by 11 percent.

These are powerful figures, especially when taking into account that Ceylon is less fertile. On Java, it takes ten trees to yield three *katties*, on Ceylon only four trees. The "native coffee" from Java fetches an average of forty-eight cents per *picol*, but the better prepared "plantation coffee" from Ceylon is sold at fifty-five cents.

If the improved quality guarantees a price increase of 11 percent, half the people engaged in the cultivation system could be freed up for other work, the government would still enjoy about the same level of revenue,

---

28. See above, §§ 191–93.

and European capital would be rewarded with sufficient interest on its investments.

§ 272   Abolition of the Cultivation System and Attendant Measures

The ultimate goal would have to be, through a gradual transition, to grant hereditary tenure to all public land (unimproved or already cultivated), to relieve the native of forced cultivation and road duties and free him up for working all this land at unabridged wages, and to have the government collect land rent from the long-lease tenants and enjoy a monopoly on exports. Such a relationship, once the new *kampong* settlements and a more natural situation had developed, would over time create the possibility for the state to take the land, by then increased in value, and parcel it out at a profit. From the proceeds the public debt could be amortized and so have its carrying cost reduced.

These changes would have to be accompanied by the following five measures: (1) to order a cadastral survey of the whole of Java and convert the land rent into proportional tax assessments; (2) to allow the road duties to be commuted into cash payments; (3) to pay village chiefs a fixed amount of surtax on the land tax; (4) to make the sale of opium subject to temporary permits; and (5) since import and export duties are the *regalia* or prerogatives of a sovereign, and since the State of the Netherlands, being the sovereign in this case, cannot of course pay itself, therefore to recognize the flag of the Netherlands as constituting a commercial unity between the mother country and her possessions that can and must levy duties on what is imported and exported under the flag of other nations but never on cargoes transported in vessels carrying our own flag.

The colonial government would then have at its disposal all proceeds from the improved tax on land, and so on (with the exception of the public lands and the *regalia* such as import and export duties, fishing grounds, and so on), while the mother county would gain the proceeds of leases, licenses, and taxes on public land as well as import and export duties and other *regalia*.

This would be offset by the costs to the mother country of installing a governor-general who would function as a state commissioner with the Indian administration, of posting customs officials at the border, and of maintaining a considerable portion of army and navy to keep the colonies, if need be, in submission and control.

Not the entire armed forces, mind you. Part of the navy and army would still have to be maintained by the colony itself, even if it enjoyed full autonomy. But the mother country would certainly be responsible for the other part that the Indies would immediately abolish if we on our part, from lack of moral energy and want of a national sense of self-worth, were recklessly to break our ties with the Indies.

PROTECTION AGAINST PRIVATE EXPLOITATION § 273

Another reason for keeping that other part with the mother country is that the Netherlands would be guilty of dereliction of duty if it were ever to abandon the peoples entrusted to its care to a small group of Europeans who have pitched their tents in the tropics.

It is undeniable that, apart from some favorable exceptions, these widely dispersed colonists decided to change domicile from purely financial, not moral motives. By marrying personal capital and intelligence they aim to profit from Java's soil and toil at a higher rate than is tolerated in the mother country. It is for this reason that we end by explicitly emphasizing the moral obligation of the government, in the face of both the Indian administration and the European capitalists, to protect the rights of the natives to develop in freedom, according to their own character and disposition.

For let it be clearly understood: we must not escape the revolution of the cultivation system in order to throw ourselves into the arms of the revolution of doctrinaire liberalism.

The thing to do is to loosen the straightjacket in order to restore freedom of movement to life itself. Whether life once freed will develop communally or individually—to mention one possibility among many—is not decided by legal rules or regulations, but by him alone who endowed the peoples of the Indies with an impulse of their own and who guides them in accordance with that impulse.

VI. THE STATE'S POSSESSIONS OUTSIDE JAVA

THE OUTER POSSESSIONS § 274

In the Indonesian Archipelago it is Java that forms the natural hub of our colonial possessions. Its geographical location, the number of its inhabitants, its history, and the nature of its soil contribute to this central importance.

Nevertheless the possessions outside Java should not be sacrificed to this colonial nerve center. This has happened all too often, both by regarding the administrative system introduced on Java as ready-made for the entire chain of islands and by treating the outer possessions in a stepmotherly fashion in order not to shortchange Java.

To the extent that this matter, too, involves principles of constitutional and international law, our rule should instead strive to (1) extend our sovereignty over the entire archipelago; (2) not proceed with this extension except at a very slow and gradual pace; and (3) let every island, under the shield of that sovereignty, develop its own distinctive conditions that suit the nature of its populace and its geographic location.

The archipelago does in fact constitute a single group of islands that belong together. A common future is therefore the best and most natural destiny for these islands. Given that the Netherlands happens to be sovereign in well over two-thirds of their populated areas, it is only natural that the unification of these scattered islands should take place under our flag.

To this extent, therefore, the inclination of the men in Batavia to continue to expand our possessions is only the expression of a natural impulse. Even the attempt at Kota Raja to at least keep out any other European or American power from the north coast of Sumatra should not be thoughtlessly condemned. We ought instead to condemn the indifference with which Buitenzorg neglected the northern coast of Borneo and passively looked on at the transfer of the Sulu Islands to Spain—evidence of myopic policies and little planning.

As is clear from the correspondence between Mr. Woudrichem van Vliet[29] and Professor Leone Levi,[30] published by the *Handelsblad*, the settlement at Brunei[31] definitely dates from the time when an Englishman

---

29. Leonard van Woudrichem van Vliet (1819–82) was a jurist who wrote critical studies about liberal policies with respect to the Dutch East Indies.
30. Leone Levi (1821–88) was a jurist, professor in King's College, London, and author of books on international commercial law and British economic history.
31. Kuyper refers to a series of letters about Brunei, a region on the north coast of the island of Borneo. Van Vliet initiated the correspondence with a number of inquiries to Levi and a short series of letters were exchanged between October and December 1878. Van Vliet was concerned the legality of grants of territory or governmental powers by foreign sovereigns to English citizens, including the possibility, in van Vliet's words, "Whether Englishmen can hold such grants without forfeiting their English citizenship?" Levi's response included the judgment that "whenever British subjects acquire dominion, it is comprehended within

could accept no other sovereignty than that of the British Crown, while on the other hand the recently published documents regarding the cession of the Sulu Islands to Spain give rise to the real question whether the part of Borneo belonging to the sultan of the Sulu Islands will long remain free and independent, or if it will ultimately be joined to the territory governed from the Philippines.[32]

RESPECTING THEIR DISTINCTIVENESS § 275

This tactic of passivity we deem exceedingly questionable. Unless we are mistaken, our government ought to keep a steady eye on the goal of regaining a free hand on Borneo and elsewhere and to extend Dutch sovereignty over the entire region of the archipelago by peaceful means and amicable settlement.

Thus not as with Achin, through overhasty breach of the peace and overwhelming force. That approach spells military and financial ruin. It gives our prestige a setback without enhancing our influence. And by offending justice it morally hampers any further expansion of our authority.

The people on this chain of islands should not have to fear the appearance of the Dutch flag, but should be able to welcome and bless it. Only then are we justified before God and man.

That entails as well what we pointed out in the second place: establishing our sovereignty should proceed very slowly. For the time being the only thing necessary—but then indispensable in every part of the archipelago—might be a fort at the mouth of navigable rivers or in inlets or harbors with reasonable depth. And if instead of gambling away a hundred million between Pulau Penang and Kota Raja[33] we had spent that sum on building such forts both in Achin and on Borneo, our name would have suffered far less and our factual power would be far stronger. Such forts, after all, if provided with torpedo boats and protected by a patrolling squadron, could easily be rendered impregnable to potential enemies.

---

the permanent dominion of the Empire." A portion of the correspondence subsequently was published at the request of van Vliet and with the permission of Levi in the Amsterdam *Algemeen Handelsblad* in January, 1879.

32. Within a few years of this writing, the Spanish authorities of the Philippines consolidated their control of the sultanate of Sulu.

33. This area marks the northern entrance to the Strait of Malacca, a region of widespread pirate activity at the time, the chief reason for the Dutch war on the sultanate of Achin. See above, § 230n10, and § 237n28.

As trading posts that collect duties from foreign vessels, they could in time pay for themselves and be a blessing for the population.

This will especially be the outcome if we also heed our third point: in every case to consult the distinctive character of the people who live on these islands. To want to force a Sumatran into the harness to which the Javanese submitted is an unforgivable mistake. Even these half savage peoples do have a distinct character. What the Javanese considers normal can offend the Sumatran bitterly. Consequently, we will not make lasting progress in the archipelago until each of these islands has a robust leader at the head who knows the people and determines what can take root among them and take hold of their minds.

Add to this, finally, that in order to work the archipelago organically, Christian missions must not rest until it has gathered its best forces in the coastal regions and the almost forgotten periphery and moves inland into the very heart and center of these populations. For, seriously, if you look at the map and compare the many mission posts in the Minahasa, on Halmahera and New Guinea[34] with our scant presence on Java and Madura, you sense that the Christophobia of the government has cooperated with the inclination of missions to avoid centralization, with the result that a situation has arisen that is exactly the opposite of what it should be.[35]

§ 276 SURINAME

About Suriname, too, we must, regrettably, be brief. Yet not so brief that we do not register a solemn protest against the indifference and coldness with which the splendid possession of this colony is usually treated at the exchange and the market in our country.

Suriname belongs to our oldest acquisitions.[36] It is no less than five times the size of the Netherlands. It has enjoyed years of production that totaled (in today's currency) more than thirty million. It enjoyed times when it surpassed Java in revenue from staples. As a colony in the Americas it can have greater political significance than our entire East Indies. In distance it lies measurably closer to us in Europe. In the stations

---

34. That is, in the more sparsely populated, far northeast of the Indonesian Archipelago.

35. So as not to upset Muslims in the interest of peaceful trade relations, the colonial government had long discouraged Christian missionaries from working on Java and Madura, assigning them instead to the more remote islands.

36. By the treaty ending the Second Anglo-Dutch War in 1667, the Dutch retained the plantations on the Suriname River in exchange for ceding New Amsterdam to the English.

of the Moravian brethren it has a model of successful missions. In the future, when the Indies get sucked into the sphere of influence of Australia, Suriname might become more important for our commercial interests than the entire archipelago.

And yet, how miserable and sad the conditions in this wonderful colony! Of its nearly 60,000 square miles little more than 200—yes, 200 square miles—are under cultivation.[37] Its population is no larger than the single city of Utrecht. Its mortality rate exceeds its birth rate. Production has decreased to a tenth of former days. Idol worship, according to the latest Colonial Report, is on the increase.

Plantation after plantation lies deserted. Every year we have to make up Suriname's deficit with several hundred thousand [guilders]. In public opinion, for anyone to go to the West Indies is such a sure sign of his general uselessness that the state of Suriname society has little to write home about.

The primary reason for this, no doubt, was the great affluence that in the middle of the eighteenth century caused the colonists of the day to slacken. This drained their strength to cope with adversities brought on by successive wars that hampered production exports and the slave market. The colonists became all too willing to mortgage their estates to Amsterdam capitalists, thus putting themselves under the power of an outside purse. Particularly in 1770, drawing on the Amsterdam money market became a frenzy that in a few weeks' time undid the independence of virtually the entire colony and established a debt on the cultivated lands of ƒ50 million (ƒ150 million in today's money).

Indebtedness of this kind could only break their energy. One does not work for outsiders. The number of colonist decreased, to be replaced by managers. Industry and agriculture lost their vigor as a result. Colonial splendor was extinguished long before the emancipation of the slaves.[38] Compensation payments to the slave owners of course ended up for the most part with the Amsterdam moneylenders. The small economy that survived the emancipation soon collapsed, and for a long time the opinion

---

37. Approximately 154,000 sq. km and 500 sq. km, respectively. The original reads: "Of its 2,800 square geographical miles little more than 10—yes, 10—are under cultivation." One sq. mi. (geogr.) equals about 21.3 sq. mi. (55.1 sq. km or 5,508 ha). Today's Suriname comprises about 63,000 sq. mi. (approx. 164,000 sq. km).

38. Slavery was abolished in Suriname when the Dutch parliament in 1863 passed the Emancipation Act.

gained ground that nothing could be accomplished anymore with this colony. On more than one occasion it was even suggested in government circles, especially among the *Indo-manen*,[39] to put the colony up for sale!

§ 277   Comparison with British Guyana

And yet, there was no real reason for such a despondent and un-Dutch view of the situation. Right next to Suriname lie Demerara, Berbice, and Essequibo. These former possessions of ours that were ceded to Great Britain[40] shared the same fate as Suriname and also find themselves today in a far from prosperous condition. Yet they are noticeably better off.

While Suriname has to come to us begging, British Guyana has a balanced budget and sometimes even enjoys a surplus. In 1871 its expenditures were only 338,000 pound sterling, as against 379,000 in revenue; in 1877 these figures were 344,000 and 364,000. For a population three times as large as Suriname it spends only ƒ4 million annually, whereas our administration would proportionally cost us ƒ5 million. Its exports amount to about ƒ30 million in total, as against ƒ3 or ƒ4 million from Suriname, which at the same ratio should be ƒ10 million. Accordingly, its trade amounted to 200,000 ton of shipping, as against only 20,000 ton from our colony, which again, at the same population ratio, should have been 65,000 ton. Only in education can we hold our heads high: thanks to the excellent services of the Moravian brethren there are 5,000 pupils to a population of 60,000 souls in Suriname, whereas British Guyana, with a population three times as large, has 16,000 school-going children. Four factors account for this situation: (1) our government system; (2) failed colonization; (3) the state of the colony's high society; and (4) the lack of enterprise among Dutch capitalists.

§ 278   Criticism of the Existing Situation

We are not saying that our government system for Suriname does not contain valuable elements. Articles 107 and 159 make both Java and the mother country envious of Paramaribo.[41] Article 107 has a provision that we would want for the East Indies: *a governor and military paid for by the mother country, not the colony* (except that it includes the capital error of

---

39. That is, lovers of all things related to the East Indies, especially Oriental religion and culture.
40. These former possessions of the Netherlands were ceded in the post-Napoleonic settlements of 1814–15.
41. Paramaribo was the seat of government in Suriname.

leaving the *regalia* and the public domains to the colony, which in the nature of the case is absurd). And Article 159 regulates education exactly in the way we would want for the Netherlands and the East Indies: *private schools the rule, government schools supplementary*—ensuring excellent results, as is well known.[42]

The mistake in this arrangement lies elsewhere. Laws copied from the British model were enacted for a non-British public, with the result that control was prematurely given up. Given a sparsely populated region and a socially backward population, to have installed a Colonial Council in Suriname, in every detail an imitation of Westminster parliaments with the right of amendment, legislative initiative, and control of the budget, was a political blunder, all the more so since in order to find more voters the whole territory was treated as a single district. This insertion into the colonial machinery lacks the moral authority to operate in a proper constitutional fashion; it divides responsibility and breaks the power of the governor.

Equally detrimental is the aftermath of the failed colonization of the Saramacca [river valley]. It is one of the saddest pages in our history: Dutch migrants were literally sacrificed and vanished as snow before the sun.[43] Despite the favorable depositions by Dr. Landré, Dr. Dumontier, Mr. Van Sypesteyn, and others, it is evident once again from the Colonial Report that the Dutch farmer is not suited for tilling the soil in a tropical climate.[44] Negroes, Indian contract laborers, and Chinese coolies are the only workers that one can permanently use in these regions. Colonization efforts can hope to succeed only if we transfer to Suriname enterprising capitalists, intelligent industrialists, capable personnel for supervisory duties, and men for small industry. Negative conclusions have quite wrongly been drawn from the failed experiment to discourage settlement

---

42. *Note by the author:* Article 158 reads: "The provision of education is free to all who can produce sufficient evidence of competence and morality." Article 159 reads: "The government sees to it, resources permitting, that the acquisition of primary skills is made accessible also to low-income groups, which it achieves by supporting private schools and operating public schools."

43. The ill-prepared settlement of Dutch Boers at Saramacca lasted from 1845 to 1853. When disease had decimated their number, the survivors moved to other districts of Suriname or returned to Europe.

44. See *West-Indië: bijdragen tot de bevordering van de kennis der Nederlandsch West-Indische koloniën*, ed. H. C. Focke, Ch. Landré, C. A. Van Sypesteyn, and F. A. C. Dumontier, 2 vols. (Haarlem: A. C. Kruseman, 1855-58).

in this colony. But a wrong impression, once imprinted deeply on the public mind, takes a long time before it has worn off.

Nor is the low state of high society good for the colony. The atmosphere is not healthy there, nor can it be, owing to the aftereffect of a sad past and the want of clean air and fresh activity. Merely recall that a man like Dr. Zaalberg was desired there as "pastor."[45] Or learn from this year's Colonial Report that of the 203 infants presented for baptism in the Reformed church, 158 were illegitimate and only 45 legitimate. The British colonists are a different run of people; wherever they go they start by looking for a church center and from there they let the dignity of the human person illumine all social interaction and professional conduct.

And what clinches the evil impact of all these deficiencies is the focus of our Dutch capitalists on clipping coupons, the absence of grit among our young people, and the exhausted state of our nation, undermined by social sin, barely able to stay on its feet, bereft of any strength to assimilate other regions of the world.

§ 279   COLONIZATION OF SURINAME

For all these reasons it would be advisable to reverse some of the limitations since imposed on the governor (a reform that would be perfectly constitutional). An energetic person could be allowed to use this unlimited power to remake and reinvigorate the colony. The inhabitants could be assisted in improving their social condition. Foreign capital and foreign entrepreneurs could be lured to the rich soil.

If Amsterdam investors then see, after others have learned from bitter experience, that money can be made from that soil, they will take courage. And then things will improve, on condition that no capital is sent over there, but that men cross the ocean—in person, with their capital, and with the intention to take up permanent residence. Colonies do not benefit from "Colonization Societies." Persons have to go over, people with knowledge and ambitions. And if these people take over the government-sponsored immigration, provide housing on the plantations for the Indian contract workers and the Chinese laborers in order to prevent collusion and mutiny, and if they encourage the Christian missionaries to work especially among these laborers, then by way of transition a kind of feudal

---

45. J. C. Zaalberg (1828–85) was a notorious Modernist preacher from The Hague who in 1885 accepted a call from the Paramaribo congregation, which he served briefly until his death.

arrangement between planters and workers could arise in Suriname that would prosper both.

All that the government would have to do is to guarantee legal security for both planters and coolies, to keep the drainage system and the canals in good repair, and to survey and map the territories in order to increase knowledge of Suriname among the Dutch people, knowledge which evidently is much needed to awaken their spirit of enterprise.

DEFENDING OUR OVERSEAS POSSESSIONS   §280

Coming at last to the critical question of how to defend our possessions in both the West and the East Indies, everyone will agree that perpetual vigilance is called for only in regard to Britain. The reason that we need not be afraid of other powers is that Britain would never allow France or Germany to take over our colonial possessions. And few today will credit the absurd notion, entertained four years ago, that a Turkish fleet might sail for Achin, seeing as the Turkish navy has demonstrated its insignificance even against the much smaller Russian ships.

Britain, however, is dangerous. Britain is dangerous because of her infinite capacity for assimilation and her insatiable greed that we must not suppose to have been satisfied with Transvaal and Afghanistan. Britain might become especially dangerous, however, if the estrangement between her and Germany were to intensify. Our country lies in between these two powers, and either power might want to secure its position by occupying us. In that event Britain no doubt would be willing to help us out again, as she did at the beginning of the nineteenth century, by taking our colonies in trust.[46]

But precisely this prospect raises the question whether we would not be wise to enter into an understanding with another power to whom we would give our possessions in trust should the occasion arise.

By her own precedent Britain has given us and that other power the indisputable right to enter into such an entente. It is not hard to guess which power alone could be considered for this. And even if we were bound by a treaty to pay for such services (if it remained limited to "trust") in the form of decent compensation in money or (if it came to war in our behalf) in territory, then one should not forget that for her services Britain

---

46. During the Revolutionary and Napoleonic wars Britian held trusteeship over a
    number of Dutch colonies.

simply took her compensation[47]—and would take it again as she saw fit. Nor should one forget that the mere knowledge of the existence of such a treaty would likely persuade Britain to refrain from taking our colonies, if only to prevent a third power from emerging in the East Indies.

---

47. In 1815, with the liberation of the Netherlands from Napoleonic France, Britain retained Western Guyana, Cape Colony, and Ceylon but returned to the new United Kingdom of the Netherlands several other Dutch colonies.

CHAPTER TWENTY

THE SOCIAL QUESTION

It acknowledges the necessity to contribute better than at present, also by means of legislation, toward making relations between the various social classes answer as much as possible to the demands of God's Word.

ARTICLE 19

I. RETURN TO GOD'S WORD

THE PROBLEM

§ 281

The social question poses the problem: What changes should be introduced in the political and social situation in order to create more satisfactory relations between those who contribute skill and muscle and those others who are rich or better educated?

Today, relations between these two elements of human society are disturbed. So disturbed, in fact, that both sides have at times felt their very lives threatened. Tensions are rife and at many points have already issued in bloody conflict.

This is a fatal interlude, causing an intransigent position to get hold of many people which holds that a resolution of tensions is no longer conceivable without plunder or bloodbath. Over against this group, only a smaller group pin their hopes on gradual reform through a change in thinking, a return to more godly manners, and a turnaround in legislation.

By an intransigent position is meant, on the one hand, the thinking of communists and social democrats who want to leave nothing standing of the existing order, and on the other the stance of reactionaries and the contented who want to make no changes at all in the existing order.

However much their starting points are polar opposites, socialists and reactionaries agree on this: the social order should reflect their interests exclusively, without worrying about the essential living conditions of the class they hate.

The slogan of both sides is therefore: All or nothing.

Unwilling to bend, they are willing to let it come to a complete break. The one side expects the triumph of fist and dagger, the other of mounted police and military force.

Since reactionaries are found among all parties, every party is confronted with the question: Will you remain politically inactive and simply wait for a repeat of 1789? Or will you use any influence you may have to shame the intransigents by means of wise policies?

To the latter question our Program gives an unequivocal answer, including the need for legislation. It answers it not just in the affirmative, but more, with an affirmation that is postulated as an inescapable necessity from God's Word.

§ 282   A Fourfold Cause

Many factors have contributed to the rise of the disproportionate relationship between the two main elements of society.

There is first of all the happy fact that the lower class has made great progress in terms of knowledge and education. Not that we are not aware of the shadow side of this progress or that we attach too much value to the kind of intellectual advancement that usually accompanies moral development. But we can be happy in the sense that the lower class of society, taken as a whole, has broadened its outlook, enlightened its understanding, and improved its ability to help itself.

Next to that we place the incredible revolution wrought by the improved application of steam power and machine production. This has freed capital almost completely from its earlier dependence on manual labor. The workingman's muscle power and his resourcefulness and traditional skills in many ways have turned into dead capital; his value now lies almost entirely in servicing machines according to set instructions. The magical operation of iron machines has unfortunately led the capitalist to regard his employees as nothing but machines of flesh that can be retired or scrapped when they break down or have worn out.

A third cause is the steady growth in population made possible by the greater production and more efficient distribution of consumer goods and promoted by shorter wars, milder epidemics, more relaxed customs, and improved hygiene. This has disproportionately swelled the labor market and increased the number of mouths to feed.

INFLUENCE OF IDEAS FROM THE REVOLUTION §283

In a society thus unhinged by this threefold cause the Revolution in an evil hour hurled its unholy torch, scorching the faith, setting fire to moral bonds, and infiltrating heads and hearts with the madness of the most blasphemous delusions moral, social, and political.

This evil was ruinous in its effect both upwards and downwards. Among workingmen, whose faith had eroded, bitter resentment came to replace earlier contentment and acquiescence in the will of God. Among the upper classes, tender compassion and kindhearted charity was replaced by reckless egoism that aggravated the bitterness without giving an inch.

Just as fatal was the effect of loosening the moral ties of trust, solidarity, and attachment that used to bind the wage earner to his employer. This effect was achieved by reducing the mutual relationship to an impersonal contract, so that the connection could be severed at any moment. The secret of a proper balance between the two was sought, for the duration of the contract, in maximizing benefit from each other and minimizing service to each other.

Once the tinder had been fatally assembled from all sides, the Revolution at last lit the fire by raising aloft the most shameful and blasphemous theories that in every sector of life confounded the concepts of justice and injustice, of honor and shame, of virtue and wickedness. Fanned by the unscrupulous language of ambitious demagogues, the masses were brought into a frenzied state by dangling before their eyes all kinds of unthinkable and impossible situations in which the flesh in unrestrained pleasure and the passions in unbridled rage would tear to shreds every bond of duty and forcibly replace the kingdom of God with a kingdom of animals. To such outrageous wickedness—never forget—the propertied classes themselves had contributed not a little, as their orgies and revelry all too often had begun to exhibit this animal trait. The effect of their immoral conduct was both provocative and contagious, now that their unprincipled theories about morality and politics had popularized a system of general ideas that, through all the gradations of liberalism and conservatism, bears a direct, genetic link to socialism.

§ 284   MEDICINES THAT DO NOT HELP

The medicine against this social sickness that is being proposed by the radicals—namely, to limit the number of mouths to feed by uprooting marriage and practicing artificial birth control and so create more satisfying living conditions for a smaller number—this medicine we reject with abhorrence. Not only is it deeply immoral and conducive to depravity, but also deceptive and unavailing. It does not reckon with sin, which with fewer numbers would immediately also dull the incentive to keep up productivity; and it will always, owing to its dangerous seduction given the various predispositions of individuals, resurrect the same sorrowful class divisions.

We expect no better results from the palliatives of the liberals who organize public lectures for the common people about political economy, who open reading rooms and smoking halls for the workingman, and for the rest know no other charms than the savings bank and the public school. Of this whole inventory, only the public school might in principle work; but now that the primary school, bereft of a higher principle, can breed but not stem socialism, it too has to be taken off the roll.

And as for those who suppose that a soup ticket or a friendly home visit or a Bible reading has the power to check the evil, we need to ask them, while appreciating their good intentions, whether they really do not see that the social question is not about the poor but about the ordinary laborer, including the office worker and the clerk at the ticket office.

By *the poor* we understand people who cannot provide for themselves because they are widows, minors, the elderly, or the sick. It is an area of life where mercy reaps its laurels and comforts those who need to be comforted.

But the social question is at best only indirectly connected with the poor, and the real factor of the social movement is not the humble poor, not even the *pauvres honteux,*[1] but rather the healthy laborer in the prime

---

1. The poor who are ashamed to beg, the silent poor.

of his life, a person who can work and wants to work but who asks—and will soon demand—that he be provided with a job that allows him to make a living wage for himself and his dependents.

Philanthropy only addresses the incidental cases when a working-man sinks into the class of the poor because his health is impaired or he is unemployed or he has entered old age. It does not address the social question itself, since the laborer with muscles in his arms and pride in his physique has a sense of honor that can't abide your soup tickets or other forms of charity.

Meanwhile, the proposal to make short work of any insurrectionists, to position cannon at every city ward, and direct a squad to every slum— or, to use the expression of the Versaillese,[2] "to crush the vermin"—resembles too much a *viaticum ad orcum*[3] as to turn a Christian away in profound disgust.

A Threefold Proposition   § 285

If you ask us what we would recommend as a better and safer route, then we admit freely that we do not for a moment claim to be able to guarantee a situation in which the inequality of property, and therefore the contrast between rich and poor, between hand and head, between brawn and brains would be abolished. Those who pretend that they can realize such a situation deceive themselves and mislead the masses. "The rich and the poor meet together; the Lord is the maker of them all," says the Old Testament; and we read in the New Testament: "You always have the poor with you."[4] These statements of course do not command us to have it *be* so; they simply note the fact that it *is* so. The experience of every age and every region of the globe, and no less the invariable fiasco of all communist utopias, testify that this is undeniably true.

Thus we are not deluding anybody with the impossible. Our proposal to resolve this problem is not aimed at *removing* the contrast between classes but at *regulating* and *alleviating* it. The contrast arose from sin, it is fed by sin, and it will be with us for as long as there is sin.

---

2. Kuyper refers here to the ruthless measures taken by the French government in the spring of 1871 to quash the rebels that controlled Paris in the aftermath of the Franco-Prussian War.

3. "A road to hell"; literally: escort money on the way to the underworld.

4. Prov 22:2; Matt 26:11.

Indeed, we want to be honest and will add a second restriction to the first: namely, that this mounting sickness will not be checked except in stages, by turning the whole atmosphere around. And even then it is an open question whether, given the ascendancy of the machine and the annihilation of what has been permanently destroyed, we can go back to a situation that will be appropriate to the present day yet be as beneficial as in former days.

Thus it is only with that double restriction that we dare to promise a relaxation and improvement of the situation. We must turn back to the Word of God, correct the political imbalance, and codify the rights and customs under which wage labor is carried out.

§ 286   RETURN TO THE WORD OF GOD

We shall devote a separate article to each of the last two points. About the first point just this:

When, as here, society splits up into two camps, each defending mutually conflicting interests, things can only end in civil war and thus in the right of the strongest, unless a moral law intervenes in time that in the estimation of both groups trumps those interests and by taking hold of their conscience keeps them from resorting to violence and injustice.

Such a law does not produce a law that issues from the state, since the ruling party in the state has the power to bend that law and make it serve its interests. It is therefore inescapable that we look for a law that lies above the state and beyond the reach of political manipulation and that is firmly grounded in him who dwells on high in holiness.

Now then, the written record of that law is the Word of God. And it is in that strict, concrete sense, not as a loose term, that we speak of a return to the Word of God.

Doing that will not only send us back to practicing charity and, when needed, make us embrace quiet submission; but it will above all send us back to debating questions of justice before the forum of conscience— that is, before the face of God—and will make us order our relationships in accordance with it.

Yes, also send us back to *practicing charity*! For the same Word of God that says "Rich and poor meet together" also calls out what is so easily forgotten: "Woe to you that are rich!"[5] The Word condemns the wanton

---

5. Luke 6:24.

spendthrift; it curses the usurer; it damns the cruel master. It charges all who fear God to do good to the brother and to love the neighbor, including the poor and the wage earner.

Yes, also make us embrace *quiet submission*. For the Lord says, "Vengeance is mine, I will repay."[6] The poor and the wage earner are not permitted to wring that vengeance from the hands of God and wrest with brute force what has not been allotted them from the hand of their Father. All the more so since the plaint, "I saw all the oppressions that are done under the sun. And behold the tears of the oppressed, and they had no one to comfort them!"[7] is invariably followed by *real comfort* from a higher power who in the midst of suffering pours a sense of bliss into the soul, distills spiritual gain from suffering, and freely bestows title deeds to a rich inheritance above.

Even so, this hardly exhausts what God's Word has to effectuate here. For that is no less than to exert such an influence on people's hearts, their thinking, moods and prevailing sense of justice that at the very core of human society egoism and its disorganizing action are banished and the love that binds together regains its capacity for creating order and harmony.

For this to happen, however, the avenues must be opened up along which God's Word can be conveyed to the heart of our society. That is to say, God's ordinances are to be paramount in the council chambers, in the public school, in Christ's church; and government is not to impede the Word's reconquest of the council, the school, and the church.

II. RESTORING THE POLITICAL BALANCE

BALANCE IS INDISPENSABLE   § 287

Our second condition is the restoration of political balance in the administration of the country.

This refers mainly to the impact that legislation and executive decisions can have for tipping the scales in favor of one sector of society at the expense of another. This situation ought to be regulated by law in such a way that the scales tip neither to the right nor to the left but remain steady, pointing like a compass needle to equity and justice.

In no way do we back away from the objection that lawmakers have no business interfering with society's course of development, that society

---

6. Rom 12:19.
7. Eccl 4:1.

must be left to the natural action of its own laws, and that therefore the social movement must never appeal to government for legislative changes in its favor.

The antirevolutionary, after all, who reckons with God's ordinances, can never overlook in Israel's social laws, which had God himself as their author, the presence of a broad series of provisions that made the relationship between haves and have-nots different from what it would otherwise have been if left to itself. Israel's laws touching usury, lending against collateral, creditors, day laborers, after-harvest gleaning, the return of alienated fields, the tithe, leaving the fruit of the land for the poor every so many years, and so much more, made for a system of social institutions that unquestionably served to restrict the powerful and to raise a protective shield over the weak. This encouraged the higher principle of mercy and charity to come to expression also in civil life. The dreadful gap between rich and poor never took root. It did not become part of Israel's national life until it came under Roman rule, and even among our present-day Jews it is still kept to a minimum by their sense of mutual solidarity. And even if you join us in recognizing that the particulars in these Old Testament laws were geared to particular national circumstances and no longer apply to us today, nevertheless you will have to admit that the pith, the purport, and the principle they express have enduring legitimacy, so that the government's duty to give guidance to society by means of laws and ordinances is grounded in divine authority.

And those who do not believe in the divine origin of these laws should seriously consider how leaving society and its various elements to its own impulses has ever had, or can have, any other consequence than that the weaker, unprotected members of society have to wrestle with the stronger ones and so will have the worst of it, and succumb. The situation would resemble the doe and the tiger living together in the jungle. Everybody will instinctively approve the more sanctified situation in which the wolf, instead of tearing the lamb apart and feasting on its blood, peacefully lies down with it, restrained by the disarming effect of the law.

And even if this were not admitted, even then one would not have the right to stand at the door of our legislature and angrily turn away the social question. Because if one disallows any legislation that would guide the course of civil society and on that account refuses the weaker ones all protection laws, then surely all laws ought also to be abolished that at present factually make the power of the stronger even greater.

There must be protection, not regulation. To provide protection is the unique task of government. Government is the repository of all rights. Only, let's not forget, each of the elements of society should in turn be recognized as the weaker and as such should share in the protection.

The lower classes are weaker than the upper classes where capital and intelligence are concerned; but they might in turn prove the stronger when it comes to muscle power and shrewdness. From this it follows that the law must not only protect the people of modest means against the educated person's money and knowledge that he could bring into play at their expense. The law must also, in the same way and to the same degree, protect the upper classes against the physical strength, shrewdness, and sheer numbers that the lower classes might employ at the expense of those who are better off.

This consideration at the same time underscores the difference between the *regulatory mania* of the meddlesome state and the obligation of government to provide *legal protection*.

The fanatic for state omnipotence, or to put it more mildly, the statesman who leans toward expanding the power of government, is not pursuing the moral goal of protecting the weak, but has the doctrinaire objective of recasting society according to an ideal model. Conversely, a protective government never acts until there is a complaint about oppression; it never has its legislation reach further than the abuse; and with the passing of every law that shifts the balance to the left it makes sure that no power deficit arises on the right that would cause the political balance to be upset.

Legislative intervention that aims at nothing more—nor anything less, nor anything different—than to offer *protection* does not erase or curtail the limits of state power. Rather, it delineates it more carefully. It is not the least of his merits that with respect to this critical point Dr. De Savornin Lohman, in his book on *Authority and Freedom*,[8] has made an airtight case for taking "conflicting interests" as a criterion for the proper scope of government.

---

8. A. F. de Savornin Lohman (1837-1924), *Gezag en Vrijheid* [Authority and freedom] (Utrecht: Kemink, 1875).

This criterion will appear all the more useful when you begin to realize the many ways in which laws can shift the balance to the right or to the left.

In general you associate legislation regarding conflicting interests with special laws for the manufacturing industry, agriculture, and wage-labor (which we shall discuss later).[9] But what you overlook in that case is that the issue of upsetting the balance or keeping in balance is at stake in almost every law and every government measure.

To convince you of this, just note how in barbaric states such as Turkey, Persia, and Bokhara[10] the absence of good laws and the abundance of bad laws have created a woeful imbalance between the elements of society. Note how in poorly run countries like Spain, Naples, and Ireland the lower classes produced paupers and brutes and still burden Naples with highway robbers and street beggars and Ireland with mass emigration and Fenian atrocities.

Or—of more immediate relevance—note how in your own country and in our colonies virtually every branch of legislation and administration can disrupt the functioning of the social network.

This became clear in the case of the colonies when we examined the cultivation system in the Indies and the poor administration of Suriname. In the case of the Netherlands itself it will be clear, if less glaring, if we but glance over a few of our legislative rubrics.

Take our civil and criminal laws. They have the undeniable effect, formally at least, of making both the summons and the defense stronger for the person of status and means than for the common person. For even though the latter may be granted the assistance of publicly financed lawyers to counsel and plead for him, nevertheless the more educated person has an enormous advantage over the person of lower status through his knowledge of the law and legal proceedings, the leisure time at his disposal, the higher stakes he can risk, and the more skillful lawyers he can hire.

Take the laws on the registration of property. As we have repeatedly pointed out above, they take away 10 percent from the little man, who is often forced to sell a house or a field, an amount that the rich man, who is not obliged to sell, indirectly adds to his capital.[11]

---

9. See below, §§ 292–98.

10. The Emirate of Bukhara, since 1925 part of Uzbekistan.

11. See above, § 222.

Take our conscription laws. They allow the sons of the well-to-do to go free, while the sons of those less blessed with worldly goods are wrenched from their jobs, their homes and families, and exposed to moral poisoning.

Take our poor laws. They discourage private philanthropy, dull the sense of duty to be generous, absolve the church, and nevertheless treat the needy in such a way that in order to escape cold and hunger the needy are tempted to break the law, preferring time in jail to relief of this kind.

Take our education acts. As the minister himself has admitted,[12] they have the effect of leaving the people of means free in the rearing of their children but applying compulsion to those who lack the means.[13]

ADMINISTRATIVE MEASURES WITH THE SAME EFFECT   § 290

With even greater justification we can point to administrative measures and decisions that have gradually distorted the entire state of relations among us.

Take, for example, the measures taken in 1815, 1843, 1852, and 1866 with regard to the churches. They could not but cause the Protestant churches to waste their energy in preoccupying themselves with internal problems and so rendered them unable to fulfill their task of providing moral guidance, especially among the lower class.

Take the measures and decisions taken to regulate the abuse of alcohol. They have caused the double evil that especially the lower class succumbs morally and has too high a sum flowing from its daily income into the national treasury. It shows as well how cruel the workingman,

---

12. Namely, in his official report to the King advising him not to accede to the People's Petition by vetoing his education bill that had passed parliament.

13. After the Education Act of 1889 granted a measure of public funding to Christian schools, Kuyper inserted the following clause in later editions: "even now that partial justice has been restored in the field of primary education." This insertion expresses Kuyper's view that the Act of 1889 made only a small beginning of alleviating the inequity. Improvements in school facilities and class size, mandated by the Education Act of 1878, had made operating a school much more expensive, putting tuition fees of Christian schools beyond the reach of lower-income families unless the school was privately subsidized. The monopoly enjoyed by public schools on funding by the central government prompted many municipalities to cancel all tuition fees, thus increasing the competitive advantage of public schools. As a result, private schools, as the minister put it in his report to the King (see previous note), increasingly became "a luxury for the rich and a form of charity for the poor." Nevertheless, the modicum of public funding for Christian schools legislated by the Act of 1889, though small, did mark a victory for the principle of parity treatment in the area of education.

who complains about being ill-treated by others, can treat his own wife and children.

Take the measures and decisions taken under King William I to focus our shipping and industry almost exclusively on our East Indies. For a time this fostered an artificial level of prosperity and a disproportionate rise in working-class families and their standard of living, only to produce the bitter fruit after a while of seeing most trade languish, shipping go downhill, and shipyards lie idle. The consequence was a considerable loss of jobs for our shipwrights, riggers, dockhands, and warehousers, as well as jobs in the supply industries.

Take the measures and decisions that have regulated the movement of capital. Partly through fictitious expansion, partly through the superior power of accumulation, they have rendered smaller businesses unable to compete and caused smaller financial assets to be wiped out during financial crises.

Take the measures and decisions that regulate imports and exports. They have caused our sugar industry, for example, to languish and our retailers to be undercut by Paris. In still other branches of industry these measures have repeatedly caused a reduction in the number of people who made a living in them.

Take, above all, the measures and the abstinence of measures that have allowed the *stock* exchange to triumph over the *trade* exchange. One consequence has been that the ordinary person lost all his small investments in Spanish and American railways. Worse, time and again a company that used to transact business, hence engaged employees, hired teamsters, and loaded ships, ceased operations; that is to say, it put all its personnel out of work and took on at most one-third that number to work in a stockbroker's office.

So let it never again be said that administrative acts and laws have nothing to do with the social question. On the contrary, it may be asserted that there is hardly a law that does not have an impact on the balance between the two groups in society. In fact, it's no use denying that relations between them would have been noticeably different in our country if smarter policies and shrewder intelligence had prevailed.

§ 291   REMEDY

Now, we do not at all demand that in view of this evil our system of laws be hastily revised and made to lean more to the side of the lower class.

This may be feasible to some extent, yet not in any effective way. First, to restore the balance, more is needed than to take care of those who are less well off. Those better off, too, need to be protected—by curbing lawless demonstrations and tightening sanctions and penalties. Government will have to learn again what it is to *govern*, something it has forgotten these many years.

Secondly, revisions, if called for, may be feasible. But what is done cannot be undone: measures of the past cannot just be reversed.

Thirdly, to restore the balance in this way is unthinkable simply because the person has yet to be born who can tell us what the right balance is.

Straightening out what has been warped will have lasting effect only if conducted in a gradual way and along normal avenues. In other words, *the element that is currently shut out has to be given a voice in the nation's representative bodies.*

Just give the disadvantaged (real or imaginary) an opportunity to stick up for themselves in the councils, to put their finger on the wound that is hemorrhaging their well-being, and to oppose the infringement upon their rightful place in life—and gradually what has been ailing will of itself begin to heal.

In former days there was no reason for this. As trades and crafts then worked, the interest of the employer coincided with the interest of his employee. When a master defended his personal interests he was at the same time fighting for his servants. This explains why Provincial States no longer seated peasants when they came to be represented by lords and knights, or craftsmen once they came to be represented by their masters' guilds. In that situation it would have made no sense for peasants and craftsmen to have their own personal input.

But when the interests of employer and employee, of lord and peasant, grow apart so that they no longer coincide but in many respects are at odds, as they are today, then to still let the lower class be represented by their superiors is nothing less than the subversion of what fairness would demand.

This situation, therefore, and definitely not certain putative "human rights," is the motive for gradually extending political rights to those who live by the sweat of their brow. At the same time it is an indication that these rights ought not to be granted in a manner that would either make them pointless or else make them defeat the purpose.

Both would be the outcome of universal suffrage. Universal suffrage would be pointless if it failed to give the floor to an advocate of the workingman, or if it brought in a demagogue who would only discredit the sacred cause of the wage earner. Universal suffrage would at the same time defeat its purpose if the lower class, rural as well as urban, were to step up its organization and in its turn outvote the well-to-do, causing legislation recklessly to serve interests, only this time of the *other* side.

It is for this reason that we opted for the guild system leading to *corporative* States, and for head-of-household suffrage, with weighted voting, for the *political* States.[14] These reforms would give the wage earner a decent chance to have his interests properly represented. At the same time they would effectively stem the danger of having the upper classes of society dominated by the lower class.

III. A LABOR CODE

§ 292   INTRODUCED IN THE SECOND CHAMBER

Nevertheless, redirecting developments to align with God's Word and restoring the disrupted balance does not at all ensure a solution to the problem we face. For that, a third requirement is that laws and regulations be enacted to bring the battlefield itself under the shield of justice.

This was the intention of the present author five years ago when in a session of the Second Chamber of the States General he suggested to the government that the ultimate goal of its intervention should be a *Labor Code*.[15]

The suggestion garnered so little support that the then sitting minister of justice,[16] speaking on behalf of the government, poked fun at it. As for the members, they merely shrugged their shoulders. And the press hissed that the honorable member who brought up the matter could himself probably not draw up a single article for such a law code.

In those days the members of the government lacked knowledge of the subject, the Chamber lacked sufficient gravity, and the press lacked the necessary goodwill to debate the issue in the hope of a satisfactory outcome.

---

14. See above, §§ 136–44.

15. See Kuyper, *Eenige Kameradviezen uit de jaren 1874 en 1875*, (session of November 28, 1874), 139–203, esp. 191–97. For full citation, see above, § 92n5.

16. Theodoor baron van Lynden van Sandenburg (1826–85), a self-styled antirevolutionary politician, was minister of justice from 1874 to 1877.

Today, however, now that it comes down to finalizing the antirevolutionary position on this critical issue, no side issues may keep us from discussing this proposal. It is our duty to speak.

And then we may be permitted to ask at once: Have the minister and the Chamber and the press taken note of the legal publication by James Edward Davis entitled *The Labour Laws?*[17] This excellent book came out in Britain exactly one year after I broached the subject in the Second Chamber. The occasion was the passing by the British parliament of labor bills that had been in preparation at Westminster at the very moment when in The Hague the mere idea of such a system of laws was decried as absurd.

What makes the case even more inconvenient for our then-sitting minister and for those who joined his chorus is that these Labor Laws were not introduced in Britain for the first time in 1875 but merely amended already existing labor laws, while the well-known Truck Act[18] dates from as early as 1831 and the amended labor laws of 1875 had first seen the light at the initiative of Lord Elcho[19] already in 1867.

If it has been the custom among British politicians and jurists to refer to this complex of laws touching on this subject by the name of labor laws, then we cannot see why anyone should find fault with the idea that the government should regard as its ultimate goal a Labor Code that would complete and harmonize these separate laws.

Commerce and Labor   § 293

The point is this: for the assimilation of what is available in the world two classes of industry are necessary: first, working up raw material into a usable state; second, bringing what has been processed within reach of the consumer.

To the second class of industry belongs *commerce*, with everything that pertains to it, such as shipping, warehousing, marketing, and so on.

The primary class of industry includes farming, mining, fishing, manufacturing, and manual labor.

---

17. James Edward Davis (1817–87), *The Labour Laws* (London: Butterworths, 1875).
18. The Truck Act prohibited the payment of wages in merchandise from the company store.
19. Francis Charteris (1818–1914), who was 10th Earl of Wemyss, 6th Earl of March, and Baron Elcho, was a member of the House of Commons and chairman of the committee that drafted The Master and Servant Act of 1867.

Differentiating between these two classes of industry in a general way, we can say that the one is entirely and exclusively characterized by the concept of *trade*, that is, taking wares for less money from those who have too much of them, to supply those who need them for more money. The other, by contrast, is characterized just as absolutely and definitely by *labor*, that is, raising the value of human exertion.

Society therefore has two areas that require rules for the often complicated relations that occur in them and which can easily go wrong. One is centered in commerce, the other is there for labor—to which can be added that commerce is mostly in the hands of the well-to-do and labor relies almost entirely on the hands of those without property.

This being so, does it not stand to reason to ask: Pray tell, if you knew enough to look after law and order for your class of industry by enacting a Commercial Code, why leave us without laws and begrudge us a Labor Code? The two cases, after all, are identical.

Both in the area of commerce and in that of labor, people rub shoulders with people; they bind themselves to one another in many ways and bring about a series of relationships, engagements, and commitments that impose obligations and beget rights.

§ 294   LEGAL DEVELOPMENTS

Originally these rights and obligations were regulated by unwritten law, that is to say, through customs and mutual engagements. Usually this customary law did not rely on arbitrary construction but on facts dictated by the succession of day and night, by the human body, by the weather, by the nature of the materials, and so on. Thus, customary law was perfectly adequate for safeguarding relations among people for as long as they continued to live in the state of dependence upon nature.

Gradually, however, this legal security came to an end as a result of three causes: (1) people acquired greater freedom with respect to nature; (2) people became more cunning in misusing their rights and evading their obligations; (3) people came into immediate contact with neighboring countries.

This development made it necessary to reduce customary law to written form and to elaborate and adjust it in order to keep up with what other nations were doing.

That is what happened in the area of trade and commerce, and in fact happened there first because (1) the merchant was less bound to his merchandise than the laborer to his materials, (2) commercial relations were more complicated, and (3) traders came into direct contact with their counterparts abroad.

Already in the early Middle Ages, the navigation laws of Rhodes came to be honored. In the fourteenth century the northern Italian republics developed the law of negotiable bills of exchange under the inspiration of Baldus and Stracha. The edicts of Colbert of 1673 and 1681 secured commercial law in a narrower sense. What had thus begun to evolve was augmented and coordinated by Napoleon in the *Code de Commerce* of 1808, which in the main has been incorporated (though improved and "Dutchified") in our Commercial Code.

Unwritten Law Code for Labor   § 295

Developments were quite different in the area of labor. Here, rights were more entrenched in the order of nature. Also, relations were less complicated, cunning infiltrated less deeply, and isolation from other nations lasted longer. This explains why almost everything in the field of labor was covered by customary law.

Customs and agreements affecting labor not only differed from country to country, but even from region to region, in fact from town to town. For example, the conditions under which a domestic entered her job varied widely: for what length of time she would be hired; within what time period she would have to give notice; how many free hours and days off she was allowed; what was owed her in terms of accommodation and meals; what belonged to her of tips and bonuses; what to do if she ruined any of her mistress's things; and so on and so forth.

The same was true of the trades: at what age one could enter an apprenticeship; what the duties of an apprentice consisted of; what the relationship was to the journeymen; at what hour the work began and ended; when and how long the breaks were for meals and rest; on what days one did not work; who supplied the tools; what to do in case of accidents with the master's property or accidents causing bodily injury; how much summer and winter wages would differ; what provisions for sickness or old age were in place; and so on and so forth. If our list went on for factory and agricultural workers, everybody would agree that customary law covered all rights and conditions of employment down to the smallest detail.

This law of usages might well have held out if the moral bond of reciprocal trust had continued to be as strong as in former days, if employers had remained as dependent on their employees as in days of old, and if their employees had remained as defenseless over against their employers as formerly—that is to say, *if no social question had arisen.*

§ 296   What Urges Codification of Labor's Rights Today

Now that the social question did arise, however—that is, now that the ideas of the Revolution pertaining to the domestic, moral, and political realms have made employers more egotistic and employees more contrary; now that steam engines and machines allow the employer to do with fewer employees and employees have acquired the means to resist their employers thanks to civil rights and labor unions; and above all, now that the totally different situation has in many ways turned customary law into unjust law—now we should not be surprised at the lack of calm minds to reform customary law or the absence of resolve to keep it as it is.

The wage earners have taken up the struggle for a new legal framework in order to have it all their way, while the wage payers have entered the lists to keep it as much as possible in their favor.

This situation cannot go on. Every country in Europe in fact stands poised to convert customary law, amended if necessary, into statute law. The process is ongoing. Once completed, the uneven nature of the various laws will automatically raise the desire for codification, resulting before long in a Labor Code.

Codification, after all, is nothing but "the systematic coordination of all the laws that have been successively enacted for relations in a certain area of life."[20]

And the reason why Britain has made much progress on that score while the rest of Europe seems to lag behind is that people have not sufficiently taken note of the fact (1) that the manufacturing industry and labor are still wrongly kept apart; and (2) that thus far agriculture has not been involved in the social question.

Once the British realize that the factory system, wage contracts, trades and crafts, and so on, fall under the same category where labor is concerned, they will no longer place the Factory Acts alongside the Labour Laws but include them as a subcategory of those laws. Similarly, the craft regulations that have been widely adopted in Russia, Germany, and

---

20. Robert von Mohl, *Encyclopädie der Staatswissenschaften* [Introduction to the political sciences], 2nd rev. ed. (Tübingen: Verlag der Laupp'schen Buchhandlung, 1872), 134.

Switzerland will certainly be booked as very comprehensive and significant elements in the Labor Code that is beginning to take shape.

As for the second point, it is obvious, for example, that relationships would certainly have been quite different recently in the German Reichstag if only wage earners, including those in the agricultural sector, we do not say had joined the social democrats, but had elected advocates for their own labor rights.

CONTENTS OF A LABOR CODE   § 297

As for the contents of such statutory regulations, they would have to include in part what at present is contained in Britain's Factory Acts and Germany's Trade Regulations, in part what is present in the Labor Laws mentioned earlier and in several articles of our own Civil Code, and in part what for the time being is subject entirely to custom.

Just as "Navigation" is incorporated in our Commercial Code, so "Manufacturing Industry" belongs in the Labor Code. Just as the Commercial Code further regulates what had in principle already been touched upon in the Civil Code, so it should be done here. And whatever labor issues have not yet found their way in statutory law should be poured into legislation if there is ever to be legal security.

Since people have asked me mockingly (from ignorance or levity?) for articles of such a code, we shall now list a number of headings that might come to be included in such a code.

The following might be included:
(1) General provisions;
(2) Wage contracts;
(3) Wage conditions;
(4) Payment of wages;
(5) Benefits and perquisites;
(6) Working hours, leisure hours, and holidays;
(7) Suspension of contract owing to sickness;
(8) Disabled workers;
(9) Lockout of employees;
(10) Workplace safety and protection against occupational hazards;
(11) Inspection of financial reports;
(12) On-the-job training;
(13) Journeymen;
(14) Foremen;

(15) Farm laborers;

(16) Factory workers;

(17) Tradesmen;

(18) Domestic servants;

(19) Master guilds;

(20) Workmen's guilds;

(21) Arbitration boards;

(22) Breaches of wage contracts;

(23) Damages caused on the job;

(24) Coercion against fellow workers;

(25) Conspiracy against employers;

(26) Paybooks and letters of recommendation;

(27) Cooperative associations;

(28) Political rights of labor corporations;

(29) Workplace inspectors; and

(30) Penalties.

§ 298   WHAT NEEDS TO BE DONE IN ADDITION

In addition, certainly, we need to watch against the exploitation of the wage earner through usury and advances and compulsory buying at the company store; also and especially against credit at the grocery store that can sometimes amount to extortion; and against so much besides.

Rightly viewed, public hygiene and decency—in fact, almost every branch of legislation—is linked in its own way to the social question. It is even linked to the church question: how can the workingman rent suitable pews and hear sermons that speak to his daily work and his place in society? But issues like these, and so many more, were not meant to be worked out here, since we inquired only into the *principles* behind the disruption that has arisen in the life of society and into the *principles* that can help remedy the existing evil.

CHAPTER TWENTY-ONE

CHURCH AND STATE

It declares that the government may not maintain or establish a state church, of whatever form or name, either for the kingdom in Europe or for the Indies; that the state has no right to interfere with the internal affairs of churches; and that in order to promote more than a so-called separation of church and state, the obligation pursuant to Article 168 of the Constitution ought to be abolished after paying the rightful claimants what is owed them.

ARTICLE 20

I. GENERAL PRINCIPLES

THE STATE CHURCH OF THE REFORMATION   § 299

The term "state church" stems from the image of a country in which the political life of the nation (taken as a whole) became ingrown in a particular ecclesiastical confession, bound itself to a particular church order, and found its highest expression in an official order of worship.

Church and state are then partners as a result of the fact that the nation, which as a whole entered into one and the same political life, also entered as a whole into one and the same ecclesiastical life. The manner in which such an arrangement usually came about was that the church community came first, which then gave birth to the political community.

In its pure form, therefore, this situation developed when the nation as a whole (as with the founders of New England) was supported for a time by the personal will of virtually everybody who belonged to the body politic. Such a theocratic situation relied initially on the sympathy of every household and benefitted all while offending none. For all intents and purposes it rested on an implicit plebiscite (a principle of sovereignty that is utterly untenable yet becomes indispensable the moment conscience enters the picture and touches someone's stance before God).

But such a pure situation remained highly exceptional and usually lasted for only a very short time.

Generally speaking, a nation *qua* nation would choose for a particular church confession in critical periods of its history but without having every branch and every cell in the national organism consciously agreeing with this decisive choice.

This scenario gave rise to the painful situation, as in our country in the sixteenth century, that the leading element of the nation married its politics to its church and cast it into a specific mold, even though the great mass of the people could not yet follow that choice or over time embrace it.

When Calvinism triumphed in our country and the Reformed state church was born, not even a third of the population belonged to the Reformed religion. Meanwhile, of the remaining two-thirds probably half were prepared, Catholics though they were, to let themselves be made over into Calvinists, depending on how events turned out. The other half, however, definitely preferred to make any sacrifice rather than be diverted from the faith of their forefathers.

As the years went by, a situation developed in the seventeenth century in which a third of the population *was* Reformed, another third *passed for* Reformed, and the last third remained Roman Catholic. That is to say, the Reformed two-thirds included the nominal ones, while the true-blue Calvinists among them at the same time had noticeably declined in their former religious fervor.

§ 300   IDEAL AND REALITY

As a result, the ideal that had animated our revolt against Spain for a part slipped into the opposite of what the heroes of that great struggle had intended.

They had intended to establish a church state in which every inhabitant, individually and all together, in full freedom of conscience, would unite under the purer religion according to God's Word, would dedicate their national honor to the glory of that Word, and would devote their strength as a nation to the flowering of the Reformed religion in Europe and beyond, and so destroy all constraint of conscience in resistance to the tyranny of Rome.

And it would have come to that if they had succeeded in persuading pretty much the whole population to embrace the Reformed religion, had preserved the purity of the Reformed religion, and had arranged the unity of ecclesiastical and political power on a firmer footing.

But when this failed, owing in part to neglect, in part to misfortune—that is to say, when they allowed the Catholic population to just remain Catholic and when they themselves strayed from the pure religion and related to each other as church and state in a way that may be called the opposite of a well-ordered relationship—then the demands of self-preservation left no choice but to resort once again to tyranny, but now under the Reformed banner. Thus the marriage between church and state caused our national life to lose its luster, both ecclesiastically and politically.

With this, the state church in our country stood condemned. Meanwhile, a number of factors brought about a change in thinking. In other countries a state church had produced the same sad outcome. Intellectual developments more and more stimulated individualism. The books of the New Testament contained not the slightest hint commanding the practical merger of state and church. The Word of God usually thrived best among the Reformed "churches under the cross"[1] that had no political support whatever. This whole conjunction of experiences and considerations led to the conviction, first in America, then in Scotland and Switzerland, and at last also in our country, that it had become a demand of faith to give up the idea of a state church.

This conclusion, however, was never taken to mean that a complete and perfect union of church and state did not continue to be our highest and most glorious ideal. After all, this is the ideal of every Christian who confesses the unity of the priestly and kingly offices of Christ and awaits the kingdom that is to come. But we confess this in the sense that this unity, given the diversity of views, cannot be realized in fact. In the present dispensation a state church hinders rather than promotes that unity. It is therefore an object of our hope at Christ's return but not a present possession.

---

1. Congregations of dissenters who broke with the state church yet were forbidden to hold separate worship services.

Given the diversity of views and the sad experience of the past, and notwithstanding the better outcomes that the opposite system has already produced, to force a union of church and state by means of political power and so create a state church would simply be to renew former suffering, keep the life of faith from flourishing, and guarantee that Rome, which is a match for any influence from the state thanks to its more powerful organization, would triumph over all churches of the Protestant persuasion.

§ 301   SEPARATION

On these grounds we choose to give up any notion of a state church and accept the divorce of the marriage of state and church once sealed in an evil hour. Yet no one should impute to us the intention to pull them apart in such a way that they would literally not have any dealings with one another anymore.

We are not even content with the restriction: "no separation between *religion* and state but only between state and *church*."

It is our firm conviction that government is a servant of God, wielding power and authority by the grace of God, called to minister to his honor, and therefore bound to his ordinances. Hence a government cannot keep itself out of touch with the religious life of the nation. And once you give in to the false idea that government should be in touch with people's religious life but not their church life, you are automatically led to the fatal conclusion we drew a quarter century ago: namely, that we can develop a kind of state religion that transcends church divisions, or else that the government should prefer that religion *that is least connected to a church*.[2]

To hold this is not to reckon with reality. The religious life of the nation is for the greater part carried on within the form of a church, and it is therefore in that form, and in that form alone, that government must get in touch with this expression of national life.

Accordingly, to our way of thinking the separation of church and state stands for three things: (1) the political unity of our nation is no longer coupled to any church unity; (2) church and state each command a unique zone in life where each functions as a minister of God and is debarred from using compulsion on the other's zone; and (3) the relation between the two should be defined *bilaterally* in the form of regular correspondence.

---

2. Kuyper alludes here to the Primary Education Act of 1857 which legislated that instruction in the common public school had to be religiously neutral, that is, teach "Christian virtues" without reference to the Bible or Christian doctrine.

THE PUBLIC-LEGAL NATURE OF THE CHURCH

Precisely with a view to the above, we strictly maintain the *public-legal nature* of the Christian denominations.

We do not mean this in the old sense of *publicum jus in sacris, in sacerdotibus, in magistratibus consistit*,[3] as if canon law still had public authority and validity in the Netherlands. We mean it in the sense that the Christian denominations have a public-legal aspect. This statement challenges current attempts at putting the church denominations on a par with a choral society, a fencing club, or a dance troupe, hence lumping them with ordinary "associations."

Our position is that the churches are unique bodies that cannot be compared to other associations. Churches can lay claim to separate treatment in the law, hold sway over their members even before any action of their will, ought to be subject to special regulations, and are not to be regarded as incidental but as one of the highest and most essential expressions of the life of the nation.

Thus our position defends the irrefutable thesis that church and state cannot each go their own way except at great harm to themselves, and that they do best when they are in regular correspondence with one another.

COMMITTEE OF CORRESPONDENCE

Some sort of correspondence was already intended by the Synod of 1619, judging by its report to the States General.[4] Such correspondence would best be assigned to a standing committee to which the government could appoint an executive consisting of three political figures and to which the churches could send delegates. These ecclesiastical delegates would have to file their denomination's official confessional standards as well as its church order or constitution and its standard liturgy, with the assurance that those documents indeed were the enduring expression of their church life. Upon proof of having a membership of, say, at least a hundred thousand souls, each denomination would be allowed to send one delegate to this committee for every one hundred thousand members.

---

3. "Public law consists of rules for temple, clergy, and magistrate." See *Justinian Code*, Digest 1.1.1.2: *De justitia et jure*.

4. In the final report from the Synod of Dort to the States General (which had convened it), the churches requested, among other things, that the authorities do more to enforce Sabbath observance.

The deliberations of this committee would have to be carried on in writing by way of curiae; that is to say, the delegates of each denomination would form a separate curia, hence would meet among themselves and not in a plenary assembly.

The government should then ask this committee for advice about all matters pertaining to denominational affairs, religious questions, and public morality. Examples would be days of prayer, marriage laws, the taking of oaths, Lord's Day observance, public education, poor relief, prostitution, public decency, and so on. Inversely, the government would give advice to this committee, or to the curiae, about regulations regarding the domain of the church: incorporating new congregations, redrawing parish boundaries, church buildings, baptismal registries, the solemnization of marriages, establishing schools, and so on. In both instances it would be understood that neither body would be bound by the advice of the other except through persuasion.

§ 304   A MORE FLEXIBLE RELATIONSHIP. DAYS OF PRAYER. NON-CHRISTIAN GROUPS

The existence of a Committee of Correspondence would automatically remove the surliness that at present so often mars and spoils the relationship between church and state. Clashes would be avoided. In any case that might arise there would be a committee, elected ad hoc, that could politely let the government know (without any restriction to mutual freedom) what the church asks of the government, and could let the churches know what the state might desire in terms of liturgy and church governance.

One particular advantage of such a relationship would be that the government in times of national disasters would, as in former days, have an organ for proclaiming days of prayer and penance with direct cooperation of the churches. At the same time the chairmen of the curiae could represent the Christian churches at official ceremonies. Another gain would be that we would have a committee that could be authorized to decide all those thorny cases in which the government itself is called upon to tend to religious life, as in chaplaincies for the army, the navy, prisons, hospitals, and the like.

And really, can any person who is opposed to a state church, as we are, yet who can acquiesce as little as we in the liberal theory that church and state should treat each other as strangers—can that person, we ask in all sincerity, in the long run escape the force of the argument that in a

Christian country of mixed population the only logical as well as work-able solution for a government that takes its calling seriously is to carry on regular correspondence on a voluntary basis with a mixed committee drawn from the Christian churches?

Of course there can be no question here of Jewish, Unitarian, or athe-ist bodies. A church ceases to be *church* the moment Christ ceases to be worshiped as Lord and Master. After all, on the basis of the most reliable research (especially that of Jacobson)[5] two things are certain: (1) that the word "church" is etymologically derived from *kuriakon* (dedicated to the Lord); and (2) that the word *Kurios* (Lord) in this form does not refer to God but to Christ. To be sure, any future revision of the Constitution will therefore have to come up with a form for religious communions of non-Christians. But in the name of proper definition they will have to be removed from the list of church denominations.

II. APPLICATION IN THE LAW

ARTICLE 168 OF THE CONSTITUTION §305

When a government pays the salaries of ministers of the church, it can do this for two reasons: political calculation or historical obligation.

In the first case, the financial tie creates a kind of state church; in the second, not at all. Especially not if this payment is simultaneously made to more than one denomination.

Since in our country Article 168 of the Constitution has its origin in for-mer constitutional provisions, which in turn rested on the government's confiscation of church assets upon acceptance of interest payments, there is no need for us to disagree that these payments still mainly represent the discharge of a historical obligation, an action that is completely foreign to the notion of a state church.

The reason why we nevertheless would like this bit of administration for the churches removed from the Article at any future revision of the Constitution, after proper compensation, is not based on any fear that the idea of a state church might sneak in through the back door, but on the

---

5. Kuyper makes a possible reference to H. F. Jacobson (1804–68), *Geschichte der Quellen des evangelischen Kirchenrechts der Provinzen Rheinland und Westphalen, mit Urkunden und Regesten* [History of the Sources of Evangelical Church Law in the Provinces of Rhineland and Westphalia, with Official Documents] (Königsberg: Bornträger, 1844).

following six observations, which we strongly like to recommend for consideration to both the political and the ecclesiastical authorities.

(1) As it is, in one and the same article—that is, Article 168—the Constitution adds a political intention to the historical obligation by paying salaries and benefits on an equal footing to churches from which *nothing* was taken at the end of the eighteenth century.

(2) The nature of a right changes over time. Although it can be argued on solid grounds that from the outset the greater portion of salaries was paid out as interest, yet one may not forget that such an original contractual and therefore *bilateral* right was imperceptibly changed into a political and therefore *unilateral* right. This depended on public opinion. And today the contractual origin of said salaries and benefits is mostly lost to public opinion.

(3) The assets confiscated at the end of the eighteenth century, if they had remained with the church, would today permit the payment of salaries by a factor of three. A church as a rule is obliged to invest her assets in real estate, to keep the level of her income in step with the rise and fall of the monetary standard. Currently she receives from the state at most four percent while the capital stays the same, meaning that the church in another fifty years, when money will again have gone down in value by half, will once again be poorer by half. If instead she were to get hold of this money and invested it in real estate, she would herself, half a century hence, as the value of money rose by 50 percent, be richer by 50 percent. Since the state is therefore incapable of supporting the church in such a way that her salaries stay in step with a rise in the monetary standard, and since the church (without such a rise) keeps getting poorer, it would seem that it is in the interest of state and church alike to settle the account.

§ 306   SETTLING THE ACCOUNT

(4) Even now there is a current of opinion that wishes to strike Article 168 *without* settling the account. Looking at the matter from the church's point of view, we would not consider this an insuperable obstacle for faith. However, a series of articles like the present, which addresses the question exclusively from the political and therefore also juridical side, must point out with some emphasis

that to commit such an injustice, inevitably causing resentment, would be morally injurious to the nation as a whole.

For this reason we think it desirable already now, while there still is time, to bend in an amicable way what might break anyway in a nasty tug of war.

(5) The payment of salaries and perquisites by someone who is not one's paid cashier but a minister of the Crown encroaches upon the right of the church to develop in freedom.

(6) Now that the salaries are increasingly inadequate anyway, it is desirable that the churches are completely weaned from the notion "Our pastors are paid for by the state," and that they use their own means, partly from the capital that will then become available, partly from annual income, to support what is required for maintaining a decent level of pastoral ministry.

The kind of settlement we have in mind would be based on these terms: (1) a complete account to be drawn up of all the incomes and benefits covered by Article 168; (2) the resulting annual sum of payments to be capitalized at 4 percent; and (3) the amount thus obtained to be paid out in, say, 10 annual installments, together with the regular but now proportionally decreasing annual payments.

We do realize that a difficult question would still need to be answered: Should these amounts be paid to the national church or to the local church or to the benefice? To decide this question, however, should not be overly difficult. After all, no one wants to go against rights. And what these rights are can be determined, either in general or in specific cases, if the government lays down that no settlement payment that is challenged can be paid out except upon a final decision of the courts.

THE CIVIL CODE §307

And yet the government would have to do still more.

After all, however much the church is spiritual in nature, still she comes into contact with relations in civil society and even falls under ordinary law the moment her material assets bring her into contact with neighboring and interested parties and give rise to property relationships.

Accordingly, as concerns the *pastoralia* (salary funds), the *bona ecclesiastica* (church assets), and the *bona ad pios usus* (diaconal or general assets), the outside world must know in what relationship it stands to the church, and the church has to have certainty about the relationship in which she stands with respect to the outside world. And it is just as imperative that a judge ultimately know which law to apply when the churches have disputes among themselves about property or control.

The current uncertainty about these matters is simply due to the fact that our Civil Code does not specify the rubric under which the churches fall. This omission in turn was caused by uncertainty whether the denominations were to be considered public-legal or private-legal bodies. This omission therefore needs to be corrected. Only then, and no sooner, will church authorities, sure of their legal status, be in a position to manage also their internal affairs.

As for what might still be lacking, perhaps we may be allowed to make a suggestion. Our preference by far would be for the main features of British legislation as most suited to church life. Of course, not for its aristocratic polity, but for its legal and political approach by which the British government binds the church denominations to nothing but their confessional, liturgical, and canonical standards.

§ 308   RIGHTFUL CLAIMS OF THE STATE ON THE CHURCH

Once the financial side of the question were settled in this vein, the state in our opinion should be satisfied with making the following demands on the church denominations:

(1) The churches shall file their confessional, liturgical, and canonical standards, inform the government at once of any subsequent changes, and guarantee that these standards are in force and will remain so.

(2) The denominations that are recognized on this basis and have seats in the Committee of Correspondence shall not make any decisions regarding certain designated topics without first seeking the advice of the government, though without being bound, other than morally, to follow that advice.

(3) All members of a church shall be assured that they may at any time withdraw from submission to an ecclesiastical authority, and all have the freedom not to be bound to their monastic vow if they wish to be released from it.

(4) With the exception of the right to criticize on the basis of God's Word, no attack upon the honor of the government shall be permitted in a public worship service, but instead prayers shall be made for all that are in authority.

(5) No church shall organize services or gatherings on public roadways except with permission of the local authorities.

RIGHTFUL CLAIMS OF THE CHURCH ON THE STATE § 309

Conversely, the government is to give the churches the following guarantees:

(1) The church shall have the right to offer advice on police matters insofar as they concern the religious and moral life of the nation.
(2) The civil authorities shall maintain law and order during worship services in and around sanctuaries, churchyards, and so on.
(3) The taking of the oath shall be kept sacred by enlisting the assistance of the church.
(4) Government shall protect the Lord's Day so that the church may fulfill her spiritual offices.
(5) Government shall make laws regarding days of penance and days of prayer for the nation as a whole through the intermediary of the church denominations.

The intention of this last point is to allow the Committee of Correspondence to propose—either via the *executive on behalf of the government or by one of the curiae to the* government—to have such a day at the outbreak of epidemics, in the event of extensive flooding, or during threats of war, or any other national disaster. If the curiae approved of such a proposal, be it unanimously or by majority vote, the king could then, over the signatures of the chairmen of the curiae, proclaim such a day of prayer and have these curiae make arrangements with each of the denominations to ensure that things are done in good order and harmony.

MILITIA. BAPTISM. MARRIAGE. § 310

Next, the church should surrender the right of her prospective pastors and priests to be exempted from military service. An adequate reason for this immunity would vanish as soon as the militia, in keeping with our proposal when discussing defense, were strictly separated from the regular army and placed "on a footing of ordinary morality."[6]

The government, on the other hand, ought to benefit the church by allowing a revision of the regulations regarding marriage and baptism.

Government has nothing to do with the administration of holy baptism. Even the provision that the officiating clergyman must first be shown a

---

6. See above, §§ 237–41.

marriage certificate [before baptizing an infant] is beneath the dignity of this holy sacrament.

As for marriage, while the church may certainly not forget that such a union also creates *material* rights, the government especially must not lose sight of the fact that marriage is a union between two *human beings*, hence a bond that touches the very foundation of their existence as *spiritual* beings. With this in mind, a settlement could be made whereby, for example, the church undertakes not to marry a couple until she has received proof that bride and bridegroom have met all relevant civic requirements, but whereby the government for its part notes the incompleteness of the act [of registration], refrains from performing any religious ceremony, directs every bridal couple to its church, and officially informs the church that the marriage has been duly registered and that there is no objection to the marriage taking place. Finally, church and state should be agreed on the degree of blood relationship that prohibits marriage.

§ 311 THE ROMAN CATHOLIC CHURCH

For the sake of completeness, this enumeration must not be silent about the exceptional position of the Roman Catholic denomination owing to its international character. We confine ourselves to noting five points:

(1) This denomination is to be left undisturbed and unabridged in the rights it gained in 1795, 1848, 1853,[7] and so on.

(2) The king is to enter into no other relation with the Pope than as temporal sovereign.

(3) Religious processions are only to be allowed in Limburg and North Brabant (with the exception of the pocket of Heusden and Altena) and elsewhere in the provinces where Roman Catholics make up more than nine-tenths of the population.

(4) In order to protect freedom of conscience, the government is to act, especially in almost exclusively Roman Catholic regions, with firmness and energy against any pressure (other than in the form of persuasion) that those of other faiths might be subjected to on the part of Roman Catholics.

---

7. In 1795, the Batavian Revolution guaranteed the equality of all religious persuasions; in 1848, the new Constitution granted the churches complete freedom of organization; and in 1853, the Pope reinstated an episcopal hierarchy in the Netherlands.

(5) The government is not to enter into relations with the hierarchy of this denomination except by way of the normal Committee of Correspondence.

CHAPTER TWENTY-TWO

PARTY POLICY

And finally, in order to encourage acceptance of these principles, the party maintains its independence, does not allow itself to be incorporated into any other party, and accepts cooperation with other parties only on condition of prior agreement on a well-defined program while leaving its independence intact. For this reason it usually participates in the first round of elections with its own candidates, and reserves the right to act according to circumstances during run-off elections.

ARTICLE 21

I. PARTY FORMATION

§ 312   THE DUTY TO FORM A PARTY

One still meets people in our circles who will tell you to your face that it is wrong to form a party.

On their view, one may never form a party. All party formation, they say, is immoral. The mere idea of "party" is reprehensible. The moment one ventures to organize a party one is on a slippery slope.

Personally these (largely elite) members of our generation, like Simon the Stylite, prefer to stay atop their pillar in lonely solitude.[1] They shirk all party ties. From their presumably lofty moral heights they do not hesitate

---

1. Simon the Stylite (d. 459) was a "pillar-hermit," famous for living 37 years on a small platform atop a pillar outside of Aleppo, Syria.

to roundly condemn your zeal for organizing a party. And sometimes, in spite of themselves, they allow themselves to fall into the same sin by acting as a party in joining other pillar saints to oppose you for wanting to form a party.

This hermitic standpoint is not ours. Nor do we yield to it. Instead, we feel obliged in our turn to condemn this standpoint as the expression of a very subtle and unconscious form of egoism.

At bottom, this refusal to participate is nothing but the expression in the political and moral domains of that same false individualism that was imported into our Christian society by the ideas of the Revolution and which runs counter to the very heart of the Christian religion. Surely the Christian faith urges community, union, and organization by reminding us of a common origin, shared responsibility, and a coming kingdom.

Christ himself is the image, the inspiration, and incarnation of the organic recapitulation of all things. It is not Christianity but the diametrically opposite standpoint that has spawned the false idea of individualism and of the nation as an aggregate of individuals.

The Christian approach is not to think of oneself as someone special, someone who therefore has to have a standpoint of his own and who has to stay on his own. It is the very opposite. It is to realize that one's views are not tried and tested until they merge with the convictions of others. It is to understand that whether one occupies a high or a low station in life, one is powerless without a conscious and concrete connection with other people. It is to know that joining hands with the least is better than holding off the best. That is how it ought to be according to the demand of those deep principles that are rooted in faith in the living God.

Now, when sin enters the picture and causes the formation of groups that do not want to side with the truth but instead oppose it, and even when sharp differences arise among those who have chosen to follow the truth, then it follows at once that the demand for coming together and uniting must lead directly to the formation of a party.

The existence of serious differences, after all, indicates that it is misguided to want to unite the whole and keep everybody together, be it permanently or temporarily. Two or more sides will spontaneously come into being, neither of which therefore comprises the whole but only a part of the whole—which is to say that each constitutes a party.

§ 313   PARTIES IN THE STATE, NOT THE CHURCH

This fact of life implies that there should never be parties in the church, but only in the state and in society. Since *party-phobia* is almost always aired by leaders in the church,[2] it is obvious that they are transferring to the political and social domains what is true and proper, relatively speaking, for the ecclesiastical domain.

Even so, only relatively speaking. The difference between church and state on this point is no other than this: the state, to be healthy, needs party formation, whereas party formation in the church is a symptom of internal sickness. That there are parties in the state is as it should be. In the church there ought never to be any parties.

So long as the church remains true to her life-principle no parties will arise in her midst, nor can they arise there. But if an element that is alien to her life-principle insinuates itself in her root, such as Modernism, Arianism, or the false philosophy, then she too will not be able to escape the push toward party formation, and all those who love her life-principle will have the moral duty to unite for the purpose of ousting the alien intruder. It is understood, however, that once this goal has been attained, "all will dwell again in brotherhood."[3] By contrast, the existence of parties as a permanent feature of the social and political domains will be a sign of normalcy.

Meanwhile, the formation of parties, be they permanent in the political domain or temporary in the ecclesiastical domain, does not at all mean that the opponent does not also harbor part of the truth, or inversely, that on our side everything is sheer gold. Nor does it mean that every person of the opposing party can be identified with the principle we combat or that every one of us has coalesced with the better principle. Reality, always relative, is far removed from such exaggerated, exclusive, and individualistic notions. Yet, that being said, your opponents will turn as a body against what is imprinted on your soul as the main cause to be defended. Inversely, the cause that is sacred to you will have begun to stir and work in the broad group of your supporters, whether out of custom, instinct, or choice of will. Now then, on that basis party formation has no other goal

2. Kuyper alludes here to Dr. Nicolaas Beets (1814–1903) and other theologians of the "ethical-irenic" school who wanted to "belong to the nation as a whole."
3. An allusion to Psa 133:1, "Behold, how good and pleasant it is / when brothers dwell in unity."

than to mobilize all available forces to repulse the attack on your sacred cause and to salvage and sustain what would be defenseless and succumb if you failed to close your ranks.

Again, this should not be understood as though we sustain the truth rather than the truth sustaining us. Rather, it means that to the extent that we are called to witness and toil and suffer for the truth, that witness, that zeal, and that cross enjoin us to unite in harmony as a bundle of arrows, according to the motto that was already known among the ancients but which only the Son of God has sanctified: that *concordia res parvae crescunt* (small things flourish with concord) but that *discordia maximae dilabuntur* (the greatest things vanish with discord).

POSSIBLE DRAWBACKS §314

If people object by saying that forming a party can easily lead to factionalism and dishonorable practices, then allow us to respond by asking: Does the risk of abuse ever absolve you from proper use? Will you condemn the doctrine of grace, for example, because of the danger of antinomianism, or the use of reason from fear of rationalism?

If the objection is that party formation leads to seeing everything in black and white—the opponents at their worst and the supporters at their best—then we should think that these moral purists had better not marry, have children, or make friends. For if one's wife or child or friend is ever involved in a dispute, everybody knows that it is simply against nature to begin by presuming that they are in the wrong or to adopt an attitude of neutrality that would be an insult to your love for them.

And, finally, if people point to the danger for leaders of the masses that party formation tends to make them disingenuous and intoxicates them with incense, then we counter by asking whether offices in the Christian church ought not to be abolished. For we all know that nothing is so hazardous for inner spiritual truth as the office of preacher and that few occupations are more exposed to corruption through overattachment than that of pastor of a congregation.

To be sure, we admit at once that party corruption is a field littered with traps and snares. Party formation is a shoal that has seen many shipwrecks and more than anywhere else calls for a bright beacon—for warnings and for prayer. Nevertheless we do not concede that these reasons permit or condone backing out of party formation.

All the more so—to note this in conclusion—because in other countries party formation, with the exception of a few sects and individuals, is the rule. It is openly practiced and functions the more soundly in the measure that public life is healthier. For really, you have to come to our highly fragmented little country of stubborn egos to encounter the peculiar plant of *politicophobia*, which elsewhere is thrown out as a weed but for too long has been honored among us as an ornamental plant.

§ 315   WE HAVE HAD CHAOS, NOT A PARTY!

But if the Christians in our country are not permitted to back away from organizing a party, they should also bear in mind how destructive it would be to halt the project halfway and walk away from finishing the job.

As things have stood among us for many years, we are said to constitute a party, yet all one hears about is internal wrangling. While ostensibly putting up a united front to the outside, inside we shake off all mutual accountability. We have mobilized forces, only to be wasted and lost owing to lack of organization. Leadership is said to be in place, yet every man does what is right in his own eyes. Incompetents often do most of the talking, while trust melts away. The sad result is that an unsettling sense of malaise is felt throughout the ranks; repeated disappointment is wearing us out; we are haunted by envy and jealousy; each blames the other. The sacred trust committed to us for safekeeping is again and again so battered and spoiled that we cannot bear to look at it and can only weep.

§ 316   POLITICAL ORGANIZATION

These woes can only be eliminated by a public and nationwide organization of the party.

We first of all have to rid ourselves of that faint and anxious sense as if participation in party activities is actually something to be ashamed of. That feeling draws everything back into the private sphere, stamps the party as a venture of obscurantists, and gives free play to the kind of outrageous intrigue that we witnessed not so long ago in a certain electoral district.[4]

---

4. This is a probable reference to the candidature of Theodoor baron van Lynden van Sandenburg in District Goes in the winter of 1878. Van Lynden van Sandenburg was recommended in a meeting of the local antirevolutionary voters' club as a "trustworthy Christian statesman" even though, as it became known later, he refused to pledge his unqualified support for the antirevolutionary demand for freedom of education.

In addition, however, we need to put the finishing touches to a well-structured, fully transparent, and fully accountable organization!

It has to be an organization that is rooted in unity of principle, tradition, and lifestyle. Thus rooted, it can over time foster a system of interrelated concepts and ideas. It will learn in a principled way to apply those concepts to the problems under discussion in the social and political domain. Thus it will induct the membership into its program, inspire them with it, and unite and coordinate their forces in order to work for its realization.

Part and parcel of such an organization would be that the members know how to sacrifice and will show others how to sacrifice: whoever has money, his money; whoever has influence, his influence; whoever can think, his intellectual labors; whoever can speak, the weight of his word.

PRESS. VOTERS' CLUBS. PARTY HEADQUARTERS. §317

Now then, lest this force, once set in motion, not work abortively and self-destruct or go to waste, it is imperative that people throughout the country join together and that everyone knows what he is responsible for.

We need our own press, not for navel-gazing but for repelling the adversary and fortifying our bulwark. That press should connect with a network of voters' clubs which, local and autonomous, nevertheless are one in program and goal and are linked to a national headquarters. These clubs are to organize whatever needs organizing during elections, and show off the bundle of arrows in the lion's claw as it once sparkled in the coat of arms of Old Holland.[5]

Finally, both the press and the clubs have to be in touch with the party's political leaders who, knowing what not everyone knows, are to indicate the direction that the action has to take.

If we had advanced to the point where we could also take action in the parliamentary sphere, this giving of direction would of course originate, as in Britain, France, and Germany, with the parliamentary caucus.[6]

But today we are only a party of the people. Those members of parliament who style themselves antirevolutionary[7] cannot be held (and

---

5. A bundle or sheaf of seven arrows in the old coat of arms symbolized the unity of the Dutch Republic of the Seven United Provinces that existed from 1579 to 1795.
6. This rule of thumb would not be followed by Kuyper himself during the MacKay ministry of 1888–91 and the Heemskerk ministry of 1908–13, both of which he criticized heavily in his columns in *De Standaard*.
7. They numbered ten at this time.

would not want to be held) to our program in all its aspects and its overall import. Circumstances therefore dictate that it should be at party headquarters, on instructions from the voters' clubs,[8] that the circle of men are to be nominated to whom the antirevolutionary party can safely entrust its future.

Once this goal is attained, facilitated by headquarters in a sound and logical fashion via the collaboration of all the voters' clubs, our strong but divided and battered group in the country will be able to welcome the hour when jealousy and envy will be extinguished and quarreling fall silent. With a party discipline that works organically and therefore morally, those who have sworn loyalty to our colors will be prevented by public opinion from giving indirect support to the opponent.

II. ISOLATION AND COOPERATION

§ 318   ANTIREVOLUTIONARY PARTY FORMATION

As we have seen, forming an independent party is not just legitimate but imperative if leading circles ignore your principle or undermine and combat it. That principle, after all, is the wellspring of your ideas, the root of your conceptions, and therefore the worldview that is sacred to you and which you hold as true. This being so, it can hardly be questioned that we antirevolutionaries are duty-bound to organize such a party.

All the facts are on our side, and all the circumstances are coming together to charge us with the mandate to form a separate party.

We are the bearers and representatives in the bosom of the nation of one of its finest and noblest traditions. That tradition still makes itself felt as we constitute a special nationality type. To be sure, this type cannot be resurrected in the form it had when it went under, but its mission is to transfer its character traits to the new type of nationality that is beginning to take shape.

As children with this historic pedigree of noble origin, we stand with our distinctive principle over against the medieval type of the Roman Catholics and the still quite fresh formation of liberals of every stripe. Our

---

8. While this may have been Kuyper's ideal, practice would often follow the opposite route. Early advice from headquarters to the voters' clubs about whom to nominate for their district would often amount to an instruction that was hard to ignore. The party's headquarters was manned by a central committee, and the chairman of the central committee was Kuyper.

principle may truly be called a root principle since it determines the nature and direction of our life in home and family, in church and state, in the broader society, and in the world of learning.

Furthermore, the recent People's Petition showed that we enjoy plenty of support for separate organization from that part of the people which in critical moments rallies around our banner. That group, which managed to mobilize upward of a quarter of the country's population within the space of a few weeks, has an indisputable right to speak and to vote in the nation's assemblies.

We used to be told that we did not belong there because our principle might be good enough for a theological system but not for politics—at least not a system that would be logically consistent and practicable. We flatter ourselves that the present series of articles will have disabused them of this convenient excuse.

The Break with the Conservatives §319

Meanwhile we are not saying that the other parties offer us no points of contact. On the contrary, we praise the conservative for his love of what has grown historically and for his respect for our glorious past. We are attracted to the liberal for his jealous attachment to our constitutional liberties. We salute Rome for its vigorous opposition to the ideas of 1789. And we admire the radical for his defense of the organic rights of society.

Yet this more favorable opinion of our opponents cannot absolve us from the duty to form our own party.

There are three reasons for this. Sometimes they want what we want, but in a *different* way. Or they want only a *part* of it. Or they want it, not as a desirable source of happiness for the people, but as a *necessary evil*.

Indeed, we will not be foisted off with the role that is often assigned to us: that we antirevolutionaries should become partners in an alliance or members of a bloc or fellow travelers in a broader party.

We did not withdraw from the house of the conservatives because of disappointment or impatience or ingratitude,[9] but simply because we do not belong there and could not stand it any longer. We would have endangered our health if we had stayed in the stuffy atmosphere of that musty building. If they had been openly indifferent to religion it might have worked for a while. But to have to look on and listen to the way the

---

9. These were actually the reasons why Groen van Prinsterer ultimately broke with the conservatives eight years earlier. What follows is the more radical stance of Kuyper.

conservatives invoked our sacred and cherished, nay, our primordial convictions, right up to the honor of the Holy God! Oh yes, they would invoke them whenever they were useful, but they always subordinated them to considerations of a lower order and calculations of political expedience. That—especially that—constricted our breathing and vexed us beyond endurance. It threatened to drown all our enthusiasm. We could not let that pass because it gnawed at our conscience and troubled us greatly.

By adopting Rome into its house a mere ten years after what happened in 1853, the conservative party as good as showed us the door. Although many did not realize it until 1869, for conservatives to play the game *against* Rome in 1853 and *for* Rome in 1863 was immoral, not because it led to an alliance with Rome, but because it was incontrovertible proof of systematic opportunism.[10]

§ 320   TWO CONSERVATIVE CABINETS

We can save ourselves the trouble of sifting all the facts of this controversy. The body of our supporters was in large numbers housed with the conservatives as early as 1840, more strongly in 1848, and strongest yet in the period after 1853.[11] They thought they were at home there and of one mind with those gentlemen. The illusion could last that long because pious customs still lingered among the conservatives, and because our own group had not yet become self-aware. This explains that as late as 1866, the general stood alone while the whole company turned to the *Dagblad* and its short-lived creation, the Heemskerk–Van Zuylen ministry.[12] But when the cabinet then resigned without even so much as acknowledging us, let alone identifying with us, the hour of separation had irrevocably

---

10. In 1853, the no-popery movement occurred; in 1863, instruction from the conservative ministry was given to remove the Bible from the public school after priests in some communities had complained that Protestant teachers were using Bible reading to promote their religion.

11. In 1840, the Constitution was revised after the breakaway of the Belgians; in 1848, a liberal Constitution was adopted; and in 1853, there were protests over the restoration of the Catholic hierarchy.

12. Kuyper here refers to the crisis that broke out after the Second Chamber adopted the motion of Keuchenius that censured the government's connivance in the king's appointment of the minister of the colonies to the post of governor-general of the Indies. Groen van Prinsterer defended the right of parliament to pass such a motion, but his conservative friends called it disrespectful interference with the royal prerogative. The *Dagblad* was the name of a conservative daily published in The Hague.

struck and under the antiphony of Miriams[13] we had our exodus from this other Egypt—praise God—and were free men once more.

And if after such a grievous disappointment there were still some who stayed behind in the hope of restoring old ties, the second conservative cabinet, the Heemskerk-Van Lynden ministry, certainly shattered this last illusion with bitter cruelty. For under the leadership of this unprincipled cabinet it became more transparent than ever that when it comes to the political chessboard the conservative politicians, for all their personal piety, will play the high and holy interests of our Christian people as mere pawns in the contest for the seats of power.

But why continue to defend the case that in all instances lies behind us and at every point was won by us?

Here we are: an independent party. All other parties have ended by acknowledging us as such.

And although there are still a few among the more senior members of our supporters who have not been able to leave the old sympathies behind, nevertheless gratitude and pride in our independence is sweeping through our ranks to such an extent that from now on the fear of ever again being absorbed and made serviceable can be dismissed as purely hypothetical.

PEOPLE'S PARTY AND PARLIAMENTARY PARTY   § 321

While proud of our independence, we must not lose sight of the fact that we are not yet a parliamentary party but still only a party of the people.

A healthy formation of a party must arise from the people themselves. A need, an urge, a higher consciousness must first awaken in the hearts of people and be quietly discussed in the privacy of their homes. From there it moves on to discussion in group settings and from there in ever wider circles, to arrive quietly and gradually at the stage where people join hands, combine their forces, and train their united strength on a select target.

This is the way a people's party is born from the people's conscience. But now to move forward and become a parliamentary party—that will require the following. (1) The thoughts that have multiplied in people's hearts need to be translated for the political domain and articulated into practical solutions for contemporary problems of government policy. (2)

---

13. See Exod 15:21.

The available forces of the party should not just join hands socially but need to be inducted into the framework of a political structure. (3) The core idea that animates such a group of people needs to be taken up by men of education and standing who can not only offer opposition in the parliamentary domain as firmly as the common people mount opposition in civil society, but who can also, if called upon, serve as the king's ministers in order to translate the people's core idea (adjusted to the demands of right and equity) into law.

We are not a parliamentary party. *Not yet.* We still lack those three requirements: a political articulation of our ideas, a political organization, and a body of statesmen. Still, we must try to become one.

With a view to this, the present commentary can serve as a first contribution toward arriving at a political articulation of our ideas and perhaps as a first step toward formal party organization. And if we succeed sooner or later in having a free Christian university[14] for gathering a circle of intelligent law students around professors in antirevolutionary statecraft, then perhaps, by God's grace, a future generation may be in a position to rely on a group of solid statesmen to inject the marrow of the antirevolutionary confession into the dry bones of our currently lifeless political institutions.

§ 322   FOR THE TIME BEING NO PARTICIPATION IN GOVERNING

So long as we have not arrived at that station, however, we are convinced of three things.

(1) We ought to abstain from any activities having to do with governance, to concentrate all our efforts on cultivating public opinion.

(2) We ought gratefully to honor those men of repute and standing who show our colors in the Second Chamber. Even if we sometimes disagree with them and harbor different sympathies, we ought to support them with our prayers and pursue them with our love, not because they represent our party in any constitutional sense, but because they are the bold tribunes who fearlessly and tirelessly stand in the breach for us whenever they become conscious of one of our cherished desires.

(3) As things stand, it is out of the question that we take over the administration under antirevolutionary leadership. We could only do

---

14. The Free University would open its doors twenty months later, in October 1880. See § 169 and its notes.

this if it were simply unavoidable (or if we abandoned our principle). Any such an administration could only *dream* of bringing about a general change in politics in an antirevolutionary spirit. It would have to regard its mandate, rather, as a passing and heterogeneous intermezzo for the purpose of finishing a narrowly circumscribed task.

COOPERATION AT THE POLLS   § 323

Finally, as far as our isolation at the polls is concerned, we should never forget that historically "isolation" in this context is the opposite of incorporation with others and therefore poses absolutely no objection to working together with other parties during elections, not to mention cooperating with others in parliament.

The only condition is that things are done in an honest way and that organs are appointed for negotiating cooperative efforts.

Prior to the elections of 1871 we stated explicitly that we did not decline some form of cooperation, provided (1) we would not be bound permanently; (2) the goal of the cooperation would be correctly defined; (3) we would be treated fully as an equal; and (4) in the first round we would be allowed to field our own candidates. And only after the *Dagblad* had firmly rejected one of these proposals did we decide to go it alone, without paying any further notice to others.

No one should conclude from that episode that we condemn every form of cooperation as immoral on principle.

On the contrary, given our dualistic electoral system,[15] it is mandatory whenever it can be done on a footing of equality and without having to abandon our principle.

We therefore continue to reiterate what we chose as our point of departure back in 1871: "We do not spurn but rather desire cooperation, by turns (depending on the circumstances) with conservatives, liberals, Catholics, or radicals, provided it concerns a properly defined program, to

---

15. Reference to the practice of having run-off elections between the two highest-scoring candidates when more than two candidates ran in a district and none gained a clear majority. This extra round enabled supporters of defeated candidates to vote for the candidate of their second choice. Thus by 1890 the coalition between Calvinist and Catholic voters included an understanding to vote for each other's candidates in run-off elections.

end when that program has been realized, and without prejudice to our unabridged independence."

§ 324   Organs for Negotiating Cooperation

But to make such an idea workable it will first be necessary that not just we but every political party in our country organizes itself on a firm footing, just like parties in other countries.

As things stand today, cooperation is out of reach because there is no opportunity for parties to openly and officially sit down with each other.

One cannot negotiate with newspaper editors. Nor with disorganized caucuses. Even less with voters' clubs that have sprung up randomly. And as for the Catholics, least of all with a bishop or a nuncio.

This makes for a situation where vague agreements are made during elections but which in no way bind anyone except morally and therefore can later be summarily ignored by the statesmen in the cabinet.

We no longer wish to make our people the victim of this situation. To escape that trap we deem it advisable that our own party give the example of an official organization, so that some future headquarters can create an organ that is elected from the bottom up by the local clubs and therefore officially invested with authority, an organ with which other parties can talk and negotiate—assuming that other parties have also organized themselves in a normal fashion. Such talks would then not be held in order to hammer out backroom deals but to establish, in black and white and open to the public, the precise conditions on which mutual cooperation is agreed upon for the achievement of specific goals.

That's how things are done in Germany, Britain, America, and France. In our country, however, all that working in secret has given rise to the wildest insinuations and has demoralized political relations.

A revision of our electoral system will have to be the first point on which such a concentration of forces will have to focus.

When that time comes, may the antirevolutionary party be ready with a fully developed organization. Ready in the very hub of political action. But to be able to be ready it will have to be ready at every point on the periphery. For the secret of our political strength does not reside in any national bureau but in the local leaders.

Speaking of local leaders, let us close with a final question: In earnest, would it not be wise to forgo fielding candidates during by-elections in districts that we have no chance of winning anyway, and to save our energies and run candidates only during general elections?

CONCLUSION

No Calvinistic Utopia §325

This series of articles is coming to a close. It has done little more than offer a rough and very cursory and unfinished sketch of our view of the state. It is not intended exclusively to satisfy a country in which none but Calvinistic antirevolutionaries dwell. Rather, our goal has been to offer to a country of a mixed population the conditions of a nobler existence and a more natural development than are at our disposal today.

Had we been asked to sketch a political arrangement for a pure, unmixed Calvinistic nation, no doubt many a line would have been drawn more firmly and many a detail would have turned out differently.

But a Calvinistic utopia is out of the question. There is only a Kingdom of the Netherlands as this factually exists in the second half of the nineteenth century. Religiously speaking, two-fifths of its population consists of Roman Catholics, plus Modernists, positivists, and atheists. Politically it consists of liberals, conservatives, antirevolutionaries, ultra-montanists, and radicals. It also has a historical past, including the history of this century, and it is therefore bound as well to the aftereffects of former wrong. Not to take all these complex factors into consideration when offering a program of political reform would have been unreal and unjust, impracticable, and unprofitable.

What the antirevolutionary party as well as the opposition had a right to expect of us was a sketch of state policies that would be in tune with the actual situation and could serve as a guide in the present day, and if the tide should turn in our favor could be worked out in a government program that can be translated into law.

What we have offered, therefore, is a sketch coming from the side of the antirevolutionaries, yet intended for the whole country. That is, it means to offer a *modus vivendi* for all parties. The program bears the hallmark of our principles, certainly, yet in nature and import it is a national program.

To what extent these articles have succeeded in achieving our goal is up to others to decide, be they sympathizers or opponents. We ask only that they do not disregard this goal.

Our sympathizers, on the other hand, should not complain that what is offered here is neither purely theocratic nor the obverse of the authentic ideal. That complaint would refer to an entirely different problem that we were not asked to resolve and which would therefore offer no criterion for a fair assessment.

But neither should our political opponents do us the injustice of looking only at those details that are especially colored by our principles. They should agree that our proposals cannot be dismissed from their standpoint until they can show that as far as they are concerned a country that is governed in accordance with the principles here developed would be less human, less uplifting, less noble.

§ 326   CONSISTENTLY ANTIREVOLUTIONARY

For the rest, it should be borne in mind, both by those on our side and by the party opposite, that what matters when aspiring to offer a national program is (1) that the antirevolutionary principles are clearly set forth; (2) that these principles can be shown to lead with some logical and historical consistency to certain conceptions about the state and its functions; and (3) that now and then these principles illustrate in detail what practical action they might lead to.

The main error of many antirevolutionaries thus far has been that they readily profess some vague propositions about God's supremacy, the importance of morality, and attachment to revealed religion, but for the rest fancy that this is all that can be said about our principles, and worse, that this moral and specifically Christian element is of no further relevance for the functioning of the state.

In this way men pass for antirevolutionary without being so. That is to say, they do subscribe to the most basic and elementary notions of the antirevolutionary system, but more in their ecclesiastical and confessional sense than in their political import. The consequence is that they do without the rich benefit of a distinctive political viewpoint and prove most antirevolutionary when it comes to the fundamental principles, but when it comes to applying them to political issues, they are either conservative or liberal.

This shortcoming in their personal education and upbringing, which has become the rule in some circles, is of course fertile soil for confused thinking and misconceptions and even cuts off any possibility of combined action.

Precisely in order to adopt a better approach that can gradually overcome this shortcoming, it has been essential to indicate again and again, at times in lengthy and seemingly redundant prose, the consequences which in real life run from the very center of the antirevolutionary principles to every point on the periphery.

The antirevolutionary party has the right to demand a hearing as a political party if and only if it can show that among its treasures it possesses principles that imply for the whole of our program an approach to national affairs that is not only useful and practicable but at the same time essential and attainable.

One Formal and Three Substantive Principles §327

Among those principles, to the extent that they have been discussed here, there is one formal principle and three principles concerning the substance of the matter.

Formally, that is, with respect to the question where knowledge of the truth can and must be found, we have repeatedly been confronted by *the fact of sin*. Acknowledging this fact has led at once to two conclusions. First, that human beings, whose minds are contaminated by sin, cannot on their own create a true conception of politics. Secondly, that human life, turbid and tainted by sin, cannot pass on the divine ideas about politics with any degree of purity. These twin beliefs condemn both the doctrinaires and the Historical School as stemming from the revolutionary way of thinking.[1] A special revelation is needed that leads to knowledge of the divine ordinances along two avenues: (1) by direct revelation of God's will; and

---

1. The Historical School of law arose at the beginning of the nineteenth century in reaction to Enlightenment rationalism. It taught that law is grounded in the spirit of a nation as it evolves over time and can be ascertained by studying its history and current condition.

(2) by shedding more light on the divine ordinances that lie in creation and in history, so that our eyes are opened to them. Opposite sin stands the Word of God. And that Word is not bound to any popish interpretation but remains free in its effect on the consciences of men.

As for the three *substantive* principles, they are contained in three ideas:

(1) sovereignty for each distinctive sphere;
(2) the nation an organism, not an aggregate;
(3) no coercion but freedom for intellectual-spiritual formation and education.

Sphere-sovereignty denotes that the right to execute authority among men is a grant, and is therefore never original. Another way of saying this is that no human authority can arise from any human will, nor from any collective will of men, but only from the free and original authority of the sovereign God.

That the nation is an organism and not an aggregate does not mean, in the sense of Ahrens[2] and the school of "organic" political philosophy, to reduce the components of the state to isolated links on a chain. It means that the human race—hence also its component parts, the nations; and hence also the components that make up those nations, the several spheres of life—has grown organically in history and that only as an organic whole can it flourish morally, socially, and politically. This forbids breaking apart the components of the state and then putting them back together again; that would be mechanical patchwork. But it does enjoin us respectfully to distinguish all those things that have been given their own life by divine ordination, so that we allow them to grow, through their divinely given articulations and in company with other parts, into an integral whole strictly held together in God alone.

And finally, there should be no coercion, but freedom, for intellectual and spiritual formation and education. That means acknowledging that the individual persons within these organic spheres of life are indeed influenced by the state community in a legal sense and by the social community in an organic sense, but that their intellectual-spiritual formation can never be any other than free, since it is too lofty and too noble to be

---

2. See Heinrich Ahrens (1808-74), *Die Philosophie des Rechts* [Philosophy of the Science of Law], vol. 2: *Die organische Staatslehre auf philosophisch-anthropologischer Grundlage* [Organic Political Theory on the Foundation of Philosophical Anthropology] (Vienna: Carl Gerold & Sohn, 1850).

brought about (albeit through human instruments) in any other way than by the direct inworking of the living God.

TRINITARIAN   § 328

As we summarize the above three principles, permit us in all reverence to pose a question. In an earlier article we recalled that even today the peace treaties between most countries begin with the solemn words: *In the Name of the Holy Trinity*. Very well, we ask all who still confess God according to his Word as "Father, Son, and Holy Spirit" whether the above three principles are anything other than the humble and joyful confession of God's Holy Trinity in its consequences for the political domain.

For consider: Christians confess that the bearer of sovereignty, as origin and efficient cause, is *the Father*.

The organic coherence of humankind is borne, in virtue of the incarnation, uniquely by *the Son*.

And the inworking that goes directly to the heart of the individual person is the work of *the Holy Spirit*.

Should someone protest that sphere-sovereignty cannot be separated from the organic viewpoint, and that this in turn presupposes the free working of the mind and spirit, then we may be allowed to ask whether this intersecting of the three rays, rather than cancelling the Trinitarian character of our sketch, instead confirms it with an unmistakable hallmark.

The Christian, after all, confesses, not only that "there are three that bear record in heaven, the Father, the Word, and the Holy Ghost," but also and just as real, that "these three agree in one."[3]

This concluding remark could not be omitted here since for those of us who cannot build otherwise than on the foundation of the holy mysteries of the Word, life's depths are fathomed neither in the theological, moral, and juridical world nor in the social and political domain so long as our investigations have not come to rest in God himself, that is, in the confession of his Holy Trinity.

---

3. See 1 John 5:7 KJV. In the original, Kuyper quotes from the Dutch *Statenvertaling*, which prefers the reading "these three are one" found in other manuscripts and followed by some editions of the KJV. Published in 1637, the Statenvertaling (literally, "States Translation") was the first Bible translation from the original biblical languages of Hebrew, Aramaic, and Greek into Dutch, commissioned by the States General of the Netherlands.

Only then can this work go out under the seal of that profound proverb from the wise men of the Solomonic circle:

Al 's Wijsheits aanvangk en beghin Steeckt in de vrees' des Heeren; En wie Hem vreesen sal, oprecht, Moet naar sijn' Woort Hem eeren![4]

---

4. "The beginning of all wisdom / Lies in the fear of the Lord; / Whoever would fear him sincerely / must revere him according to his Word." Unknown source; but the verse appears to be based on Prov 9:10.

APPENDIX

DETAILED TABLE
OF CONTENTS

ABOUT ABRAHAM KUYPER (1837–1920)

Abraham Kuyper's life began in the small Dutch village of Maassluis on October 29, 1837. During his first pastorate, he developed a deep devotion to Jesus Christ and a strong commitment to Reformed theology that profoundly influenced his later careers. He labored tirelessly, publishing two newspapers, leading a reform movement out of the state church, founding the Free University of Amsterdam, and serving as prime minister of the Netherlands. He died on November 8, 1920, after relentlessly endeavoring to integrate his faith and life. Kuyper's emphasis on worldview formation has had a transforming influence upon evangelicalism, both through the diaspora of the Dutch Reformed churches, and those they have inspired.

In the mid-nineteenth-century Dutch political arena, the increasing sympathy for the "No God, no master!" dictum of the French Revolution greatly concerned Kuyper. To desire freedom from an oppressive government or heretical religion was one thing, but to eradicate religion from politics as spheres of mutual influence was, for Kuyper, unthinkable. Because man is sinful, he reasoned, a state that derives its power from men cannot avoid the vices of fallen human impulses. True limited government flourishes best when people recognize their sinful condition and acknowledge God's divine authority. In Kuyper's words, "The sovereignty of the state as the power that protects the individual and that defines the mutual relationships among the visible spheres, rises high above them by its right to command and compel. But within these spheres ... another authority rules, an authority that descends directly from God apart from the state. This authority the state does not confer but acknowledges."

ABOUT THE TRANSLATOR AND EDITOR

Harry Van Dyke was born in Rotterdam, Holland, and at the age of twelve moved with his parents and six siblings to Canada. He earned a BA at Calvin College and a DLitt at the VU University Amsterdam. He has published a score of articles, numerous translations, and a book, *Groen van Prinsterer's Lectures on Unbelief and Revolution* (1989), besides editing anthologies of the writings of S. U. Zuidema and M. C. Smit.

For twelve years he served as research fellow and instructor in theory and philosophy of history at the VU University Amsterdam, then taught history at Redeemer University College for twenty-three years. Since his retirement he has given direction to the Dooyeweerd Centre for Christian Philosophy and has been involved in several translation projects. He and his wife have two adult daughters and two grandchildren. They reside in Hamilton, Ontario, where they are members of a local Christian Reformed church.

INDEX